Song school, town school, comprehensive:

A history of Inverness Royal Academy

Song school, town school, comprehensive:

A History of Inverness Royal Academy

Robert Preece

First published 2011

ISBN: 978-1-905787-46-3

The publication of this book has been assisted by
a grant from the Inverness Common Good Fund

Any surplus from the sale of this book will be devoted to the
development of the archive in Inverness Royal Academy

Inverness Royal Academy:
www.invernessroyal.highland.sch.uk

Printing and binding by
For the Right Reasons,
Printers and Publishers,
60 Grant Street, Inverness, IV3 8BN
Scottish Charity Number SC037781

*Title page: the original building for Inverness Royal Academy in Academy Street,
possibly photographed around 1895*

CONTENTS

List of illustrations
on pages 283 to 326

Appendices 1 and 2 (pages 355–363) contain images of all the Rectors for whom an image could be traced

Appendix 4:

Permission to reproduce illustrations has been granted by:
Aberdeen Journals (*Press and Journal*): 19.1
Aberdeen University: 2.1
Am Baile/High Life Highland (formerly Highland Council Library Service) [photographer Ewen
    Weatherspoon]: 2.4 a-b, 6.1, 9.6, 12.1, 17.2, 17.5
George Outram/*The Herald and Evening Times*, Glasgow: 18.3
Headland Archaeology and Tulloch Homes, Ltd.: A4.5
Highland Council Archives: 2.3, 2.5, 9.3 (part)
Highland Folk Museum, Newtonmore/*High Life Highland*: 7.1, 11.1
Highland News Group (Scottish Provincial Press), Inverness: 18.5
Highland Photographic Archive, Inverness: 11.2, 15.2, 17.7
Jimmy Thomson (Inverness Press Photos): 18.6
National Archives of Scotland, Edinburgh: 4.1
National Library of Scotland, Edinburgh: 1.1 a-b, 7.2, 7.4
National Maritime Museum, Greenwich, London: 10.1 a-b
National Museums Scotland, Edinburgh: A4.2, A4.4
Noël Wilkins (Galway) and the Royal Dublin Society: 7.3

The author has supplied the following photographs: 9.1 a-b; 17.4.

Scans of documents and photographs taken from items in the Royal Academy archive: 2.2, 4.2,
    5.1, 5.2, 8.1, 9.2, 9.3 (2 parts), 9.4, 9.5, 10.2, 12.2, 13.1, 13.2, 14.1, 14.2, 14.3, 14.4, 14.5,
    15.1, 16.1, 17.3, 17.6, 18.1, 18.2, 18.4, 18.7, 19.1, 19.2, A4.1

For several items the original photographer cannot be identified or else the photograph or
    illustration is now out of copyright.

Acknowledgements

Inverness Royal Academy: the recent Rectors, teaching and administrative staff, especially the various school librarians over the years

Highland Council Archive: Bob Steward (formerly Archivist) and Susan Beckley (currently Archivist) and their staff

Highland Council Libraries Service: the staff of Inverness Public Library, especially in the Reference Room, and the staff of the *Am Baile* website

Highland Council Museum Service: Inverness Museum: Catharine Niven (Curator) and her staff

National Archives of Scotland: especially the staff in the Historical Search Room in HM General Register House, Edinburgh

National Library of Scotland, Edinburgh, especially in the Manuscript Room and Map Library

Also to:

University of Aberdeen: Library and Marischal Museum

University of Edinburgh Library

University of Glasgow: Archive and Business Record Centre

Dundee City Council Archive

Perth and Kinross Council Archive

Cambridge University Library: Adam Perkins, Royal Greenwich Observatory Archivist, Department of Manuscripts and University Archives, for access to material on the scientific work of James Weir and Matthew Adam

Royal Dublin Society Library, in connection with research on Alexander Nimmo

Dr Gordon Munro, Lecturer in Academic Studies at the Royal Scottish Academy of Music and Drama, Glasgow, for advice on early Scottish song schools

Dr Sally Mapstone, St Hilda's College, Oxford for advice and comments on the *Inverness Fragments* material in the National Library of Scotland

Dr Alison Sheridan, Head of Early Prehistory, National Museums Scotland Archæology Department, for discussion and information on the archæology in the Cuduthel Area (see Appendix 4)

Professor Noël Willkins, Galway University, Eire, for discussions and information on the career of Alexander Nimmo

Highland Family History Society for information about gravestones in Inverness cemeteries

Jim Brennan, former colleague at Inverness Royal Academy, for research especially with regard to the overseas connections for funding the Academy, and for identifying the architect and workmen of the 1792 school building

Christine Horne, for genealogical research, the meanings of various archaic terms, and comments and advice on drafts of the material, etc.

Donald Preece, for comments and advice on drafts of parts of the material and proof-reading
and many others

Permission has been granted by Mainstream Publishing to use a quotation on pages 251-252 from *The Root of the Matter* by Father Anthony Ross.

The extract from the Fraser of Reelig papers on page 137 is reproduced with the permission of the Fraser family of Reelig

Preface

Considering that Inverness Royal Academy is now well over 200 years old, it is surprising that there is no full-length published history of the school to date. Three people have gone some way to starting the work on such a history:

1: Peter J. Anderson, former pupil, historian and librarian of King's College Library, Aberdeen, who researched the various rectors and medal winners of the school, publishing a booklet in the first decade of the 20th century.

2: Evan M. Barron, also a former pupil, a lawyer, turned historian, turned newspaper editor, and key figure in the Old Boys' Club, who partially completed a study of the period before the school opened in 1792 but who, due to the First World War and family circumstances, never managed to get far beyond that point, even in his retirement; his only published work on the school in 1921 never claimed to be comprehensive but was merely offered as a contribution to the history of the Academy – it hardly mentions what happens after 1792.

3: Margaret MacDougall, Burgh and County Librarian from 1952 to 1960, who seems both to have worked on her own, and in association with Evan Barron, on researching education in Inverness up to the 19th century, but does not appear to have ever published any of this work (although typescript copies of papers written by her are held in the Highland Council Archive).

This volume aims to fill a gap: not just for Inverness and the many former pupils of the school who have, as I have been working on this material, been regularly enquiring about progress (and even phoning up to check whether they had missed their copy as the book might have already sold out!), but for a much wider educational and social history audience, both academic and lay, throughout Scotland. Most academic works, tracing a part of the history of Scottish education, say nothing about Inverness Academy (as so little has previously been published), or repeat some of the half-myths and errors caused by earlier writers such as Joseph Mitchell.

The impetus for this history came from the Bicentennial celebrations of the Academy, held very successfully in 1992. However 2007 marked another milestone in the history of the Academy with the centenary of the private Act of Parliament which transferred the school from one run by a Board of Directors to one fully under the control of the local authority: School Board, County Council, Education Authority, and probably other names through the years.

My full-time teaching job (until retirement in 2003), and my other interests, meant that progress on this history was slow until the last few years. I am not particularly a historian by training, and this book could not have been written without tremendous help from many people. They are too numerous to mention every one (even if I could remember all the names), but the key ones are the staff of Inverness Royal Academy (both teaching and administrative), and the staffs of the Highland Council Archive and the National Archives of Scotland. Particular thanks are due to Jim Brennan for discussions and advice on aspects of the historical context of the school's history (especially with regard to the West Indian connection), Christine Horne for genealogical research and much else, and to my brother, Donald, for reading and correcting drafts of some of the material. A full list of acknowledgements appears on page 8.

The reader may now judge if this work can join the long tradition of accounts of the history of well-respected Scottish schools. I shall be pleased if it provides a useful account of how the history of Inverness Royal Academy differs, at least in part, from that of many other long-established Scottish schools.

Robert G. Preece
November 2011

Conventions

Three conventions used in the text need to be explained here:

1. Year dates: until 1600, the Scottish civil year started on 25th March – the Feast of the Annunciation. As a result dates in legal documents for January, February and most of March will have, for the modern reader, the year date of the previous year. Modern transcriptions may show dates as 'Old Style' or 'New Style': the date of 3 February 1556 (OS) and 3 February 1557 (NS) are in fact the same date. Sometimes this will be written as: 3 February 1556/7. To save confusion, although it is really only relevant in chapter 1 of this book, all dates up to 1600 are given in the new style.

This change took place 152 years before the same change took place in England! It also only applies to the date of the new year – not to the change from the Julian to the Gregorian calendar, which involved the missing out of 11 days in September, and the revised rules for the calculation of leap years. This change took effect throughout the whole of Britain and the Dominions in 1752.

2. Currency: Until well on in the 18th century, money values in Scotland were expressed in a variety of units. Merks and Pounds Scots are the most common. The conversions between Merks, Pounds Scots and Pounds Sterling are generally accepted as:

1 merk = 13s 4d Scots, or alternatively 3 merks = £2 Scots: this did not change
In the 16th century £4 Scots was equivalent to £1 sterling. By the 17th century the value of the Pound Scots had fallen and the approximate conversion was £12 Scots = £1 stg. The first payments in £ stg. do not occur until about 1725. Where units in pounds are important, Pounds Scots or £ stg. are specified: however at times it is not clear from the original material which unit was being used.

It is assumed that most readers will recognise pre-decimal forms of representing money where:

12d made 1s or 1/- [12 pence = 1 shilling]
20/- made £1 [20 shillings = £1]
£4 2 6d is four pounds, two shillings and six pence.

Due to inflation, as precise conversions are rarely of importance, translations into modern £ and p are not given in the text for values prior to about 1895.

3. Spelling: *Personal names:* In early Scots/English, as used in the Highlands, certainly until well into the 18th century, spelling was not fixed and personal names may appear in many different versions. From time to time it is not clear that it is necessarily the same person who is being mentioned. However to avoid confusion for the average reader, in this text a person's name appears only in one spelling, using the one that this person most frequently signed themself by, where this can be identified – but where there are special problems over spelling, comment is made in the text.

Place names: Due to a lack of an adequate orthography for Gaelic until recent times, Gaelic place names may have variations in spelling through time. Major corruptions have also taken place. Original spellings are kept where this is relevant, especially in quotations. The modern form of the name is given in square brackets after the original spelling, to allow the reader to locate the place.

Quotations: In most quotations, the original spelling of words has been retained, unless there is clearly a mis-spelling. The early form of the letter 's' which looks like a modern 'f' has been transcribed as an 's'. Where the spelling of a quotation has been modernised, this is stated.

Abbreviations for references and notes

Abbreviations used in the chapter references and notes are as follows:

IRAA = Inverness Royal Academy Archive
ITCM = Inverness Town Council minutes, housed in the Highland Council Archive
HCA = Highland Council Archive
HRC = Highland Regional Council (existed 1975-1996)
NAS = National Archives of Scotland, now merged into the National Records of
    Scotland (NRS)
NLS = National Library of Scotland

Chapter 1
Setting the scene

... And after the above business was gone through the Directors with a considerable number of the Subscribers proceeded from the Guildry room to the Academy; And after convening the masters and students, the Academy was opened with prayer by Mr Rose one of the [Inverness] Ministers, and an Introductory Lecture suitable to the occasion, was delivered by Mr Weir the Rector.[1]

This entry in the Directors' Minutes, for 16th July 1792, records the launch of Inverness Academy as it then was – the *Royal* was added only in the following year, with the purchase of the Royal Charter. But this launch, although a new beginning in one sense, was more a reaffirmation of the form of academic education as it had been developing in Inverness in the second half of the 18th century.

The story probably begins more than 500 years before, with the establishment of the Priory School associated with the Priory of Black Friars – the Dominicans (not the Grey Friars as most Inverness people believe). According to Spottiswoode, the post-Reformation Scottish chronicler, Inverness Priory was founded by Alexander II, King of Scotland, somewhere between 1233 and 1240, one of nine such houses created in Scotland around that time.

The Priory was built on a piece of land given to the Friars by the Abbey of Arbroath, who were the superiors of the Parish Church, on a site to the north of what is now the Old High Church in Church Street. In 1240 the Priory received a further gift of land – the area known as the Maggot – round about the area from the present telephone exchange towards the modern-day Friars' Bridge. This gift included the rights of fishing in the River Ness in the area still known as The Friars' Shott.

A key part of their work as friars was in the realm of education, and every priory would have friars who would be well versed in theology, with a doctor of theology who would lead the teaching. To maintain the number of young men as recruits to their priory, there would probably have been several "schools" – more what we today might regard as subjects or classes – one of which would undoubtedly have been theology. It is very likely that there would have been a reading and writing school, and a Latin school. Latin would be an important element of the course of study as church worship took place in Latin, although the Friars themselves would preach publicly in the local language. Collectively the various schools would be under the control of a *Rector Scolarum* – the Rector of the Schools.[2]

A key piece of evidence of the existence from an early age of an Inverness school comes from one of the signatures on a charter by John of Inverallan on 18th October 1316;[3] one of the witnesses was a Master Felan[us], described as "Rector of the School of [Inverness]". The word 'master' here, and until perhaps the eighteenth century, meant someone with a master's degree from a university. This proves the existence of some sort of school, but perhaps not the priory school, with educated staff, from at least early in the 14th century. It also shows that, as another of the signatories is the perpetual Vicar of Inverness, the schoolmaster was a person distinct from the Vicar [priest/minister] of the Parish Church.

At some point the Burgh became involved with education and some of the classes in the school would have been opened both to members of the order and to members of the laity, including local boys and perhaps the sons of gentry sent in to the Town from the country. However no date can be put on when this might have happened, although Watt says that he considers it unlikely that Master Felan[us] was a member of the Dominican order, and that the location of the school close to the Priory grounds (see below) was coincidental.[4] By implication Watt is suggesting that Burgh involvement in education had started certainly by the beginning of the fourteenth century.

The second piece of evidence for an early school at a site to the north of the present Old High Church comes from 1574, when the provost of the time, Provost William Cuthbert, took the lease of an area of land where the school had been. The text reads:[5]

> ... the laarycht [= site of building] of the auld scule lyand at the eist pairt of the Freiouris wall betuix the said wall of the Freiouris yard at the west, the Hie Kingis Gett passis to the Chapell yard at the eist, the said Freiouris wall at the northt, and the commoun wennall [vennel = lane] passis to the wattir of Ness at the southt...

This clearly locates the site of the school as being at the north end of Church Street at its junction with Friars' Lane, and it must have been adjacent to the Priory entrance. Nothing now remains of the priory or of its school, other than a single pillar and the effigy of a knight in the wrongly-named Greyfriars' graveyard lying behind the city telephone exchange.

The Inverness Sang Schuile
Prior to the Reformation, in 1560, little else can be discovered about schooling in Inverness, but modern scholarship has turned up a little information on what was probably happening in the school, or one of the schools, in the months, perhaps even weeks, prior to the Reformation changing the religious order in Inverness.

The Priory would make extensive use of music in the church services. As much of this music, before the Reformation, was very complex and sung in Latin, there would be a sang schuile [song school] attached to the Priory.[6] Durkan[7] found that one James Auchlek/Auchinlek, Town and Parish clerk of Inverness from late 1538 or early 1539, was:

> ... to rule the school, to instruct and teach the chaplains and scholars coming thereto in the art of music, not only in chant but in organ playing.

Sadly, very little material seems to remain about the Inverness sang schuile attached to either the Priory or the Inverness Parish Church (or perhaps serving both), unlike the situation in some other parts of Scotland where there is considerable information available.[8]

Song schools (in a variety of spellings, as at that time written Scots did not have any fixed spelling system) existed right across Scotland, from Kirkwall to Melrose. Perhaps the best-known of them was that at the Chapel Royal in Stirling. Dunkeld clearly had a good one as a writer in 1517 declared that the church there had the best choir in Scotland. The writer went on to give details of the various priests and vicars choral, showing them to be well educated, often with university degrees, and with a range of interests outside the church, including one who was a keen gardener![9]

The discovery of some fragments of church music and parts of two Latin grammar books amongst the binding of a manuscript feudal law book may now have shed some light on the subject of the Inverness song school. Apparently the law book was given to the Abbey Library in Fort Augustus in about 1940 by Captain William Mackay, an Inverness solicitor. The material is now the property of the National Library of Scotland.[10] The book itself was bound around 1575, some years after the Reformation had made the music redundant, with reformed ministers being in post in Inverness from 1560. The Latin grammars were also by that stage regarded as dated. The book was the property of a William Cumming, an Inverness burgess, and for a period the Town Clerk and a notary public starting in the 1560's. The scribe was Gilbert Duff, who signed many of the pages that he had written. He was also a Town Clerk.

In 1973 the Abbey authorities finally allowed the book to be taken apart in what was then the Scottish Records Office (now the National Archives of Scotland). During the binding of the book, much damage had been done to the sheets so that what remains is only fragments, which is why they are now known as *The Inverness Fragments*[11] [Figure 1.1 a-b]. These contain, amongst other items, music for use mainly in the liturgy of Holy Week, and the Office of Compline during Lent. There is also a sequence of settings of music for use during the Palm Sunday procession, and six different polyphonic settings of a psalm in Latin for Easter Sunday. These were perhaps for the training of boys in the song school before they moved on to higher things, such as the grammar school.

Originally it was thought that the music had come from Beauly Priory, but the music had not been derived from the correct source for it to have belonged to a Valliscaulian house such as Beauly, which followed Cistercian monastic practice. The material is based on the Sarum form, i.e. from the practices at Salisbury in the south of England. These practices reached Scotland shortly after 1070 following the marriage of King Malcolm III (Malcolm Canmore) to the English-Hungarian Princess Margaret. Sarum use spread across the cathedrals of Scotland, in an Anglicisation introduced by Margaret. However by the time this music was written in the sixteenth century, it is likely that the Sarum influences were coming more indirectly through France or Belgium, rather than directly from England.[12] The nature of this music also suggests that it was more likely to have been used in a parish church rather than in a monastery [Figure 1.1a].

Other items rescued from the binding are two papers relating to the Inverness Burgh Court, including an Inverness marriage contract of about 1543, and a letter dated 1553 regarding a business transaction. The pages from the sixteenth-century printed Latin grammar, of Scottish origin, have a large number of handwritten marginal notes, perhaps by the schoolmaster himself or, as Dr. Sally Mapstone of Oxford University believes, by some of the author's pupils, and the notes are sometimes in a mixture of Latin and Scots. There are also parts of another as yet unidentified Latin grammar.[13]

The book itself is a manuscript collection of Scottish acts and legal treatises[14] from the time of David I to that of Queen Mary, and was much copied in the fifteenth and sixteenth centuries. This copy was completed about 1575 and is heavily annotated. Some of these notes are 17th century schoolboys' graffiti including: "Robert Ross is a boss, the greatest in all his class".[15] This comment starts in Scots, and then changes to Latin [Figure 1.1b]. Hence Robert Ross is probably the first pupil's name to be recorded in the history of Inverness Burgh education.

These "Inverness Fragments" of music and the pages from the Latin grammar books then, assuming the attribution to Inverness is accepted (and Dr Mapstone is fairly categorical about its provenance), represents information from a period immediately before and after the change in church government around the time of the Reformation. On balance therefore, it seems likely to represent the first evidence we have of actual books and music used in an Inverness school, and therefore in a predecessor of the Royal Academy. It is not possible to decide from the evidence of the Inverness Fragments whether there were two separate schools in Inverness immediately prior to the Reformation: a song school and a reading school. Perhaps there was even a separate Latin school. Many towns had reading schools, which provided elementary training in Latin grammar, where a pupil might spend two years before moving on, perhaps to a grammar school.

Education and the Burgh Court Records
Local affairs in the sixteenth century, and up to 1636, were under the control of the Inverness Burgh Court, which at that stage controlled both administrative and judicial matters. Unfortunately the earliest volume or volumes of their records have not survived and the first material available is from November 1556. Later there is a gap in the record from 1586 until 1602, representing probably another missing volume. Nevertheless the surviving volumes are another valuable, although fragmentary, source of information

about schooling in the Town.

One specific piece of evidence from these Burgh Court records (and from much the same period as the "Inverness Fragments") is an entry where the schoolmaster's salary in 1557 was fixed by the Burgh Court at £4 in money and 12 bolls of victual, stented on the "common rents and possessors of them".[16] A stent is a tax, and those taxed were all those who rented land in and around the town. The full quotation reads:

> The consell hes condiscendit all in ane voce thair be twelf bollis wyttell [victual] stenttit on the commone takis and possessors of tham to be gyfin yerle to the Master of Sculle for his fee and fowyr pundis mone in pencion to be payit to hym yerle at twa termis for techyn of the scull, quhilkis wittuallis salbe payit to hym at Candylmes and Pasche and fowyr pundis mone at Mertimes and Whytsunday; quhajs nams efter followis that ar stentit, viz:- *[here follows the 24 names]*: And als the prowest, balzes [baillies] and commone consell hes consingit Thomas Waus, skynner, and Necoll Kar of his awyne dissyris [desires] to refund content [= payment in full] and pay hym his fowyr pundis pencion yerle quhilk salbe allowit to thame tha hef the Master acquittance lyk of payment as the same hed beyne payit to our Thesaurer.

Basically this means that the schoolmaster was paid partly in money and partly in grain, probably oats, mainly at the legal quarter days. The money was to be paid at Martinmas (in November) and Whitsun (in May), with the grain handed over at Candlemas in February, and at Easter (Pasche). This salary was probably for the schoolmaster of the reading school, in which the Town Council would take a greater interest than in a school that was primarily for the training of clergy.

Post-Reformation Education in Inverness
The coming of the Reformation to Inverness, as elsewhere in Scotland, would lead very quickly to the abandonment of the Latin music, only sung by what amounted to a professional choir, and this perhaps is why the fragments ended up as part of the binding of the law book, as paper was too valuable to throw away if it could be reused. Most song schools were closed in 1560 (although the one in Edinburgh was reopened only a few years later), so the music sheets would be of no value to the church. Singing in future would involve the whole congregation and be in the vernacular, and be biblical in origin, for instance the psalms and paraphrases.[17]

In 1579 Parliament passed an act directing that song schools with qualified masters be re-established in all burghs. However we have no direct information on whether Inverness complied with this order, or perhaps had something already in place which would have satisfied Parliament. Certainly by 1628 there was such an appointment when the master received £36 [Scots] for his salary. A similar amount was paid in 1634.[18] This sum was meagre compared with that paid in other burghs at this time.[19] Unfortunately, there are no names recorded. The master of the music school under the new regime would normally also function as precentor in the church, and perhaps as session clerk.

The Reformation in Inverness was not a violent affair: the deposed clergy, or those who switched to the Protestant faith, retained a large proportion of their revenues from Friary lands and were active in civic life. Priests continued for many years to fill the role of Town Clerk, and the old feast days survived although in a diminishing way. Nevertheless the Friary was closed, presumably sometime in 1560. An order in 1568 was the second attempt to stop the demolition of the Friars' Kirk and other buildings until the Town formally controlled the land. The text does not indicate whether or not the former school building was included in this.

We have more information about what can be called by this stage the Grammar School, but, as already stated, when the school moved more under the control of the Burgh is not clear. Nor is it clear when the school moved from the Friary entrance to some other location in the Town. Barron[20] suggests that this move would have been some years after the Reformation, but this seems unlikely in view of the attempts to demolish the priory buildings. He then suggests that its new location was in a building on the site of the former *Inverness Courier* office at the foot of Bank Lane, beside the River Ness and close to the main bridge. The lane which passes here was at one time called School Vennel, and only changed its name when the Bank of Scotland built offices there. In the absence of any other information, this site is the prime candidate for the location of a grammar school in the late 16th century and for nearly seventy years in the 17th century.

From 1561, details in the Burgh Court Book concerning salary and appointments of masters become more frequent, perhaps representing the change from ecclesiastical to Burgh control. By 1562 one Master Thomas Howieson (with a wide variety of spellings) was the schoolteacher, on a salary of 50 merks. This salary abolished a requirement that had been in place for the previous couple of years to pay part of the fee in terms of a day's meat, supplied by 24 named people. But by June 1565 Howieson was minister of the Town.[21] According to a list of Scottish clergy Master Thomas was a Roman Catholic priest, but joined the Reformers and was the second Protestant minister in Inverness[22] – the first was a person by the name of David Rag.[23]

Rag had been something of a woman's man and within approximately a year of his appointment he was accused of committing adultery. The minister was acquitted but his reputation must have been dented and within a year or two Howieson was in place, perhaps as Rag's direct replacement. Howieson clearly had several jobs, and the Town gave him permission to appoint an assistant to do the teaching in the school. This person would be called the Doctor or Usher (terminology varied from town to town and time to time).

In 1564 and 1565 Master Martyne Logye (again with several spellings) is twice named as Master of the School,[24] probably as Doctor for Howieson and paid out of Howieson's pocket. In the earlier entry Logye is admitted by the

Burgh as a stallanger [= stall-holder], presumably to supplement his meagre income from teaching. He also practised as procurator in the Burgh Court. As both Howieson and Logye were specifically named as 'Masters', they must have attended a university and graduated with a master's degree.

The second entry about Logye concerns a bizarre incident when a woman called Margaret Cuthbert burst into his house whilst both he and his wife were out and their child was being looked after by a nurse at the fireside. Cuthbert took fuel from the fire in the hearth and threw it all over the nurse and child, burning the child and her clothes.

At the Burgh Court meeting on 2nd February 1566 a Sir Patre [Patrick] Anderson was appointed[25] – the 'Sir' here meaning a person with a bachelor's degree from a university. Anderson had been (and to some extent still had the emoluments of) the Chaplain of Saint Michael's in the Parish Church of Inverness. In modern English spelling, his contract runs as follows:

> ... the said Patrick for the pleasure and desire of the Provost, Baillies and Council, who are Masters and Patrons, and by their desire and supplying of him by their fortification and help to inbring his yearly duty and anvellis [annual income], becomes bound and obliged, and by the tenour of these presents binds and obliges himself faithfully to be Doctor under the said Master in teaching of the said school for all the days, years, and terms of his lifetime, and shall await thereon by the desire of the Master to the furtherance and profit of the Bairns that are and are to come there, for which the said Master Thomas binds and obliges himself faithfully by the faith of his body to thankfully content and pay yearly to the said Patrick the sum of 10 merks, or else shall assign the same to the said Patrick to be uplifted of the Town from the Provost and Baillies out of the said Master Thomas's pension, which the town is obliged to pay Master Thomas by virtue of the security of the said Town made to the said Master Thomas, and the same to be paid unto him for his lifetime in sickness as well as in health, and this contract to remain for both the said parties...

He remained in post at a salary of 10 merks probably until some time in 1570. Soon after this Howieson offers as Doctor an Andro McPhaill, who was both the Gaelic minister of Inverness and the minister at Petty (a parish a few miles east of Inverness). Howieson demands from the Burgh officials the money (which had been withheld during a vacancy) to pay his doctor at the same salary.[26]

Of the pupils themselves we can learn little: perhaps the Robert Ross, whose graffiti appear on the law book mentioned above, was one of the pupils at this time, although Allenson dates him as a pupil in the seventeenth century (see above). The removal of what was regarded as the excesses of the previous ecclesiastical regime are mentioned, when in 1569 John Reid was instructed to hand over the brass he had received from the schoolboys and which they had taken from the stone of the High Altar and the new Aisle of the Parish Kirk:[27]

> John Reid son of Schir Johne Reid is decernit be the jugis to rander and delywer to William Cuthbert thesaurer of the burcht [burgh] of Inverness all and haill the brass rasauit [received] be him fra the scollaris of the scule tane be thame of the

stane of the hie alter and new ile within the kirk of Innernis.

Sixteenth-century teenage vandalism! However this John Reid was no angel either, despite his father being a university graduate. He was constantly in trouble with the authorities, including charges of theft. When he was in prison for one offence he burned the Town's firlot, a grain measure, which he was ordered to replace.

Before the gap in the records, that should have taken our story into the 17th century, the only other significant entry is the one previously quoted, concerning the renting of the old school land to the Provost in 1574. The Friary building had clearly been abandoned by this time: timber from the Friary church roof was used to repair the roof of the Parish Church, and the building stone and other useful products had been removed from the site, so in the last quarter of the sixteenth century the traces of the Friary and its school all but disappeared.

Chapter 2
The Grammar School of Inverness

As the years move on through the seventeenth and eighteenth century the references to the Grammar School, and later a range of other schools, become more frequent. It is clear that the grammar school served the Town for something over 200 years, from the disappearance of the church school round about 1560, or perhaps even earlier, until the grammar school was formally closed with the opening of the Academy in 1792.

The *Records of Inverness*, which provide most of the quotations from 1560 until 1688, provide only a few clues for the remaining period of the Inverness Burgh Court, which did not split its legal and administrative functions until 1637, when the administration passed to the Inverness Town Council.

Perhaps a shortage of people who could write competently led to the employment of youth labour when the Court decided to pursue its debtors in 1613:[1]

> 20 December, 1613. Giffin Patrick Clerk, messinger, to summiond alters [= various] men anent the reduction of the horning [= debt] 5 lib. Item, to the boyis that maid coppis thairof and to the relaxatioun 13 ss 4 d.

The word "relaxatioun" is an old Scots legal term referring to the document confirming that, in this case, the debt had been paid. However, this copying suggests a good level of literacy amongst the grammar school boys. Apart from a minor payment for rent for a period around December 1617, the only other information that is recorded is the salary of £40 Scots paid to William Ross, master of the Grammar School, in 1617,[2] and Peter J. Anderson's entry for about 1636 when a John Duff was Master.[3]

The early schoolmasters
Soutar[4] claims that in 1646 the Burgh first paid salaries to teachers, and in a sense this may be true, as previous payments probably came from the rentals of the church lands, which after 1560 gradually came under the control of others. Certainly in April 1650 Robert Forbes, appointed in the previous year, was asking the Town for an increase in his salary[5] "in regaird of the scairctie of the zeire [year]" – food prices had increased – and he was given a bonus of £10. Forbes' appointment is the first where we get a clear idea of how the Town appointed its schoolmaster, with limited church involvement. In July 1649 the Town Council record reads:[6]

> That day compeirit [appeared before a court (here the Council)] Mr. Robert Forbes and Mr. James Dunbar, and gave vpe thair names to the Towne Counsell for giwing thair tryallis anent [with regard to] thair qualifications and abilitie for dischairgeing the dewtie and function of ane scholemaister at the present waiking [doubtful transcription from original; probably = 'Latin'] schole of Innernes. The Counsell hes assignit to the saidis Mr. Robert Forbes and Mr. James Dunbar the 17 of August nixt to give tryall of thair literatioune and qualificatiounes for the said functioune at Innernes befoir thame and the brethrene of this presbitrie, and the

21

man found most able efter tryalll to be presentit and preferit to the place; And the Counsell, with adwyse of Mr. William Fraser, one of thair ministeris, hes givin out in leassone to the saidis scolleres the 16 Od of Libri opidum of Horace, the first 16 lynes of that Od to be handled be him the said day of tryall, and that they use ane harrang befoir they handle the leassone, and that the said leassone be handled according to the custome of scolleres usit in the lyke caices.

This extract proves very valuable in providing information about schooling in the mid-17th century. The use of the term 'Mr.' again implies that both candidates had Master of Arts degrees from a university, probably one or other of the Aberdeen Colleges, assuming they were local to the Highlands. Indeed people of both names appear amongst the lists of graduates of King's College, Aberdeen, in the preceding two years.[7]

The use of a "crit" lesson, loathed even today by trainee teachers, in front of members of both the Town Council and the Presbytery of Inverness, was often used as a device to select teachers, akin to a sermon preached by a minister before being called to a new charge. The 'harrang' would not have had the present-day meaning of a tirade or noisy speech, but would mean an explanatory talk. The text selected, a section of the classical author, Horace, gives a clear indication of the nature of the education carried on, but for the modern reader it is unfortunate that the instructions for the conduct of the lesson simply say 'business as usual' and do not provide the details.

An Alexander Dunbar took over from Robert Forbes only eighteen months later, but no reason for the change is recorded.[8] By January 1654 Dunbar had resigned and an Alexander Fraser, son of Alexander Fraser, litster [= dyer], was asked to take over[9] until someone more qualified was found. Clearly no-one better was found, as the *Wardlaw Manuscripts* (an account of the Clan Fraser written around 1700) tragically record that in August 1661 Fraser was drowned in the Town harbour whilst trying to rescue one of his pupils.[10] The story is recounted by Newton.[11] Two boys, Donald Bain of Tulloch and Hugh Fraser of Reelig, got into difficulties. Fraser saved Bain but died when he attempted to rescue Hugh Fraser. Attempts at resuscitation failed when his still-warm body was dragged out of the water.

Fraser had been a graduate of Marischal College, Aberdeen in 1657, so he must have been only in his early twenties when he died. The fact that he was teaching in the Grammar School while completing his degree, would not have been uncommon, as university terms were very short, recognising that many students had to earn a living as well as study. Graduation also took place at a much earlier age than we expect today, as many students went to university at age 14 or 15 and would graduate by age 19 or 20.

One of Alexander Fraser's pupils must have been a James Fraser [Figure 2.1], third son of another Alexander Fraser, of the Farraline branch of the family.[12] His father was the minister at Petty (a parish to the east of Inverness). James left the Grammar School in 1660 at the age of 15, and went to King's College, Aberdeen, graduating with an M.A. in 1664. He went on to become the first Secretary of Chelsea Hospital in London, a post he held for thirty years, and was also librarian of the Royal Library and Licenser of printing. He made considerable donations to King's College, and in his will left money to provide a regular income for the Inverness Kirk Session Library. However, he did not forget his old school, and endowed two bursaries for pupils of the Inverness school, one bursary to be in Theology linked with the Library Keeper of King's College; the other bursary to be in Philosophy, with this person succeeding the Theology bursar after a four-year period.

The only other information that has survived from the middle of the seventeenth century, before another gap in the Town Council records from 1655 to 1662, was an order in June 1651[13] for all those owning a horse to:
> lead ane fraught [= load] of staine and sand to calsay the schoole wyne [pave the school lane]

This could well have been a repaving of what we now know as Bank Lane. By 1663 the Council were concerned about the quality of the school building. Two sites, one at the east port and another at the back of David Robertson's house and yard (the exact location is not stated), were surveyed for building a new school.[14] Neither was very suitable, and the Town then considered repairing its own building at the bridge end. This did not go ahead, and by July 1664 it was decided by the Council to construct a building of '4 couples and 2 hewn gables'. The outstanding stents [= taxes] were to be collected, presumably to finance construction.

Even this building was not erected, and a year later the matter was still under discussion:[15]
> ... and finding that ther is ane absolut necessitie for looking out for a sufficient hous fitt for accomodatione of the children, as also that in the said hous ther be a chamber off loft qrin their will be a bedd, a taffie [= a small table], and a chimney for the use of the mr.; ... and authorise [3 councillors] to promise in behalfe of the Magistrats and Counsell for sick a hous, furnisched as aforsaid, the soume off fiftie merks yeirly for the space of three or four yeirs after Mertimis nixt ...

Yet again nothing appears to have happened, but either in or very soon after 1668, the Dunbar Hospital building in Church Street, which had been purchased by Provost Alexander Dunbar (of Barmuckety and Westfield), became available, and under his instructions the room on the ground floor at the south end of the building became the grammar school for around the next 125 years [Figure 2.2]. He was Provost from 1666-1668.

The building which clearly was in such need of replacement was probably the one previously mentioned as identified by Barron.[16] A deed of 1749 describes it as an ancient house with a timber house above. It became the property and possibly the home of Provost John Hossack, shipowner, merchant, and Chief Magistrate from 1735 to 1738, and again from 1741 to 1744. Hossack, generally a very powerful figure in the Burgh, challenged some of the brutality following the Battle of Culloden, and this led to him being thrown in prison.

The gap in the Town Council records from 1655 to 1662 covers the period when the Town was under the control of a military garrison in Cromwell's fort. But the restoration of the monarchy (with Charles II as King) in 1660 brought another change which affected the appointment of schoolmasters, namely the reintroduction of bishops to control church affairs. Bishops had been removed in 1592, and abolished again in 1638 at the time of the National Covenant. Reintroduction of bishops was not popular in 1662 but lasted until 1690, when a new constitution for the Church of Scotland was ratified by William III. Amongst its provisions was the abolition for all time of bishops in the established church; church affairs were then controlled by presbyteries and the General Assembly.

James Stewart [or Stuart] replaced William Cumming as schoolmaster in December 1663, Stewart having won the "dispute"[17] – another form of examination where questions were posed to the candidates to identify the one with the highest standard of education. However this method seems to have had little to do with teaching ability. Stewart stayed in post until September 1669, when he resigned to go into the ministry.[18] In preparation for the new appointment, the magistrates decided on their powers of appointment:[19]

> The Magistrats and Counsell being interrogat be the Prowest, whither or not they would allow the presenting of ane person pitched on [= selected] by themselves to the School of Invernes, as they are patrons thereof, or that ane edict should be emitted and served for ane free disput to be the state of the questione yea or not, and, it being put to the voyce, is caryed affirmative as follows, – that is to say, that according to their friedome and libertie they present a man of their own appointment, without any dispute. ...

There were in fact three candidates, John Cuthbert, a native of Inverness, and therefore presumably known to the magistrates, a candidate called Michael Fraser put forward by the Bishop of Moray, and a third person who had put his own name forward. Cuthbert won on a majority of votes.[20] This Bishop (Murdo Mackenzie, formerly minister in Elgin) however seems to have delegated to the local Presbytery the examination of Cuthbert as to his religious acceptability. During a meeting of the Presbytery in Inverness in 1672, the local ministers declared themselves:[21]

> well satisfied with the thriveing theirof, and reported that they were well pleased with yr schoolmaster.

Pupil numbers seem to have been higher than usual whilst Cuthbert was schoolmaster, and by June 1671 he was requesting assistance[22] and the Council authorised the appointment of a doctor, or second master. This is the first time in 100 years that a doctor had been mentioned. John Munro was appointed for one year in the first instance, and allowed 6s Scots per scholar, whether from town or country, over and above the 40 merks given him by the Session and £20 Scots from the schoolmaster. This settlement seems generous for the period, but the payment by the Session suggests that he may also have been Session Clerk.

Cuthbert resigned in August 1673, and again the Council, even though they clearly saw themselves as patrons of the school, debated whether to nominate or to have a "dispute"; after some time-wasting, they simply appointed, by a majority vote, Master Alexander Rose, "lawful son to David Rose of Earlfinlay", but referred him again to the Bishop to check that he was (religiously) suitable, and if so a contract was to be drawn up.[23]

By 1682 a George Dunbar was resigning as schoolmaster, to be replaced by John Munro, late governor to Lord Lovat, who was appointed unanimously.[24] He was called before the Council and instructed to go to the Bishop of Moray (Colin Falconar)[25] for approbation. His trial was the third Ode of Horace. Less than two years later, Munro indicated he would resign the following 1st May (1685), but the Council were keen for him to stay in post. He did not want to stay, but his teaching methods were so highly regarded by the Council that they wanted his replacement to work with him during his closing months as schoolmaster.[26]

A native of the county of Inverness, Alexander Sutherland, took over, with the approval of the Bishop,[27] in May 1685 at the usual salary and emoluments. The salary is defined the following year[28] as "eight score and ten merks money", i.e. 170 merks, from the mort-cloth money. The Town made some of its revenue from hiring out a mort-cloth to cover the coffin at a funeral. A local merchant was made responsible for this, and as far as is known, this is the first reference to the schoolmaster's salary being paid from these funds, as the previous year the money had come from the Common Good Fund and the feu duties. For many years around 1700 the keeper of the mort-cloth was one John Hatmaker, his name suggesting his occupation or that of his forebears. Sutherland was the last schoolmaster to be appointed with the approval of the Bishop, prior to the abolition of bishops in the Presbyterian church in 1690.

The printed *Records of Inverness* come to an end in October 1688. However Margaret MacDougall, one-time librarian and museum curator in Inverness, transcribed a summary of notes about schooling from the Town Council minutes, up to the last reference she could find in 1795, following the opening of the Royal Academy. These currently remain unpublished, but provide the source of much of the remaining material in this chapter. Doubtful references have been checked against the originals where they could be specifically identified.

In 1690, Sutherland was replaced by Thomas Jaffrey, previously schoolmaster at Cromarty. He was a native of Aberdeenshire, and at some point schoolmaster in Elgin.[29] He served the Town for seventeen years, and in 1691 appears to have been preaching during a vacancy in the High Kirk, in spite of an attempt by some of the ministers who had met in Elgin to oust him from that job and put in place the minister from Cromarty. The issue seems to have been political, as much as religious, as the minute concludes:[30]

They are unanimously of ye judgement that ye said proposal be declined in respect of a call they formerly gave to Mr Thomas Jaffrey Master of the Grammar School a person everyways well qualified & affected to the present government to supply the same.

Souter[31] claims the magistrates favoured an Episcopalian candidate and it was some time before a Presbyterian minister was in place.

Several mentions are made in the Minutes about payments to Jaffrey, although at that stage it was necessary for the schoolmaster to petition the Council or the Kirk Session for his salary.[32] It was not automatic that payment would be made. However, no record has been identified of payment being refused once a precedent had been established. Jaffrey died in the early days of 1707.

The eighteenth century

In August 1707 the joint Presbytery of Forres and Inverness examined Robert Thomson, schoolmaster in Inverness, for Jaffrey's job. Presumably he was the master at one of the other schools at the time. They found him satisfactory as far as his scholarship in Latin was concerned, but:[33]

... several questions being proposed to him anent his method of teaching and specially his way of training up the youth in the principles of the Christian religion and satisfying answers being made, he was exhorted to diligence and encouraged in his work, and appointed to have serious thoughts about the Confession of Faith that he may be in case to subscribe it how soon the Presb. shall require him to do it.

Subscribing to the Confession of Faith appears several times in the coming years. That afternoon the Presbytery visited the school and examined the two classes in the various classical authors they were studying; the minute concludes by saying that the details of the work were to be recorded so next time they visited the progress of the scholars "may be better known".

For some unknown reason it took the Town Council until the following April to appoint Thomson, and even then it was on a temporary basis until a "dispute" was held on 5th May. Unfortunately, a page is missing from the Presbytery minutes, so full details of the arrangements for the examination do not remain, but Thomson was duly appointed. His examination was quite extensive:[34]

The Presbytery ... did take tryal of Mr. Robert Thomson ... by expounding an Ode of Horace ad aperturam libri at the Moderator's desire, as also a piece of Cornelius Nepos, and at Baillie Fraser's desire a piece of Buchanans History of Scotland, and at the desire of one the Council a piece of Terence, and likewise by writing a theme and version ex tempore, and the Magistrates judging these steps enough for tryal [asked the Presbytery to visit the school].

Thomson had been appointed synod bursar in 1705 for four years, and the minutes of the Town Council in 1709 state that he was given a certificate as schoolmaster at the time of his resignation "to continue his studies elsewhere".[35] He went on to be minister of Clyne and then of Kirkhill.[36]

Alexander Matthew, previously schoolmaster at Calder [Cawdor], replaced Thomson, but within months the Town Council was asking him to resign due to his "want of authority".[37] If he did not resign, they intended to declare the post vacant. Conveniently he decided to resign, leaving his salary to their discretion, but this was paid in full. Several payments were due to the school, and he had to leave a list of them so they could be collected through the court if necessary. Reading between the lines, it seems that the Town Council actually had a replacement in mind, a John Laing, previously doctor of the Grammar School of the Cannongate (then a separate Burgh, but next to Edinburgh]. He was in post by January 1710, even though Matthew had resigned only in early December.

Laing left no time in petitioning the Council[38] that the:
> ... former practice of giving long series of vaccancies [holidays] to the scholars was a great hindrance to their education particularly the tyme of fastens even [= Shrove Tuesday] by which they lost a great deall of their learning & did nothing else but begg cocks up and down the country to the great hazard of their health & incurred their parents displeasure...

He asked the Council to change the holiday dates, which they did, declaring that the Fasten's Eve [= Shrove Tuesday] holiday should not start until the Thursday before the holiday and to reduce undesirable practices declared:
> for that effect enjoyn the Master that NOE schollars be obliged to bring above two cocks to the school.

Cock-fighting was a major spectator sport, and took place in the classroom, providing the master with quite an important source of income. Barron describes the activity.[39] The schoolroom was turned into a cock-pit for the day; the master presided, collected the money and judged the fights. The master would also claim the defeated birds and those that ran away, only the victorious birds being returned to their owner. This practice would not have died out until well into the 18th century.

Laing was in post for about five years, and provides us with the first surviving document directly associated with the Grammar School, with his salary claims for 1710-1712,[40] where his signature appears against his petition for payment. Mort-cloth money was still being used for this purpose, with a payment of 110 merks for 1711 [£73 6 8d Scots]. His total salary seems however to have been greater than this. In his early petition he also asked for a visitation (these days what would be called an inspection) at least once a quarter, and an examination with parents present. The Council approved his suggestions and a visitation is recorded as having taken place in July 1710.[41] He resigned in 1712, and the Council minute says it was "for reasons contained in his petition". These turn out to be about his poor health and the cost of living in Inverness.[42]

After an attempt to replace Laing with a teacher from Aberdeen,[43] the schoolmaster at Ferintosh, James McKenzie, was appointed. A sticking point seems to have been McKenzie's unwillingness to sign the Confession of Faith. At its meeting in February 1713,[44] the Presbytery of Inverness (now no longer joined with Forres) put the matter off a second time, and its seems likely that he never signed the document. McKenzie was also described as Master of the Humanity School, the only time this old-fashioned term is used for the Latin or Grammar School. The Council seem to have been well satisfied with him[45] as in February 1717 they wrote to the Earl of Cromartie asking if McKenzie could stay in Inverness another year. (No explanation has survived as to why permission was necessary.) This seems to have been granted, but he resigned either in December 1717 or at Whitsun 1718, the Town Council and Presbytery accounts varying.[46]

In May 1713 McKenzie was allowed to recruit a doctor, as his contract allowed when the number of scholars exceeded 30. He claimed that the number was well above that and increasing daily.[47] Kenneth Tuath was appointed, being paid 100 merks a year later (after considerable pleading on the grounds that he was about to leave town), to be replaced the following May by Alexander McPhail, appointed on a similar salary, but with a third of the quarterly fees in addition.

Three candidates appeared for the "trial" to replace McKenzie,[48] McPhail, the doctor (or sub-doctor, depending on the record) applied, but as he refused to sign the Confession of Faith he was not examined any further. The competition between a Wm. Munro and George Steele was won by Steele, who did sign the Confession of Faith. He was another Marischal College graduate, and had been Chaplain to the Laird of Lethen. His salary was to be 170 merks plus 13/6d Scots quarterly per pupil. McPhail seems to have resigned immediately, and Steele petitioned for a doctor "to instruct the inferior classes", as he had six classes. He also complained about unauthorised competition at Muirtown.[49] Several doctors came and went [see Appendix 1], and Steele finally resigned in June 1723[50] "he having resolved to travel abroad for his further instruction".

David Fraser, the doctor at the time, and another native of Inverness, was asked to take over in the interim, and was formally appointed in November of that year.[51] His salary claims and receipts for part payments have survived.[52] His tenure lasted just under four years. He was replaced by a fellow King's College graduate, Thomas MacPherson, who had served under Fraser as doctor. His salary claims and receipts also survive,[53] being the first ones to be, at least in part, in £ stg. Times were obviously hard as Robert Niddrie, the doctor around 1730, asked for and got a salary increase, immediately leading to MacPherson asking for and getting one.[54] Accounting was clearly not a strong point with the Town Council, as the mort-cloth accounts for 1723 to 1735, used for paying some of this salary, were not presented for approval until 1743,[55] along with many years of the Burgh accounts [Figure 2.3].

MacPherson remained in post from 1727 until 1750, by far the longest tenure as Master or Rector of the Grammar School until this time, and apart from his salary payments appearing in the Burgh Accounts, sometimes listed between the ministers' stipends and the salary of the Burgh hangman, little else can be gleaned about his time in office. MacPherson seems to have died in early 1750 whilst still in post. His replacement, Alexander Fergus(s)on from Prestonpans, was given £10 stg. to encourage him to move north, although the Magistrates could not afford to provide him with a rent-free house.[56] His salary would be 300 merks [about £17 stg]. It was claimed that pupil numbers could be 140, or even more, under a good head teacher. Mention is also made that there were mathematics and music teachers working in the Town. Following a visitation to the Grammar School by the Town Council in June 1750, a vintner was paid £19 16s for food and drink to entertain Fergusson and his staff, with a further £7 4s spent later in the year.[57] In 1751 a similar entertainment cost £14 0s.

A scandal led to Fergusson's dismissal in January 1755.[58] He had neglected his charges:
> ...to the manifest prejudice of the Town & Country, & had made himselfe obnoxious to the reproach of eitheir, who have withdrawn their children from the Town & School. That he is meditating defamatory informations agst. Magistrats Councillers & others, & that he is now accused of gross immorality.

The school was declared vacant from Candlemas (2nd February). A petition in the National Archives of Scotland, from Fergusson's wife,[59] tells more of the story. She petitioned for a warrant for the commitment of Janet Cumming, servant at Dunean [Dunain] and alleged prostitute, for exposing her child and for suspicion of child murder. A note on the reverse, from John Hossack, J.P., the former Provost, indicated that Fergusson was already in prison for other reasons, and had a connection with the misconduct of Janet Cumming. In modern language, it seems that he had fathered a child by her, and she attempted to murder the child. The matter was referred to Edinburgh for legal determination.

Hector Fraser as schoolmaster or Rector
If Fergusson's appointment was a disaster, despite promising references, the magistrates' next choice in 1755 was, as it turned out, inspired, with the appointment of Hector Fraser,[60] the one master of the Grammar School whose name is still known to pupils in the Royal Academy in the twenty-first century. Fraser was another native of Inverness, and had been a bursar, both for arts and for divinity, at King's College, Aberdeen, under the James Fraser bursaries. Hector Fraser had become master of an Academy at Bethnal Green, now part of the east end of London. He would have been in his forties when he came back to Inverness, having first graduated in 1732 probably at about age 18 or 19.

Fraser accepted the appointment and took up post at Whitsun, later being given £15 stg. for transporting himself and his family from London. He clearly saw the way forward for the school as an Academy, where the various subjects taught were brought under the control of one person – the Rector. Consequently he petitioned the Town Council.[61] Presumably this scheme would be similar to the arrangement at Bethnal Green, and was beginning to take hold through England (see Chapter 4). It also in part matches a scheme which had been introduced in Ayr in 1746, where three departments were established, one for classics, one for teaching English subjects, and the third for various branches of mathematics such as arithmetic, book-keeping, geometry and navigation. However, the Council in Ayr does not seem to have agreed a planned course of study through these departments until 1794.

Summarised, his petition stated that he had provided himself with a house fit to provide accommodation for young gentlemen, and as a result (numbered as in the original):

1. he proposed that there should be another school, called the mathematical or writing school, which would be near or contiguous to the Grammar School for reasons he then states:

2. the master of this department should be under his direction and superintendence, to the extent of boarding with him and being paid by him if he received the salary from the Town; if a suitable assistant was allowed, he would look out for one;

3. that the assistant would attend as required in the grammar school:

> he shall wait on such gentlemen as shall make writing, cyphering [= simple arithmetic], merchants accompts [accounts], navigation, etc., their only study from ten a clock in the morning till noon, from two a clock till five & the residue not specified here to be employed in a subserviency to the writing and cyphering of boys at the Grammar School, & in such manner as Mr. ffraser shall direct....

After consideration, the Council decided to proceed with his plan, and ordered the salary established for the teacher of mathematics, and the rent of his school house, to be paid to Hector Fraser. Within a year the Council also gave him, his family and his servants, free crossing of the old stone toll bridge over the River Ness.[62]

Nothing else is heard of Fraser until April 1777, when he must have been approaching 65 years of age. This silence in the minutes presumably indicates that the Council had no cause to complain, and probably were very satisfied with his service. In that year the Provost reported[63] that there was reason to believe that Mr Hector Fraser, Rector of the Grammar School [the first recorded use of the term 'Rector' in connection with the school], would willingly demit office in order to pass the remainder of his life in ease and retirement. In consideration of his having served the community for many years with fidelity and reputation they judged it a part of their duty to testify their sense of his service by bestowing an annuity of twenty pounds stg. on him, which they accordingly promised him. He accepted the offer and retired as from 30th April 1777.

Fraser made his first will in 1784, and the codicil to it was written on his death bed in 1786. After various family matters were attended to, and money given to the library fund of Inverness (the forerunner of the present so-called Kirk Session library, mentioned above in connection with James Fraser), he decreed that after the death of his wife (which did not take place until 1795):[64]

> Item: I bequeath the sum of one hundred pounds stg. in order to promote and establish an Academy at Inverness, reserving to my said trustees or the survivers of them & after their decease to the Provost & Eldest minister of Inverness whom I hereby appoint as trustees, the power of presenting constantly & successively a student to the said Academy of the name of Fraser, son of a burgess of this town, or one of the name born in the town or parish, and until such Academy is established I request my said trustees or the surviver of them, or after their decease the provost & oldest minister of Inverness for the time to lay out the said sum upon interest for the purpose of helping at the writing school of Inverness the education of two boys of the name of Fraser, sons of Burgesses, or of the name born in the town, & failing of these two of the name born in the Parish of Inverness.

This amendment to his will was made only a matter of days after the initial meeting of the local Commissioners of Supply in November 1786 to promote the idea of an Academy in Inverness (see Chapter 4), but possibly reflected his knowledge of the spread of such schools in England in the middle of the eighteenth century, and the beginning of their spread in Scotland.

Fraser is buried in the Chapel Yard in Inverness,[65] and he was held in such high regard by many of his former pupils that for many years there was a dinner held in his memory. The first such event for which there is evidence was in September 1792.[66] By 1811 his reputation was such that a marble bust of Fraser was ordered:[67]

> On Wednesday last, the Gentlemen educated at the Grammar School of Inverness under the care of the late Mr Hector Fraser, held their Annual Anniversary Meeting in Bennet's Hotel, Angus Mackintosh of Holm in the Chair, and George Inglis, Esq. of Kingsmills Croupier. The day was spent with that great conviviality and good humour that has invariably distinguished this Meeting; and as a mark of the estimation in which these gentlemen hold the memory of their venerable Teacher, it was resolved that a Marble Bust of Mr. Fraser, value one Hundred Guineas, should be procured, and placed in the Hall of the Inverness Academy.

That bust, sculpted by Richard Westmacott (who was also responsible for some of the carving on Marble Arch in London), was put up in the Hall of the original Academy building in 1812 and still stands in the Library of the Royal Academy to this day [Figure 2.4a]. There is no surviving evidence of how his likeness was determined for the sculptor. Hector Fraser had from his own funds also donated to the Grammar School a bell, which has moved through each of the Academy buildings, and is now on display in the Culduthel building [Figure 2.4b]. These two specific reminders of his time as Rector survive to this day, although the third, the bursary, has been subsumed into the general Academy endowments.

Following Fraser's retirement, there were only two more Rectors of the

Grammar School. Alex. Simpson, his usher, agreed to take on the post of Rector at a salary of £31 stg.[68] Simpson was a native of Aberdeen, but once again a graduate of King's College, and as he graduated in 1771, he might have been roughly aged 25. However, the arrangement of having the mathematics school under the control of the Grammar School Rector was discontinued following Fraser's retirement, and the salary was paid directly to the mathematics teacher from that date. There is little mention of Simpson, except when he was asked to look out for staff for the other Town schools, until he resigns in December 1790.[69] In March 1791 he took the lease of a farm for 19 years at "Mains of Drakies, now Seafield".

A candidate from Glasgow was appointed but in the end declined, leading to the appointment of Ebenezer Young, late Rector of Queensferry Grammar School.[70] More will be said about Young in Chapter 6, as he became the first Latin teacher in the newly-established Academy eighteen months later.

School life in the eighteenth century

The records provide little information about the life of the grammar school scholars (probably entirely boys) in the seventeenth century, but as with the other information, references become more numerous as we move into the eighteenth century. Barron[71] mentions a document called "Note of the form of teaching Boys in the Grammar School of Inverness, taken in the said school this 24th March 1726". Unfortunately this document cannot now be traced, so it is necessary to rely on Barron's interpretation of it, and his comments probably reflect conditions only in the first half of the eighteenth century. The only three subjects mentioned are Latin, Greek and religious instruction, and he implies from the other evidence that reading and writing also formed part of the curriculum, although not in the same building. It is unlikely, although this did happen in some other towns, that all the subjects were taught at the same time in the same room to different groups of pupils.

In the Grammar School class itself, all instruction would have been given in Latin, all conversation would have been in Latin, and on school premises the boys would not have been allowed to speak in any other language. Latin, perhaps with a little Greek, was the pinnacle of education, allowing those trained in it to converse with scholars throughout Europe and beyond, regardless of the local language. By 1733 the age of entrants to schooling in Inverness seemed to have been somewhat younger than it had been in the past, and in response to this, the Town Council restricted the winter hours of attendance, to allow the pupils some free time, especially on Tuesdays and Thursdays.[72]

Soon after this we find the first mention of the orations – a feature of the Grammar School, and the Academy to follow, for over a hundred and fifty years. These were a form of public performance at the end of the school year in August or thereabouts, where the pupils recited sections of the classical authors in front of family and invited guests. The guests would have included the ministers and other local dignitaries, and the wording of the entries suggests that the scholars had some say in who was invited. Some nineteenth-century programmes for the orations have survived (see Chapter 9).

From 1736 the Town paid for an entertainment for the scholars and their guests. To our eyes, the quantity of alcohol consumed at this event is incredible, but in terms of other entertainments funded from the Burgh funds, the £10 16s [Scots] paid to the vintner for the 1738 event is modest.[73] Fruit, nuts and biscuits also appeared on many of the accounts, as well as the cost of broken glasses. By the 1740's the event cost the Town about £15 Scots. This type of entry appears almost every year thereafter until the 1840's or so.

Prizes seem to have been introduced in the late 1770's, when the first entry appears, both for the writing and Grammar schools. The sum of 9s 7d was made available by the Town for the Grammar School (with £1 the following year), and 11s 6d for the writing school.

From time to time petitions were received by the Town to support the education of deserving scholars. Paul McPhail in 1740[74] was claimed to be "a promising genious" and got free education in the Grammar, music and mathematics schools. Donald Campbell, son of Angus Campbell, souper [= sweeper up, cleaner] was given a similar privilege in 1747.[75] Bursaries for further studies were also funded by the Town, and about 1739 [date difficult to determine] Donald Fraser, the orphan son of a labourer, sought help for college expenses.[76] It was claimed he had a "genius for education" in cyphering and book-keeping. George Watson, son of the Deacon of the Tailors' Guild, had been appointed a free scholar in 1744 in the Grammar and music schools,[77] and had temporarily acted as usher in 1753[78], before resigning this post to continue his studies at Aberdeen, although he returned as doctor in 1754.[79] In 1746 the Burgh officer's son was given help with the costs of his studies in Aberdeen.[80]

During 1745-46 the Jacobite rising greatly affected Inverness, and the Town was soon under occupation by Government forces and remained so until 18th February 1746, when the retreating Jacobites reached the Burgh, eventually making their headquarters at Culloden House. There is no record of the magistrates meeting during the Jacobite occupation, and most of those loyal to the Government side (including all of the magistrates) would have kept a low profile at that time. The result of the battle at Culloden on 16th April brought into the Town new government forces, under Cumberland and Hawley.

The situation clearly affected the Grammar School, as it was used as military hospital after the battle. Nothing can be learned about this period from the Council minutes, but entries in the Burgh Accounts for 1746-48[81] show payments for half a pound of brimstone at a cost of 2 shillings for "smoking the Grammar School after using it as a hospital", and £133 3s for replacing the desks, seats and tables as they had been burned [Figure 2.5]. A new door lock also had to be fitted.

One other incident has for some reason survived from 1750. John Shaw, father of one of the Grammar School pupils, petitioned the Town for the commitment of a vagrant who had torn the hat of his son, William, when he was on his way home from school.[82] Unfortunately, what happened to the vagrant seems not to have been recorded!

By August 1792, the Dunbar Hospital room, used as the Grammar School for about the previous 125 years, was out of use. Some of the seats and desks were donated to the Raining's School (see Chapter 3), and the rest locked up until a decision was made about their future,[83] and the last recorded entry about the Grammar School in the Town Council minutes was of the same date, when it was agreed:

> ... the old school room & weigh house are no longer used for these purposes to which they were destined by Provost Dunbar, the Mortifier of the house, & considering how much a Poor House or Hospital is wanted in this place They therefore appoint the provost, [former] Provost Phineas Mackintosh and the Dean of Guild or any two of them as a Committee to meet with the ministers & Session & conclude with them about the manner of employing the house in the strictest conformity to the original destination...

Chapter 3
Eighteenth Century Education in Inverness

The Grammar School was certainly not the only school operating in Inverness in the eighteenth and probably also in the seventeenth century, although the evidence in this earlier period is more scarce. There was a music school from at least 1628, and an English and writing school must have existed, either as part of the Grammar School, or as a separate institution, to provide the basic education that was necessary to allow the boys to move on to learn Latin grammar.

Reading and writing were regarded as separate subjects, writing being less important. Reading was seen to be the key to education as it allowed the reading of the Bible. In fact in many, if not most, reading schools, the main, and possibly only, textbook would be the Book of Proverbs from the Bible, which both provided simple material, and a moral and Christian framework in which pupils would be brought up. Most girls would never have progressed beyond this stage, and more advanced education for girls, where this took place, would have been primarily for the daughters of the gentry, and have taken place within the home, possibly with private tutors, or as boarders in nearby towns, although there is evidence that, even in the seventeenth century, girls did attend the music and dancing schools. Attitudes changed, and by the very early years of the Academy, girls were included in classes there.

All the official schools were under the patronage of the Town Council, and other unauthorised schools were from time to time suppressed by the Town Council. The first such events that have been noted were Acts in Council of 1662 and 1673. Only four years later the Council was closing down three of these schools when a delegation from the Council reported back on their visits as follows:[1]

> ... they did sie sewerall children learning the Prowerbs & several wther books in Rorie Sinclers hous & Issobell Fraser hir chalmer [chamber = room], & diverse and sundrie children learneing to read & wrytt in George Anderson his hous; qlk report sua mad, and the Magistrats & Counsell being therwith maturelie adwysed, and considdering the great prejudice that may aryse to Johne Innes, present precentor, and to this place also be reasone of keiping and wpholding sewerall shooles without warrand had from tham; they therefor all in one woice haue discharged, and be ther presents discharges the forsaids thrie shooles, with certificatione to the upholders of tham that iff they or aither of tham presume under quhatsoewer cullor or pretext to teach a shoole heirefter they salbe lyable in the peyment of 40 lbs. Scots *toties quoties* [= each and every time], & that by & attour the dischargeing of the shoole...

John Innes, as precentor, would probably also have been the teacher of elementary reading and writing, authorised by the Council. This arrangement seems to have run for many years, as Robert Edwards (of whom more later) petitioned the Town for a salary for teaching writing and music.[2]

In the same year Mary Cowie was instructed not to teach "beyond the Proverbs". She probably taught what was called a "Dame School", run by widows or women of "genteil manner". They would teach elementary material and this would have had little effect on attendance at the Town school. There would also have been "Adventure Schools", private ventures which charged very low fees, attracting pupils whose parents could not afford to send them to the Town school. The three closed down were probably Adventure Schools. A century later, in 1753, Alexander Fergusson, master of the Grammar School, complained about an unauthorised school at Lochgorm (now Millburn Road), and the teacher (Archibald Henderson) had to submit to the magistrates' jurisdiction.[3] But what of the official schools?[4]

Writing and English

Little specific information appears about the writing school in the early eighteenth century. In 1753 John Boyd, who had been invited to Inverness, presumably by the Council, to teach writing and French (the only time French is mentioned, apart from in 1756 when a John Brulet sought a job),[5] seeking a salaried post, with the support of Fergusson in the Grammar School.[6] Around 1759-60 a schoolmaster by the name of Alexander Munro is mentioned in the Burgh Accounts. In 1773 Andrew Tolmie, the owner of the now-demolished 'Castle Tolmie' (on the site of the present office block and restaurant on the corner of Bridge Street and Castle Road beside the main bridge), sought an order for repossession of a house let to a Thomas Gordon, described as "writing and schoolmaster".[7] Gordon failed to appear at the hearing before the Burgh Court, and an order was issued against him. There is a more specific reference after Hector Fraser retired in 1777, and the writing and mathematics school was split from the Grammar School under Alexander Fraser.[8]

By the 1770's, the writing and English schools seem to have become largely separate from the Grammar School, as different staff were appointed. An English teacher is mentioned in 1778, when the Burgh Accounts show payments of £6 17 5d to make up a deficiency in his emoluments, and for £3 10/- for the rent of a room in Castle Wynd.[9] In the following year the sum of 3d was paid for the cartage of desks to this room. References to English teachers then appear regularly until the opening of the Academy. William Cook, appointed in 1783 from Leith Grammar School, found only 14 pupils and was given £5 stg. towards his removal expenses. He soon petitioned for a higher salary, claiming that his work was a "tedious and laborious task". The Council decide to pay him £5 stg. a year to employ a sub-doctor.[10]

The final appointment as an English teacher before the opening of the Academy, was in 1790, when William Hoyes seems to have taken up his post. Although considered for the English post in the Academy, he did not get the job and all trace of him is lost. The final appointment as writing master was James Will(i)s from Glasgow who arrived in Inverness in the summer of 1788. He transferred to the Academy, serving that school for 27 years, before dying in July 1819, aged 67. He is buried in the Chapel Yard in Inverness, close to his colleague, Ebenezer Young, classics teacher, who had died eleven years earlier (see Chapter 9).

Mathematics

The first reference to a specific mathematics master appears in 1721 when John Carson was paid £2 stg. for the rent of his schoolhouse for the previous year, and the Town agreed to repair at their own expense the steps up to the schoolroom.[11] It is not clear when he was appointed, or perhaps authorised to teach, but in 1725 he was described as "teacher of the navigation and other parts of the mathematics", at which point he had deserted his post and was dismissed.[12] Thereafter Robert Whittingdale, probably from Glasgow, was appointed on a salary of £10 per year plus £2 for the rent of the schoolhouse and the usual emoluments – presumably the fees from the pupils.[13] He died late in 1739.

Two petitions survive from those interested in taking on Whittingdale's job[14] and one of the petitioners, John Sa(u)nders, took over for only a couple of years until he was apparently dismissed. He was allowed to teach book-keeping, arithmetic, practical geometry and navigation, but was prohibited from teaching writing and vulgar arithmetic, which he also professed to be able to teach. An Edinburgh teacher, Robert Barbour, was invited by the Town to come north, and was in post for about 12 years before he died in August 1753, at which point his widow had to petition the Town to be put on poor relief, as she had four children and was destitute.[15]

Barbour had petitioned the Town very soon after he arrived that he had very few pupils and other teachers were going far beyond the reading and writing that they were permitted to teach, although he claimed they were ignorant of these subjects.[16] The Council did nothing until he again wrote to them in 1745, when they increased his salary from £12 to £16 stg., and forbad others to teach arithmetic and other similar topics, under penalty of a fine of 40/- [£2] stg.

When the Castle was blown up by Prince Charles' troops in February 1746, the sundial on the stone bridge was damaged. Barbour was later paid a substantial fee for "finding the meridian" and for setting up a replacement sundial. During the winter of 1751/52, Barbour apparently taught mathematics to James Wolfe, when he was stationed in Inverness.[17] Wolfe (the general who surprised and defeated the French at the capture of Quebec in 1759) spoke very highly of his teacher. In 1753 Matthew Fraser, a shoemaker, sought free education from Barbour for his son who it was claimed had a "genius for education".[18]

Following Barbour's death, there appears to have been no mathematics teacher until Hector Fraser made his first appointment following his educational plan put to the Town in September 1755 (see Chapter 2). This brought the mathematical school directly under his control, and little information remains other than the payment of the salary of the teacher through Fraser. When Hector Fraser retired in 1777, Alexander Fraser was teaching mathematics, and from then onwards he operated on his own account, receiving the full fees from the scholars. However, as often happened following a teacher retiring on a pension, Alexander Fraser did not receive any salary, but was promised one when Hector Fraser's pension ceased, presumably when he died. Alexander Fraser became one of the Parish ministers in Inverness in January 1779. He recommended Robert Graham as his successor, and Graham received a salary of £10 plus the fees of the class.

From May 1784 for a few years a Mr Gray was in post. During his time the Town Council agreed to purchase from London a pair of globes, to which was to be attached an inscription plate reading "Presented by the Magistrates and Council to the Mathematics School of Inverness 1785".[19] One of these globes would be terrestrial, covering the earth; the other would cover the constellations – a celestial globe. These globes were generally 1 foot [30 cm] to 2 foot [60 cm] in diameter, and formed an important part of the equipment of any mathematics school. Physical geography and astronomy were seen at this time as branches of mathematics.

Gray's replacement was sought in 1791, without any obvious success, until the mathematics school became incorporated into the Inverness Academy the following summer.

The Music School

The sources provide much more information about the music masters, and to a lesser extent the dancing masters. Parliament had passed an Act in 1579 (see Chapter 1), declaring that all of the main burghs should establish a song school, with qualified staff. This Act is known as the 'Act of tymous remeid'. It is unclear whether Inverness responded to this, whether it still had a song school in place, or whether nothing happened at that time. Certainly in both 1628 and 1634 a music master received £36 Scots.[20] By this time a Scottish Psalter had been published, and in the 1615 version of this psalter twelve common psalm tunes were clearly established. This suggested a need for a precentor or qualified person to teach these tunes to the congregations and to the young people in the schools. In 1673 the Town Council's Act in Council (see above) forbad unauthorised teachers from encroaching on the privileges of the music master.

By 1686 William Niven had been appointed and in that year was admitted to burgess-ship and created a guild brother.[21] Within a year Niven was summoned before the Council:[22]

> That day Bailiff Duff presented a letter in Counsell, direct to him be Jeane Cuming ... vindicating herself of that scandalous report made against her be William Niven, Professor of the Musick School ... and calling of the said William Niven, who compeired [appeared before them], and having interogat him how he being

38

her master & having her under his government & tutelage and being as in vice of a parent to her could have betrayed his soul & trust in offering to circumveine and cheat a child at school ... and having interrogat him whither or not he was maried with the said Jeane Cuming and had carnall copulation with her, declared affirmative that he was married with her on Halloweven last, and that he had carnall copulation with her ... In consideration off the cryme it was voted in Counsell that William Niven be keiped in sure & firme prison till they have advyse from the Privie Counsell what course to take in the said matter, and in the meanetym declares his place vaccand. ...

Jean Cumming was the daughter of the Minister at Edinkillie (a rural parish south of Forres), but was boarded in Inverness with Bailie Duff's wife. The report then details the examination of various witnesses from the family, who claimed she had not slept with him at night, but had attended the school during the day, until her father came and took her home. The following day, Niven was given the freedom of the upper room in the Tolbooth prison so that he could find caution that he would not escape,[23] the penalty for escaping being a fine of 1000 merks Scots. Munro[24] has managed to trace Niven through to a trial in Edinburgh in March 1688, where the Register of the Privy Council records that he was thereafter "banished from the kingdom ... not to return under pain of death".[25]

The passage quoted also shows that some girls received a musical education, although ministers would be amongst the better-paid members of the community and therefore able to afford both the school and the boarding fees. It seems unlikely that much of the music taught would be sacred, and it is probable that Jean Cumming was learning to sing and to play various instruments.

Munro says that Niven's replacement was an Alexander Munro, who was by 1709 to be found in Elgin. However an Alexander Bishop was master of the Music School before 1699 when he was made a burgess and guild brother,[26] something that seemed to happen about a year after a new teacher took up appointment. Bishop, like the writing school masters, had problems with unauthorised competitors, as in 1704 he was asking the Council to revive the 1673 Act of Council. The Council then acted against two sisters, Anna and Isabel Inglis, who were teaching vocal and instrumental music to both adults and children.[27] Bishop had died by 1707, and two part-time teachers, who were perhaps Bishop's pupils, were asked to carry on for a while.

William Cumming from Elgin was appointed in January 1709, which is perhaps why Alexander Munro was offered the Elgin job. As before, Cumming had no salary or allowance from the Town for his work, although he would have had protection under patronage. In consequence, following a petition from him, he received up to £20 Scots for rent of a schoolhouse and later he became a burgess and a guild brother. He was dismissed as unsatisfactory in April 1715.

Then follows a significant period when a father, and then his son, both called Robert Edwards, ran the Music School, and further scandal is recorded. The father took up post at Martinmas (November) 1717, and was given protection against competitors, as unauthorised teachers had established themselves during the vacancy. He used the minister's manse as his schoolhouse, and the Town repaired it for him in July 1722. His clientele seem to have been "gentlemen's children from the country". It took the Council eight years to make him a burgess and guild brother, at a time, according to Margaret MacDougall, when he was at the height of his popularity. A petition to the Council survives from 1730, in which he says he will leave Town if he does not get a salary for teaching both music and writing.[28] It was however the following June before the Council agreed to give him 100 merks Scots a year, from which date a couple of receipts survive.[29]

Edwards (snr.) was certainly a good teacher, but seems to have been a person of uncertain temper and rather outspoken.[30] By September 1733 he was in prison, having allegedly uttered disrespectful words about Bailie Thomas Alves (Treasurer of Dunbar's Hospital and at one point Dean of Guild), whose Shipland estate lay just east of Inverness. From jail, Edwards petitioned the Council either to grant him bail or start the prosecution. He was later fined and dismissed, but then reinstated. He was once again dismissed in October 1736, but the Council records do not indicate any reason. However about the same time he had been brought before the Kirk Session accused of drunkenness and under suspicion of adultery. He admitted being drunk, but claimed "no man indulges in more than one sin at a time". As Session Clerk he recorded his own case in the Kirk records. He was found guilty on the first charge but not guilty on the second, was fined and reprimanded by the Moderator, but was not dismissed from his church positions.

This shows once again the link between the secular music master's post (and the teaching of writing) and the church's post of Session Clerk and Precentor. Edwards was obviously very popular locally, as a public petition in January 1737 wanted him fully reinstated. He also petitioned the Council in September of that year to return his salary and rent to the level that it was before Martinmas 1736, to which the Council agreed. His death occurred towards the end of 1742, as in the following January, his son, also Robert Edwards, was petitioning the Council for a salary and fees.[31]

By October 1744, the son was seeking permission from the Council to go to Edinburgh to learn the latest music. The Town Council minute records:[32]
> ... that the petitioner had by their [i.e. the Town Council's] goodness been appointed Master of their Musick School & Church Presentor in his early years when his improvements & his education was below his genious[?] which might be improved, but that in this place he could attain it, nor was he in condition even tho' their Honrs. were pleased to allow him time for education to bestow on it. That their Petitioner was of opinion, that if their Honrs. were pleased to grant him a leave of absence for some months for his education at Edinr., and to bestow of

their bounty upon him, he apprehended he would improve it much & become more usefull & seviceable to their Honrs. & to their community for instructing & educating their children & occassion a greater resort of Children from the Country for the public benefite of the Community ...

Not only did the Council agree to his going to Edinburgh from November to March but they also gave him expenses of £8 stg., paid to him as £96 Scots.[33] He returned to Inverness only six months or so before Prince Charles raised his standard at Glenfinnan, and Government forces took control of Inverness for a few months.

What Edwards learned in Edinburgh would have covered a range of instruments and styles, including both classical and folk music.[34] The classical instruments would have included the violin, cello, flute, the harpsichord and the spinet. He may well have attended meetings of The Edinburgh Musical Society, which had been formally constituted in 1728. This Society was then in a period of ascendancy which lasted until about 1760. With a membership of about 60 and a large music library, it held regular classical-music concerts. These were performed largely by amateurs, and were generally totally unrehearsed, although some professionals from outside Scotland were paid from the funds of the Society. The music would be by continental composers such as Corelli and Handel (although Handel was living in London by this date), as well as music written by local composers. Oratorios and other large choral works were also performed, as well as solo vocal items. The folk music (which would not appear in the concerts) would include Scottish fiddle music, including music for dancing, based on Scottish tunes, but partly adapted to classical styles.

Regardless of what new music he had learned, we hear nothing more of Edwards until January 1751, when an inspection of the music school by the magistrates found his work unsatisfactory. By March 1752 the Provost reported to the Council that Edwards was neglecting his duty. By October Edwards submitted his resignation, saying that it did not "suit his convenience" to continue.[35] A candidate from Edinburgh was considered as his replacement, but this could not proceed as the Inverness Kirk Session would not dismiss him from his church posts, an indication perhaps of the Kirk Session refusing to submit to the secular authority of the Town.

Edwards tried to regain his position with a petition in 1755,[36] but the Council refused to reinstate him, although they granted him permission to teach privately if he wanted to. He was obviously in financial trouble as Duncan Forbes, a merchant, petitioned the Council in June 1756 for two year's rent of £40 Scots for Robert Edwards' schoolhouse.[37] The Council agreed to pay the rent, in order that the room would be available when a new teacher was appointed. However they refused to recognise Edwards as their music teacher.

The last mention of Edwards was in December 1761 when he was recorded in the Council records as "late master of the music school". At this point he was ill and destitute, as was his mother. By unanimous decision, the Council gave them the sum of £1 stg., the Treasurer being instructed to pay the money "in divisions to make it more serviceable to them". He seems to have lived in Bridge Street, and had a feu in Academy Street which was bought off him by Hector Fraser, who was, according to MacDougall, collecting subscriptions for the building of New Street (now Academy Street) from about 1756. This development lay just east of the old Town limits, and the street itself replaced a derelict ditch and wall.

In 1758 John Pearson took over the post of music master, receiving the salary and the schoolhouse rent.[38] Apart from these payments, almost nothing is known about Pearson. In his later years he was in poor health and died in about March 1791. His job was advertised in the Edinburgh newspapers (there was not yet an Inverness newspaper), and applications came from various quarters, including Dundee and Greenock.[39] Neither of these applicants got the job and one Maxwell Shaw took up the post. His hours were determined by the Council. From April to October he was to teach from 10 a.m. till noon and from 3 p.m. till 5 p.m.; from October to April the morning hours remained the same, but in the afternoon it was from 2 p.m. till 4 p.m. Quarterly concerts were to be held, in addition to the concerts held at the time of the visit of the Circuit Court to Inverness. He could also teach privately as long as this did not interfere with the public school.

Shaw was still the Town music master when the Academy opened in 1792, and his classes are mentioned in the opening advertisement for the Academy. He remained in post perhaps until 1796, when a petition from Robert Rose, Moderator, on behalf of the Session, says that the music master's job should be linked to that of Precentor.[40] Certainly by May 1797 Bailie Inglis had appointed Keith Thomson. He was to be paid the usual salary and emoluments plus £5 for travelling expenses. However, the Kirk Session refused to appoint Thomson as precentor and session clerk, apparently largely on the grounds they had not been consulted by the Town about his appointment.

By September 1803 the Town tried to make up a bit for this problem by increasing his salary to £20 stg. a year, and gave him permission to charge 25/- [£1 5s] per pupil per quarter in the public school and whatever he wanted for private pupils. Physically Thomson was not very strong, and at some point round about 1810-15 he tried to resign, but the Council changed his mind by increasing his salary to £30 and the pupils' payments to two and a half guineas [£2 12 6d]. By 1818 his salary was increased to £40. His salary receipts survive for most years from 1819 to 1852.[41]

He obviously was a skilled teacher, and in October 1811 the Council awarded him £40 to purchase a "piano forte" for the "young ladies to practice on". MacDougall also says he intended to open a music warehouse, but she could find no evidence that he did. The year 1846 saw the passing of the Patronage Act which thereafter prohibited the Council from favouring one teacher over another, but Thomson's salary from the Council continued until 1852. He died in November 1855, aged 83 years, having taught music for almost 60 years in Inverness.

Isabel Anderson, who was his pupil when she was aged seven, paid tribute to her former teacher with these words:[42]

> There never was a teacher more respected and beloved than old Mr. Thomson. He was a perfect gentleman, and his snow-white hair, his refined face, and venerable form can never be forgotten by his pupils. To the very youngest and smallest among them his manner was the personification of courtesy, and his patience never failed, even with the idlest and most stupid. How vividly the mention of his name recalls his low and courtly bow, his mild accents, his encouraging smile. He was a teacher who cared little for showy execution, but taught his pupils to play with taste and feeling; in fact, he used to say that he had never enjoyed listening to the music of anyone who had not first learnt to *feel*. It was a favourite practice of his to place his watch on the back of any pupil's hand, to ensure its being kept in the right position, and though this always caused great trepidation, the watch was never known to fall.

The location of the music school in the early years cannot be fixed with any certainty. As music teachers generally provided their own schoolroom, it would have moved from time to time. In 1741 there is a reference to a narrow lane leading to the river which was "commonly called the Musick school lane".[43] This could have been one of several such lanes, now streets, which still exist. In 1758 the Council purchased a "great new kiln" on the High Street, at the end of what is now Meal Market Lane. The word "kiln" here refers either to a malt kiln (a key, but declining, industry of the Town) or to an old Scots meaning of a wooden-framed building. The building was considered a serious fire risk, requiring a high insurance premium. The ground floor later became the meal market, and a room upstairs became a music school room.

This arrangement saved the Town money as they did not have to pay rent for another room. However by 1791 the building was so ruinous that a new site was purchased on the south side of the junction of High Street and Eastgate, which was to function as meal market, dancing and music schools, a fire station and a fish and green market. This building was bigger, but there was a problem with soundproofing between the music and dancing classes. This was eventually resolved by having classes at different times. A long corridor on the upper floor functioned as a cloakroom, but was also crammed with musical instruments. Concerts were held here quarterly, when the parents, Magistrates and Town Councillors would attend as guests. This seems to have been a sort of payment by results, as, presumably, if the councillors did not like the quality of the concert, they could withdraw the teacher's salary!

This building, immediately west of the foot of the Market Steps, was used until the late 1830's when it was replaced by the former Post Office building, still in commercial use today as a bank.

The Dancing School

The first evidence recorded about a dancing master is from 1720 when the Guildry protested about the Town Council continuing to provide patronage to Peter Gould, who had apparently left the school in 1715 to fight in the Jacobite army. He had taken part in the Battle of Sherrifmuir, before returning to Inverness and his job. Even though the Council were non-Jacobite (but not necessarily anti-Jacobite), and Gould had refused to subscribe to the Test Act which gave loyalty to the King and Government, this had been ignored as Gould seems to have been a good teacher. The Guildry petition forced the Council to dismiss him and threaten him with a fine of £100 Scots and imprisonment if he did not qualify himself. MacDougall suggests that he probably did qualify himself and continue as teacher. Dancing was extremely popular amongst the upper classes, and large balls and similar events were held frequently, bringing the dancing master considerable income.

There is a petition in about 1743 from Daniel Murray,[44] requesting support from the Town to run a dancing school on a salary, but it is uncertain if he was appointed. Certainly someone was in post in 1745 at the time Robert Edwards went to Edinburgh to learn the new music.[45] No further information is available about the dancing master until Bailie Rose was instructed in 1756 to find a new teacher who was to be of a "sober and virtuous nature". Certainly by 1760 a William Alexander was in post as there is mention of payments to him in the Burgh Accounts. He also petitioned the Council on an unrecorded matter a couple of years later. But in February 1765 Alexander was charged by the Kirk Session with adultery, and the Town Council dismissed him due to "having youth of both sexes under his care". He was immediately replaced by John Kinnaird from Morayshire. The speed of this appointment suggests that the Council were well aware that there was a problem, and were only waiting for the Kirk Session to find him guilty.

The dancing would have included country dances imported from England, along with dances designed to be performed to Scottish folk tunes. The reel was also popular, and from the 1760's the Strathspey was appearing in dance programmes. Various books of new dances were published from about 1740 onwards. The minuet had also been imported from the continent but was based on classical, rather than, folk music. The dancing master would generally accompany his lessons on the fiddle, adapting tunes to fit the solo instrument, although at more formal balls and gatherings a small band of musicians would play, and this may have included violins or oboes, and a cello. Bagpipers might also perform for some of the dances.[46]

Kinnaird was the first dancing master to get a salary, which from 1779 was £5 5s stg. a year, plus pupils' fees and help with the rent of a schoolhouse. However after the Meal Market building was erected he moved there alongside the music room. On 24th March 1783, he was dismissed following complaints about his conduct and behaviour, to be replaced by Andrew Laughlan who came north for the job. His salary was the same as Kinnaird's, and he had free use of a schoolroom, with an assurance that he would have no competition. His name is also mentioned in the opening advertisement for the Academy.

In 1802 Laughlan moved on to be a customs officer, and was replaced by John Dean, previously the dancing master at Tain. The Council increased his salary in stages from £5 to £20 by 1818, and various receipts for his salary remain.[47] He probably moved across the High Street from the Meal Market Close building to the building on the site of the Old Post Office. MacDougall claims that Dean was the last of the patronage dancing masters (patronage becoming illegal under the 1846 Act). The surviving receipts include one in 1825 paid to "widow Dean", suggesting that John Dean died during the early part of that year.

Raining's School

Two other patronage schools require mention at this stage. The first of these is still remembered in a local feature, the Raining (or Raining's) Steps or Stairs. John Raining was a merchant in Norwich and died on 18th March 1723. In his will he left £1000 to establish a charity school in the Highlands, with a further sum of £200 for the building of a schoolroom. It is not clear why Raining should have left this money for use in the Highlands, but thousands of Inverness children in the eighteenth and nineteenth century were grateful for his charity.

The General Assembly of the Church of Scotland put this money in the care of the Scottish Society for the Propagation of Christian Knowledge (SSPCK). The first mention of this bequest is in a paper in the General Assembly collection in the National Archives of Scotland.[48] Inverness, Tain and Fort William were all regarded as possible locations for the school, and each put forward its case, but Inverness decided to put forward various inducements.

The Town Council offered to maintain a building for seven years and the Kirk Session offered to donate money from the Duncan mortification.[49] A temporary school was established in Inverness and the first master, Alexander Moncrieff, took up his appointment at Whitsun 1727. His salary was £25, but he was forbidden to charge fees, as this was a school primarily for the education of the poor. As Moncrieff came from Stromness in Orkney,[50] he was probably not a Gaelic speaker, so fatherless children, aged at least 12 and able to speak both Gaelic and English, were employed to assist him as a type of pupil teacher.

The curriculum was similar to that taught between the writing, mathematics and Grammar schools in the Town. As the school was overseen by the General Assembly, religious instruction was an important aspect of the work.

45

The master had to lead his pupils to Church each Sunday and later examine the pupils on the sermon, requiring them to be able to quote the book, chapter and verse of the text. When the school opened, 125 pupils were admitted.

By 1740, the General Assembly were inclined to move the school to Fort William, but various delays and the 1745 Rising meant that this did not happen. Finally, in 1747 the school was established formally in Inverness, and the Council donated a site on Colt Hill (or Barn Hill), on the edge of what is today known as the Crown district. Building finally started in 1756,[51] and the following year the passageway, still known as the Raining's Stairs, was created down to Castle Street.

From 1749 the headmaster was Gil(l)es Ker(r). He produced a spelling book, part of which was used in SSPCK schools throughout Scotland. He also had it printed at his own expense, and petitioned the Town Council[52] to encourage its use in all schools in Inverness, which the Council agreed to for at least seven years, and it was to be used alongside the Shorter Catechism as a key book. From 1759, the headmaster, now known as Rector, was Robert McComie or McOmie, who received a salary of £30, the highest-paid SSPCK teacher in Scotland. He had at that stage 208 pupils, and had an assistant paid £20. The roll dropped a little at the end of the century, but generally was not far short of 200. McOmie died in 1806. A later master was Thomas Mackenzie, who was sent to Aberdeen to learn navigation so that he could teach it in the school, suggesting close links with the sea trade of the port.

Raining's School was never seen in any way as a competitor to the Grammar School or to the Royal Academy, as it was specifically aimed at poorer pupils, and in the early days did not charge fees. By the 1840's, the school became so overcrowded that additional accommodation was built, but at the Disruption in 1843 Mackenzie joined the Free Church and soon became master of the Free Church Institution in Ardconnel Street. This later became the building for the High School which moved in 1880 to a new building, now the Crown School. Changes in the structure of education following the 1872 Act lead to changes in the role of Raining's School, and it was finally closed as a school in 1899. John Raining, whose grave is in St Giles' Church in Norwich, left Inverness an important educational legacy.[53]

The Girls' Boarding School

The last of the patronage schools was the shortest-lived of all. Girls' education had been very restricted up to the earlier part of the eighteenth century. Daughters of the gentry, after 1745, were sent south for education, whereas previously they had come for at least some time to Inverness. So in 1766, the provost of the time reported that Miss Margaret Ker, with her assistants, would set up a boarding school for girls. The boarding fees were £16 a year, with additional charges of 5s per quarter for simple thread work, 10s for more advanced work, such as Dresden work (a form of white on white embroidery), Japanning (black lacquer work), stell work and gum flowers. It is not clear what the last two of these art forms involved.

Nothing more seems to have been said about this school for many years, although there is an item in 1783 where an Isbel *[sic]* Junner sought an increase in salary due to rising rents.[54] However this may refer to some other school. The schoolmistress's salary continues to appear in the Burgh Accounts until 1784. Miss Jean Low, who had taken over from Miss Ker at some time in 1784, requested permission in 1786 to take only day pupils to increase her numbers and the financial viability of the girls' school. She was not receiving a salary, unlike her predecessor and there was not a "sufficient succession of boarders". In her two years in post she had had a maximum of eight boarders, and at the time of the petition had only three.

She was granted a salary of £10, with an allowance of £3 towards the rent of the school. Within a year she had lost the last of her boarders, and was again appealing for permission to take day pupils such as daughters of local merchants. The Town Council, ignoring the fact that the country gentlemen were still sending their daughters south for education, refused her plea and dismissed her! Even Mrs McLelan from Perth, appointed in June 1787, could not recruit enough boarders, and she abandoned the school, leading to its closure by the Council.

For about 10 years nothing happened, but in July 1799 a widow from Ayr, Mrs Mitchell, was appointed at a salary of £25 plus pupils' fees. She was given permission to take day pupils. Even this did not work out financially and rumours must have spread that she was wanting to leave, as a document in the National Archives of Scotland[55] sent to Jane, Lady Grant (of Grant Estates on Speyside) looked at the possibility of establishing a boarding school if Mrs Mitchell left. She received a grant of £20 from the Town to meet the cost of provisions (which had risen during the Napoleonic War), but no increase in salary. She continued to run the school until 1809, when she closed the school without notice and left town. Miss MacPherson, her assistant, carried on for a short while, but left during 1810, when the job was advertised at a salary of between £25 and £40 per annum.

Miss Fleming was appointed but her health was not good and she died in early or mid 1811. The last incumbent of the post was Mrs Rachel Gibson who was given a gift of £20 from the funds of the community. Her salary was gradually increased, and by 1818 (from which time her salary receipts survive)[56] she was paid £40. However she was related to one of the Magistrates and there were accusations of favouritism. Her term in office lasted until 1823, by which point education for girls, in academic subjects at least, was available through the Academy, and "womanly" subjects such as needlework were less in demand. In her letter of resignation in January 1823 she said:

the trouble and great responsibility attenting the situation I held has not been

compensated in any degree by the profits arising from it.
This led to the final closure of the Girls' School as a patronage school, and various ladies from time to time tried to provide such a service at their own expense. Mrs Gibson herself continued for some years as a private teacher with a reasonable income.

It can be seen then, that in the later part of the eighteenth century there was a wide provision for academic education for the better-off children in Inverness and the surrounding region, although mainly for boys. There was also some provision for children of the "working classes" to gain basic education, although, apart from the operation of the Raining's School, much less information is available. Hector Fraser's attempt at combining the Latin and mathematics classes under a single control, a Rector, perhaps showed the way towards the establishment of the Academy that was to open only fifteen years after his retiral and less than six years after his death. Provision outside Inverness was much less satisfactory,[57] despite the operation of the Acts of 1616, 1633 and 1696, which attempted to establish a school in every parish in Scotland. These acts applied to rural areas, and not to the burghs, and proved almost impossible to implement in some parts of the Highlands,[58] until the operation of schemes under the auspices of the SSPCK. This lack of provision in rural area allowed the burgh schools to dominate throughout the eighteenth century.

Chapter 4
Funding the Academy

In the late summer of 1786, the two Universities in Aberdeen, King's College and Marischal College, put forward a plan to unite the two seats of learning into a single university. This was neither the first nor the last time this was attempted, and the union was not achieved till 1860. Copies of a document, *Outline of a plan for uniting the Kings and Marishall* [sic] *Universities of Aberdeen with a view to render the System of Education more complete,* were sent to various authorities in the north of Scotland, including both Inverness Town Council and the Commissioners of Supply for Inverness-shire. These Commissioners were a form of early County Council made up of the main heritors and landowners in the area.

The Town Council considered the document at their meeting of 25th September,[1] and their decision was clear:

> ... they are unanimously of the opinion that an union of the two colleges at Aberdeen upon a proper plan and under suitable regulations would be attended with beneficial consequences and would tend greatly to the advancement of literature and science in the North of Scotland ...

The matter was not raised again at any subsequent meeting.

Some eight weeks later the Commissioners of Supply considered the same document but the result was completely different[2] (perhaps as they had a controlling interest, providing some of the funding to the two colleges):

> The meeting having considered the outlines of a plan laid before them for uniting the Kings and Marischal Universities of Aberdeen & they (all in one voice excepting four of their number, magistrates in the town of Inverness) disapprove thereof.

They then listed five points of opposition, the first four of which were:

- competition between the two universities encouraged high standards
- it might affect donations and so strangle the combined university financially
- population was on the increase, and it would be "impolitik to clogg the avenues to erudition" that have flourished for many years
- difficulties of having classes on a split site, and it would be better to favour King's College in Old Aberdeen "as possessing the better air, and better buildings" than Marischal College and "at a greater distance from such amusement as frequently are apt to divert young men from a due attention to study".

The fifth point provides the key to the establishment of Inverness Academy:

> ... This meeting humbly apprehend that in place of enlarging the sallaries of the present Professors or adding any unnecessary classes to any of these colleges which appear to be the principal object of the foresaid plan, that if it is thought expedient to annihilate one of them, that it would be proper to dispose of the buildings of the other and to employ the price thereof and of any other surplus after restoring proper sallaries of the Professors of the remaining college in establishing an Academy in some central Royal Burgh in the Highlands which wd.

prove of very great national importance ... (and as a great part of the funds which at present supports one of these colleges was granted by natives of this county they consider that the town of Inverness has the best claim ... and its local and most central situation to be the place of such an establishment)

The Commissioners then went on to appoint a committee to work with the magistrates of Inverness to establish such an Academy. In effect, the Inverness magistrates had to do an about-turn under such pressure from the Commissioners. What went on behind the scenes to bring about this change of heart by the Town Council will probably never be known.

Within a fortnight, the committee received its first commitment of money (although they would not get access to it for another ten years), when Hector Fraser, the retired Rector of the Grammar School, wrote into his will the conditions of his bursary for educating boys of the name of Fraser (see Chapter 2).

A joint meeting from the Town and County was held on 29th January 1787,[3] with an attendance of eleven, including some of the key people who would figure in the details of the establishment of the Academy in the next few years. These included the Provost of Inverness (William Mackintosh) who was chosen as Prases [= Chairman], the sheriff depute, Bailie William Inglis (merchant, banker and ship-owner, and Provost from 1797 to1800), Dr John Alves (physician and son or grandson of Thomas Alves who had been insulted by Robert Edwards in 1733), and two local ministers. They agreed that an Academy was a very good idea and:

that a subscription should immediately be begun for raising a fund to enable the Directors, to be after mentioned, to carry the said plan into execution and the meeting think that at least the sum of £4000 will be necessary for beginning this undertaking. They are also of the opinion that every gentleman subscribing the sum of £50 should be a Director for life ... and that the ordinary Directors and patrons should be the Provost, four Baillies, the Dean of Guild of Inverness for the time being ...

Various other local dignitaries, Sheriffs Depute from Elgin to Caithness, and all the local Ministers, were declared extraordinary Directors. Subscription papers were approved and the clerk of the Committee was to get them printed as soon as the Commissioners of Supply and the Town Council had both approved of the committee's actions. The Commissioners of Supply gave their approval only two days later, and the joint committee met again later the same day, when £365 15 0d was pledged, ranging from £50 each from Phineas Mackintosh of Drummond and John Bailie of Dunain, to five guineas (£5 5s) from Campbell Mackintosh, writer [= solicitor], who was soon to repace Charles Mackintosh, W.S. as Burgh Clerk (see Chapter 5).

Surviving printed copies and the Directors' minutes book both give the text of the Subscription Papers, dated 29th January 1787,[4] with the resolutions of the Committee:

1st. That the present state of education in this, and the other neighbouring Counties is defective and imperfect, and will admit of considerable improvement.

2nd. That an academy for the education of Youth in which the most useful and necessary parts of learning should be taught in a more perfect and complete manner, than is usually done at colleges, would be the greatest utility to the Northern parts of Scotland.

3rd. That the Town of Inverness being centrical to the Northern Counties; the place where the Circuit Court of Justiciary meets twice a year; in a healthy part of the Country and having a good market, affords the best situation for such an academy.

4th. That though there is no reason to doubt of the utmost exertions of the Magistrates and Town of Inverness, in a matter of this kind, yet as their funds will fall very short of the sum that will be wanted to form and support an academy upon that liberal and extensive plan that will be proper to answer the ends of such an institution, it is therefore necessary to open a subscription, for obtaining an adequate fund for this purpose.

5th. That some account of the motives, extent and design, of the intended establishment should accompany the subscription, for the information of the public; and a paper for this purpose being read and approved of, that the same be printed and the subscription immediately be set on foot.

Within two weeks papers had been sent to some 45 people, in places ranging from the Highlands to London, and also to the East and West Indies where significant numbers of Inverness people were working. Some 85 or so other people were advised as to who in their locality had the subscription papers. Key people were asked to send the documents on to others who they knew would help. Lord Lovat, in Edinburgh, responded immediately,[5] not with money, but wondering if the promoters had put the cart before the horse, by inviting subscriptions before formulating a plan for the proposed Academy. He stated that he had for the last three years been putting forward an idea for an Academy in the north of Scotland, and felt that academies should be places where practice went hand-in-hand with theory.

The copies of the correspondence and the summary of action, both in the minutes book, identify only one major issue raised by the distribution of the subscription papers. In Ross-shire, both Sheriff Macleod of Geanzies and Frances Humberston Mackenzie of Seaforth expressed concern about possible competition with the planned Fortrose Academy. In letters to both of them any such idea was rejected:[6]

... The Fortrose Academy will we hope prove very useful to the surrounding Country especially to such as cannot afford the time and expence required for a more liberal Education. But our plan is upon a more extensive scale comprehending every branch of Education usually taught at College – Logick, Metaphysick, & Moral Philosophy excepted which no doubt are useful parts of learning but are chiefly so to divines, & students of Divinity are under a necessity of having University Education in order to intitle them to degrees in their profession, every other branch of education will be taught here & we flatter ourselves even in a more perfect manner than at College, because double the time will be employ'd in teaching that is allowed there, & we trust we shall be enabled to offer such liberal encouragement to masters of the first abilities as shall induce them to settle amongst us. ...

There was a feeling that university education did little for many who went there, and was relevant only to those who were to become ministers, doctors, lawyers and schoolmasters (with many schoolmasters using that job as a stepping-stone to getting an appointment as a minister). The type of college proposed would provide education for those intending to enter the world of business. The letter also set out a plan of the various "schools" that would be established within the Academy, the lengths of terms and holidays, the likely Directors and how they were to meet. It also stated that the school was to be under the control of a Rector.

The concept of Academies in Scotland

Through the eighteenth century the spread of commerce in Scotland, together with the ideas of the Scottish Enlightenment covering intellectual, literary, scientific and artistic achievement, made many people conscious that there was a need to move on from an educational provision that was primarily concerned with the classics. Despite Inverness's Highland location, there is plenty of evidence that these developing ideas were prevalent in Inverness, even though the Enlightenment is perhaps most associated with the cultural and intellectual life of 18th century and early 19th century Edinburgh.

At this time there were many complaints about the poor standard of tuition available in both burgh and parochial schools, as well as in the universities. There was a need to educate merchants, burgesses and craftsmen, and Withrington[7] puts the start of this new thinking at a time before the Parliamentary union with England in 1707. Inverness had, to some extent, widened the educational pattern after 1707, as was shown in Chapter 3, by establishing English and Mathematical schools, distinct from the Grammar school, but nevertheless under Council patronage. Schoolmasters were keen to increase the number of subjects taught, as, high inflation in the first forty years of the eighteenth century had seriously reduced the purchasing power of teachers' salaries, and Councils were reluctant to increase these salaries. New subjects meant that extra fees could be charged, and thus improve schoolmasters' incomes.

It was not a very large step for Councils to draw the various subjects into an 'Academy', and Ayr was the first town in Scotland to do this, in 1746, although in a general way [Table 4.1]. Perth was the first to establish an Academy by name, but not really in a form we would recognise, being only one of several separate "schools" in the town, and it was distinguished from the grammar school, for instance, by the subjects it taught. It will be seen that Inverness was the fourth or fifth Academy to be established in Scotland.

Perth Academy, from which Inverness Academy gained much in its early years, was first proposed in September 1760,[8] and largely the idea of the Rev. James Bon(n)ar, minister of the West Church within St John's Kirk in

1746	Ayr	earlier model of an Academy, but not called by that name
1761	Perth	several separate schools, one called "Academy": (in one building from 1807 called "The Seminaries")
1786	Dundee	ran for two 3-year periods, closed 1792, new version 1802
1791	Fortrose	
1792	Inverness	initial proposal 1786/1787; charter 1793
1794	Ayr	in a more formalised way
1801	Elgin	initial proposal 1790
1801	Annan	
1802	Dumfries	
1810	Tain	initial proposal 1800; charter 1809

Table 4.1: Dates of the opening of the early Academies in Scotland

the Town, who was keen to develop the teaching of science (in a rather wider sense than we would use the term today). The first Rector was a future Duke of Atholl, although this appointment seems to have been largely an honorary one. Within a few months the accommodation was "two storeys above the Corn Mercatt", and two staff were in place. By 1769, one of them had resigned and the other had died, leading to Robert Hamilton, son of an Edinburgh bailie and bookseller, being appointed. He was later to be Professor of Natural Philosophy at Marischal College, Aberdeen. Within three years, Hamilton needed an usher, and John McOmie (various spellings) was appointed. McOmie was later to become Rector in Inverness with a testimonial as to his abilities from Hamilton (see Chapter 6).

It was not until 1807 that the building in Rose Terrace, familiar to many Perth residents, was opened for education, but even then, the schools within it were still separate, self-governing, institutions – the former grammar school (with a rector and two doctors), the Academy itself for arts and sciences (with a rector and a doctor), an English school, a French school, a writing school, and a drawing and painting school (each with one master). Only in 1873 were all of these brought together as a single institution, following the 1872 Education Act.

The Fortrose Academy was on a much less grandiose scale. Withrington[9] quotes from a manuscript in Aberdeen University archive. Writing to Robert Hamilton at Marischal College, James Smith, the minister at Avoch, said:

Our Academy at Fortrose will not probably interfere in the least with Alma Mater's interest, being chiefly intended for the benefit of those who cannot afford the time or expense of a compleat course of University Education. Besides this, almost all the University students from Ross and our neighbouring Counties are picked up by Mr Macleod of King's College and his connections, for all the clergy here except myself, having received their Education at Old Aberdeen, are perhaps too partial to that College.

Mathematics would form a key part of the course at Fortrose, with the master running a course on a two-year cycle, to include in the first year arithmetic, algebra, book-keeping and a complete course in geography. The second year would cover geometry, plain and spherical trigonometry, land surveying, gauging, the elements of fortification, navigation and some astronomy. This is very similar to the course introduced a year later in Inverness Academy. (Several staff moved from Fortrose to Inverness during the first twenty years or so of the two Academies.)

Withrington[10] also outlines the plans in Elgin, taken from the *Records of Elgin*. In 1790 Elgin Town Council approved a petition from the local population to unite the various schools and soon produced a plan for an Academy with three departments – the first to be English, French and church music; the second writing, arithmetic and the elements of mathematics; and the third the traditional grammar school subjects of Latin and Greek. However by the following year the Elgin councillors were proposing a scheme "on the lines of the Inverness Academy", with four masters, where arithmetic and mathematics were separate departments, and ancient and modern geography was added to the classical studies. Nothing seems to have happened to this plan until 1800, when the council went back to a plan, similar to that then operating in Montrose, of three separate schools. It was not until 1801 that Elgin Academy opened.

Clearly the academies were aimed at a rather different group of boys from those who would go on to University, to study for one of the professions that specifically required a University degree. However, a boy could attend an academy for some years and complete some of the more 'practical' subjects, before moving on to University, perhaps only to attend a selection of classes, and not actually graduate. Some of these university classes might be the public classes of the professors; others might be their private or extracurricular classes.

Over the final decades of the eighteenth century, the ideas underlying the movement towards academies moved on from the Perth arrangement of 1760 which took students on from where the grammar school left off (for those who did not require the traditional university subjects). By 1790 or so, when Inverness was launching its academy, science (in its widest definition) was seen to be part of general education, and this could lead on to the further study of these topics at a university, who were also introducing new subjects.

The academies provided mainly for the middle to upper classes of society, with some provision of bursaries for the poor but able boy (it is not known how many of these academies accepted girls). They were publicly organised, with the church to some extent sidelined in their organisation, and were usually financed by subscription funds. Many students would not need to leave home for long periods, as was necessary for boys from the Highlands

54

attending either of the universities in Aberdeen, although generous bursaries were available for many of those who did continue their education there.

It is interesting to note that none of these new academies was in the major cities of Scotland and therefore close to the four city-based universities (including the two in Aberdeen) then existing in Scotland. However, Edinburgh and Glasgow would have had plenty of private teachers available to provide what the smaller towns sought to promote by establishing their academies. Even the school still called 'Edinburgh Academy' and opened in 1824, was a private institution run much more on the lines of an English 'public' school, although as a day school rather than a boarding school.

Raising the money[11]

Within months, local gentry and merchants promised subscriptions (though few offers were from tradesmen). These came increasingly from abroad, where there were high hopes of large sums of money from the West Indies and India. Without an appointed Cashier [= Treasurer] no subscriptions could yet be received. The Commissioners of Supply at their April meeting were impressed with the promise of £50 from Mackenzie of Seaforth.[12] In the original minute, the word 'unsolicited' has been inserted in the margin, but this can hardly have been the case as a letter to him survives, written only six weeks previously by Provost Mackintosh (as Chairman of the Steering Committee), trying to convince him that there was no competition with the planned Fortrose Academy, and inviting him to subscribe:[13]

> ... the Committee will expect to be aided not only by your example, but also by your influence in bringing into effect a Plan which promises such great & lasting benefit to the North of Scotland.

Seaforth, along with a number of other influential subscribers, was to be invited to serve on the Committee although largely as a figurehead.

At the first general meeting of subscribers on 1st May 1788 Thomas Gilzean, a person who was to figure very prominently in the affairs of the Academy until his retirement through illness in 1833, was appointed Cashier. The son of a small Elginshire proprietor, and by training a lawyer, Gilzean had come to Inverness in April 1783 when he was appointed as Comptroller [= Controller] of Customs, a not very well-paid job. In 1791 he also became Collector of Stamp Duties and Distributor of Stamps for Inverness-shire, a much better-paid job. Later he held almost every public office in the Town, including, for four years, that of Provost. Throughout this time he continued to practice privately as a lawyer. As the School Cashier, as was standard at that time, he would operate the accounting through his own funds, finding from others caution for his actions (a financial bond), as a sort of insurance policy.

At that same meeting a sub-committee was given power to purchase land and erect a suitable building.[14] Four days later the meeting approved the first outline of the building,[15] although this plan is not what was actually implemented. Other decisions concerned future trustees, the appointment of

Directors once the Trustees were in place, and at what point the staff could be appointed and the regulations approved. It was agreed that the staff would consist of five teachers, with three of the classes running rolling programmes of instruction. Subscriptions were sought through press advertisements, followed, in some cases, by personal letters. The former Gibraltar merchant, Charles Mackintosh of Bathford (near Bath), a member of the Essich part of the family, took two years to reply,[16] and then pled poverty. He may never have paid, although later he did contribute to the Northern Infirmary project.

The committee's hopes of contributions from India had been pinned on Warren Hastings's immediate successor as Governor of Bengal, Sir John MacPherson, Bart., a Skye man and former M.P. He had returned to Brompton in London, while the letter requesting that he circulate subscription papers had still been on its way to India. A second letter was sent to him in London, but his reply said that he was now unable to seek subscriptions from his friends in India. He also offers his views on what sort of education was required:[17]

> The principal objects to be recommended to the attention of the Academy should be, in my humble opinion, a grammatical knowledge of the English language, with a master to teach, not so much the English pronunciation as a proper discrimination between English and Scotch phrases and idioms, and the meaning of words as they are pronounced in both countries. ... If it is attempted to make it [the Academy] a *half-College* and *half-Academy* Institution it will not succeed in either line. ...

Money from the West Indies was more forthcoming. In July 1789 John and James Wedderburn living in Westmoreland, Jamaica, gifted £100 each, in return for which the Town Council thought it "highly proper" to give them the Freedom of Inverness.[18] This branch of the Jamaica planting and banking Wedderburn family, which had Dunbar kin, had moved to Cantray in 1750 from Grangehill, bought from its Dunbar owners by Sir Alexander Grant of Dalvey, a Jamaican millionaire who would eventually become M.P. for the Inverness Burghs. Later, in 1797, James Wedderburn, who had been born in Inverness in 1751, left the Academy a legacy of £200.

Other Jamaican money had begun to arrive during 1789, through Fraser of Torbreck's brother, Hugh, a cousin and eventual legatee of James Wedderburn, who was their millwright in Jamaica. In particular money came through Lewis Cuthbert, fourth son of George Cuthbert of Castlehill, Sheriff Substitute for Inverness (appointed by Lord Lovat). George had died when he fell from his horse on the Millburn Road in 1748. After the death of his father, Lewis had been brought up in London, and eventually became a Jamaican merchant dealing in slaves. From 1778 he had leased the office of Provost Marshall General of Jamaica, a lucrative legal post which administered bankruptcy debts and the island slave code, bringing in around £7000 a year, with £2000 going to the patentees. Lewis could, and did, afford to use his younger brother, George, as his deputy for much of the 1780s, and so took his wife and young family to settle in Bath. George died unexpectedly in

1789, leaving, it would seem, very large debts. Lewis had therefore to take up the office again in Jamaica. The lease was nearing expiry, and renewal, paid for in advance, needed to be urgently settled. Lewis needed to borrow money.

In late 1791, with the Academy building well advanced, Cuthbert, back in Bath, and now laird of Castlehill, was disposing of Shipland estate (to the east of Inverness between roughly what is now Academy Street and Harbour Road), which had been surrendered to him as caution when Thomas Alves (his cousin and the heir of Dr John Alves of Shipland, an Academy founding committee member, whom Lewis had made deputy for the Montego Bay area), failed in 1790. This sale did not meet the approval of Baillie of Dunain, an Alves kinsman by marriage and one of the sale commissioners. Lewis dismissed his objections and the sale went ahead, probably enabling him to finance the payment for just over £800 of Jamaican subscriptions that he had brought back with him, though he gave bond for (i.e. borrowed) rather less than half the total, paying the Academy roughly £17 a year interest until the state of his affairs after his death in 1802 forced his executor into a long drawn-out legal action in the Court of Session, and, for a time, too, Chancery in London. Gilzean, who accepted the deal, soon became the Castlehill factor.

Insufficient detail remains to establish just how much money came from the West Indies, but it was certainly well over a quarter of the total.[19] Readers today may express surprise that a significant proportion of the funding came from money linked to slavery in the Caribbean. However at the time this would not have been regarded as a issue – much more as a sign of how well some Inverness businessmen had succeeded in the commercial world of the day. This is very different from the situation in Perth some fifteen years later, when almost all of the money for their new Academy was raised locally.[20]

Lewis's elder brother, Seignelay Cuthbert (or de Colbert), third son of George Cuthbert of Castlehill, was the Bishop of Rodez (near Toulouse in the south of France).[21] In the 1680s the sons of Louis XIV's minister, Jean-Baptiste Colbert, had discovered a family connection with the armigerous Cuthberts, through which they successfully claimed the status of *noblesse de l'épée* (the top rank of French nobility), and had since taken in two of Lewis's uncles. The uncles took in Seignelay, who had been given a forename taken from a Colbert title, and put him into the Church. With his pedigree affirmed by the Inverness magistrates, he soon became vicar general of Toulouse, standing in for his Archbishop, Lomenie de Brienne, a future chief minister of France, in meetings with Adam Smith, and corresponding with David Hume. He was appointed Bishop of Rodez in 1782, becoming a member of the Second Estate (the House of Clergy) of the States General, the summoning of which in 1789 led to the outbreak of the French Revolution. Rodez sided with the modernisers, and was the first French bishop to throw in his lot with the Third Estate, the Commons, to be carried on the shoulders of the

May 1787	£1095 13 6d	
1 August 1787	£1610 18 6d	
8 October 1787	£1670 18 6d	
7 January 1788	£1828 13 6d	
7 April 1788	£2138 13 6d	includes subscriptions from London
1 May 1788	£2290 18 6d	
6 July 1788	£2342 18 6d	
24 November 1788	£2384 18 6d	
28 January 1789		£753 12 6d actually collected
21 April 1789	£2471 13 6d	further £230 7s collected
1 May 1789		further £141 10s collected
20 October 1789	£3112 8 6d	includes £551 10s from Jamaica; further £272 19s collected
5 March 1790	£3661 15 6d	further £508 17s from Jamaica; further £343 5s collected
1 May 1790		further £88 14 6d collected
22 November 1790		further £116 16 6d collected; arrears of £1694 6s not collected
2 May 1791	£3757 10 6d	further £212 collected
23 May 1791	£4060 9 6d	further £314 9s collected
5 October 1791	£4402 17 0d	further £67 10s collected, including subscriptions from Jamaica
26 October 1791	£4468 12 0d	further £198 10s collected
10 January 1792	£4479 2 0d	further £241 10s collected
19 October 1792	£5580 12 0d	further £802 8 3d from Jamaica through Lewis Cuthbert
22 December 1792	£6277 5 3d	including total of £1271 0 3d from Jamaica

Table 4.2: Subscriptions for IRA promised and paid, 1787 to 1792

mob through Versailles in celebration. He voted for the Declaration of the Rights of Man. Not surprisingly, Rodez was not easy for the Academy to contact,[22] and in the end Lewis paid his one hundred guinea subscription. In 1792 the Bishop went into opposition and, soon, exile, as he refused to sign the Civil Constitution of the Clergy, which put the French Church firmly under the State. Later the Academy used him to nominate some of their French teachers.

Lists of subscribers were printed in the Edinburgh and London newspapers from time to time, and by May 1791 the total subscribed exceeded £4000 [Table 4.2].[23] This was the original minimum figure that the steering committee considered necessary to allow them to proceed with the project. The local Church Presbyteries made their contributions, and it was suggested that if any Presbytery donated £50 or more their Moderator should become a perpetual Director. The Highland Society of London made their first donation, something which would lead to the financing for several years of the salary of the teacher of Gaelic. By October 1791 the committee felt they were on target to open the following Whitsun (May 1792), with adequate funds.

A further trust fund was made available when the Rev. David Denoon, the minister of Killearnan (in the Black Isle) and former Grammar School pupil and doctor/usher, left £100 from his estate as a fund to educate a virtuous young man as a bursar at the Academy.

The land and the building
Various plots of land were considered for the site of the school, the first of which, in 1787, was a waste area on the west side of Church Street, usually at that time called the First Minister's manse (the building here having been used around 1720 as the music school – see Chapter 3). In May 1787 it was agreed to purchase this land, but this does not seem to have happened. In December 1788, land was purchased in Church Street (now on the corner of Church Street and Baron Taylor's Street) for £70 from Captain John Macgregor.[24] The committee later concluded a bargain to buy a garden next to it for £50, but at a committee meeting in April 1789 it was decided that this site was too restricted.[25] Within a month it was decided to sell it. It should be noted that most of the Academy Directors were also members of the Town Council and leading figures in business, or lawyers winding up estates, so they would know well what other property development and sales might be about to take place in the Town.

By October the Town Council was offering to buy the Church Street land for the establishment of a fish and green market, which appears at that stage to have been held in the streets. The deal included the Town paying not just the purchase price but all the costs of the transactions as well. Gilzean, as cashier, was authorised to do the necessary conveyancing – in effect he was wearing two hats, one for the Academy, the other for the Town, something he was to do many times thereafter. Shortly afterwards the members of the Northern Meeting bought the land off the Town to construct their meeting rooms (which survived until the 1960's) and the site is now occupied by shops and an office block.

Three other sites had been identified and in April 1789 one of these, an area in New Street (now known as Academy Street), was selected, probably today the site of Farraline Park. The disposition for this land survives,[26] stating that it was purchased for £315 from James Fraser, a smith and burgess in the Town, and one-time Deacon of the Hammermen's Guild. The various surrounding landowners and their forebears are stated in detail, and the land is also defined as having the common highway, fosse or foulpool on the west.

(This New Street had been laid out in 1765 along the line of a defensive ditch [fosse] which had encircled the Town until the mid-fifteenth century. Thereafter it had deteriorated and become in part a stagnant pool.) Fraser's site was later judged to be unsuitable for building the school, probably as there were tenants with leases on this land. In November 1790 the land was sold on to Simon Fraser of Farraline for the same sum as it had cost the Academy subscribers.

By March 1790 Bailie Inglis was authorised to negotiate with William Cumming, a glazier, to buy another site in New Street.[27] The cost was £700 – over twice what they had recently paid Fraser for his site. Nevertheless it was decided to go ahead and the tenants on the land were to be warned, so that full possession could be taken of the land at the next legal term-date, which would have been Whitsunday [15th May] 1790. As a result of this sale Cumming was able to pay off debts which had resulted from the failure of his brother as a merchant.

Even though the site had changed a number of times, a plan of the building had been produced and estimates sought. The meeting in October 1789 had decided on the size of the building:[28]

> ... the dimension should be eighty seven feet in length and twenty three feet in breadth within walls and the height of the ceiling of the two principal stories thirteen feet and the attic storey nine feet of wall finished with a coach roof and the staircase to be thrown in Tympanum behind [tympany/tympanum = gable in the middle of a house-front, but more likely here meaning a round back-stair tower] with a closet for an observatory at top and the lobby at entrance twelve feet in width at least ...

The building that was finally constructed is about 100 feet (30 metres) long.

The architect was Alexander Laing, an Edinburgh architect, using a design that he prepared for the High School of Edinburgh, but probably modified locally.[29] The only mention so far identified about Laing was a payment to him of £5 5s "for designing and drawing a plan and elevation of the Academy buildings".[30] This seems a very small sum, even by the values of the day, for the complete design of the building. (Laing was also the architect responsible for the (Royal) Northern Infirmary and possibly for the tower of the steeple in the Town centre.) The modifications were perhaps done by Simon Fraser, wright, who also received the sum of £5 5s in May 1790 for drawing plans and producing estimates.[31] Alternatively William Sibbald, the superintendent of works who came from Edinburgh, may have made the modifications.

For the subscribers' meetings in March 1790, two estimates for the wright-work [joinery] were available, one of which survives [Figure 4.1].[32] William McDonald's estimate was for nearly £400, and, together with that of Hugh Sutter (mason) and John Davidson (a slater), it was the one which was accepted as the more reasonable. The unsuccessful wright, Simon Fraser, was, as just mentioned, paid five guineas for his trouble. A cautioner was appointed for the proper execution of the work, and the contracts were drawn up on 15th March 1790.

Building started immediately the land deal was settled in May 1790, and a sum of one guinea (£1 1s) was paid for drink for the masons for the laying of the foundations.[33] An inscribed parchment was put in a corner stone.[34] Work must have proceeded very rapidly as by late that year the roof was in place, and it was suggested that the structure would be completed by the following summer.[35] From October 1791, the sub-committee concerned itself with the finishing details.[36] By early 1792 the seating plan had been agreed for the second (classics) and third (writing, arithmetic and book-keeping) classrooms, and a decision taken about the land for the "necessary offices" (presumably the toilets) and the coal house. These contracts were agreed in February, with Hugh Sutter getting the job for the mason work of the extra building, and for some paving work. Only one estimate had been received for slating, so this matter was held over. No further details are recorded in the minutes, although the accounts book records progress. An old kiln on the land was demolished and the materials sold, although Sutter, the purchaser, had to leave a proper boundary wall onto the street.

As the construction was under the control of a sub-committee, more details may have been available in their records, but these have not been traced. By June or early July 1792, the building was ready [Figure 4.2], although later comments in the minutes suggest that not all of the classrooms were fitted out by the opening day. Plans for the Rector's classroom were not considered until early 1793,[37] after Weir returned from London (see Chapter 5). Gilzean's *Client Account Book* allows the final cost of the building to be calculated.[38] The total, excluding the cost of the land, was about £950 for the main building, with about £680 for the additional building work and the furnishings, such as the seating and presses [= cupboards]. Sibbald, the superintendent of works, received 40 guineas (£42) for his efforts.

The First *Statistical Account of Scotland*,[39] written perhaps only six months after the opening, says that there were six "spacious apartments for classes, library and philosophical apparatus", with a central hall. Rooms would have been available for each of the five named classes with one available for the Gaelic class. Certain aspects of the building did not prove satisfactory. Within six months more paving was required behind the building, and porches were built for the Latin and English "schools".[40] From later evidence it seems that the Latin class was at the north end of the building (nearest Strothers' Lane), and by implication the English class was at the south end (nearest the present-day railway station).

Chapter 5
Staffing and administration for the opening

With the building well under way, in October 1791 the general meeting of the subscribers turned their attention to the staffing and administration of the school. At this time the five Directors to be appointed by the Commissioners of Supply had not been elected, and would not be until their annual meeting on 30th April 1792, but Charles Mackintosh, a Writer to the Signet in Edinburgh and the Burgh's Agent, suggested that a sub-committee should be appointed to advertise jobs – one application having already been received. In addition the subscribers were keen to apply for a Royal Charter, something they felt that they could not do until the official board of Directors was in place, although Mackintosh had begun work on this.

A new sub-committee was established with Provost William Mackintosh in the Chair. By November the basic outline of staffing was approved.[1] There was to be a staff of five:
- a Rector, with a salary of £50, teaching mechanics, natural and experimental philosophy (basically physics) and natural history
- an English teacher, with a salary of £30
- a classics teacher, for Latin, Greek and French, with a salary of £40
- a teacher for writing, arithmetic and book-keeping, with a salary of £30
- a mathematics teacher, to include geometry, algebra, mensuration, solids and surfaces including surveying, and in addition geography, navigation, fortification and gunnery, with a salary of £40.

It was accepted that the details might have to be changed depending on the staff who were appointed, and additional staff would be taken on if funds permitted and there was sufficient enrolment. Although Perth had at least five staff in their various schools, this number exceeded the staff in most if not all of the schools in the other Scottish towns. Dundee employed only three staff, as did Fortrose. Mention was also made that a Gaelic class would be established in Inverness, supported by the Highland Society in London.

Appointing the staff
Newspaper advertisement were placed almost immediately, with the advertisements to appear in the Edinburgh newspapers, including the *Evening Courant*, and the London *Chronicle*. Application were to be sent either to Provost William Mackintosh or to Charles Mackintosh, W.S., in Edinburgh. Various applications were received very quickly, sometimes starting as enquiries, and sometimes in the form of recommendations from people of distinction.

By February 1792[2] the three staff in post in the Grammar and related schools had all applied and were regarded as qualified – Ebenezer Young for the classics post and James Wills for the writing, arithmetic and book-keeping class, whilst John Hoyes, the English teacher would be recommended "unless a native of England" was available. This seems to have taken on board Sir John Macpherson's desire for English, rather than Scots, to be taught. Applications for the mathematics post had been received from all over Scotland, and James Weir, the person to be appointed the first Rector, had made his initial enquiries, perhaps, as will be shown in Chapter 6, aware that his job in Dundee Academy was in danger, with his second three-year contract coming to the end.

A month later, the general meeting of subscribers gave the sub-committee full powers to appoint. Weir had handed in his application to Charles Mackintosh in Edinburgh, after he was given assurances that the Inverness post was on a permanent basis. In April the sub-committee received an application through Charles Mackintosh from Robert Douglas of the Marine Academy in Edinburgh, and Weir, Douglas, Young and Wills were formally appointed on 10th April 1792. These staff were asked to attend on 1st May 1792 so that they could be installed in their posts, and from the letters of Douglas[3] and Weir[4] a fortnight later they seem to have travelled to Inverness as requested. Young and Wills of course were already in town.

Letters had been sent to the Rev. Donald Maclean in Mitcham (now part of the south side of London) concerning finding an English teacher, and through him a Mr Vatchell, "a native of England", was appointed. It was claimed he was proficient in elocution, understood the French language and was versed in classics and "several polite branches of education". However, despite being named in the opening announcement, Vatchell never arrived in Inverness, causing the Directors a major headache when the Academy opened in July. The Rev. Maclean eventually sent from London a person called Crisp (see Chapter 6). Hoyes, the existing English teacher in the Town, did not get the job, and he disappears from the records immediately, presumably leaving Inverness for a job elsewhere. The appointment of the Gaelic teacher was held over, and the post was not advertised until October 1792[5] and even then there was no progress until a part-time appointment was made in February 1793.

The Commissioners of Supply made the necessary appointments of five of their number to be Directors of the Academy at their meeting of 30th April,[6] leaving the way open for the first formal meeting of the Directors on 2nd May. Later in that month one of the most significant decisions concerning the establishment of the Academy is recorded, namely the decision by the Town Council to close the Grammar School and spend the money previously allocated for this purpose on funding the salaries of Academy staff:[7]

> Thereafter the Magistrates and Council considering that for some time past endeavours have been used for establishing an Academy upon an extensive scale in this place, and that when the scheme was first proposed they did from the great prospect of benefit to the Town and the County at large resolve to give it every support in their power in their public and private character; and in particular they did agree that the Latin, English and Writing Schools now under the immediate patronage of the town should in future form part of the classes in the Academy, and that in lieu of the sallarys payable to the masters of these different schools the

sum of seventy pounds sterling should be annually paid by the treasurer of this Burgh to the hands of the Cashier for the time to be appointed by the Directors of the Academy, the said sum of seventy pounds sterling to be in particular applied in all time coming towards payment of the sallarys of the three classes in the Academy in which these branches are to be taught: And now seeing that the sum subscribed towards this useful establishment the Directors chosen by the Town and County find themselves authorised to determine on opening the said Academy upon the 16th day of July next, and they have for that purpose engaged proper teachers for these and for the other branches of Literature, the Magistrates and Council do therefore hereby confirm the Agreement entered into upon the part of the Town as above narrated, and empower their Treasurer to commence the payment of the said sum of seventy pounds sterling into the hands of the Cashier of the Academy when the salarys of the Masters in the Academy shall become payable; and the Council do further recommend it to the Town Clerk to enter in a Book to be kept for that purpose a full copy of the Institution and Regulations for the Academy, a complete list of the subscribers towards it, the names of the first Directors and Masters, and in short every other step taken towards the establishment of this seminary, that posterity may see at one view when and how the plan of it has been carried into execution.

From this extract it is clear that the Academy was seen as a direct replacement for the Grammar School, providing a development of the educational provision in the Town. The book mentioned in the last sentence of the quotation may or may not have been written up, although the information is provided in the Directors' Minutes books. The Town was not always up to date with its payments, and was in arrears several times in the 1820's.

Robert Douglas wrote to Bailie Mackintosh, brother of Campbell Mackintosh, on how he wanted his classroom fitted up, enclosing a plan.[8] Although the letter survives, the plan does not. His requirements included a round table with a three-foot radius. He asked the Directors to find a suitable house for himself and his family, if the house intended for the Rector, adjacent to the school, could not be repaired in time. He also included an outline of his course which included Euclidian geometry, trigonometry, geography with the use of globes, surveying of land and sea coasts, navigation, various branches of architecture, and including fortification and practical gunnery. The last two items would be of great relevance as international tension was then high and the Napoleonic War would break out the following year. The practical gunnery presumably was the calculation of trajectories, rather than experience with actual guns!

Weir was also busy, drafting a newspaper advertisement, a form of timetable, and regulations for the consideration of the Directors. Weir was probably the best qualified person in Scotland to do this, as he had had control of Dundee Academy since its opening in 1786, although there he only had two other staff working under him. He had been empowered by the sub-committee to purchase apparatus, writing on 2nd June asking when he was to do this.[9] There were problems with the house he was supposed to occupy, which was uninhabitable. This house continued to cause trouble for the next ninety years.

Advertising continued to recruit pupils; one clipping has survived in the Academy archive which comes from the *Edinburgh Evening Courant* of 21st June 1792 [Figure 5.1], setting out the classes, the fees, and the names of the staff. Although not mentioned in this advertisement, the music and dancing classes in the Town (see Chapter 3) were mentioned in later advertisements. The main advertisement was repeated several times in the run-up to the opening day, with the addition, on Saturday 7th July, of an advertisement about a dinner for subscribers on the opening day.

Mention was made of boarding arrangements and the fact that staff and others would have suitable accommodation. In the copies of this newspaper in the National Library of Scotland, immediately under the advertisement announcing the opening, there is another one by Mrs Gordon of East Street (presumably now Eastgate) offering to take boarders. Four days later Ebenezer Young was also advertising for boarders aged 14 or under. In a letter to one enquirer,[10] a J. T. or J. J. Jones of Swinbroke Park near Bradford, rates for boarding were quoted as from £14 to £22, washing included. It was suggested that about £25 a year would cover both boarding and education. Provost William Mackintosh in a later letter to Jones[11] said that the Rector would not be taking boarders "as he was a single man":

Inverness 29th Novr. 1792

Sir,

I received by last post the honor of your letter dated 20th. I observe with pleasure that you continue your intention of sending one of your sons to be educated at the Academy of this town, and I have not a doubt, that the result will be to your satisfaction.

The Rector of our Academy being a single man has of course no accommodation for boarders, but the masters of the different classes have, and as soon as you let me know to which you wish your son to enter I will secure board for him with the master of it. The terms of it are very nearly what I formerly mentioned to you.

There are several excellent vessels constantly employed in the trade twixt London and this port. One of them the Buxar, Captain Rey will sail from Hawley's Wharf about the end of December, which will suit the opening of the next session well.

You have been strangely misinformed as to the quality of our River water, it being uncommonly fine, nor can a better proof of the salubriety of our water and air be given that the great numbers of vigourous old people to be seen on our streets, many beyond 80 and from all corners of the World. There are besides our River many wells in those parts of the Town most distant from it. I have the honor to be Etc.

It is not recorded if the Jones boy ever came to be educated in Inverness, regardless of the quality of the river water!

At the end of June the Directors appointed their first Janitor, a Chelsea Pensioner by the name of Alexander Fraser.[12] They also decided to purchase gowns for the staff and the Janitor, which were to be "of the same pattern as at the High School of Edinburgh".

The Rules and Regulations
The early weeks of July saw discussion on the rules and regulations for the Academy,[13] which were to be "writ out, neatly framed, and hung up in the Public Hall for the perusal and direction of all concerned". These rules and regulations were confirmed at the major meeting of Subscribers and Directors on the opening day[14] and many of them had their origins in the correspondence with people such as Seaforth, and Weir's suggestions in his letters to the Directors. The Directors would also inspect the school quarterly themselves.

The rules were as follows:
- there would be two sessions in a year: 16th July to 20th December and 5th January to 10th June
- the various classes were fixed as:
  1. English – to be taught grammatically
  2. classics
  3. writing, arithmetic and book-keeping – writing to be taught to the scholars of the grammar school from 12 to 1, and from 1 to 2 to "young ladies who cannot attend at the ordinary school hours"
  4. mathematics – Euclid, algebra, trigonometry, mensuration, geography with the use of globes, navigation with lunar observations, naval, civil and military architecture, practical gunnery, fortification, perspective and drawing; with the geography taught between 1 and 2 p.m.
  5. natural and civil history, natural philosophy, chemistry and astronomy
- hours of attendance would vary between summer and winter (obviously reflecting the lack of adequate artificial light): for the first four classes hours in summer were to be from 7 - 9 a.m., 10 a.m. - 12 noon, and 3 - 6 p.m.; and in winter from 9 a.m. - 12 noon and 2 - 4 p.m.; the Rector's class however would be held in summer from 8 - 9 a.m., 11 a.m. - 1 p.m., and 3 - 4 p.m., but in winter only from 11 a.m. - 1 p.m. and 3 - 4 p.m.

These timings would allow some students to attend both the Rector's class and parts of another one. A supply of ink and Dutch pens (made from quills passed through hot ashes to remove fat and moisture) was included in the fees of the first two classes.

The regulations were more concerned with the staff and their duties, and the holidays:
1. the Rector and teachers were to be in post until the Directors removed them, or they gave three months' notice
2. the Rector was to lead prayers in the main hall in the morning, and each teacher was to conclude the afternoon with prayers in his own class
3. the Rector was to visit the classes frequently, and examine them at least once a month, keeping a record of his findings but not direct or control the other teachers in the presence of the pupils

4. the Rector was to lead the masters and pupils to church on Sunday, and then meet with them on Sunday evening for an hour for instruction in religion and morality
5. Saturday afternoons would be free of lessons for the first three classes, but the mathematics and science classes would have the whole of Saturday free; there were to be no other holidays except for special reasons, although at the time of the Sacrament in the church there would be a break from the end of Wednesday afternoon until the following Tuesday morning
6. each teacher was responsible for discipline in his own class
7. the supply of coals was to be controlled by the masters and money to purchase them was to be collected from the scholars
8. the Janitor was to have a salary of £3 plus 6d a year from each student;[15] his duties were to keep the building clean, light the fires and help the masters, especially the Rector
9. students can repeat a class if they want to, free of charge, and the masters were not to interfere with the work of other masters

Almost all of these regulations were to cause problems, in some case within months, and others within years. The first one in particular was to be challenged by Matthew Adam in 1815, in a major legal case which gave him life tenure of office. The third rule, concerning the Rector visiting the classes would be challenged by Douglas early in the second session of the school. The religious element of the education was also clearly stated, and it would not be until the 1830's that the rule on Church attendance by all the pupils would be abandoned.

The Royal Charter
As early as 1789, the Subscribers were keen to incorporate themselves, as the minute says, "into a body politick",[16] so that they could handle funds and hold property collectively with greater security. In the eighteenth century, the normal method of doing this was by purchasing a Royal Charter:[17]

> Thereafter the meeting resolved that it was highly proper to apply for a patent for incorporating the Directors into a body politic and appointed the said James Grant of Corrymonie and James Fraser of Gortuleg and Mr Charles Mackintosh, Writer to the Signet, as a Committee with power to take the necessary steps preparing a scroll [= draft] of a charter to be laid before the general meeting of Subscribers upon the first lawful day of May next for their consideration.

Work proceeded slowly on this draft over the next couple of years, and it was not until October 1791 that a draft was ready.[18] Further details were agreed the following October,[19] including the request that the names of both the Directors and those who had subscribed at least £50 should be included. In February 1793 Ebenezer Young was translating the Charter into Latin, and he was also asked to translate the Warrant. At the April meeting Gilzean reported that the Charter had been obtained from King George III:[20]

> incorporating the subscribers into a body politic and corporate by the name and title of the Managers and Directors of the Academy of Inverness.

Account of the Expense of the Charter incorporating the Directors of the Academy at Inverness			
1792 Oct.	Drawing Petition to the King for a Charter	£1 5 -	
	Two Copies thereof 6 pages each	- 4 -	
	Drawing Royal Warrant for the Charter	2 10 -	
	Two copies thereof 12 pages each	- 8 -	
Nov.	Paid advertising for a Gaelic Teacher in three Edinr. Newspapers	1 1 -	
1793 Feby.	Fee to Lord Advocate for his report on the Petition to the King	21 - -	
	His Clerks fee	3 3 -	
March	To the Bank of Scotland's draft on Messrs Coutts & Comp. remitted Mr Alex ffraser to pay fees at the Secretary of States office & Mr ffrasers own fees	82 6 6	
	Making out scroll of the Charter 6 sheets	2 10 -	
	Copt thereof for the Chancery 12 pages	- 6 -	
April 9	Director of Chancery's fees	15 - -	
	Clerks in Chancery	12 12 -	
	D. money 5 . 5/- Livery 9/- Servant 5/-	5 19 -	
	Lord Keeper of the Great Seals fees	6 13 4	
	Deputy keeper	2 10 -	
	usher	2 4 5¹/2	
	Appender & Wax 2. 7 Depute 1. 1. -	3 8 -	
	Writers fees 10 . 10 . - − Clerks 2 . 2 . -	12 12 -	
	Copy warrand & Charter for the Press(?)	- 9 -	
	Paid for printing the same	2 7 6	
	Inserting notice in Newspapers	- 7 6	
	Sundry postages from London & Inverness	- 10 -	
		£179 6 3¹/2	

Table 5.1: Cost of purchasing the Royal Charter, 1793

The cost of obtaining the Charter was large, being £179 6 3¹/2d [Table 5.1][21] – about the cost of two years' salaries for the staff. From this point the school could be called Inverness *Royal* Academy, although the 'Royal' was little used for many years. Mention was made however of the Royal Charter in the newspaper advertisements for the third session of the Academy due to open in July 1793 (in the early years a session lasted six months). Charles Mackintosh in Edinburgh had sent north eighty printed copies of the Charter and the Royal Warrant on which it was based (at least three copies still survive).[22]

The Warrant (often with the spelling 'warrand') is in English, but the Charter itself is in Latin – presumably Ebenezer Young's translation [Appendix 3]. The original Charter, on vellum with its Seal of Scotland [Figure 5.2], was presumably sent north at the same time as the printed copies. As a result of changes in the management of the School over the years, with control passing to Inverness Burgh School Board in 1907, the Charter is no longer relevant, but it provides an important link with the early history of the

Academy. As with the rules and regulations, this Charter was to cause the Directors major problems over its interpretation, especially in 1814-1815 when Matthew Adam took them to court over his tenure of office (see Chapter 7).

For many years the original charter was missing, but it was discovered in 1942 in a lawyer's office in Inverness and was then returned to the school. The seal however was broken, although still attached to the charter by its appender. The whole charter was restored and framed at the time of the school bicentenary in 1992, the work being funded by the Inverness Common Good Fund, and is now on display in the School. Modern conservation work has made the seal appear almost undamaged.

Purchasing the apparatus

From the time of his appointment, Weir had been in discussion with the sub-committee about the purchase of appropriate apparatus for his class. In a letter to the Directors in June 1792,[23] Weir set out his views on how it should be purchased:

> An apparatus or Instruments for explaining Mensuration, Geography & Navigation & for exhibiting experiments in Philosophy & Chemistry must be procured. Without them the 3 former of these branches cannot be concluded nor the two latter begun. Of these instruments, some can be purchased ready made; the greater part however must be commissioned. Every thing depends upon the accuracy of their construction & this can only be determined by one who is perfectly master of the subjects to which they apply. They can therefore only be procured by a person so qualified, & in the accomplishment of this his best method will be, to go to those places where they are to be found cheapest; to purchase such as he finds made that will suit, & to get the others made under his inspection & according to his order. This method is no doubt tedious, but as it seems to be the best, no objection should arise from its requiring 3 or 4 more additional months. It was in this way that the greater part of the apparatus, of the Dundee Academy, was purchased by me.

> As it is not probable that there will be any fit for attending my classes the first session; (& even altho' there were without any apparatus I could not pretend to begin) I should wish to undertake the charge of procuring the Instruments provided the Directors will agree to pay my expences. This will no doubt be attended with additional expence, but they will be most probably be so much the better, or better adapted at least to my purposes. If the Directors agree to this I would go over immediately to Edinr. being acquainted with several Instrument makers there and order such as I think could be obtained cheaper there than at London. Then after opening the Academy at Inverness on the 16th July, & seeing that all the Masters are going on properly, I should set of to London, & buying one Instrument here & another there as appeared best; do every thing in my power to procure a valuable apparatus, at the cheapest rate. I am exceedingly anxious to have proper Instruments; my usefulness in the Academy is particularly connected with them: & it would grieve me very much were they procured of such a nature, as not to answer properly.

Weir does not seem to have been permitted to purchase any of the apparatus before the opening day, but very quickly thereafter the Directors considered his list and he was authorised to go to London.[24] However he was granted only £200 (four times what he had been allowed for the same purpose in Dundee!), and allowed expenses of 30 guineas (£31 10s). By early October Weir was in London[25] and from there sent nine boxes of materials by sea to Inverness. He had also commissioned some items in Edinburgh, which he collected on his way back to Inverness. Sadly no list of what he purchased remains.

By Christmas 1792 he was back in Inverness, having overspent by almost £40, with his own expenses amounting to £20 more than he had been allowed. One of the ministers was instructed to look at what Weir had spent,[26] and the Directors did what they did several times in the future, and avoided the issue by paying Weir £10 for his expenses in moving to Inverness but refusing him the extra £20 the London visit had cost him. Eventually the Directors accepted that all the equipment was needed, and they agreed to pay the outstanding balance of £28 17 8½d.[27]

So, by the summer of 1793, a year after the school first opened, most of the main issues concerning the administration of the Academy were under control, although many other issues attended the running of the school in the first few years of its operation.

Chapter 6
The early years

When Weir gave his opening lecture of 16th July 1793 in the presence of the subscribers and Directors, there were only four staff in place: Weir himself, having moved from Dundee, and Douglas (mathematics) from Edinburgh, together with Young (classics) and Wills (writing, arithmetic and book-keeping), these two continuing their work in Inverness. As mentioned in Chapter 5, Mr Vatchell, "a native of England", although appointed, had failed to arrive. John Hoyes, who had taught English in the Grammar School (or the school linked to it) had not got the job. There is no record in the Directors' Minutes of the formal appointment of Mr Crisp as the replacement. His name first appears in the accounts in September 1792 and by December he was wanting to start a private English class.[1] In October 1792 he must have been in post, as the English class was described as "very big" and extra accommodation was required. He was named as English teacher in the advertisements for the start of the second session in January 1793.

Little information is available about Douglas, Young or Wills, prior to their coming to Inverness, and nothing is known about Crisp, other than that he came from London. However considerable information about James Weir has come from a batch of papers in the National Archives of Scotland in the Fraser-Mackintosh collection,[2] covering the period 1789 to 1827. Weir appears to have come from Craignethan, near Lanark, but his date of birth is not known, although it was probably about 1763 or 1764. By 1780 he was studying at Edinburgh University, and so he might have been aged 15 or 16 at this point. His studies were in Greek, mathematics, natural philosophy and moral philosophy, and a couple of years later he attended a class in logic and another one in Greek.[3]

He became Rector of the newly-opened Dundee Academy in October 1786, which operated alongside the local grammar school. The salary was £50 per annum, with a fee of two guineas from each scholar. The appointment was for "three years certain",[4] and he was asked to acquire suitable equipment for his classes at a sum not exceeding £50, a sum which he overspent. This overspending lead to problems with the Town Council who in the end did pay the extra £10 or so. Weir and his two fellow staff were re-elected by the Council at the end of the first three-year period in 1789.

In early 1792 the French teacher walked out and Weir was asked to find a replacement. Instead, in April 1792, Weir announced that he had accepted "of an offer which had been made to him of being Rector of the Academy at Inverness".[5] Probably as a result of his resignation, Dundee Academy did not reopen for its third three-year period, and the school was not replaced until the Messrs Websters of London (although natives of Dundee) funded a new Academy which opened in 1801.

Weir had first enquired about the post of Rector in Inverness in December 1791,[6] following this up the following February with a letter enquiring about the permanency of the post. Reassured on this, perhaps at a time when it was clear there was a serious problem in Dundee, Weir put in his application to Charles Mackintosh in Edinburgh. Provost William Mackintosh (not directly related) enquired of Charles Mackintosh what he thought of Weir, but the reply said that the conversation when they met was so short that he had no opinion on the subject. (An 1822 Dundee book described Weir as "a gentleman of considerable abilities, but rather a projector".) The formal appointment was made on 10th April 1792, and Weir seems to have visited Inverness on 1st May.[7] Thereafter he produced a detailed plan of his ideas on the newspaper advertisements, the roles of the various staff, and the appropriate rules and regulations.[8]

It is not clear how long Weir was in Inverness, following the opening ceremony, before going to Edinburgh and then London, to purchase the apparatus (Chapter 5), and little is said about the Academy classes during the early months. Clearly Weir did not have a class (as he had thought likely in his May letter when he sent in his proposed regulations). Salaries were paid early, at the end of November, not at the end of the session on 20th December, presumably to help Douglas and Weir cover their travelling expenses to Inverness, although Douglas did at the same time receive the sum of ten guineas towards the cost of moving his family and furniture to Inverness, and Weir received a similar sum in January 1793. On the last two days of the session the Directors examined the classes. The advertisement for the second session of the school, which appeared in the newspapers in the closing days of 1792, indicated that there were about 200 scholars attending the school, and that Mr Crisp would teach French as well as English. The advertisement also claimed that Inverness was free of vice!

Weir obviously took up his duties in the school in late 1792, and these included the requirement to visit the classes of the other teachers, something which at that stage was very unusual as teachers in grammar schools were virtually independent of each other, and in many towns there was only a single teacher anyway. Weir was also dealing both with the apparatus which was arriving by boat, and with the issue of how the coals were to be provided for the classroom fires. In January 1793 the Directors appointed Ebenezer Young to deal with the coals for that session, to be followed by Weir in the next session, and declared that students would pay 1s 6d a year for coal and candles.[9]

By February 1793 the first major crisis hit the Academy, and this revolved around Weir's visits to classes. The leader on this issue was Robert Douglas. An anonymous and undated letter in the Fraser-Mackintosh collection[10] has a pencil note on it saying '1792' but might be from very early 1793. It says that it is essential that teachers are as independent of each other as possible, with the Latin teacher looking to his former University professor for guidance on his work. The writer, who may well have been Douglas, says that there was no precedent for a Rector to control the work of other masters – not quite what he then goes on to describe. The example of problems in the Grammar School of Glasgow in the early 1780's is quoted. The dispute, it is claimed, came to an end with the death of the Rector of the school, and the magistrates then put all the staff on an equal footing. It is also claimed that the High School of Edinburgh had been for many years "in a state of civil war" over the same issue, and several law processes were in hand.

The Directors' meeting on 20th February received three letters, from Douglas, from Young and from Wills, about the Rector visiting their classes. Douglas' letter is by far the most extreme:[11]

> ... to suffer any man to examine the various classes in the Academy supposes that man not only a judge of the various branches professed by the masters, but better acquainted with their particular moods of methods of teaching – even than the particular teacher himself. ...
>
> ... the students ... will conclude their particular teacher inferior to the Rector in knowledge, even in those branches which have been the particular study and daily practice of their teacher, and which the Rector has never practiced in his life – hence the teacher will sink in the scholar's esteem till at length they come to despise his instructions ...

Young's letter is much more moderate in tone:[12]

> Placing a superintendent supposes superior knowledge or experience in the person who superintends. I have reason to think that Mr Weir's visits can be of no service to my classes as he had no experience or practice in teaching the branches in my department, but on the contrary loss of time & putting the classes out of order and method.

whereas Wills' letter indicates he is not very happy with the arrangements for class visiting but looks at two other issues, proposed by Weir:[13]

> There were also some other innovations proposed by the Rector, such as fines, in order to enforce punctual attendance, calling over a catalogue of all the names in the morning &c. – The first of these, in my opinion is unnecessary, as I have seldom had cause to complain of my class for that neglect, all the time I have been in Inverness. – The last must occasion a considerable loss of time.

Young also found the concept of fines for late-coming ridiculous:

> the absurdity of this is too obvious to require any observation ...

He also suggests that some pupils might turn to crime to get the money to pay the fines!

After calling in the staff individually and questioning them, the Directors decided to reduce Weir's visits to one a month. It was also decided that each teacher should call the catalogue (the register in modern terms) in his own room before proceeding to the hall for prayers led by the Rector. Late-coming punishments were left to the discretion of the individual masters, but the Rector was to report any master who did not enforce prompt attendance.

The minute of this meeting apparently reached Douglas on 6th March and he penned his resignation the next day:[14]

> ... I have therefore taken the liberty to beg you will inform the directors particularly

the members of that Committee, that after having deliberately read and considered the minute, I find it simply impossible for me to comply with what it enjoins, and therefore hope they will consider this as a full resignation of my Office at the end of the present session ... from the day I was appointed Teacher of Mathematics, I considered myself as having no superior in the Academy but the Directors. But altho I acknowledge the Directors as my superiors, I never did nor never will acknowledge a power in them to subject me to another ... Yet I did not desire they should alter the Law but humbly beg'd it might be suspended ... But the committee so far from granting my humble, my reasonable request, have confirmed the Rector in his Dictatorial Office, and limited him to assume the character of Inspector General only once a month ... *(underlinings in original)*

Douglas goes on to claim that the Directors were making him a tax gatherer by collecting the Rector's fees. His only conciliatory comment is concerning Wills, whom Douglas considers to be overworked in his writing and arithmetic class.

The Directors accepted his resignation at their next meeting,[15] and, as they had received complaints about Crisp, they decided not to re-employ him after the end of the session. So, within ten months of the official opening, two of the staff would be leaving. Weir, a few days later, put forward a plan to reorganise the staff, as he claimed that three of them were overworked, and he also provided a plan of education to be completed by age 16:[16]

... children coming to the Academy, & taking a complete course at it, which should always be aimed at & inculcated; would be employed during their attendance in the following manner. By nine years of age, they might be masters of the English; & in 4$1/2$ years more of the Latin. During this time by occasional attendance on Mr Wills, they should have learned writing; & the half of the day during the last year at Latin should be devoted to Arithmetic & French. Against the 14th, they may begin Mathematics; & this year alongst with the study of it, French & Arithmetic & Book-keeping, should also be prosecuted. The last year by this means is spent on drawing, Geography, Navigation, Philosophy, Chemistry & History, Drawing being more detached & unconnected than any of the other branches, may be studied any of the last 3 years.

The personal papers of Alexander Macgregor, covering the period from 1789 until his death in 1805 and now in the National Archives of Scotland, provide us with further details of the operation of the Academy.[17] Macgregor, who appears to have married in central Scotland and fathered a child before apparently leaving his wife, was teaching in the Grammar School in Alness (in the parish of Kiltearn, Ross-shire). He was lodging with Rev. Harry Robertson, the local minister, who recommended Macgregor for the mathematics and French post in Inverness. In the recommendation letter from Robertson[18] we get some more information about the size of the Academy classes. Douglas seems to have had 20 scholars learning geography and 12 mathematics, with a few ladies learning to draw. He also kept nine boarders in his house.

The session would have ended on Monday 10th June, following the examinations on 6th to 8th June and the orations on the final day (Monday).

The next term was due to start on 16th July, and William Haig (although he was not immediately available) was appointed to take over Crisp's English class. However just before the start of the new term Bailie William Inglis received a letter from Weir concerning his health: this cannot have come as much of a surprise as Weir had had an epileptic fit in mid-May in front of Young's class, when he was conducting one of his monthly visits,[19] which "made so strong an impression on some of the boys as to render their parents very unhappy".[20] His letter said his health had deteriorated during the last six weeks of term, and he had travelled from Inverness to Leith by sea in the hope of recovery. He also disclosed that he had been affected with epilepsy for the previous two years or so, but claims he was not convinced he had a problem until after he was appointed Rector in Inverness.

The Directors were quite sympathetic over the illness, and told him not to return until he had recovered. He proposed taking a further sea journey to London, but in the end decided it would not be beneficial.[21] He was treating himself with a nostrum, a patent medicine for which only the maker would know the recipe, which he claimed was helping. He continues:

> From your letter I observe that the people are alarmed, & though the disorder is not infectious, yet it is surely of that cast which of most others is hurtful to a teacher. It need scarcely be observed that whatever others may feel on the occasion can be but trivial when compared with that distress of mind to which an epileptic patient is continually subjected. For near these two years I have been under the necessity of shunning most kinds of company & public places. Riding on horseback has seldom or ever been attempted but with a companion, & even the sea has been considered as dangerous. It was with trembling I walked the streets, & when in Church render such anxiety of mind as is not easy to be described – never at ease but when alone or with some friends I could confide in.

He also stated that he was aware that there had been no applicants for his class, and so an immediate return to Inverness was not essential. Weir apparently never returned to Inverness, and was dismissed by the Directors in December,[22] having in effect given him six months' sick leave. He may never even have taught a class in the Academy. The Directors assured him that they were totally satisfied with his abilities and conduct as Rector and wished him success in whatever he might be able to do. Weir did appeal against his dismissal, but to no avail.

Weir by this point had gone to London, where he became involved in work with the Board of Longitude and the Rev. Nevil Maskelyne, the Astronomer Royal. This work involved trying to produce a more satisfactory arrangement for operating an artificial horizon, an instrument used to determine longitude at sea (or on land) when the horizon is obscured.[23] He travelled between London and Edinburgh (and presumably Craignethan where his father was still living in late 1793), working on his apparatus, but no information survives about his health. He died some time in the summer or autumn of 1797, aged perhaps only about 35 years, but the cause is not recorded. His brother, a surgeon on board a British ship fighting in the Napoleonic War, did not reappear in London to settle the estate until early 1803.

So, eighteen months after the opening, the Academy had lost its third original member of staff.

Appointing the second Rector

Alex. Macgregor had started work in Inverness as mathematics teacher in the summer of 1793. William Haig had taken up appointment as the English teacher some time in the autumn, and was living in the Rector's house. For all practical purposes the Academy ran without a Rector for the whole of the two sessions from summer 1793 to summer 1794. Perhaps the tradition of teachers working independently in the grammar schools helped the school survive. Alternatively, perhaps the departure of Douglas came as a relief to the other teachers.

Weir's potential dismissal must have been obvious in Inverness by October 1793, as Macgregor was by then in correspondence with his former teacher at Perth, John McOmie (with a variety of alternative spellings), about the emoluments of the Inverness job. Both Macgregor and McOmie seem to have been interested in jobs in Dundee in 1792: in fact Macgregor was appointed to the job of French teacher there[24] (his father was French teacher in Perth) but turned it down due to concerns about security of tenure, and McOmie was at least considered for the job as Rector there.[25] Macgregor clearly had a high regard for his former teacher and there was a regular correspondence between them until the time they were both in Inverness.

Testimonials for John McOmie were sent from the Church of Scotland and Episcopalian ministers in Perth, from Robert Hamilton (his former Rector, now at Marischal College in Aberdeen), and from others.[26] Several of the testimonials, according to McOmie, were unsolicited.[27] Macgregor also wrote a sort of testimonial,[28] but was somewhat cautious in his wording as he was already employed in the Academy, and the Rev. Harry Robertson had advised him to take care in what he wrote.[29] McOmie was formally appointed on 1st May 1794,[30] after some haggling over the salary, and a claim that he had another job in prospect.[31] He was introduced to the Directors at their meeting on 25th July,[32] and at their next meeting the Directors agreed that the Rector should in future attend all their open meetings.

No major issues arise in the next few years, but the few snippets of information available suggest that classes settled into a reasonable routine. McOmie's tact and experience, as described in the testimonials, presumably got round the issue of the Rector's visit to classes.

Inverness Presbytery library (these days generally known as the Kirk Session library) had been established in the early 1700's. During the early months of the Academy it had been agreed to house the library in the Academy hall, and bookcases had been made at a cost of £50. The transfer of books was complete by July 1794, and the library remained in the Academy until 1817 when it was moved back to the old Library Room in the Dunbar Hospital as the books were not being properly cared for.[33] The Directors also appointed official booksellers in the Town, and the teachers were prohibited from selling books to the pupils. The bell of the old Grammar School, presented to it by Hector Fraser, had been moved to the Academy during 1793.

March 1795 saw 'the itch' affecting pupils, and about the same time Macgregor appears to have gone to Perth to attend his father's funeral.[34] Discussions took place about adjustments in the hours of some of the classes. Thomas Fraser, the Gaelic teacher, who also assisted James Wills with arithmetic, writing and book-keeping, resigned in July 1795 for a better job, to be replaced by William Mackintosh. The Gaelic class did not always have pupils, and there was some doubt about Mackintosh's ability as a teacher to assist Wills, but he was later judged to be satisfactory, although he was told to exert more authority over his pupils. By September 1796, the Directors decided that the Gaelic class could continue only if the Highland Society continued their allowance, as funds were beginning to be stretched.[35] By the following summer Mackintosh was told his salary would only be the £15 from the Highland Society. If he was unhappy with this, it was suggested he should resign. Mackintosh did resign in the summer of 1798, to be replaced by William MacRae.

The start of the summer holiday was delayed from mid-June to the end of June in 1795, but this was changed yet again to the start of June the following summer. With the death of Hector Fraser's wife, the Fraser bursary was instituted in late 1795 for a son of a burgess by the name of Fraser, or someone at least of the name of Fraser. The original Janitor died in the autumn of 1797. By this stage the Napoleonic Wars were in progress, and McOmie was thanked by the Provost for the contribution of £40 from the school towards Government funds.[36] It is not stated how this money was collected.

The wide-ranging ages of the school pupils came to light in 1798 when William Haig petitioned the Directors not to admit to his class scholars under the age of five, as the work of the older pupils was affected,[37] and this was agreed to. That summer the programme of orations was widened from Latin (and possibly Greek), to include English, French and, if possible, Gaelic, the Gaelic oration to be a passage from Ossian's poems if a pupil was competent enough. These poems were created by James Macpherson in the 1760's/70's, allegedly by translation of original Gaelic material, but now shown to have been written largely by Macpherson himself.

McOmie himself had not been well over the winter of 1797/98, and had missed a considerable amount of teaching as a result. There was also a complaint from the Directors that he had been seen in the street at a time when they felt he should be at work. However he requested, and was granted permission, to go to London on business in mid-May, two or three weeks before the end of the session – the reason is not stated but it could be related to his health or that of his wife (who was to give birth to a stillborn child in early 1800). It was agreed to examine his geography and drawing class early, there being no pupils in the natural philosophy class. His visit to London was clearly fairly extended as a further copy letter in the minutes book concerns a boy who was expected to attend the Academy but had not appeared, perhaps due to the danger of the sea passage from London during the Napoleonic War.[38] It was suggested that he could come north by coach with the McOmies when they returned.

The remaining years of McOmie's tenure as Rector seem to have been relatively peaceful, and few issues seem to have developed. One that did was the attendance at church by the staff and the pupils, an issue that was to recur frequently until compulsory attendance at church was abolished in 1830. The Directors' meeting of 17th September 1800 decided that the pupils were to take their place in church on a Sunday in the order they had achieved in class on the previous day. The only exceptions were those of the English class (which would include the youngest pupils) and those whose parents did not belong to the established church. Deviation from this regulation was to be punished with flagellation, and finally expulsion. In addition the rules on religious instruction in class were to be observed and this work would be examined.

One other event is well worth recording. There was a gunpowder explosion in Baron Taylor's Lane (now Street) which happened on 11th March 1801, and details appear in *The Times* of London, and in *The Scots Magazine* (there was no local newspaper in Inverness until 1807). A candlemaker, Robin Goodwin, had left his shop and when he was away, a fire developed which spread to six barrels of gunpowder nearby, causing a massive explosion. Seven townspeople were killed, and widespread damage was caused, both by the explosion and by flying debris. Buildings damaged included both the Northern Meeting Rooms (in Church Street) and the Academy. The candlemaker disappeared from the Town and one version of the story says that his body was found in the River Clyde. The cost to the Academy, mainly from broken windows, was £68 9s 11d, but the Directors only required the company that was responsible to pay £50.

Further changes took place amongst the Gaelic teachers. In September 1800, an Alexander McCommie or McOmie was appointed, but there is no specific information as to whether he was a relation of John McOmie, the Rector. A testimonial, preserved in the National Archives of Scotland,[39] records Alex McOmie as a teacher in Fortrose starting at about Whitsun 1793, and the Old Parish Registers for Inverness[40] name his wife and record the baptism of two children in 1799 and 1800. In the 1799 entry he is recorded as "Master of the Grammar School past seven years" *[transcription of last three words doubtful]*, but the 1800 entry (for November) records him by that date as "Teacher in the Academy". He stayed in post only until February 1802. That same year, the Highland Society wrote with a view to withdrawing its grant for Gaelic teaching, as no report had been received about how their money was being used. The Directors responded, and the grant continued.

Overall numbers in the Academy seem have been well over 200 at the start of the nineteenth century, but John McOmie resigned through poor health in March 1803. He returned to Perth where he served as Secretary to the Literary and Antiquarian Society until his death in 1819, aged 63. His obituary in the *Inverness Courier* reflects something of his character which had been stated previously in his testimonials:[41]

> At Perth, on the evening of Sunday se'ennight [= last week], after a very short illness, John M'Omie, L.L.D. long known in this town as a diligent and zealous teacher. This amiable and respectable individual was, during a period of 11 years, rector of the Academy here, but the state of his health having rendered it necessary for him to retire from that situation, he returned to Perth, his native city, where he continued till his death to employ his leisure hours in giving private instructions in drawing and geography. With manners mild and conciliating, he was universally esteemed and beloved; and it may be truly affirmed, that by his death society has lost a very valuable member, while the cause of religion and philanthropy has been deprived of one of its warmest advocates ...

The statement that he had served eleven years was inaccurate – it was only nine years. McOmie was awarded his Doctorate by Marischal College, Aberdeen in 1795.

Macgregor appointed Rector

A number of people applied to replace McOmie as Rector, but the Directors did not seem satisfied by any of the applications. A sub-committee was appointed to look for suitable candidates. This committee included the Hon. Lord Woodhouselee, Simon Fraser of Farraline, Charles Mackintosh, W.S., James Fraser, James Grant, W.S., and Colin Mackenzie, W.S.

There had been correspondence with the Rector of Perth Academy, and from this we learn that the Academy roll was claimed to be around 250.[42] There were five classes and young ladies were attending drawing, geography and French classes. The Directors (at least in the person of Provost Mackintosh) had an idea of the ideal candidate:

> ... a very young man would not suit, as we wish for a man if possible who not only by his abilities but his respectable character may command the dignified attention due to him not only from the students but from the other teachers.

The front-runner seems to have been Gilbert Wright from Perth Academy, but he was discounted on the grounds that it was not believed he had sufficient discipline, although he was well-qualified. The committee recommended Alex. Macgregor, even though he does not seem to have formally applied for the job, despite having apparently hinted that he might be interested:[43]

> That Mr Alexr. McGregor now teacher of the Mathematics and the French language in the Inverness Academy has not only given general satisfaction in his present situation (which he has occupied for about 10 years) but that he also possesses a general knowledge of the other sciences taught in the Academy, and

such other qualifications as seem to indicate his fitness for discharging with propriety the duty of Rector in this Academy.

The Committee feel the less reluctance in giving this as their unanimous opinion that by the constitutional laws of the Academy no office bearer can be continued longer in office, than he shall in the opinion of the Directors continue to be deserving of the situation.

At the same time the Committee declare they have no cause to fear any disappointment in the choice they now recommend to the Directors. ...

Macgregor was called into the meeting, and at the age of 33, became the third Rector of Inverness Academy. He retained his mathematics class, but dropped French teaching to take natural philosophy and chemistry. A new teacher for French and geography/drawing was to be appointed, although this did not happen until Robert Mudie (also a spelling of Moodie) of Pittenweem was appointed the following summer (1804) for the geography and drawing classes, with John Tulloch from Reay in Caithness taking the French class and assisting Ebenezer Young in Latin. William Haig, who had served the school for 14 years, was dismissed early in 1804 (with effect from the end of the session), following poor examination results,[44] to be replaced by Alex Campbell, another teacher who moved to Inverness from Fortrose. Haig then taught in Dumfries for 18 years before his death in 1822.

From the start of 1804, there is a printed list of all staff, with their class numbers.[45] This was produced by Matthew Adam, the fifth Rector, in 1835 when he was trying to prove that the Academy was not in a state of decline. Although there are some errors in this list, it provides a useful summary of the staffing and state of the school over a thirty-year period at the start of the nineteenth century. There also exists the first specific list of pupils, as a class register survives covering the period from 1804 to 1810,[46] which lists names (predominately male but many female) and addresses (not just from the Highlands, but from the West Indies, Canada, and elsewhere). Unfortunately no ages are given. Three Macrae brothers from Jamaica are identified as of mixed race, and were probably the illegitimate sons of an Inverness emigrant. The only earlier evidence of a pupil's name is a receipt, signed by Ebenezer Young, for fees of ten shillings paid by a pupil, Hugh McDonald, in October 1793.[47]

From these documents it appears that there were just over 200 pupils in the school in 1804, with some pupils enrolled for more than one class – not as many as suggested in the correspondence about Gilbert Wright applying for the job of Rector. The gross number is given as 237, of whom 86 were in the English reading and grammar classes (17 of these coming from the Caribbean). More than 50 pupils were in the arithmetic, writing and book-keeping classes and also in the Latin classes. French had 15 pupils, mathematics 21, but the geography and drawing class was closed for the first session of 1804 (although after Mudie's appointment it had 20 or 30 pupils, roughly evenly split between the two classes). After Alexander Nimmo became Rector in 1805, total numbers did reach over 250, before declining to below 200. The highest figures for the early nineteenth century were round about 1815/1816, in the early years of Matthew Adam's term as Rector, when 304 pupils enrolled.

This register also includes details of what was taught in most of the subjects. The subjects with larger numbers were split into classes, sometimes up to 5, 6 or 7 classes, with the girls in some subjects separately listed as a class. Some of the main subjects also had private classes, presumably at a higher fee than that charged in the public classes. There is confusion as sometimes the 1st class is the top class; sometimes the highest-numbered class is the top class. Some of the topics of study, based mainly on the 1804 registers, were:

- English: Alphabet and Spelling Book in the 1st class; *Tyro's Guide*[48] in the 2nd or 3rd class; the Bible and the Catechism in the 3rd or 4th class; grammar and *Scott's Lessons* in the 4th or 5th class
- Writing, arithmetic and book-keeping: the 4th class in 1804 seems to have been the lowest, studying addition and proportion; the 3rd class studied decimal fractions; book-keeping, reduction and interest calculations seem to have occupied most of the time in the 2nd and 1st class (entries indicate certain pupils from this class then went on to the mathematics class)
- Mathematics: due to small numbers this was not always separated into classes, but topics mentioned include algebra, fluxions (in modern terminology differentiation), geometrical problems, the elements of Euclidian geometry, trigonometry and mensuration [measuring]
- Latin: *Rudiments* in the 1st class; Eutropius and Cornelius Nepos[49] in the 2nd or 3rd class; grammar, Caesar, Ovid and Virgil in the 4th class (by this stage pupils were often in their 6th or 7th (half-year) session of Latin)
- French: the 2nd class studied the Rudiments; the 1st class *The Travels of Anacharsis*[50]

The books listed for English and Latin are very similar to those used in other schools in Scotland at this time.[51] The geography and drawing class lists do not specify content. There was no Gaelic class at this time. Two or three pupils were listed as studying natural philosophy in addition to other subjects, but there is no separate class list for this group, or indication of the class work.

Little is said in the minutes concerning Macgregor's term of office until his death, following an illness, on 24th March 1805 at the age of 35, as reported at the April 1805 Directors' meeting. The papers which survive about the winding up of his estate provide a valuable insight into his life.[52] He employed a servant called Janet Smith, who was paid at a rate of two pounds sterling for a half year. His illness apparently began in the first few days of 1805 as a doctor and a surgeon attended him from 6th January, supplying medicines to the value of £5 0 1d, and advice and attendance to the value of five guineas

(£5 5s). During this illness it appears from the 1805 register entry that Robert Mudie taught the mathematics class, and this continued until Alexander Nimmo was appointed as Rector in the autumn.

After his death, Macgregor's estranged wife, Maxwell Shiels, was left to sort out the estate, although it is unlikely she received much money as he was heavily in debt. In August 1801 Mrs Macgregor had come to Inverness with her brother, a farmer in Renfrewshire, possibly to try for a reconciliation with her husband. In the end she got a promise of an annuity of twenty pounds a year for maintenance of herself and their daughter, Janet, then aged about 12.[53] The Rev. Harry Robertson at Kiltearn, with whom Alexander had stayed when teaching in Alness, was to be one of the guarantors for this annuity. Macgregor seems to have tried to avoid payment, as in the next few months his wife's brother, and then the minister at Rutherglen, wrote letters to try to get the bond made out.[54] The minister implies that Macgregor made himself out as a single man during his time in Inverness.

A local writer [solicitor], Alexander MacDonell, was appointed by Mrs Macgregor to wind up the estate on her behalf, and a letter exists from Janet, the daughter, requesting a few mementoes of her father.[55] A roup [= sale by auction] was held over three days in July 1805, based on a fifteen-page inventory of goods and effects, including over 300 books, some of which he had borrowed, as in October of that year the Rev. Harry Robertson was still trying to retrieve his books from the executor, as many had been sold during the roup. Bills were also outstanding to John Young, a bookseller, for £82 17 2d, and to a tailor (£1 3 9d). The roup made over £56 on the sale of the books, and the household furniture in the Rector's house made over £98. Other minor accounts which survive include the fees of the executors (£21 16 1½d) and the cost of the bellman (£1 4s, with a discount of 2s) for announcing the roup around the Town.

It is presumably through Alexander MacDonell (acting as executor) that these papers have survived, and passed into the Fraser-Mackintosh collection in the National Archives of Scotland. Much of the material consists of letters from the Rev. Harry Robertson's daughter, Anne, to Macgregor. These were written on a basis of one every seven to ten days, and comprise social news.

Financing the Academy
Full accounts, showing income and expenditure, were not properly considered by the Directors between 1804 and late 1811, when sixteen pages of accounts appear in the minutes book. The total level of subscriptions continued to rise for only a short period after the opening of the school, reaching £5520 in October and £6277 in December 1792. Clearly, after payment for building work, funds were tight, and there are frequent references to attempts to get those in arrears to pay what they had promised.

The only regular income the Directors would receive over the coming years was the sum of £70 promised by the Town, which had previously been allocated for the salaries of the Grammar School staff. In addition the Town agreed to take a loan of money temporarily not required, from Whitsun 1793 and pay 4^{1}/$_{2}$% interest. This was approved in May 1793[56] and a bond for £1400 made out in September 1793.[57] The bond was not redeemed by the Town until 1829.

At its meeting on 30th April 1793 the Commissioners of Supply for Inverness-shire had received a request for aid out of the contingency funds of the County. The meeting agreed to pay £200, "payable in two moieties" (parts), but the meeting felt it necessary to consult the landowners, who made up the membership of the committee. As a result, the following February Arthur Forbes, their convenor, wrote to the heritors, and a copy addressed to Sir James Grant of Grant, then resident at Grantown on Spey,[58] has survived. At the meeting on 30th April 1794, even though the minute says that it was a very acceptable idea, funds seem to have been stretched, and it was agreed to postpone the matter until the following year "when they entertain no doubt but the full amount required by the Directors of the Inverness Academy be granted".[59] But the following year the matter was not even mentioned, so presumably the money was never paid.

By the end of 1796 the Directors were so concerned about a shortage of funds, that they were to consider major savings unless money was soon forthcoming. The rate of interest on the bond with the Town was to be increased to 5%, and Lewis Cuthbert, the main fundraiser in the West Indies, was to be written to, to recover outstanding sums there. He did manage to send over £120 in subscriptions in October 1797.[60] By 1803 Lord Lovat's contribution was twelve years in arrears.

Early in 1793 porches were built for the Latin and English classrooms, probably the two rooms at the opposite ends of the school on the ground floor, at a cost of £29, but even by the end of 1794 some of the tradesmen had still not been paid for the work on the main building. The Directors then agreed to purchase an iron chest to keep the main papers relating to the building and the school, including the rights to the ground and the Royal Charter. The Academy grounds, which lay behind the building, had been let for agricultural use, and the two years' rent paid in 1801 had brought in over £20.

The Fraser legacy (see Chapter 2) became available in early 1796, and the first Fraser bursar was appointed in November 1797, one Alexander Reid, son of James Reid, flaxdresser.[61] The Wedderburn legacy of £200 (see Chapter 4) was paid in the summer of 1798. A third legacy, for £100, was received in 1802 from the estate of the late Provost William Inglis. This document[62] is very interesting in that Thomas Gilzean signs the document in two capacities: as cashier to the Academy and as receiver of legacy duty, and also describes himself as Sheriff Substitute, and therefore enforcing the laws on money transfer.

The Clark bequest

A major legacy became available during 1801, when letters both to the magistrates and to the Directors[63] informed them of the death in Naples in December 1799 of James Clark, a native of Inverness. This legacy included money to the value of £725, from his estate in England, but more significantly he bequeathed to the Academy a painting of *The Holy Family*, then claimed to be by Sassoferrato, which was to be placed in the hall of the school. After expenses and duty, the Directors received £681 10s of the £725, and it was decided that the money that could be spared was to be invested. The money appears to have been loaned to Fraser of Torbreck, who then did not pay the interest on the loan promptly.

In 1919 the Inverness Scientific Society (now better known as the Inverness Field Club) had a lecture by William Simpson, their President, about Clark and other local artists.[64] Clark's father had been Provost of Inverness in the early 18th century, and James, by sponsorship from local gentry, was able to follow the pattern of training of many artists of his time by going to Italy and copying many paintings by the Old Masters. He eventually settled in Naples, at a time when Sir William Hamilton was British ambassador to the Court of the Kingdom of Naples. Hamilton was a major art dealer and collector, and Clark acted as his agent. Clark also acquired an important collection of antique pottery, including Etruscan vases and antique rings. He left an estate worth over £8000 and in his will he asked Thomas Coutts, the banker, to administer his estate in England. Coutts declined, and it fell to Clark's brother in London to do the necessary work. The Italian estate was administered by two friends, one of whom was the British Consul in Naples.

The picture itself [Figure 6.1] was very slow in reaching Inverness, and by July 1804 it had only reached London. The frame had been damaged and had to be repaired. The committee hoped that it would be sent carriage free, but were disappointed when it arrived in September with carriage charges of over £27 due, which they were forced to pay. It was agreed that the picture be hung in the Academy hall under these conditions:[65]

> That the hall be kept shut on all occasions, and none of the students admitted, except at public examinations or when public prayers are given; that the different classes shall assemble each in their own private class, and when the rector and masters are met in the hall the students shall be conducted to it to hear prayers, and shall be conducted back to their respective classes immediately after prayers are finished; that the doors leading from the two low rooms to the hall shall be shut up, and the street door constantly locked, except on public occasions, the only ordinary access to be for the future from the back door, the key of which is to be constantly kept by the rector; and it is earnestly recommended to the rector and masters to pay particular attention to these regulations to ensure the safety and preservation of this valuable mark of Mr Clark's good-will to the place of his nativity, and to the Academy possessing it.

Obviously the Academy and Town were very proud of their new acquisition.

The person who was claimed to be the artist, Sassoferrato, was named after the town of his birth. His full name was Giovanni Batista Salvi, and he lived in the province of Ancona in Italy from 1605 to 1685. Examples of his work are found in Britain, for instance in the National Gallery in London. The painting is on wood and has suffered the ravages of woodworm, and one restoration was carried out in 1840 by Alexander Macinnes, a local artist. However Charles Fraser-Mackintosh, in his book *Letters of Two Centuries*, indicates that he thinks that the painting that actually arrived in Inverness was not the one bequeathed to the Academy, and that another one had been substituted which was of little value.[66] Fraser-Mackintosh did not give any proof for his assertion, and modern scholarship says that it is an original work, but by an unknown artist about a half-a-century earlier than Sassoferrato.

In 1845 a suggestion was made to sell the picture, and two local valuations priced it, one at between £500 and £800, and the other between £2000 and £3000. An attempt was made to get a price from London, but there was strong opposition to the sale, and a suggestion that the sale might be illegal. The matter was dropped at that stage, but revived in 1868 when funds were low.[67] One estimate had again given a value of at least £2000. The recommendation was that it should be valued in Edinburgh, and, if thought valuable, sent for sale in London. More strong feelings arose about the conduct of the Directors, and the value placed on it in Edinburgh is not recorded. It was moved from the Academy hall to the drawing classroom of the Ladies' Institution of the Academy, until removed to the Town House in 1886, where it now hangs at the top of the grand staircase. Exactly who painted the *Holy Family* is a matter for the art experts to decide: it is even not clear who actually owns the picture today: the Academy or the City of Inverness, but probably by default as a result of local government reorganisation the question is irrelevant, as both are now controlled by Highland Council.

Early written accounts
The Academy was founded just in time to receive a mention in the (First) *Statistical Account of Scotland,*[68] which was published in 1793, although this adds little to what is available in other sources. A few years later the Englishman Thomas Garnet toured the Highlands, publishing his *Observations* in 1800.[69] His account seems to be partly a paraphrase of the First *Statistical Account*, somewhat updated, but his comparison of Scottish and English education is interesting:

> This useful institution possesses many advantages. The situation of Inverness is in the midst of an extensive country; the town is pleasantly situated, healthy, and not too large, board is likewise very reasonable. From the popular way in which the directors are appointed, as well as from their respectability, they are likely to keep up the spirit of it, and prevent abuses. Though it has not the name, it possesses most of the advantages of an university, and may serve as a place of complete education for all, excepting those intended for the learned professions...

> I cannot avoid observing here, that the inhabitants of North Britain have much

juster and more liberal ideas of education than my countrymen; and I cannot but express a wish, that many of the large schools in England, which are so nobly endowed, but in which the dead languages only are taught, were modelled according to the plan of the Scottish academies and universities. At the time of the foundation of these schools, these languages were deservedly in repute; they were the keys which unlocked the learned lore of antiquity. ...

... Is it not therefore better that the abilities of youth should be exercised in gaining a knowledge of things, instead of sounds? Instead of tormenting the young mind during that period when a store of useful knowledge might be laid in, with studying Latin and Greek for seven years, would it not be infinitely to their advantage to instruct them in history, geography, mathematics, mechanics, and other branches of experimental philosophy; particularly chemistry, which is a science of such importance, that there are few situations in life which would not be benefited by a knowledge of it? ...

In 1810 an anonymous comparison was made between Inverness and Perth Academies,[70] and, as this forms part of the Earl of Morton's papers in the NAS, was most likely prepared in connection with plans to modify Perth Academy. That academy was still only one of the schools in that town (see Chapter 4), although all by this stage in the Rose Terrace building. There were four staff, but only about 80 pupils (although increasing yearly), compared with Inverness' five staff and some 200-300 pupils. Pupils generally remained in the Perth Academy for two years, studying arithmetic, simple mathematics and French in the first year, and more advanced mathematics and physics in the second. The fees charged in the two schools are also listed. Much more detail is provided about Inverness than Perth. No ages for admission to Perth Academy are given, but it seems from the topics studied that most pupils must have been aged perhaps 11 or 12 before being admitted, having already studied English and Latin in the other parts of the Perth school system.

Chapter 7
Nimmo and Adam: engineer and scientist

From the death of Macgregor in 1805 until 1839, the school was under the control of two people whose names should be much better known in Inverness, namely Alexander Nimmo (Rector, 1805-1811) and Matthew Adam (Rector, 1811-1839). Nimmo moved on to become a surveyor and engineer, working largely in Ireland, and much of his legacy of engineering works there still stands today. Adam was more of a scientist, having an interest in meteorology and navigational instruments. Nimmo is beginning to be recognised in Ireland, but apart from mention in Joseph Mitchell's book *Reminiscences of my Life in the Highlands*, he is hardly known in the Highlands today. Adam is almost unknown, even in Inverness.

Alexander Nimmo
Alexander Nimmo according to some early biographies was born in Kirkcaldy, Fife, but was more likely to have been born in nearby Cupar in 1783.[1] His father was originally a watchmaker, but subsequently kept a hardware store in Kirkcaldy,[2] where Alexander may have attended the Burgh school. In mid-1796, aged 13, he had been awarded one of the Bayne bursaries, valid for four years. These bursaries, whose patron was William Ferguson of Raith (on the western edge of Kirkcaldy), were worth £120 Scots (£10 stg.) a year at the University of St. Andrews,[3] and were available for students whose families were fairly poor. The bursary was actually paid out by the magistrates of Cupar, suggesting that the Nimmo family still had links to that town. He then spent two years at St. Andrews, registering in early 1797, and another two years at Edinburgh University. Attendance at University from about age 14 was common at this time. Nimmo became an accomplished scholar in Latin and Greek as well as in various branches of mathematics and natural philosophy (physics). There is no evidence that he actually graduated from university, but failure to graduate was common at that time.

After being a tutor in Edinburgh, Nimmo became, in early 1802, aged 18 or 19, second master at Fortrose Academy, teaching mathematics.[4] His salary was £35 a year, plus class fees from his fifteen students; he also oversaw a boarding house for scholars, as was common at that time. In 1805 a new Rector, James Tod, brought a harsher regime[5] but Nimmo seems to have been keen to move on even before Tod was appointed. Following Macgregor's death, Nimmo applied for the Inverness job, even before it was advertised.[6] The two men almost certainly knew each other, as they were both mathematicians and so had similar academic interests. There would be few other similarly qualified people in the Highlands at that time. The mathematics curricula then taught at both Fortrose and Inverness Royal Academies seem very similar, reflecting the needs and interests of the time, and included arithmetic, book-keeping, surveying, architecture, fortification and gunnery.

The Royal Academy Directors, despite Nimmo's application, decided to advertise in the Edinburgh papers to fill the vacancy. Four candidates responded: Nimmo, John Tulloch (already on the staff), a Mr Pollock of Glasgow and a Mr Adie from Nielston, near Glasgow. At their May meeting, the Directors decided to invite some of the professors at Edinburgh University to make the choice. In some sources details of the appointment procedure are misleading, as details of the length of the examination and who the examiners were are presumably correctly given in the copy letter in the Minutes Book after the minutes of the meeting of 13th July 1805. The text reads:

Edinburgh, 27th June 1805

Report Etc. to be laid before the Directors of the Academy of Inverness.

Agreeable to the request of the Directors of the Academy of Inverness signified by James Grant Esq. Provost of Inverness in his letters to Professor Playfair of the 22nd May last and 5th curt. we the undersigned met this day at the College Library to examine such candidates for the place of Rector in the Academy of Inverness as might come forward to submit their qualifications to a comparative trial. There appeared before us only Mr Nimmo at present of the Academy at Fortrose who was accordingly examined by us on the subjects of Mathematics, Natural Philosophy, Chemistry, the Greek and Latin and French languages in all of which he acquitted himself very much to our satisfaction. In the sciences above named in which he underwent a long and particular examination he showed great accuracy and extent of knowledge as well as ingenuity and soundness of judgment. We can have no doubt therefore in recommending him the said Mr Alexander Nimmo to the Directors as possessing the qualifications which they require in the Rector of their Academy in an eminent degree and as likely to discharge the duties of that office much to his own credit and the satisfaction of all concerned.

(Signed)   Jo. Hill, Litt. Hum.
John Playfair, Prof. of Natural Phil.
James Finlayson, Prof. of Logic
Thos. Chas. Hope, Prof. of Chemistry

It will be seen that Nimmo was examined by four professors (not three as given in some sources), and for only one day (not three). John Hill was Professor of Humanity (Latin), although the signature does not fully indicate this. He retired about this time and died soon thereafter. Of the other professors, John Playfair is probably the one best remembered today. He was a mathematician, but in 1805 had changed his professorial chair from mathematics to natural philosophy, through his interest in geology. He was an original member of the Royal Society of Edinburgh. It is very likely that Nimmo had attended Playfair's mathematics lectures in the years he was at Edinburgh University, and probably knew him previously when Playfair was tutoring Ferguson's sons in Kirkcaldy.

Nimmo was clearly the only candidate who went to the examination. As a result of this report, Nimmo was duly appointed. Pollock also had very good certificates, but had objected to the comparative trial by the professors, and was given expenses of £21.[7] The Directors decided that some 'grovelling' would not be out of order, and the following appears in the minutes:[8]

> The meeting cannot avoid expressing the obligation the institution lies under to the gentlemen who have examined into and certified the qualifications of Mr Nimmo. It will be undoubtedly very creditable to the Inverness Academy to have the merits of its Rector ascertained by such eminent gentlemen and tho' the discharge of so useful and patriotic a duty is of itself sufficient recompense to persons of their sentiments yet the Directors in justice to themselves do request that Provost Grant will return to the different gentlemen through Mr Playfair (who has occasion to take particular trouble in this business) their most sincere thanks and acknowledgements for the services they have done to the Inverness Academy.

Nimmo took up his duties either at the start of, or very early on in, the autumn session of 1805, the third teacher to come to the Royal Academy from the academy at Fortrose.

Soon after his arrival Nimmo had requested and been authorised to purchase globes, but his request to start a library was received with doubt by the Directors who referred this idea to a committee (the 'Kirk Session' library was at this time in the Academy hall). They did agree that Academy staff could teach in the Girls' Boarding School (see Chapter 3) if it did not affect their teaching in the Academy. Various minor adjustments to classes and timing were also considered by the Directors, following suggestions from staff.

A visitation committee had been appointed in December 1805 but no report of their work, nor of the second visitation committee, was entered in the Minutes Book. The Directors were concerned about the number of scholars who missed the December examination in 1807, and at their next meeting decided to examine the absentees on 12th January.[9] In future, they said that absentees would be punished or expelled (although there is no evidence this was done). Some of the work produced for the examination was not satisfactory, and the teachers were told to be careful about what was produced. Spelling was to be checked regularly and James Wills was to teach English dictation to those who were capable of benefiting from it. Nimmo had failed to get his report ready for this meeting, but promised it in a few days.

The third visitation committee reported in March 1808.[10] Nimmo was not in his classroom at the time of the visitation, and was severely reprimanded for taking some of his pupils to the field for practical surveying, when they should have been in the classroom. Although the Directors did not doubt the value of this 'field work', they felt it should have been done in Nimmo's own time, so that the rest of the class could get the full lesson! Another complaint concerned Moodie's geography and drawing class which met at noon on a Wednesday. Every fourth Wednesday was a half-holiday so this class was losing a quarter of its teaching time. Moodie was instructed to teach the class on these Wednesdays until 2 p.m. when he could have the rest of the day for relaxation. Church attendance was also highlighted (see Chapter 9).

The only recorded major incident involving Nimmo was in 1810. A letter was produced at a Directors' Meeting from Major Thomas Fraser of Newton, whose son Hugh who was in the writing and arithmetic class, and also studying Latin:[11]

My son Hugh Fraser has attended the Academy for some years and I believe he behaved like other boys of his age and without giving much trouble to his Masters from disobedience or disrespect. It was therefore with much concern I learned that on Monday 29th ultimo he suffered a most cruel beating from Mr Nimmo, who, not satisfied with using his fists, seized a heavy mahogany ruler and with it beat the boy upon the shoulders, back and thigh. The marks and bruises are evidences of the usage he received which might, and still may prove of very bad consequences. However, I shall not at present enter into a more detailed account of the injury received, as that will best appear from the evidence of the medical gentlemen and the masters who saw the boy afterwards as well as the testimony of the other boys who were present.

Nimmo was censured:

The meeting having taken into consideration the facts admitted by Mr Nimmo himself respecting the manner and degree of chastisement inflicted upon Hugh Fraser are unanimously of opinion that he erred extremely in both, of the necessity of chastisement they are perfectly aware when necessary, but they are convinced it ought invariably to be inflicted with solemnity and a severity proportioned to the offence but in no case whatever with any other instrument than a tawse. They therefore recommend to Mr Nimmo in future to beware of yielding to suddenness of provocation or hastiness of temper and if the offence is of a serious nature to call the Masters and scholars of the whole Academy to the public hall and cause the master of the offending boy to inflict the chastisement there.

In early 1811, Nimmo was suggesting a scheme of work for pupils to progress more consistently through the various subjects during their time in the school, rather than study a single subject then drop it.[12] The Directors did set up a sub-committee to consider these proposals[13] but no formal report ever came before the committee, presumably as Nimmo's resignation was presented to the meeting on 11th June, and the matter was dropped. The January 1811 meeting also told Gilzean, the Treasurer, to enquire into costs of repairs to the Rector's house done a couple of years previously, but at the May meeting the Directors refused to fully fund the repairs – one of many occasions when they took this line – and the Deacon Convenor was told to claim the balance directly from Nimmo.[14]

Nimmo as a surveyor and an engineer
In December 1804 Nimmo was the sole author of a report presented at a meeting of the Royal Society of Edinburgh, although it was actually read to the meeting by Playfair. The title of the paper was 'An account of the removal of a large mass of stone to a considerable distance along the Murray Firth' [sic]. Unfortunately the report was never published in full, but from the title it is clear that Nimmo had been observing coastal erosion, transportation and deposition along the shores of the Firth.[15] On 1st January 1811, shortly before he changed from schoolmaster to engineer, Nimmo was elected a Fellow of

the Royal Society of Edinburgh, and in their register, he is described, even this early in 1811, as an 'engineer'. He was proposed as a Fellow by Sir George Steuart MacKenzie of Coul (Ross-shire), a person with whom Nimmo had stayed in 1807.[16]

In the same year as he was observing sediment movement in the Moray Firth, he was also making observations on Loch Ness in the company of his friend Simon Fraser of Foyers, Foyers being on the banks of the Loch. They were trying to discover the temperature of the water in the lower layers of Loch Ness, and lowered a half-gallon vessel to a depth of 120 fathoms (720 feet, or about 220 metres). How they constructed the vessel to take the water samples is not known. During the experiment they drifted about a mile up the Loch even though the little wind that was blowing should have driven them in the opposite direction. They put this down to a return current of water deep below the surface of the Loch.[17]

It is clear that Nimmo had an interest in surveying. A document which has turned up in the Highland Folk Museum collection includes a thumbnail sketch of Fort George [Figure 7.1].[18] A note on the reverse says "Drawn by Mr Nimmo – in May 180?". It unfortunately is not clear what the last number is – it is either a 5 or 6, and has been changed from one to the other. This is the first specific document that survives showing Nimmo's surveying interests.

In the summer of 1806, during the school holiday from 6th June to 1st August, Nimmo surveyed the boundaries of Inverness-shire, Ross, Cromarty, Sutherland and Caithness and these were incorporated in Aaron Arrowsmith's map of Scotland, first published in 1807 [Figure 7.2]. The Cromarty boundary was particularly difficult as that county, consisting of the lands of the Earl of Cromarty, was in many separate sections spread through Ross-shire. The Black Isle area also required great attention to detail, as at that time parts of four counties were included. Arrowsmith was born in Co. Durham, but moved to London in 1770, becoming a map publisher in 1790. He had been commissioned by the Government to produce a new map of Scotland. Nimmo's work was an extension of this commission to improve the accuracy of this map. His diary recording his work on the Highland county boundaries includes references to his journey, the people he interviewed, the meanings of place names, and two sketch-maps.[19]

Nimmo had been identified by Thomas Telford, the engineer, for this work, but how Telford came to know about Nimmo is not known. Telford had recently completed surveys in the Highlands on fisheries and on roads and bridges. The Report of the Commissioners for Highland Roads and Bridges records as follows:[20]

> The boundaries of the counties were not marked in the large survey, and are difficult to ascertain in the Highlands; but it being necessary that we should possess an accurate knowledge of them, we therefore requested the assistance of the proprietors of the adjacent lands, by letters addressed to the several county meetings, and appointed Mr. Nimmo, rector of the academy at Inverness, to

investigate and perambulate the boundary of the shires of Inverness, Ross, Sutherland, Caithness, and Cromarty; and he has performed the task with a zeal and intelligence surpassing our expectations; having not only marked the boundaries on the large map, but also transmitted to us an historical statement of the erection and boundaries of these Northern counties; which we have thought proper to insert in the Appendix, as likely to be useful towards ascertaining and explaining the state of these boundaries, the lands being much intermixed, and the boundaries themselves being different for different purposes.

For this work Nimmo received £150 from the Government, with a further £29 13s paid out for surveying equipment. The sum of £150 for seven weeks' work was greater than what he would have earned in the whole of the school year.[21] It also took Nimmo longer than he expected, and he was not back in Inverness for the start of the new session. In a letter to John Rickman, Secretary to the Commissioners for Roads and Bridges, Nimmo says that he had "exceeded the time allowed from my occupation here. I was given to understand that my return [to Inverness Academy] was much wished for...".[22]

A couple of summers later, in 1808 or 1809, Nimmo was again active in surveying when he surveyed the route of a road – never actually built – from Kylerhea (on the mainland and the traditional crossing point from Skye) to Killin in Perthshire, via Rannoch Moor. The report on this route was published in 1810, and so it is likely that the work was done in the summer of 1809, rather than 1808.[23]

Nimmo wrote various articles, both while in Inverness and after he left for Ireland, for *The Edinburgh Encyclopædia*, then being edited by David Brewster, Fellow of the Royal Society of Edinburgh. Brewster may well have been a classmate of Nimmo at Edinburgh University.

Nimmo's resignation
Joseph Mitchell, the civil engineer who learned his trade on the Caledonian Canal with Thomas Telford, and who later became Inspector of Highland Roads and Bridges, was living in Inverness just after Nimmo's time as Rector. Mitchell was a pupil at the Academy starting in about 1814, from age 11, for three and a half years, but no school record survives to confirm the details.

His *Reminiscences*,[24] however, do not seem to be completely accurate. After saying that Nimmo had established an admirable curriculum, Mitchell goes on to say:

> Students came from all parts of the surrounding country. About three hundred used to assemble in the Hall on Sundays to hear a prayer, and, headed by their masters in their gowns, they marched in procession to church. Nimmo, who was very social, used sometimes to neglect this duty on Sundays. The magistrates, austere men, particularly when their authority was questioned, censured him, and he resigned his appointment, to the great loss of the institution. He was immediately employed by Telford, and sent to Ireland as his assistant engineer.

The numbers claimed by Mitchell are rather high, the highest recorded gross number (derived from the numbers attending each class) being 268 in 1810,[25] and the actual numbers were probably below 250. Nimmo may well have failed in his duty to lead the Academy to church regularly on Sundays, but his resignation was much more to do with the fact that the Commissioners on the Bogs of Ireland had appointed him as an engineer from 5th January 1811 for a period of three years.[26] He was required to work for 720 days in that period, at 2 guineas per day of actual employment. This would earn him a much greater sum than he was receiving as Rector of the Academy, and the 720 days could easily have been worked with a starting date late in 1811. It is likely that he resigned to take up this much better-paid job.

For the next twenty years Nimmo worked mainly in Ireland, in the first instance on the reclamation of bogs, and then on harbours. The harbour work included the use of an early diving bell. From 1822 he was given charge of the 'Western District' of Ireland to provide work and create public amenities during and following the potato famines.[27] He had an office in Dublin built by his brother, George. Other work included a bridge and docks at Limerick, planning a railway from Dublin to Kingstown (now Dun Laoghaire), and also around Liverpool. When Liverpool Corporation prosecuted the Mersey and Irwell Navigation Company in 1827 over diverting some of the water into the navigation channel and thereby affecting river flow, Nimmo's evidence, which involved significant mathematical calculations, swung the case for the defendants.

Nimmo died in Dublin in January 1832, aged 49. *The Times* said that he had long suffered from rheumatic pains, with "a dropsy", a condition now called oedema, which usually follows rheumatic fever.[28] The legs and feet swell due to the retention of body fluids, frequently causing death. A marble bust of Nimmo, sculpted in 1845 by John Edwards Jones (1808-1862), stands in the premises of the Royal Dublin Society [Figure 7.3].[29] Jones had trained under Nimmo as an engineer, but gave up this occupation around the age of 40 to become a sculptor.

The appointment of Matthew Adam

In 1811 Matthew Adam applied for the post of Rector as a result of an advertisement in one of the Edinburgh newspapers, giving his address as "Mathematical Academy, 2 George Street, Glasgow", an address that was close to the buildings then used for the University of Glasgow.[30] Adam offered to provide certificates of character from various Glasgow professors, but also from Professor Playfair in Edinburgh, as Adam had corrected the proofs of an edition of Playfair's *Elements of Geometry*.[31] He claims to have edited the second edition (published in 1804), although at the time this editing would have been done, Adam was still studying in Glasgow. It is possible that it may have been the third edition of the book which Adam edited, as this came out in 1810, although his name is not mentioned in either edition.

Adam's background is known, thanks to a published *Roll of Graduates* and the other records of Glasgow University.[32] He was born on 20th February 1780 in Ayrshire, and whilst a lad worked as a blacksmith, selling nails made from cast-off horseshoes. The money he earned from this took him to Glasgow University, where he gained an M.A. in 1808, having studied Greek, logic, ethics and physics between 1800 and 1805. All students at that time also required a certificate in mathematics, even if they did not study it. Adam obtained a certificate from James Millar, the professor of mathematics in Glasgow from 1795 until 1831. Edinburgh University cannot trace any class of Playfair's which Adam might have attended, but, as there is no other information about the period from 1805 until his graduation in 1808, it is possible that he spent some of this time in Edinburgh under Playfair. From 1808 until 1811 Adam taught at his own school in Glasgow, presumably the "Mathematical Academy" named in his address.

Two other candidates applied for the Rectorship, but the Directors' Minutes do not record the names of the other applicants.[33] Adam was appointed unanimously "during the pleasure of the Directors" – key words around which so much of the future acrimony revolved. He arrived in Inverness near the end of August 1811, but within days was in dispute with the Directors over his potential salary:[34]

> ... Mr Adam the Rector, appointed at the last meeting having come to Inverness about eight days ago he entered upon the charge and there was produced a letter from him addressed to the Chairman expressing his disappointment in finding that the salary and emoluments of his office were not equal to his expectations and craving that the Directors would augment his salary, and also make an allowance for his expence in coming to Inverness and which being considered they decline making any allowance or addition of salary to Mr Adam reserving his claim for after consideration in case the salary and emoluments shall not amount to £230 Stg. in the year.

William Allerdyce, from Banff, appointed as English teacher soon after Adam's appointment, was also to complain within weeks of his arrival that his salary was inadequate.[35] The following June, Adam was given ten guineas (£10 10s) for travelling expenses, but no increase in his salary.[36] A later minute, though, suggests that this was not paid until late 1816.[37]

Disputes between Adam and Simon Fraser, teacher of writing and arithmetic, arose during 1812. Fraser refused to call the register before prayers, and disputed the amount of coal money collected by the janitor from his class. The Directors also received representations about the system of fining for misdemeanours that had recently been introduced, and this became optional. Fraser was later dismissed, but attended the examinations in June 1812. As a result, at their meeting on 3rd June 1812, the Directors banned him from attending the ball the following day as well as banning him from the building.

Adam taught both mathematics and geography, and in January 1812 he was given authority to spend money on new maps and atlases at a cost of £23 19 6d:[38]

- two general maps, one Mercator and one stereographic projection: £4 16s
- roller maps of Europe, Asia, Africa, North America and South America: £7 17 6d
- a frame to suspend them on: 16s
- a good modern atlas: £10 10 0d
- some canvas for mathematical figures, etc.

That summer some of the Directors became concerned about Adam's competency in mathematics, a topic on which two letters survive.[39] The first is from Provost James Grant, as Chairman of the Directors, to Professor John Leslie, professor of mathematics at Edinburgh University from 1805 (following Playfair's move to the natural philosophy chair). This letter is probably a draft, as it contains a number of changes and corrections. The second letter is a note from Wm. Fraser Tytler, another of the Directors and the Sheriff Depute, saying that he entirely approved of Grant's letter, other than to suggest that it should be made clear exactly which branches of mathematics were at issue, and that Leslie's reply should be in the form of a letter to the Directors, rather than as a certificate to Adam. Fraser Tytler obviously knew Leslie, as he too had an interest in science.

The key sentences from Grant's letter are:
> ... There has an unfortunate rumour prevailed that he is not competent in the teaching of Mathematics, which as it is equally injurious to his public character as to the Reputation of our seminary we are anxious to have removed & the fact ascertained – Informed of your distinguished character for Mathematical knowledge we naturally attach the highest importance to any thing connected with that Branch of Education to which your name could be procured. Mr Adam has very creditably to himself agreed, most readily to undergo an Examination by you of his Attainments in Mathematics and of course to submit to the Result. Indeed his success here seems entirely to depend on removing this predudice against him. ...

This enquiry does not merit a mention in the Directors' minutes, but Adam was paid 12 guineas (£12 12s) in November for his expenses in travelling south during the previous vacation. Any reply from Leslie has not survived, nor is it recorded in the minutes book.

By late October 1812, Adam was writing to William Fraser of Culbokie, another of the Directors, about his salary claim:[40]
> Had the Provost in his letter to me of 3rd July 1811 stated what the emoluments of my situation consist of, instead of stating their amount, my present claim might have been doubtful, or but ill founded. In that case however I would not have been a candidate without making further inquiry. If the Provost gave the information contained in his letter without authority from the Meeting of Directors, I have no doubt that he alone is liable to make it good.
>
> ... I am well informed that the Directors can neither dispense with my services, nor refuse the payment of my Salary, without being able to show a proper cause for such decision (as required in their Charter) i.e. to prove that, by misconduct on my part, I have forfeited my office, which, on trial, I am persuaded they will find

impossible. But on the supposition that I could not remain, & insist upon full payment of the Salary held out to me in the Provost's letter, I would in that case be undoubtedly entitled to such in name of damages, as would be sufficient both to compensate the loss I have already sustained, & that which I might be likely to sustain until I should obtain another situation equal in value to that which I left in Glasgow.

He claimed that he could prove that his earnings in Glasgow had been about £240 a year.

Adam's letters tend to be very long-winded, but he goes on to say that, like the Rectors of other "seminaries", he should be invited to attend Directors' meetings, so that he could be consulted where relevant. He then continues:

I beg leave however to state that if the Directors shall agree for the time that is past, to make the emoluments of my situation equal to £230 a year, (as stated in their own Minute respecting my letter of 31st August 1811) & thereafter to add £50 a year to my present salary until the improved state of the Funds shall enable them to increase my Income to the Amount mentioned in the Provost's letter to me above quoted, I shall be satisfied. If however the proposal be not accepted by the Directors at their first meeting, or within two weeks thereafter, I shall not consider myself bound thereby, but at full liberty to demand the whole, &, on refusal, to raise an action of damages before the Court of Session. (For I have been so advised.)

In a postscript to the letter he then avers that Nimmo was unable to live on his emoluments, receiving £50 a year from his father, and at the time of his departure to Ireland his brother (George) had paid off his debts of about £180. He also claims that Macgregor's debts were not paid off in full following his death. Adam also points out that he was not the highest paid member of the Academy staff. This would have been either the Latin and Greek, and/or the writing and arithmetic teacher as they taught large numbers of pupils.

Prior to the Directors' meeting on 11th November, Bailie John Mackenzie had worked out Nimmo's assumed emoluments,[41] which he assessed as worth on average £219 a year, well short of the £250 that Grant and Mackenzie had worked out Adam would get. Mackenzie accepted that the two of them had originally miscalculated the sum. He also comments that Adam had not filled in the "Record" – the register – as he said it was nearly finished, but had not bothered to ask for a new one, although he had been very keen to ask for repairs to his house. Mackenzie finished his note to Grant by asking that his letter about gowns be discussed first, before certain of the Directors "get into bad humour". It was agreed to purchase new gowns at 3 guineas (£3 3s) each in "tweeled stuff cloth". There is no mention of Adam's salary claim in the minute of this meeting, but it clearly was discussed, in the light of subsequent correspondence and minutes. A proposition was put to Adam which he requested time to consider. By the meeting on 30th December he had still not made his decision, but did reply with an agreement, for the meeting on 5th January 1813.[42]

The terms of the agreement were that Adam would accept the difference between Nimmo's assumed emoluments of £219 and the £230 which it had been agreed at the September 1811 meeting would be the sum that would trigger a review. If Adam agreed to this he would give up his claim to the sum of £250 which Provost Grant had suggested in his initial letter to Adam. Adam's letter says:

> Gentlemen,
>
> I have deliberately & repeatedly considered this proposition, & have at last resolved to accept of the terms offered, in regard that the present Funds of the Institution do not seem to admit of more being allowed, & that I am unwilling to subject individuals Directors, who have acted through mistake, but with good intention, in the expence of making good my claim. But I request that, in justice to the present & future Rectors of this Institution, copies may be entered upon your Minutes of the Documents upon which the present incumbent preferred his claim, & of the reasons for which he at last agreed to relinquish it, that these may have the due weight in the minds of the Directors, should any favourable change in the pecuniary circumstances of the Institution take place.

The minute contains Adam's agreement and signature:[43]

> And Mr Adam having been this day again called upon to the above effect he declared his acquiescence in the terms of the foregoing Minute and in testimony thereof he adhibits his superscription upon this and the two preceding pages.

The legal case in the Court of Session

The following year, 1813, the Directors were taken up with the "Inverness-icus" controversy (see Chapter 8), but at the beginning of the next year Adam was once again complaining. This complaint was about Dr. John Inglis Nicol, one of the Directors and a local surgeon, seeking permission for the second year in a row to use a classroom for chemistry lectures.[44] Adam had not got his facts right, and within four days had to withdraw his complaint. Things reached a head, though, when Adam complained about the absence of Alex. Campbell (Latin and Greek – having changed from English teaching in 1811) and William Allerdyce (English). Fraser Tytler, seconded by Mackintosh of Holm, moved that all three teachers should be dismissed at Christmas 1814, but Fraser of Farraline, seconded by Bailie Alexander Mackenzie, moved as an amendment that only Adam be dismissed. The amendment was carried "unanimously ... by a majority of votes".[45] Campbell and Allerdyce were to be censured for their conduct, and the Secretary was to inform Adam of his dismissal.

Over the summer Adam took legal advice in Edinburgh from George Cransto(w)n, and this advice is quoted as an annex to a letter to Gilzean as Chairman of the Directors. Cranstown, not surprisingly, was clearly of the opinion that the Directors had no right to dismiss Adam. The extract reads:

> 1st.: I am of the opinion that the Directors of the Inverness Academy are not entitled to dismiss the Rector of the Academy duly elected in terms of the Charter without a just cause.
>
> 2nd: In so far as I can judge from the facts stated in their Memorial and the letter and papers relative to the complaint against Messrs Campbell and Allerdyce I am of the opinion that the Directors of the Academy have dismissed Mr Adam without a just cause (signed) Geo. Cranstown

Adam declined to produce the full statement to the Directors,[46] and Col. Fraser of Culduthel moved that the whole matter be referred to Counsel for an opinion, and a sub-committee was set up to deal with the matter.

Adam went to the courts and initiated a Bill of Suspension and interdict. This move was considered by the Directors at their meeting on 23rd December 1814, and the decision was taken to oppose the Bill. Mackintosh of Raigmore and Mackintosh of Holm however disagreed with this course of action, and this had further implications when Adam later sued for damages. The court case proceeded through the spring of 1815, from which the main papers survive in the Court of Session records of the National Archives of Scotland.[47] From later information we learn that Adam spent 17 days in Edinburgh in the summer of 1814, and 42 days the following summer to pursue his case.[48] The details of the case are tedious, but the outcome was that the Bill of Suspension was passed in Adam's favour on 7th July 1815. In effect, Adam had secured life tenure for his job, and not just tenure during the pleasure of the Directors, and he could only be dismissed if a just cause could be shown.

At a meeting on the 18th July, the Directors decided not to go any further in the litigation. However, Adam had raised a summons for £1000 for damages, with the expenses of the action, against the Directors, either individually or collectively. Fraser Tytler moved that this should be resisted, and an agent employed to fight it. This was passed "unanimously", except that both Holm and Raigmore declined to vote on the grounds that they had signed a protest against the measure going to the Court of Session. These gentlemen only assented to the resolution in as far as it was necessary to protect the Academy, but claimed that the school was not liable anyway. The argument about damages went on from mid-1815 until September 1816, and was finally settled when a payment to Adam of £130 was agreed.[49] This dispute, which lasted for five years, was to affect relations between Adam and the Directors for the twenty-four more years that he was Rector, and certainly affected the Directors' actions through fear of further litigation.

Adam the scientist – the meteorological observations
Although Matthew Adam had been granted permission to purchase maps and an atlas in 1812 for his geography class, in 1817 he was refused (on the grounds of a shortage of money) up to 40 guineas (£42) for equipment for a series of lectures in natural philosophy and astronomy. In 1819 much of the existing equipment, most of which were the items that James Weir had originally bought in 1792, was in need of repair. The clear hostility between Gilzean (Chairman) and Adam shows in a circular letter addressed to all the Directors by Adam in which Adam says Gilzean had refused to call a meeting of the Directors before the summer to agree to the repairs.[50] This refusal was on the grounds that the matter was not sufficiently important. However Gilzean was forced into a meeting a fortnight later due to the death of James Wills, who at that stage, through illness, was only teaching book-keeping. It was then agreed to get estimates for the repair of some of the mathematical

instruments, and to purchase an artificial horizon, one of the instruments which Weir had been developing after he left the Academy for London. A year later the horizon had still not been purchased, and its purchase does not appear until the 1825 accounts, when payment was made to the estate of James Allan, the maker. Some repairs on the existing equipment were eventually carried out, such as on the school theodolite, repaired in 1822[51] and again in 1827.[52] Some of the repairs were funded by the Directors, but they refused to pay for some of the others.

There was also a dispute about the security of the Academy apparatus. In late 1821 Dr. Nicol had proposed that the apparatus should be under the control of a committee, and Adam (who was the only teacher likely to want this apparatus) would have to request what he needed on a regular basis.[53] Adam refused to comply with this directive, stating that in effect his contract of employment implied that he was responsible for the apparatus. The dispute carried on for many months through 1822, fuelled by animosity between Dr. Nicol and Adam.

It is not until almost the beginning of the 1820's that Adam's interest in practical science outside the classroom begins to show. Certainly by early January 1821 he had started taking weather readings at the request of the Royal Society of Edinburgh (RSE). At first these were just temperature and air pressure, with comments in his register on the wind and the general weather.[54] Adam did not have an anemometer (for wind speed), hygrometer (for humidity) or a "rain gage" [sic]. The Directors had turned down Adam's own requests for the additional instruments during 1821,[55] and only authorised the purchase of a thermometer at a cost of 7s 6d, on the grounds that the circular from the RSE had said that the other instruments were only desirable. The note inside the front cover of the register, presumably written just before it was sent off to the RSE in early 1822, states that Adam felt the Directors would respond positively to a direct request from the RSE to purchase additional instruments:[56]

> The prices stated in this estimate sent by Mr Adie [instrument maker in Edinburgh] varied considerably, particularly that of a barometer varied from 12 to 4 or 5 guineas. But in his letter to the Meeting of 1st May the Rector neither suggested any particular process, nor solicited from them any one of these instruments. It is therefore difficult to discover just grounds for the allegation either that these instruments were wanted by the Rector, or their prices amounted to £21.17.6. The terms & spirit of this minute dictated by the Chairman seem intended to represent the Rector as a troublesome person teasing the meeting for unnecessary & expensive instruments. Although the Rector's letter (of 13th Jan 1821) soliciting Sir G. Mackenzie to procure this estimate was written at the special desire of this chairman & read to & approved of him before it was forwarded.

Adam, according to notes in the 1821 records, used his own thermometer and barometer in the first instance [Figure 7.4]. With the 1822 report he also sent in a paper on what he claimed to be the physical cause of the reflection of light from the surface of bodies, whether polished or not, but this paper does not seem to have survived. He also records the fact that weather readings were being taken at the Caledonian Canal by an Andrew May. The 1823 weather records are interrupted twice in January. The first was when he was called to Edinburgh as a witness in a court case for defamation by Fraser Tytler, Sheriff Depute, against Mackintosh of Raigmore; the second time when he was aboard the *HMS Cherokee*, as part of some work in connection with the Board of Longitude (see below). Someone else must have been assisting him with the readings later in the year, as when he was again at sea the record is complete.

In early 1824, Dr. Brewster, Secretary of the RSE, who had previously had dealings with Nimmo, wrote to the school asking the Directors to support Adam in his work:[57]

> Mr Adam has transmitted to me two years of observations made with great judgement and accuracy, but as he has no other instruments than the thermometer, and I believe a common barometer, the observations are on that account defective. Mr Adam would require at least a good Barometer, a rain gauge and a self-registering thermometer which will not cost a large sum. The Marquis of Huntly was so good as to procure at my suggestion a complete set of meteorological instruments by which a most complete register has been kept at Huntly Lodge by Mr Murdoch. If such a register was kept at Inverness it would not only be of benefit to science but would attach a scientific character to the Academy which might promote its reputation and add to its number of pupils. I would not add what you must be well aware of that Mr Adam's talent, zeal and industry fit him in an eminent degree for carrying on a set of meteorological observations.

This time the meeting did agree to purchase the appropriate instruments up to a maximum sum of £16, although a thermometer and the rain gauge (or maybe a replacement gauge, as records for rainfall start on 4th February 1824) was purchased (or perhaps paid for) in 1827 at a cost of £5 6 6d.[58]

The surviving detailed records cover up to the end of 1824, but a summary exists for 1825, perhaps as a result of less information being requested from observers in and after that year. But the readings did not end at that point, as Adam's recordings were used by Sir Thomas Dick Lauder in his account of the Moray Floods of August 1829.[59] The other readings quoted in Lauder's book were taken of behalf of the Marquis of Huntly at Huntly Lodge.

Adam the scientist – the astronomical observations
In 1812 Adam had written to the *Inverness Journal* about observations of sun spots. These letters produced a response from a Simon Fraser, but only a couple of his early letters were published. Two originals survive, one of which is marked 'rejected' and the contents of this letter suggest that an earlier one had not been published either.[60] This Simon Fraser, who originally wrote under the pseudonym 'A Constant Reader', may have been the teacher of writing and arithmetic who had been dismissed in the summer of that year.

From the middle of 1822, Adam was in correspondence with, at first, the

Admiralty, and then the Board of Longitude, in London, over an improvement he claimed he had made in the method of taking the altitudes of heavenly bodies when the horizon is obscured either by fog or by land.[61] His development involved a modification to the eyepiece of the telescope used in quadrants, sextants and reflecting circles. Some, but not all, of the correspondence survives in the Board of Longitude papers.[62] At this time the Board was much less active than it had been in Weir's time, and in fact it ceased to operate about six years later.

By January 1823 the Admiralty had arranged for Adam to sail on *HMS Cherokee*, a brig of war, but this was delayed by the weather. During the delay he was summoned to Edinburgh to act as a witness in the trial of Tytler *v*. Mackintosh of Raigmore mentioned above. While he was in Edinburgh he ordered a new piece for his own sextant. From 22nd until 28th January he was sailing in the Cromarty Roads and off the Caithness coast. However he was severely affected by sea sickness in the open sea, and this restricted his observations.[63] The ship's captain, Captain Keats, was favourably impressed with the instrument, but his report, submitted to the Board of Longitude, has not survived. In addition Adam sent a letter to the Commander in Chief at Leith: it has not survived either, but the duplicate of this letter, sent to the Board of Longitude, has.[64] Following his return to Inverness, Adam experimented with a platform suspended on gimbals, to try to compensate for the movement of the ship.[65]

As he got no immediate reply from London to these reports, Adam sought help from the Duke of Gordon, who passed on his letter to the Admiralty, who in turn passed it to the Board of Longitude.[66] From this point some of the correspondence is clearly missing, but in the summer of 1823 Adam was in the English Channel on *HMS Seringapatam*, a frigate, and at the end of October his third period at sea was again off north-east Scotland on *HMS Clio*, a sloop of war.[67] During this period the school records indicate that there was no proper geography class. Captain Strangways *[sic]* of the *Clio* sent in his report in late November,[68] and various letters take the story on until a minute of the Board of Longitude confirms that what Adam had done was to incorporate some form of spirit level into a telescope.[69]

By April 1824 a copy instrument had been made, so that the Admiralty could carry out trials at sea, but Adam was not happy with the copy. There are further gaps in the correspondence, and the final surviving document is a letter from Adam enclosing a description of his "improved inverting telescope with Nautical eye tube".[70] His description has survived, though, and the details of the instrument, with drawings, are in an article in the *Edinburgh Journal of Science* in 1826.[71] Very soon after this, meetings of the Board of Longitude became very infrequent and ceased altogether in 1828, so what happened to Adam's invention is not known.[72]

Adam's time as Rector following the settlement of the Court Case

Following the final settlement of his Court of Session case in 1816, Adam was again active seeking the support of the Directors. There were frequent requests for repairs to his house, as it was smoky, damp and draughty. These repairs were generally refused, but it is clear that the house was in a very poor condition, and too big for his needs as he did not marry until 1826. A decision was even taken in December 1821 not to rebuild the house, but to keep it in a habitable state, although a committee report had suggested giving the Rector an allowance to rent a suitable house elsewhere.

At the annual meeting in May 1817, another "long letter", only summarised in the minutes, was laid before the meeting, requesting that:
- the cost of certain repairs to his house should be paid
- the Directors would pay a further £4 in costs for the court case
- they would allow him to use the grass of the Academy park for his own use (presumably to keep animals – he certainly kept pigs[73] and a horse)
- he should be given £42 for apparatus (as mentioned above)
- there should be some changes in the examination arrangements.

The first four were refused, and the points about the examination were referred to the next meeting when the examination arrangements would be made, although little specific is mentioned in the minute of that meeting. A further letter from Adam in December 1821 upset the Directors:[74]

> ... Upon hearing the letter read over the Meeting considered it to be couched in such disrespectful & insolent terms as not proper to be inserted in their minutes and was handed over to the Secretary.

As the letter has not been traced, we do not know what Adam was writing about on this occasion.

The year 1820 was taken up with the Glengarry dispute (see Chapter 8), and Adam also got embroiled in this, but his lack of drive on the matter suggests that he knew that his case was weak. In 1821, the Rev. J. Clark (writing and arithmetic teacher) was accused of charges of a serious nature which he partly admitted, *viz.* refusing to lead the prayers when it was his turn, and contempt for the Rector. In return he made charges against Adam.[75] This matter was remitted to a committee to examine.

In January 1822 the nature of the charges brought against Adam become apparent:
- the bell was not being rung ten minutes before assembling
- he was irregular in attending morning prayers, and others had to take prayers when he was late
- he was frequently absent from church on Sundays
- the janitor had been sent to his house on one occasion and found him still in bed
- the monthly examination of the classes was not being carried out
- he took no part in the religious instruction of the school, or enquired how others were doing it.

Adam was severely censured, perhaps the strongest thing that the Directors were prepared to do fearing the possibility of a further court case. He was to:

> ... understand distinctly that everything connected with the moral and religious instruction of the students in the Academy forms an important part of his, the Rector's, duty ...

A complaint about Adam's discipline was made in July 1822, although he was exonerated:[76]

> The Chairman produced a letter addressed to him by William Falconer, Esq., accompanying the report of the Committee upon the complaint of Mr James Mackintosh [of] Kinchyle and which report is of the following tenor:-
> In compliance with a reference made to us by the Directors of the Academy at the general meeting, respecting a complaint made by Mr James Mackintosh against the Rector for having struck his son with a ruler, we attended at the Academy and after hearing what the Rector had to say and having examined the boy, we found that he had been struck accidentally on the face by the taws, that there was little reason for complaint, had Mr Mackintosh enquired into the conduct of his son – and we presume that he must have misunderstood the information he got ...

The exam reports in December 1823 censured him for failing to attend the meeting about the dismissal of the janitor for misuse of the admission tickets (see Chapter 8).[77]

A strange incident took place one evening in October 1824 when some pupils entered the building during one of Adam's evening natural philosophy lectures, and stole the candlesticks, locked the hall door, melted the candlesticks down and threw some of the metal into his house, with an "insulting address" [possibly = shouted remark] and comment to his maidservant. Adam managed to identify the culprits and examined witnesses in front of Peter Scott, the recently-appointed classics teacher. A full report appears in the minutes book from which we learn the names of some of the pupils, and also some of Adam's nicknames, which were, presumably as he kept pigs, "Matthew Pig, Esq., alias singed face".[78] As the Directors seemed slow to act, and the Provost (Provost James Robertson), chief magistrate, said there were no funds to prosecute the offenders, the teachers put an advertisement in the local papers calling a meeting of the Directors.[79] Adam was again censured for this action.

Adam married in the summer of 1826,[80] but there is no mention of this in the minutes book or any other school record. The ceremony was held at Mount-pleasant in the parish of Dyke and Moy (just west of Forres in Morayshire). His wife, Ellen Moffat Atkinson, from St. Anne, Jamaica, aged about 23, provides another link with the British colonial expansion of the time. Adam was aged 46, so there was a significant difference in their ages. Over the next nine years he seems to have had five or six children, although two of the children appear to have been born within eight days of each other, and his first boy may have been stillborn, as a later boy, who died shortly before his seventh birthday, is referred to on the gravestone as his first son. Two girls also died very young, with his last one dying aged only 15 days in 1835, to be followed six days later by the death of her mother at the early age of 32. Soon thereafter Adam was to receive over £304 as compensation, following the abolition of slavery, for Jamaican slaves who had been owned by his wife.[81] She, and the three children who died in childhood, are all buried in the Chapel Yard in Inverness.

A surviving son, William, grew up to graduate from Glasgow University (as had his father), and become a teacher, and in turn his son also graduated from Glasgow University before becoming an engineer and electrician in Glasgow, and later London.[82]

No major issues seem to have brought Adam into conflict with the Directors in the second part of the 1820's and during the early part of the 1830's, although reports on the operation of the school were prepared by subcommittees (see Chapter 8) in 1828 and 1834, this later report leading to a new set of regulations being prepared. Adam was clearly unhappy about some aspects of these, especially a comment that the school was less efficient than it had been in the past. It is from his reply to the proposed regulations, linked with his annual report to the Directors in 1835, that the table of staffing and pupil numbers covering the period from 1804 to 1835 survives.[83] Only the first paragraph of the report itself was ordered to be entered into the minutes, and Adam presumably felt it necessary to have the rest printed to put over his point of view that the Academy was not in decline. Much of the document is a thinly-veiled personal attack on Dr. Nicol, who Adam did not get on with. Much of the rest criticises the Directors for repeatedly introducing new regulations, and about them allegedly making decisions on topics about which they were not, according to Adam, qualified to comment.

Adam's resignation

Like most matters involving Adam, the process which led to his resignation was a long drawn out affair. Much of it revolves around the issue of the state of his house. His wife had died in 1835, and in early 1836 Adam once again wrote to the Directors.[84] The Directors proposed that he should be given £25 to rent another house from Whitsun 1836, and Adam agreed to this but requested permission to reap the crop in the garden for that season (which certainly included fruit trees). Adam also suggested that if he was given a bonus of £15 he would stay in the house, and this lead some of the Directors to think that a new house was not necessary. He claimed that he wanted to live close to the school so that he could easily get books, etc., from his house. He claimed he had spent his own money on a new porch, painting and papering, and on gas fittings, at a total cost of at least £22, as well as developing the garden. For all of this he asked for compensation.

Although the minutes do not say so directly, it appears that Adam did move house at this point, as by the 1837 annual meeting consideration was being given to feuing the area of land on which the house and garden stood. This fell through and by December the house was actually let.

By March 1839 a matter, the substance of which is not stated, caused the Directors to declare that Adam's conduct involved a gross violation of duty.[85] They resolved that by the May meeting he was to:
- produce an accurate list of his classes with numbers and fees since 1826
- produce a return of the number of students in the Mackintosh of Farr fund (see Chapter 10) taught by him in the same years
- produce the record of weekly proceedings of the staff from May 1828 to May 1836 as required by an 1828 regulation
- provide anything else the committee required
- assemble all the apparatus so it could be compared with the inventory.

The Secretary was to give a copy of the resolution to Adam and get a receipt for it.

By the next meeting in mid-April some of these returns had been produced. Adam had also handed in a complaint, again not specified, against James Falconer, the writing, arithmetic and book-keeping teacher. The apparatus had still not been set out for checking and the Directors were "very much displeased" with the delay. They also wanted to know the rent which Adam was paying for the house he was staying in.

Adam, now aged 59, decided he had had enough and handed to one of the Directors a proposal to resign on a pension of £60 a year, in the form of an annuity. This was agreed to, but with the proviso that:

> ... their acceptance of Mr Adam's offer proceeded from considerations noways affecting their persuasion that they are legally entitled to dismiss him without any allowance whatever...

They may have felt that £60 a year was a small price to pay compared with the possible costs of further legal action by Adam against them if they tried once again to dismiss him. Adam however insisted on payment of the value of his current house rent and his usual salary, both up to Whitsun 1839. The Chairman (W. H. Colquhoun) accepted his resignation on behalf of the Directors.

The report in the *Inverness Courier* actually provides more information:[86]

> Mr [Robert] Smith, the secretary, then read a report from the Supervision Committee, containing a detailed account of alleged misconduct, carelessness, disobedience, &c. on the part of Mr Matthew Adam. One part of the report excited some amusement in the meeting. After describing various instances of neglect, respecting the classes, apparatus, &c., it then went on to relate a transaction between the directors and the Rector with regard to a dwelling house. The house belonging to the institution, inhabited by the Rector, was reported to be in ruinous state; and he importuned the directors to make an allowance by way of rent, so that he might inhabit a safe and suitable dwelling. The sum of £25 per annum was his lowest amount consistent with the dignity of his situation in the Academy. The sum of £25 was granted and the Rector immediately removed to a house of £16 rent, thus Jewing the directors out of £9 per annum, to support the dignity of his situation as Rector!

The motion respecting the Rector was unanimously adopted. It said: "That the meeting give to Mr Adam the sum of £60 per annum on the condition of his resigning his situation in the Academy.

The debate about the payment of his annuity went on for three years, not coming to a conclusion until the annual meeting in May 1842. At first the Directors wanted to secure the annuity on the Academy ground and buildings, but Adam either wanted £640 in cash in lieu of the annuity or heritable security on most of the value of lands at Fairfield, west of the River Ness. Later, various insurance offices were approached for terms, but the annuity was finally purchased in early 1842 from the National Debt Office. This involved the sale of Government Stock held by the Directors, and a small sum from their cash reserves to cover the expenses of the discharge.

At last Adam was off the Directors' hands. Although Adam was someone who made enemies very easily, and was not much liked, either by pupils or adults, it is clear to the modern researcher that there were serious faults in the way the Directors managed the Academy. Lord Henry Cockburn's comments about the Directors (Chapter 10) over the appointment of Adam's successor show that the problem was not one-sided. Directors' self-interest was a key factor in many of the decisions. Adam returned to Glasgow, where he taught in his own house for ten years, before moving to Ayr, and he died there on 10th December 1853, aged 73.[87]

So ends the period of tenure of two of the more significant early Rectors of the Royal Academy. The school was to change somewhat, and to settle down, over the coming years, but before considering these changes, mention is needed of other issues from Nimmo and Adam's times in post. At least one of these issues can now be seen to be farcical.

Chapter 8
More Controversy and Argument

The period from 1809 until 1820 saw three major disputes affect the Academy Directors, and these shook them, although briefly, out of their complacency. The early 1830's brought a fourth problem. Two of the disputes, one already considered, involved Matthew Adam; in the other two he became involved on the sidelines. Towards the end of 1808 Lachlan Mackintosh of Raigmore returned to Inverness a wealthy man and tried to take a leading place in local affairs. In 1814 and 1815 Adam took the Directors to court to secure life tenure in his job (see Chapter 7). In 1820 Glengarry tried to force his own candidate into the vacant position of classics teacher, and in the early 1830's a major report, compiled by the Directors, accepted that some of their actions were ill-judged.

The return to Inverness of Lachlan Mackintosh of Raigmore
In the autumn of 1808, Lachlan Mackintosh of Raigmore returned from Calcutta, to take his place as a Director. He was to be both a strength and a major thorn in the flesh of not just the Academy, but many aspects of Inverness life. The first Directors' Meeting which he attended was that on 12th November 1808, at a time when Nimmo was still the Rector.

He brought with him from Bengal, India, promises of subscriptions of £2605 5s towards the Academy and the Northern Infirmary (which was also being promoted at this time), with an actual draft for £2300 of this money.[1] He said that most of the money was for the Academy, so it was agreed that £2000 would go the Academy, and the balance of £300 to go towards the Infirmary. £205 2s came from Prince of Wales Island, a name then used for the island known as Penang in the Malay peninsula. It had been renamed in 1805 when it became the fourth Presidency of the East India Company. The project did not thrive and the East India Company abandoned the island, so the name reverted to Penang. Raigmore's money was a lifeline to the Academy as subscriptions from other sources had largely dried up, although the figures given in the Minutes do not quite add up correctly.

A summary of these subscriptions appeared in the *Edinburgh Evening Courant*, the following month.[2] Apart from Mackintosh's own contribution of £150, the largest subscription from Bengal was from a General McDonald (£125), with several subscriptions of £60 10s, including one from the Military Paymaster-General in Bengal. The only major subscription from Prince of Wales Island was one for £105 from Col. McAlister, the Governor. The minute, reproduced in the newspaper, continues:

> Deeply impressed with due sense of the zealous and patriotic exertions of Mr M'Intosh, in thus promoting the advancement of establishments so intimately connected with the welfare of his native country, the Meeting anxiously embrace this opportunity of expressing in their own name, and in that of the public at large, the very great obligation they lie under to him, and to the above respectable

Subscribers, who have contributed so liberally towards the support of the institutions under their management. ...
The signature to the advertisement was that of Thomas Gilzean, as Chairman of the meeting.

Only a few other donations were received in this period. In the following year (1809) a John Smith (son of Donald Smith, merchant in Inverness) sent £75 for the Academy and a similar sum for the Infirmary from Seringapatam in south India.[3] This was the site of a victory by East India Company Troops in 1799 when the local sultan was killed. In early 1811 a William Grant of Green Island, Jamaica (who had been educated in Fort Augustus), sent a bill [= draft] for £50 as the subscriptions for himself and his brother.[4]

About this time an unsigned document can probably be attributed to Mackintosh of Raigmore, in view of the various issues that are raised:[5]

Proposed

That the ground belonging to the Academy, originally provided for the exercise of the Students, be reassumed.

That in order to render it fitter for its purposes in wet weather as well as in dry, leave be given to all persons so disposed to take away as much of the earth on the surface to a depth of 2 feet as they may think proper, replacing it with an equal quantity, or with as much more as may be considered of equal value to the earth removed (for the higher the ground the more appropriate for its object) of small clean gravel – the work to be carried on subject to the approval and under the superintendance of such person as the Provost shall be pleased to appoint.

That Mr Normanville (or such other person, native or foreigner, as may be found qualified from character and capability to fill the situation) be appointed to teach the French language under Mr Tulloch, and that the Provost be requested to adjust the Terms.

That all meetings of the Managers of the Academy and Infirmary be previously advertised in the Inverness Journal.

The reference to Mr Normanville dates this document to a few days before a Directors' meeting early in 1809 following a recommendation by the Bishop of Rodez that Normanville be appointed as the French teacher.[6] All the matters mentioned were discussed at that meeting, with one decision being that the grounds were to be turned into a playground and the farming tenant was to be asked not to put down a crop that year. Normanville, who had taught privately in Inverness since August 1808 as "M. de Normanville", was duly appointed with a salary of £20 together with the class fees, and Tulloch was given £5 for supervising his work. Normanville took an army commission in Dillon's Regiment in spring 1810, and was replaced by Pierre Villemer (also recommended by the Bishop of Rodez) (see Chapter 9).

In 1810 Mackintosh established what is now known as the Raigmore Medal:[7]

The said Lachlan Mackintosh Esq. of Raigmore signified in course of his correspondence respecting the subscriptions procured by him in India for the Academy and remitting the same herewith, that a sum equal to his own personal subscription be set apart as a capital the interest to be applied half-yearly in giving a medal bearing an appropriate inscription at each (half-yearly) examination alternately to the best proficient in the classics and in the mathematical class, the medal deliverable at the summer vacation to be gold and at the winter vacation silver, the gold medal to be alternatively given to each class, the Directors and visitors attending to be the judges of the comparative excellence of the candidates. The inscription to be "Adjudged by the Directors and Visitors attending to --------- for proficiency in ---------" the year to be below and the whole to be surrounded by a snake the emblem of eternity on the scales of which will be inscribed "To the most deserving" on the reverse of the medal will be inscribed "To the Royal Academy of Inverness from Lachlan Mackintosh Esq. of Raigmore in testimony of his zealous wish for its prosperity".

During 1811 some of Mackintosh's proposals were put into effect. A handball wall was built (shown on John Wood's 1821 map of Inverness [Figure 8.1]), but he opposed a plan to build a wall across the back of the Academy which would cut off two-thirds of the grounds. He entered his dissent in the Minutes Book in his own handwriting, and claimed that, if this wall was built, students would resort to the streets, and:[8]

associate with the boys of the lower order begetting (as they must from such companions) ideas and manners that must sap the principles and proper pride which it is the object of the Directors and should be the duty of the Masters of the Academy to instill into them, but which the foresaid example must weaken and in a good measure destroy ...

Although the wall had been built, a special meeting of the Directors in September agreed by a majority to pull the wall down and rebuild it at the east end of the Academy property.[9] The same meeting also established new regulations for the conduct of the Directors, which included a requirement for quarterly meetings, and an advertisement in the *Inverness Journal* in advance of meetings. The annual meeting on 1st May (required by the Charter) was to inspect the accounts, and matters were tightened up on how money on repairs and expenses was to be spent. It is clear that the operation of the Directors had become very lax, and Mackintosh was probably quite right to take the line he did on these matters, even though it upset some of the more conservative members of the committee.

A meeting in early 1812 went even further and drew up a list of regulations for the conduct of staff and students.[10] Two of these might raise a few eyebrows today:

10. That no student for any offence whatsoever, be beaten or struck with a ruler or other improper instrument. He shall not be sent to the Academy prison without the order of the Rector nor shall he be expelled from the classes in the Academy without the sanction of Directors
11. That no student shall bring within the walls of the Academy or playground, any sword, gun, pistol, or other offensive weapon. That for every such offence the student shall forfeit such weapon, besides being fined at the discretion of the Rector.

Just what was meant by the Academy prison is a matter of conjecture, as this is the only mention of such a place.

"Invernessicus" and the *Inverness Journal*

However Raigmore's actions between 1813 and 1817 are the ones which are of most interest today. In early 1813, an attack on the Academy and its Directors appeared in the columns of the *Inverness Journal*, signed by "Invernessicus" (at that time many writers of letters in the newspapers used pseudonyms). Hon. Col. Fraser of Lovat requested a special meeting of the Directors,[11] and this was called for 13th April 1813. Fourteen Directors attended, but Raigmore said that he could not attend, as he was allegedly busy supervising workmen planting a boundary hedge, and hinted at his support for the letter-writer (which was not surprising since it turned out later that he was in fact "Invernessicus"). Four issues were raised:

- John Clark, assisting with the Latin class, was in Aberdeen pursuing his studies (according to the minutes – but, according to "Invernessicus", as a travelling tutor to Provost Gilzean's son), even though he had been told to return to his job in Inverness
- Adam was seeking a higher salary
- decisions were being taken behind closed doors
- the Academy was in a declining state

After a failed attempt to adjourn the meeting, the charges were declared to be groundless by nine votes to none against.

At the annual meeting on 1st May Raigmore was present and launched an attack. He tried to get the vote of censure on Campbell rescinded (see Chapter 7), but failed. He enquired about Fraser of Lovat's subscription, the interest due on which had not been paid. The Directors, probably from fear of alienating one who was so prominent in the County, agreed not to demand payment of this interest. Fortunately Lovat himself was not present at this meeting. At this point Raigmore admitted that he was "Invernessicus", and the meeting was adjourned for two days (this meeting was on a Saturday), when the charges would be discussed in full.

On the Monday, Raigmore expanded on his letter, but the details of his arguments are long and involved, and the argument about Adam seeking life tenure in his job has been discussed in Chapter 7. All the charges were dismissed (although Raigmore declined to vote) and a letter was to be sent to Mr Young, the editor of the *Inverness Journal*, setting out the minutes of the meeting. In December of that year (1813), John Clark was given a proper salary for his job as assistant in the Latin class, at the rate of £30 per annum, backdated.[12] Clark had been a pupil in the Academy, and by teaching at a salary of £10 a year he had forfeited a bursary of £6 a half-year University session. He had supported himself mainly by private teaching. His letter of thanks to the Directors, survives.[13]

Raigmore did not let matters rest, however, and all the correspondence and arguments were published as a book,[14] dealing not just with the Academy but with issues such as the Northern Infirmary and the Inverness Banking Company. By modern standards it is very difficult to read, but reflects the type of argument so common in the first quarter of the nineteenth century. He concludes the book with his explanation of what he sought to achieve:

> Invernessicus had no personal object to gain; he farms a part of his own property, and his ambition is bounded by his farm; neither the town nor the county have any thing to give which he wants, except their justice; in the measures he has pursued, he had no friend to serve, no enemy to vanquish, for he had no difference with any one of the parties, except such as arose out of these discussions; no motive therefore but in the expected consequences of the painful task he undertook; none but in the anxious desire to liberate his country from trammels which have weighed its energies to the dust; which, for the advantage of a few, a *very* few (insensible themselves of the extent of the evils they inflict), destroy not less the prosperity of the present, than the prospect of the future.

In early 1814 he also tried to borrow the Directors' minutes book, but a note written on his letter says this would only be possible with the permission of the Directors.[15]

Despite what he stated in the quotation above, in 1815, following the death of the original proprietor of the newspaper, Raigmore purchased the copyright and plant of the *Inverness Journal* for the sum of £7000, and soon thereafter had to pay another £1000 to stop the disposers of the rights starting up another newspaper in competition with the *Journal*.[16] By the standards of the time this was an enormous sum to pay for a business in Inverness. Raigmore, although he did not publicly admit that he was the owner, immediately started to attack, through the pages of the *Journal*, all and sundry who held any position of authority in the Burgh and the County. It was this stance by Raigmore which led to the establishment of a competitor, the *Inverness Courier*, in December 1817, so that the balance could be redressed a little.

The first major attack on the Academy in the *Journal* followed the award of the prizes at the end of the session in December 1816. Remarks had appeared about partiality in awarding them in the issues dated 27th December 1816 and 3rd January 1817. Matthew Adam and most of the rest of the staff tried to reply on 20th January, but the *Journal* refused to print the letter, and made further comments on 7th February, which included garbled extracts of the staff letter. The staff were forced to produce their own booklet to get their point of view over to the public.[17] Raigmore (who is only alluded to, as was the custom in letter-writing at that time) had not even attended the examination, nor had many of the rest of the Directors and clergy. Adam and the other staff said Raigmore should attend the next examination, so that he could see that the system of allocation of prizes was fair.

Raigmore dissented from the reappointment of Gilzean as Chairman at the annual meeting on 1st May 1817. In his book he had attacked the fact that the Town Council was very largely self-appointed, and worked for their own

111

advancement and that of their immediate friends. This dissent was obviously part of the same campaign. The following year the Town was actually disenfranchised by the Court of Session over this issue (see below).

In the early part of 1817 the janitor, John Paterson, died. Paterson had been in post since 1811, when his predecessor, Alex. MacBean, then aged about 80, was allowed to retire on a pension, which he enjoyed until his death at the end of June 1818.[18] The Directors allowed Paterson's widow and step-son Daniel, aged 11, to take over the job originally for two sessions (one year).[19] This arrangement lasted for several years, but at the annual meeting in May 1822 it was agreed to advertise the post. There were nine applicants, including Daniel Paterson, the step-son. There was also a petition signed by 120 pupils for him to be retained. The Directors agreed with the petitioners by 22 votes to 4, with three abstentions, on the strict conditions that he kept to his duties, and did not keep animals in the Academy park [= grounds]. His salary was to remain at £6 per annum, plus the fees of 1s per session from the pupils (which generally brought his emoluments up to about £26 a year), together with a rent-free house (built in 1811), free coals, a garden, the grass of the park and dung.

In August 1822, "a Director of the Academy", almost certainly Raigmore himself, wrote to the *Inverness Journal* about the situation. It was a further attack on the hierarchy in power in the Town:[20]

> It will be recollected, that Provost Robertson's quondam [= former] *Chambermaid* – a young and very good-looking woman – was appointed to a situation, such as certainly neither Housemaid nor Chambermaid ever filled before, viz Janitrix to the Inverness Academy – superintendent of the exercises of 300 boys, (some of them stout fellows from 16 to 20, whom it was her duty to horse [= punish] for flagellation when necessary), &c. &c. – because that appointment is worth between £40 and £50 per ann. The Provost's gardener had previously held it; she was married to him a year when he died, and the thing being too good to be let out of the family, was transferred to her, and a son of the gardener, a boy of *eleven years* old, appointed to assist her.

The writer of the letter then went on to say that a committee, enquiring into school discipline and which had reported the previous year, was almost entirely made up of Provost Robertson's friends. It had reported that all the teachers were against Mrs Paterson and the son filling the post of Janitor. On the other hand the petition from the boys had been accepted by the Directors even though, according to Raigmore:

> ... those very boys who, from her inefficiency, had indulged themselves, to the bodily danger, and mental depravity, of their companions, by introducing gunpowder, and dangerous implements, horses, blackguard companions, &c. into the play-ground, as reported to the Committee.

The letter runs to perhaps fifteen hundred words, and goes on to allege that Adam had told him that the son had been employed as a clerk in the Provost's wine shop, when he should have been working for the Academy. Adam complained about this comment at the meeting on 6th August, and this lead to an enquiry, for which the report runs to five pages – his offhand remark had become a "fact" – Paterson had been writing up his own books to show to the shop owner. Adam was ordered to be more careful in his comments in the future.

The final part of the story regarding the janitor, although it does not specifically involve Raigmore, occurred in December 1823, when Adam complained about the misuse of the class admission tickets and the breaking open of his desk where the tickets were kept. Some Latin books were found in Paterson's house and it was alleged that he was trying to get a loan of money. He admitted his guilt and plead to be forgiven,[21] although the letter is signed in a formal way as 'Donald Paterson', rather than as 'Daniel', the name which had been used previously in the minutes book. However, he was dismissed[22] and a new janitor was appointed early in 1824.

The Glengarry controversy – the background
As Matthew Adam's legal dispute over length of tenure of appointments has been discussed in Chapter 7, the next, and completely farcical, dispute was over the appointment of a new classics teacher in 1820. Alex. Campbell, the previous teacher, resigned in December 1819 to take up an appointment as the Minister at Dores (at the north end of Loch Ness). He had been teaching classics since 1811, following the departure of John Tulloch. Prior to 1811 he had taught English for seven years in the Academy. He recommended John Clark, his assistant, as his replacement, who he described in these words:[23]

> ... none could show more zeal, more temper, or more regularity. In fact he uniformly acted as if the whole responsibility rested upon himself, and I cannot better discharge my graceful [sic – could be misprint for 'grateful'] sense of his able assistance, or leave a more valuable legacy to my beloved pupils, whom I must now leave with affectionate regret, than by recommending Mr Clark as my successor, who I know will be found in no ordinary way to combine the rare faculty of tempering firmness with familiarity, and modesty with a thorough knowledge of his duty.

The class size had reached 125, twice what it had been when Campbell came to the Academy in 1804. Some press commentators later claimed that this was the largest classics class in any school north of Aberdeen.

The controversy over Campbell's replacement was first chronicled by Evan Barron in 1909 for the Inverness Field Club,[24] although a few of the references he used have not been traced. Some additional material has come to light during research for this book.

Colonel Alexander Macdonell of Glengarry was first appointed as one of the Directors nominated by the Commissioners of Supply, but at his first meeting in 1813 paid his £50 to become a Director in his own right. Immediately Campbell's resignation was announced in 1819, Glengarry put forward the name of Ewen Maclachlan, the Librarian of King's College, Aberdeen, to fill the post. The Directors however decided to advertise the job, and Glengarry was told to bring up his nomination at the appropriate meeting. He, like Raigmore, had an impulsive nature, and was not, according to Barron, very popular. He did not like opposition, and was not an easy person to get on with. As a Highland chief, his dress was flamboyant, in public wearing full Highland dress in the way he thought it had been worn in the past.

Glengarry had supported Ewen Maclachlan during his studies at King's College, Aberdeen, where he had taken first place in the bursary competition. Maclachlan soon became assistant librarian in the College and assistant teacher in the Grammar School in Aberdeen, rising to headmaster of that school in 1818. He also translated the *Iliad* into Gaelic, and became the leading Celtic scholar of his day. Glengarry produced a letter from Dr. Skene Ogilvie, Parish Minister in Old Aberdeen, to Maclachlan expressing a high opinion of him. However, the letter was dated the 30th September 1819, some nine weeks before Campbell's resignation was announced, although he had been presented to the parish in August, and the resignation was therefore expected. There had been an enclosure in Skene Ogilvie's letter, the contents of which were not disclosed, but Barron is certain that it was a letter from Glengarry to Maclachlan advising him to apply. Had Glengarry not interfered, John Clark would probably have been given the job, without it being advertised. Glengarry's determination that his candidate be appointed led to a strong feeling against Maclachlan.

At the Directors' Meeting on 9th February 1820 the method of selection was considered, and it was agreed that the appointment would be made on 1st April. According to Glengarry, in a letter to the Chairman dated 14th February,[25] it was decided that the vacancy would be filled by a trial of comparative merit before competent judges. Glengarry claims that the newspaper advertisement in the *Inverness Journal* said that the vacancy would be filled by comparison of the respective candidates' certificates. He goes on to hope that this mistake was an unintentional blunder on the part of the Chairman (Provost Gilzean), and that an amended advertisement would be published, requiring candidates to appear personally. The letter up to this point, although written in the flowery language of the time, is quite civil, but the "N.B." after his signature has a sting in the tail *(underlinings in original)*:

> Considering the advertisement in last Journal to have done more harm than good; I beg leave to mention, lest (in case) *[inserted later above the line]* you should fail to insert a fresh one in the first Journal, that I transmit, by the same post, a copy of this letter to the Editor of that Paper; as my protest against such proceedings.

It should be remembered that the *Inverness Journal* was by this time under the control of Mackintosh of Raigmore, who was a friend of Glengarry. In the coming months a very lively correspondence took place in both the columns of the *Journal* and of its rival, the *Inverness Courier*, over the tactics used to select the candidate.

Barron transcribes some letters which appeared in the *Inverness Journal* of 3rd March[26] following a letter from Glengarry. One of these, dated 4th February, is from John Clark to Glengarry, seeking his support, on the grounds that he had served the school faithfully for ten years on a low salary.

However Glengarry would not accept this:

> I confess [your letter] surprised me, not as coming from a person unknown to me even by sight, but from the nature of your pretensions, founded so gravely upon false data. You allege to me "private friendship" as the groundwork to which Mr Maclachlan founded his claim to my support. But in that you are perfectly mistaken, and no less so in your idea that I would support any man but the best qualified ... and if ... you or any other, can outstrip Maclachlan, you may rest assured whoever does so shall have my vote, and the support of every independent Director who enters into the real interest of the Academy and of the public.

Glengarry obviously did not know the staff in the school for which he was a Director. Soon after this Clark withdrew as a candidate. With regards to scholarship he would have had no chance against people like Maclachlan, and Archibald Carmichael, schoolmaster at Crieff, the eventual successful candidate.

At the Directors' Meeting on 23rd February, Glengarry appeared with three of his supporters, including his factor and a member of his clan, all of whom promptly paid the £50 which entitled them to become Directors. It is almost certain that these three people were given the money by Glengarry to enable them to become Directors, with a view to swinging the vote in Maclachlan's favour. William Falconer of Lentran, who had children at the Academy, and was opposed to Glengarry, added enough to his previous contribution for him also to become a Director. Glengarry also entered a protest against John Simpson, interim Dean of Guild, acting as a Director.[27] This was part of a separate dispute outside the Academy, with the matter still under determination by the Court of Session, following on from the disenfranchisement of the Burgh of Inverness, after claims that the elected councillors were illegally appointed some years earlier.[28]

After a vote, Simpson was declared eligible by seven votes to six to act as a Director, with one abstention and Simpson himself declining to vote.[29] The vote set some of the Town Directors against a group of mainly County Directors, when Mackintosh of Raigmore, Grant of Corriemonie, and Macdonald of Barrisdale (a member of the Macdonell clan) sided with Glengarry. An amendment was made to the advertisement, to indicate that the candidates would be required to attend on 1st April, but an amendment proposed by Corriemonie, to state that "a comparative trial may be required", was defeated.

As Carmichael was unknown in Inverness, whereas Maclachlan was perhaps one of the best known Highlanders of his time, Carmichael resorted to petitioning some of the Directors, and also appealing in a sort of election address through an advertisement in both Inverness newspapers.[30] Its appearance in the *Inverness Journal* was the only significant statement in his support in that paper, as Raigmore, the paper's owner, openly supported Maclachlan.

At the meeting on 1st April thirty-nine Directors were present, the largest number to have attended a meeting up to that point, and of these, sixteen were new Directors, having just paid the £50 necessary to secure the right to vote. Of these sixteen, thirteen lived in or near Inverness, and three came from Glengarry country. Some of the new Inverness-based Directors were people who had professional dealings with either Glengarry or Raigmore, and so could be relied on to support them, or risk losing their business. Five of the new Directors were solicitors, several were merchants and tradesmen, and one was the Bank of Scotland agent in Inverness. From the six applicants for the teaching vacancy, only Carmichael and Maclachlan appeared as required. The letter of withdrawal by John Clark was also tabled. John Simpson, interim Dean of Guild, was, by a majority, not permitted to vote. Sixteen documents were then produced in favour of Carmichael and twelve in favour of Maclachlan.

Glengarry's side moved that the meeting send the two candidates to the Professors of Latin and Greek at Glasgow University, whereas the Inverness contingent moved a motion to appoint immediately. The first motion was passed by twenty votes to nineteen, of which one of those against was presumably Simpson, given after protests in view of the decision earlier that he be debarred from voting. In a further vote of twenty to seventeen against, it was agreed that the professors' decision would be final. The report would be presented to the annual meeting on 1st May, and advertisements were to appear in both local papers as to these decisions. The unsuccessful candidate was to be paid his expenses for going to Glasgow.

However, this tactic misfired on Glengarry when Professors Young and Walker in Glasgow declined to act, perhaps fearing the consequences from whichever side lost. A tactful letter, dated 9th April, was sent back to Gilzean[31] but the postscript to this letter suggests that Gilzean in his letter had not indicated the closeness of the vote to remit the matter to the professors, and they received this information from another source, perhaps Professor Cooper, also in Glasgow. Barron's article then explains what had been going on:[32]

> It subsequently transpired that Glengarry had himself written to the Glasgow Professors immediately the reference to them had been determined upon, and that Mr Peter Anderson, solicitor, Inverness, had written to his brother-in-law, Professor Cooper of Glasgow, on Carmichael's behalf. Glengarry alleged that Professor Cooper in Carmichael's interest had persuaded the two Professors to refuse to undertake the task, a charge which a letter addressed by Professor Cooper to Carmichael does something to justify, but looking to all the facts in the case, and especially to Glengarry's own interference with the Professors, it is probably safe to say that these gentlemen saw they had been invited to mix themselves up in a squabble which they were better out of.

The letter from the professors declining to act leaked out long before the scheduled meeting on 1st May and the controversy was renewed in the columns of the Inverness newspapers with an increased intensity right up to the day of the meeting. Many of these letters were written under noms-de-plume, some certainly by either or both of Glengarry and Raigmore. It is not possible to determine which were written by Raigmore and which by Glengarry, in support of Maclachlan, although the violent tone of the letters would have done little to support their candidate in the minds of many readers. One of the writers accused the agent of the Bank of Scotland, a person of great power in the Town at that time, of using his power and knowledge of the financial position of some of the Directors to threaten them with financial penalties if they supported Glengarry. Glengarry also got his factor to instruct both candidates to report to the professors of St. Andrews University to get an opinion on their respective merits. Maclachlan did so, but Carmichael refused to carry out this instruction. Maclachlan also wrote from Glengarry House to the Duke of Gordon,[33] requesting the Duke to produce a letter of support by writing to Col. Gordon of Invertromie and any of his friends who might influence the vote.

The Glengarry controversy – the final vote
It was clear that the result would now be determined by whichever side could produce the largest number of supporters on the day. However, the meeting had to be postponed until the 2nd May due to the Commissioners of Supply meeting which took place on the 1st. The Directors' meeting was held in the Court House, a squalid place, then adjacent to the Steeple on the corner of Church Street and Bank Street. Large numbers of the public appeared and the room was so packed that it had to be partly cleared before the Directors could get in. Ten more people had qualified themselves as Directors before the start of the meeting, and another twelve paid up at that point, bringing in to the Academy funds a further £1100. How many of these sums of £50 were paid by Glengarry personally may never be known.

When order was established, it was found that there were sixty-three Directors present. As this was the annual meeting, the first business was the election of the Chairman for the forthcoming year. Even this produced controversy, but in the end Provost Gilzean beat Raigmore by thirty-five votes to twenty-five, largely on the basis of Town against County. This vote was not without dispute as the right to vote by three Directors was questioned. In addition Matthew Adam protested that his vote was not accepted. He claimed that, by his concession of not claiming the £60 for personal expenses in 1816, incurred during the legal dispute about his security of tenure, he had in fact donated to the Academy a sufficient sum to register him as a Director. As usual for Adam his claim is in the form of a long-winded letter, but the minute records nothing about discussion with regard to his claim.

The letter from the Glasgow professors was then read, and Gilzean as Chairman, indicated that the Directors were back to the same situation as they were at the start of the meeting on 1st April. Glengarry's dealings behind the scenes, as outlined above, then became apparent. Considerable discussion took place and Fraser of Reelig, seconded by Fraser Tytler

117

(Sheriff Depute), proposed a vote of censure on Glengarry for his conduct. The minute of the meeting records Glengarry's response:

> Glengarry stated that it might have been irregular for that he was no regularly bred man of business or lawyer but he had acted (as he conceived every independent Director had a right to do) on the resolution of a majority of the Directors with the knowledge that there was no time to summon a second meeting and that he had no intention of giving offence or offering disrespect to the Directors. With this explanation the Directors were satisfied and the motion was withdrawn.

The two candidates were then proposed by their respective supporters, and the Rev. Donald Fraser of Kirkhill suggested that the meeting be cleared of "strangers", but after a long discussion, this motion was withdrawn. Dr. John Inglis Nicol, the Inverness surgeon previously mentioned in Chapter 7, tried to get other professors to examine the two candidates, but the counter-motion won by thirty-six votes to twenty-six. As a result, the business of the meeting moved to the final vote as to who would be appointed. The whole meeting is recorded in the pages of the *Inverness Courier*, and this notes that several of the Directors prefaced their votes (probably taken by roll call) with speeches explaining the grounds on which they were voting.[34] Carmichael won the day, again by thirty-six votes to twenty-six. Glengarry and his supporters (including Dr. Nicol) stated that they had voted for Maclachlan under the express reservation that it should be competent for them to take any legal action they wanted to, to set aside the decision that a comparative trial was not required. However, in the end they did not pursue this line.

Provost Robertson moved that Maclachlan be paid £100 out of Academy funds to cover his travelling costs during the contest. Fraser Tytler moved a resolution that it was highly creditable to the Academy that two gentlemen of such calibre should present themselves for the vacant post, and this was adopted as reflecting the view of the meeting. One of Maclachlan's supporters, James Lyon, an Inverness ironmonger and a leading figure in the move to disestablish the Burgh, moved that Clark should receive an additional £10 on his salary for the Latin class, and £10 for the drawing class. This motion was actually seconded by Macdonell of Glengarry, a somewhat different response to the snub he had given Clark in his letter of 19th February. These were the only votes of the day that were passed unanimously, but the grants could be easily afforded as the contest had raised £2090 for the funds, a sum which could never have been expected six months earlier.

By this point it was eight o'clock in the evening, and the meeting was adjourned until noon the following day when the meeting would be reconvened in the more spacious Town Hall. At this second part of the meeting Glengarry moved a motion that all the testimonials be entered into the Minutes Book, together with the letter from the St. Andrews University professors on Maclachlan's qualifications. This was done along with this statement: "with the explanation, that no reference was made to the Professors of St. Andrews by the Directors of Inverness Academy".[35] (These certificates and letters take up some forty pages of the Minutes Book.) Next a committee was established to look into the level of the teachers' salaries. James Grant of Bught then proposed that the Glasgow professors should be thanked for their letter. Glengarry, supported by Raigmore, indignantly moved an amendment that they did not deserve any thanks, but the vote on Glengarry's amendment was lost by thirteen votes to twenty-one. In a final act of generosity, it was agreed that Grigor Urquhart, a former pupil and the son of the Church Officer, would be paid £20. He was at that time in Rome and pursuing studies in art, but had helped out in the classics department in the absence of the regular teacher while he was still in Inverness.

It is clear that Maclachlan was the better scholar and Carmichael would not have stood a chance in a comparative trial, but Barron points out that scholarship is not the only requisite for a good teacher,[36] and he feels that there was some defect or handicap which persuaded some of the Directors that Maclachlan was not the right man for the job. However Glengarry's behaviour may largely have determined the outcome. He stated that if Maclachlan was appointed he would take a house in Inverness and send his son to the Academy. Having Glengarry in Inverness might have been just too much for some of the Inverness society, and paying £50 to become a Director was a small price to keep Glengarry in Lochaber. Barron's analysis of the voting is interesting:

> Of the twenty-six Directors who voted for Maclachlan only four were Directors before the beginning of February 1820, the remainder were Directors manufactured for the occasion. Of the thirty-six who voted for Carmichael sixteen were old Directors and twenty faggot Directors *[a term Barron used for those who paid the £50 to be allowed to vote]*. Many deductions could be drawn from these figures, but it is sufficient to point out that they make it perfectly clear that the real Directors were opposed to Maclachlan in the proportion of sixteen to four.

Maclachlan lived for only a couple of years after the contest, dying in March 1822, aged 47. His wish was to be buried in Lochaber, and, when his body arrived there, Glengarry, accompanied by a large number of his clansmen dressed "in their native garb", escorted the body to the grave.

Carmichael served four years in Inverness Academy, before moving to the newly-opened Edinburgh Academy, where he taught until his death in 1847,[37] keeping in contact with Adam at least once, over gymnastics as a subject. He was particularly a Greek scholar, and published several books. He married in 1821, and two of his sons went on to be classics teachers, one in the Edinburgh Academy, the other in the Royal High School in Edinburgh.

So ends one of the most ridiculous stories in the whole history of Inverness Royal Academy, which lasted for some ten weeks. In the end a good teacher was appointed, and the accounts of the school benefited by over £2000, something which took the school out of another looming financial crisis. Few other schools can ever have had anything which approached this farcical situation, apparently brought about by the arrogance of one of the landed gentry in the County of Inverness, and one of his landed gentry friends.

Rules and regulations
Various committees had reported during the 1820's on different aspects of the running of the Academy. One of the more important of these, appointed in 1825, did not report back until the annual meeting in May 1828. The main points that they raised were:
- there had been a big improvement in discipline
- the number of pupils was increasing
- there had been some changes in administration tried out since the appointment of the committee, and these had met with some success and were to be continued
- it was accepted that there had been too much interference by the Directors in the day-to-day running of the school
- the Rector's fee of 2s 6d per pupil was very unpopular – it was agreed it should be removed
- the registers were to be kept properly
- in August 1827 daily morning assemblies had been discontinued and replaced by Saturday morning meetings, and this had been beneficial
- a letter from the staff on changing the holiday dates should be seriously considered
- all fees were to be paid quarterly in advance

A full list of interim regulations was suggested:
1. the Rector was to keep the general register properly
2. the teachers were to keep their class registers properly
3. each teacher was to lead prayers at least once a day with their class
4. the general meeting on Saturdays was to commence with prayer, and then deal with discipline and business matters
5. a book was to be kept of the business conducted at the Saturday meetings
6. the proposed hours of attendance were stated
7. the annual examination should take place in the first week of August, and then there should be a six weeks vacation with only 8 or 9 days of a break at Christmas – in effect creating only one session a year
8. there should be an interim fee to cover the period from June to August in the current year to allow the changeover to the new summer holiday dates
9. the fees were to be paid quarterly in advance, instead of half-yearly
10. a committee of eight should be established, and members of it would visit classes at least once a month, superintend the Saturday meetings and all other matters concerning progress, and report back to Directors' meetings

It was agreed to adopt the report and, as a temporary measure, to adopt the regulations. From this point the records show only one annual session, compared with the previous arrangement of two six-month sessions a year. The Rector's fee from the pupils would be replaced with a payment of £40 a year. This was accepted by Adam.

At the annual meeting in 1833 Gilzean retired after nineteen years as Chairman, and also from the Treasurer's post which he had held for 45 years. Mitchell, in his *Reminiscences*, describes Gilzean in these words:[38]

> These three *[Gilzean, James Grant and Dr. James Robertson]* lived among themselves, and much apart from the rest of the community. Gilzean was very taciturn, got the credit of great wisdom, chiefly because he seldom spoke, lived in a miserly style, and died about 1830, leaving a sum of £50,000 or £60,000, a large fortune in those days. ... If Provost Inglis did much for Inverness, these men did nothing. They were great Tories, and prosecuted parties with much severity who indicated Liberal or Radical opinions.

Once again Mitchell's account is inaccurate, as Gilzean did not die until 1843 aged 86.[39]

As Chairman, Gilzean was replaced by John Edwards, but the Treasurer's post was not immediately filled. Dr. Nicol once again tried to take control of Academy matters when he gave notice that he wanted to submit a motion about the future management of the Academy, and the result of this was that he was appointed at the next full meeting to chair a committee of seven to examine the state of the school.[40] Various matters, including the comments of a supervision committee appointed in 1828, were passed to this new committee for their consideration. The most significant of these was a suggestion that, following vacancies, replacement teachers should be appointed only on a year-by-year basis, without salary, although in receipt of fees from the pupils.

There was a significant reaction in both of the local newspapers, with the *Inverness Journal* campaigning bitterly against this proposal, whilst the *Inverness Courier* was equally opposed but in a more moderate way. In both cases anonymous letter writers and the editors put forward their views.[41] These included a statement that the fees were too high, one writer saying it cost 11 guineas (£11 11s) a year to educate a boy if he attended all the classes. Also suggested were higher salaries to attract the best talent, or combining classes to save money.

The new committee produced an interim report within three weeks, which stated that there was a need to appoint teachers to the vacant classes and to appoint an interim treasurer. They felt there was probably a need to widen the remit of the committee so they could consult Counsel about the terms under which teachers could be appointed. This interim report was accepted, the modern languages, writing and arithmetic, and drawing posts were to be advertised, and Roderick Reach, solicitor, was appointed interim Treasurer.

The 1834 report

The final report of the committee was ready by the Directors' Meeting on 12th April 1834, and it was decided to print 100 copies of it, with the Royal Charter as an appendix.[42] It runs to sixty-two pages of print, exclusive of the introduction, but the appendix of the original report was not printed. This had dealt with legal opinion, accounts of expenditure to date, the original regulations, possible rules for the use of the library, and a specimen form for the class register. A significant part of the report provides a summary of all aspects of the history of the school over the preceding forty-five years or so, and part of the first section tries to establish the relationship between the Academy and the Burgh, concluding that the Academy was not a Burgh school, although many people, including the teachers, thought of it as a Burgh school. The members of the committee also said that they felt that the Directors did have the power to amend anything they wished in the Royal Charter, if they believed it was in the best interests of the school.

Some of their major suggestions in the report include repairs and improvements to the school building, such as providing a staffroom in the old wooden belfry, and improving the paved space behind the school and keeping it free of mud. There is discussion on the role of Directors and who should be a Director, as well as defining the role of the Chairman. A warden, possibly paid, might be appointed to provide general supervision, as the committee of supervision had not really done its work properly. Clearer rules on the appointment and dismissal of teachers were required, but Counsel's opinion was needed in view of the conflict between the wording of the Royal Charter and the decision in Adam's legal case against the Directors. The roles and duties of the Rector and janitor were also considered.

It was suggested that seven subjects be taught:
1. English, reading, grammar and modern history
2. Latin, Greek, ancient geography and history
3. writing, arithmetic and book-keeping
4. drawing
5. French and other modern languages
6. mathematics, mechanical philosophy, chemistry, geography and astronomy
7. elocution

Teachers would be appointed for each of these subjects, and in addition occasional courses of lectures on natural history, botany and similar topics should also feature. The monitorial system, often used in charity schools, was not regarded as suitable for teaching in "seminaries for higher studies", such as the Academy. Also gymnastics, a topic on which there had been considerable debate across the country in the preceding few years, should not be taught "because an impression now prevails extensively that such exercises are of questionable utility, and hurtful to the unformed constitutions of youth". Adam had first put forward the idea of gymnastics two years earlier, based on information he had received from Carmichael after his move to Edinburgh.

Mention is made that the orations, which dated back to the former Grammar School days, had been discontinued at some point but had by 1834 been revived, with a large attendance of the public (see Chapter 9). The committee recommended that they be continued, but were concerned about the "deeply rooted provincial accent acquired in our nurseries", and this was the reason that an elocution class was suggested, to be conducted by a Mr Calvert, for six to eight weeks prior to the close of the session. The Academy had been offered the Northern Institution's museum, and the Directors accepted the committee's view that the Academy should take over the running of this museum. The final section of the report stated that revision of the rules was long overdue, as the 1828 experimental rules had never been confirmed. When agreed, a copy of the rules was to be hung up in the Academy.

The concluding remarks say that it was important that the constitution of the Academy should be clearly defined, and little could be sorted out until this was done. But the Directors accepted that their role in the past was frequently inappropriate. The final paragraph reads:

> Of the teachers, therefore, we should say – let them henceforth be supported by your personal friendship, rather than visited by the ostentation of your authority – let the high order of their responsibilities and of their attainments be recognised by the tenderness of personal regard, rather than with paralyzing indifference and chilling contempt, – let their energies be sufficiently encouraged, and their labours amply rewarded – let the patience of this Board be extended to them in all things – and it will be discovered that the industry and zeal, the integrity and courtesy of a worthy and useful Teacher will, through the faithful and satisfactory discharge of his duties, do more for the security of his individual rights, and for the fulfilment of the expectations of the public, than could ever be accomplished by all the eagerness and vigilance of a Board of Directors.

It took two years for many of the changes to be implemented, although at the 1834 annual meeting it was agreed to take over the Museum by paying the debt up to a maximum of £80.[43] The premises in Inglis Street were leased for another year, and a committee was to determine its future, but in 1835 the material was transferred to the Academy building. The following year £15 was allocated to add a mineral collection and an herbarium to the collection. George Anderson, solicitor, was appointed curator, with some remuneration, and he was asked to produce a catalogue. The skeleton of a Bengal tiger was added to the collection in 1838.

The recently-appointed Treasurer, Roderick Reach, produced summary accounts since the establishment of the Academy, as well as the current accounts. Adam also produced his first annual report for some years, showing that numbers had reached 246, a big increase compared with the 156 students at the same time the previous year. He goes on to say that there is "no just ground to allege, as in the committee report, that the Academy does not at present possess the confidence of the public". He also claims that he had been unable to teach certain subjects due to the lack of repairs to the apparatus.

Discussion continued about the terms of appointment of new teachers, one view still being that new teachers should be appointed without a fixed salary. James Falconer, who had been appointed on a temporary contract, had his contract renewed for a further year, and he was paid for teaching the French class in addition to his work in the writing, arithmetic and book-keeping class. At the annual meeting in 1835 his post was made permanent.

The committee was empowered to seek the opinion of Counsel on whether there was a need to make fundamental alterations in the existing constitution, or even to seek a new charter. By May 1835[44] it was decided to print two documents: *Remarks and Suggestions relative to the Election and Dismissal of Teachers in Seminaries of Education* and *The Queries and Answers by the Dean of Faculty together with the Queries and Opinion of Mr Rutherford.* Neither of these seem to have survived, nor have they been entered into the minutes.[45]

Adam's 1835 challenge to the Directors
Adam's annual report, dated 30th April 1835, is partially entered into the minute. A printed copy of the full report has survived[46] which provides us, on the first page, with the table of the sessions, staff names and pupil numbers (albeit with some errors and omissions), starting in January 1804. (This has been extensively used in the previous four chapters of this book.) The second and third pages of this report are a thinly-veiled attack on Dr. Nicol and the 1834 report. A footnote says that only the first paragraph was read to the Directors "and ordered to be entered in their [the Directors'] minutes". The main theme of the report is an attempt to disprove the assertion that the Academy was in decline. It refers to "Dr Nicol's lengthy, but most incorrect, injudicious, expensive and *justly rejected* Report ...". As with all documents written by Adam, the text is verbose, and the document was presumably printed to get his point of view over as most of the text was not to be entered into the minutes.

Following Adam's signature, a further five long paragraphs attack the frequent changes of regulations. It seems that this section was not written until after the printing of the revised regulations in September 1835, and therefore Adam's report, in the printed version, was not available until perhaps October of that year. Modern readers might have some difficulty following this extract:

> ... it is generally and confidently believed that, whatever may be professed, the real object of a large proportion of Dr Nicol's newly proposed *Prussian, scholastic, despotic and domiciliary visiting code of bye laws*, (inspection of which was refused to the Rector, even after they were printed), closely resembles the spirit and objects of the *Chaldean decree against Daniel*, in so far as they cannot but know that, in consequence of their inexpediency and injustice, the Teachers cannot be expected to submit to them, and consequently that they have it in view to annoy the Teachers even at the hazard of materially injuring the success and dissipating the funds of the Institution. ...

There is also a further attack on the proposal that the Rector would have to borrow the philosophical apparatus from the committee when it was required for his classes. The passage finishes with a claim that the teachers would be safer under the Royal Charter and common law than under the proposed new rules.

Adam's attack seems to have been ignored at first. Over the months of May and June 1835 various discussions took place over the revised regulations, and a further committee under Mr Edwards, the recently appointed Chairman, worked on them. This committee reported in September with a draft of the regulations, which were then duly accepted and signed. Various copies of the regulations survive[47] and the main points are as follows:

1. future meetings of the Directors would be held in the Academy hall, on a more formal basis;
2. the roles of the Chairman, Secretary and Treasurer were defined, and a committee of management, with a warden annually appointed, would supervise the running of the school; the janitor would be on the premises throughout the day and not have any other employment;
3. the staff were to be appointed by a majority vote, and Directors could not vote if they had a vested interest; appointments were to be during the pleasure of the Directors, but with dismissal possible only with a two-thirds majority and six months' notice, except for grave offences;
4. the Directors could fix the salaries of the teachers, and these could be changed on six months' notice, and would vary based on the number of students – salaries for new teachers would depend on their success as teachers; the fees were to be fixed for two sessions ahead;
5. the teachers were individually responsible for their classes, and were to keep weekly registers to be submitted through the Rector to the Secretary every Monday morning; the Rector was to keep a general register, along with a diary of staff attendance at morning prayers; a book recording pupil discipline was to be kept;
6. the grounds for instant dismissal were agreed, with votes of censure for lesser offences;
7. the length of each session was to be 157 days, including the exams, with no more than 11 days' vacation in the winter and 40 days in the summer (thus returning to the two-session year that existed up to 1828); the hours of teaching were fixed, with a half-day on Saturdays; the arrangements for the examinations were stated;
8. the janitor was to ring the bell 10 minutes before the start in the morning and 5 minutes before the start after a break; young ladies (who had always attended in small numbers for certain classes) were to enter five minutes after the boys and leave five minutes earlier; prayers would be held in the hall each morning; no firearms, gunpowder or weapons were to be permitted; the punishment of students was left to the individual teacher with certain reservations for serious issues;
9. religious instruction would take place on Monday mornings, covering Scripture and the catechism, and psalms and hymns were to be committed to memory; those who were not of the established faith could be exempted on application from their parents; the local clergy would be invited to visit the school during religious instruction;
10. the museum, library and the equipment were to be under the direct

control of the committee and items would be issued as required and returned at the end of the session.

The rules were to be printed and a copy pasted up in the hall of the Academy.

Adam's printed report from the 1835 annual meeting led to a "Reasons of Protest" from the Rector and teachers,[48] which was read to the preparatory meeting before the 1836 annual meeting.[49] It was resolved that the matter would be raised again at the annual meeting two weeks later, on 2nd May. Some amendments were then considered and accepted:[50]

1. this regulation to be unchanged;
2. the Secretary and Treasurer were to be separate appointments; the post of warden was abolished, and the powers of the committee of inspection were adjusted;
3. the restriction on voting by Directors with vested interests was removed, and the conditions of withdrawal of salary if dismissed were eased somewhat; notice of resignations was reduced from six to two months;
4. the rules on fixed salaries was rewritten, with the salary to be based on the average number of students over the previous five years, but, if this produced a figure thought to be too low, an extra sum could be given;
5. a section on motions from the staff to the Directors was eased, and the mention of weekly registers and a staff diary were deleted; the rules on prayers in class were moved here, and teachers were instructed to develop a Christian ethic in the pupils;
6. the notice for a meeting to consider the dismissal of a member of staff was reduced from one month to ten days;
7. the attendance was changed to 279 days a year, with at least six hours a day on weekdays, with three hours on Saturdays (this implied a return to one session a year);
8. this regulation was deleted;
9. this item, including the religious education syllabus, was deleted;
10. this item was renumbered as no. 8, and it was agreed that the committee could name a person to be responsible for the apparatus.

As a result of these regulations, Matthew Adam's own class register for the final three years of his tenure of office has survived[51] (see Chapter 9). Whether these revised regulations satisfied the staff, or whether they felt they could make no further progress, is not recorded, but no other complaints about the regulations appear in the minutes book, until a further change was proposed at the annual meeting in 1839, at the time of Adam's resignation. Despite the Directors realising that they were being too officious, they did not seem to give up easily the power they felt they held.

Chapter 9
The School in the early nineteenth century

Despite all the arguments and problems, especially during Adam's period as Rector, school life went on, and, as the joint tenures of Nimmo and Adam cover a period of more than thirty years, people were perhaps much less conscious of the problems than a modern reader might be from this account of the period.

School life under Nimmo

In May 1807 James Wills, the writing, arithmetic and book-keeping teacher, complained that Robert Moodie, who was to assist him with some of the classes, was holding a private class and was not available when required.[1] There were also complaints that discipline was poor. However, by the next meeting of the Directors in December (the meetings do not seem to have been held too frequently at this time) Nimmo had resolved some of the problems, and Moodie had ceased to run his private class.[2] An improvement in discipline was noted.

The building had been improved during this period. Following the joisting and flooring of the English classroom in 1805, the same was done to the Latin classroom in 1808. Over £550 was spent between 1805 and 1811 on new building, and on alterations and repairs both to the school and to the Rector's house. Funds in 1811, just after Nimmo's departure, stood at £3750, with an average annual expenditure of £314 14 1d,[3] of which £262 was required each year for salaries, a figure which had fallen to £240 by 1821 (excluding in both cases the class fees payable to the staff by pupils), when assets were £3850.

Church attendance was once again highlighted in the March 1808 report,[4] and seven rules on the conduct of classes on Sundays were set out. Part of the report reads (as handwritten):
> 3 That they walk to church in the following order -
> The Rector follow[d] by his class
> Mr Tulloch followe[d] by his
> Mr Wills follow[d] by his
> Mr Moodie follow[d] by his &
> Mr Campbell – by all the children above eight in his class
> each of those classes in which places are taken to walk in the order in which they stood at dismissal on Saturday
> 4 That the boys whose parents are of the episcopal persuasion be permitted to turn towards Bishop McFarlanes chapel immediately opposite the church yard gate
> 5 That the classes sit in the church in the follw[e] order –
> The Rector ~~in the seat~~ immediately behind the Masters on the side next Cullodens seat – Mr Wills's behind them
> Mr Mudies behind them
> Mr Tulloch's immediately behind the masters on the side next the magistrates & Mr Campbells behind them – none of the inferior classes to sit in the same pew with the superior ones & the two last classes to sit in the order of their places

6 That the Masters & scholars return to the Academy hall in the same order in which they left it

7 That on Monday at 12 o'clock the catalogue be examined & absentees punished in the manner most likely to be effectual – the committee conceive that to fine grown lads and threaten the young boys with corporal punishment, & in certain cases to inflict it may be the most proper mode.

Within a month Robert Moodie submitted his resignation,[5] and part of the text of his letter reflects his view on the way in which the Academy was being governed:

The principal cause of dissatisfaction, and that which involves all the others, is, that suspicion and jealousy with which the teachers of the Inverness Academy are watched. It is unnecessary to enquire what may be the reason for this watchfulness. I merely hint that it completely overturns the respectability of the Academy, and must in time fritter down the character of the most consciencious and assiduous teacher to a mere time server, and thus the institution, like some others of the same kind, may be revised to death, and that from the best of intentions. It becomes, of course, unsafe for a man, who considers teaching as his business for life to remain long in such a situation, although it may do very well for those who are travelling towards the church, through the office of a teacher. These I mention with the greater freedom, as it must operate upon those whose labours are of importance and whose loss would be felt. While such expressions as "keep them to their duty", they must be looked after & are bandied about from mouth to mouth. Those who would keep themselves to their duty will remain as short time as possible.

He had accepted a job in Dundee Academy, but within weeks he had reapplied to the Royal Academy, a request which was turned down. He seems to have stayed in Inverness for some time after this, as his name appears in the class registers against a drawing class of 6 pupils in the spring of 1809,[6] before Donald McLeod, a portrait painter, was appointed for the autumn session of that year.

With the publication of the *Inverness Journal* from 1807, and the *Inverness Courier* from 1817, sources of information about the Academy, other than from the Directors' Minutes and the surviving documents, became available. The first newspaper report of a school dance comes from summer 1809:[7]

In the evening the young gentlemen attending the Academy gave an elegant ball in the Northern Meeting Rooms. The display of innocent gaiety and the attractions of the youthful group, which consisted of nearly 300, were extremely interesting; but too few parents came to witness the blameless mirth and endearing graces of their offspring; a scene of all others the most gratifying to parental affection.

The ball seems to have been a feature in most years of the nineteenth century. A later edition of the same newspaper records Alex. Campbell, the English teacher, opening a private Gaelic class,[8] a subject which had dropped out of the main curriculum by this point.

Staffing problems would dominate part of Nimmo's time as Rector. Ebenezer Young, who had been appointed to the former Grammar School in 1791 and then been appointed to the Academy, fell ill during the autumn of 1807. The

Directors appointed John Tulloch (who had been assisting him) as interim first teacher, and John Clark (recently appointed to assist Alex. Campbell in English) to assist Tulloch. It was claimed that funds were not available to assist Young during his illness, although it was decided to continue his salary until the summer of 1808. He died on 5th September 1808, aged 49, to be survived by his wife (who died in 1812), and his four boys, three of whom served in India, and one in Jamaica. Both Young and his wife were buried in the Chapel Yard, Inverness, where the slab erected by his children, and stone erected by his grandchildren, can still be seen, although the railing has disappeared [Figure 9.1a]. Young's death was "universally regretted" according to the report in the *Inverness Journal* of 9th September 1808.

Staffing under Adam
In 1812 James Wills, the only remaining member of the original staff of the Academy, sought the backing of the Directors to obtain a suitable position for his only son.[9] His son had been a pupil in the Academy, and had then attended Aberdeen University, before qualifying as a surgeon in London. The Directors used their influence by writing to Charles Grant (senior), Chairman of the East India Company, and the M.P. for Inverness-shire.[10] By January 1813 the son had an appointment as an assistant surgeon in the East India Company. His father continued to teach in the Academy until his death in 1819 when this tribute appeared in the *Inverness Courier*:[11]

> Died here, on the 2nd curt., in his 67th year, universally regretted, Mr James Wills, who had been one of the teachers to the Inverness Academy since its institution. The life of Mr Wills was wholly devoted to the faithful and zealous discharge of his professional duties; and his exertions as a teacher were rewarded by the veneration and grateful affection of his pupils, in every quarter of the globe, and by the general esteem of his fellow-citizens.

Wills' grave is in the Chapel Yard, Inverness [Figure 9.1b], close to that of his former colleague, Ebenezer Young.

Isabel Anderson in her book describes some of the staff in the years before 1820, in the first decade of Adam's tenure as Rector:[12]

> Mr [Hugh] Urquhart was adored by all his pupils, both boys and girls, and the first day he appeared in the Academy, after returning from his marriage trip, they all met him at the door, with loud cheers and congratulations, and many demonstrations of affection. For many years after leaving Inverness, he was pastor of a church in Canada, and in that country he died.

Urquhart was appointed to teach English to replace Allerdyce in May 1816, and resigned in 1822, having been refused a salary increase in 1819. He became the Rev. Dr. Hugh Urquhart. He was replaced as English teacher by John Cumming of Forres. After listing the other staff of the time, Anderson continues:

> [There were] two gentlemen who each bore the name of John Clark, but one of whom had a Reverend before his name. The last-named taught arithmetic and writing, and his colleague, Mr John Paterson Clark, M.A., taught drawing. These two gentlemen were designated by their pupils – in order to prevent confusion

from the similarity of name – by the titles of "Black Clark" and "Red Clark", owing to the colour of their hair. Mr. John Paterson Clark, who rejoiced in the latter title, was an amiable and kindly little man, who afterwards acquired celebrity as dentist to the Prince Consort *[Prince Albert]*, who wrote a book called *The Odontalgist* (which was published in 1854), and purchased the estate of Fingask (now known by the name of Clunes), in the Aird *[west of Inverness]*, from which, after only a short residence, he removed to spend the few remaining years of his life in London, where all his wealth had been acquired.

The two Clarks were apparently cousins.[13]

J. P. Clark's book, *The Odontalgist*, has been traced in the National Library of Scotland and in the British Library. On his resignation in 1824 he attempted to sell his art collection to the school, but this was turned down at a time when funds again seem to have been low. His replacement, Davidson, was appointed at a salary of only £30 compared with the £40 that Clark received.

Pupil fund-raising for charity is not something that has taken place only in recent years. Cumming, the English teacher, was in December 1822 proposing a competition in recitation amongst his pupils with the proceeds going to the fund for the building of the Northern Infirmary. The following year he asked for separate hours for teaching the boys and the girls,[14] and changes in his hours were agreed.

Anderson refers to Adam, but makes no comment about him, perhaps as he does not seem to have been very popular. Another verdict on Adam and other members of staff of the Academy comes from an autobiography by James Kennedy, Raigmore Gold Medallist in 1831:[15]

> ... If I remember rightly, I was two sessions in the classes for Arithmetic and Mathematics. I made fair progress in both, but I cannot say I applied myself much in either. The teacher of arithmetic *[Rev. John Clark]* was kindly, very fond of a joke, but very passionate, and, when angry, he gave such wacks! The mathematical teacher, the rector *[Adam]*, was not a favourite. It was said he knew a great deal, but he could not get out with it. I was in the classical department continuously from July 1826, to August 1831.

> I have pleasant recollections of the five years I spent in this department. I gave myself diligently and successfully to the work carried on in it. My only unpleasant recollection of that period was in the first few months, when those entering on the study of Latin were made over to an assistant – a fine young gentleman in look *[T. Davidson – resigned at end of 1826 to study divinity in Edinburgh, as the Directors refused him leave of absence]*, with a gold chain attached to his watch, who had no patience with mistakes, and deemed it the proper thing to drive us with the tawse into diligence and accuracy. I remember yet how I trembled when my time came to decline a noun or conjugate a verb, lest I should make a slip, and my poor body should be made to suffer for the dulness of my mind. The other classes under the head-master *[for Latin and Greek]*, Mr Peter Scott, were taught in the same room, and it was evident he regarded this beating with entire disgust. He succeeded in getting the Directors of the Academy to dismiss this fine gentleman, and I am sure the sight of his back going away was the most pleasant thing we ever saw in him. We then came under the teaching of the head-master, and I think

we all felt we had got from a stormy sea into a peaceful harbour. There was no assistant teacher afterwards.

Early in 1811 Pierre Villemer, a French exile, became the French teacher,[16] and he was to stay in post until his death on 1st December 1825, when his widow and daughter, both from London, were given £15 to cover their expenses to travel back there "or otherways".[17] Anderson describes him as "a man of culture", and says he also taught Spanish and Italian. He had asked for an increase in his salary in 1818 to pay for a visit to Aberdeen, but he was refused this increase although he was told that he could go to Aberdeen if he wanted to! In summer 1819 Villemer petitioned the Directors again, and this was refused on the grounds that the Directors were short of money.[18] He petitioned a third time, probably in spring 1820[19] during or after the Glengarry controversy (as he mentions "the improved state of the funds"), but this petition is not recorded as having been specifically discussed by the Directors (although all staff salaries were examined at this point, with a report the following year). He states that his income comprised his annual salary of £30 together with fees of twenty-four guineas a session from his eight boy and sixteen girl pupils, which made a total of £40 4s a session (£80 8s a year). To make ends meet, he claimed he had to teach privately until very late at night, and this was affecting his health. By 1824 he was in debt.

Villemer is remembered by a poem in French, *Astronomie*, published in a second edition in 1824.[20] The poem, which runs to 91 pages, was published with the help of subscriptions from friends and former pupils. Styled on French Classic writings of the 17th century, it treats the stars and planets in reverential terms, but also explores phenomena such as gravity, the number of moons, the physical characteristics of the planets, the seasons, and festivities related to the stars, as well as the Christian orthodoxy of the Creation story.

On his death, Villemer was not immediately replaced, and Peter Scott, appointed the previous year for classics, was to take the class if qualified. Scott had received a very positive report in the examinations in the previous summer, and continued to do so in subsequent reports. However, it was only after an appeal to the Directors that he was awarded the salary of the class for session 1825-26. C. T. Journet (various other spellings appear in the minutes), who had been living in London, was appointed on a trial basis in August 1826, but the following May he was dismissed with effect from the end of the session,[21] when the Directors became dissatisfied with his work. He was given his salary up to the end of the session, and £10 to cover his costs to return to London. He appealed, and from this appeal it appears that he was so heavily in debt that a creditors' meeting had been held in his classroom on 9th May. In a second letter to Gilzean he says that he had a wife and a six-week old daughter in London, and they were about to come to Inverness. His creditors were prepared to suspend action against him if he was reinstated. At the time of writing he claimed he only had two shillings to his name, together with two valuable pictures. He apologised for the quality of the paper he was using for the letter as he could not afford anything better. His debts, run up since arriving in Inverness, amounted to £232 18 2d, with funds of only £28 available. Apart from a debt of £61 16s due to a banker, the biggest debts were to booksellers and innkeepers.[22] The Directors heard his pleas on 30th May, but decided against reinstatement in view of the size of his debts.

In 1829 Armend Fabe (perhaps Fabé) was appointed to teach French, and achieved good results according to the August 1830 examination report, but he left for France over the holiday period and failed to return. There was no appointment until October 1831, at which point a number of candidates were considered, the best qualified of whom the Directors thought would be better paid by staying in his existing job. In the end Claud Guiot from Haute Marne, who had been teaching in Wells, was appointed, but he left during the cholera outbreak in the autumn of 1832 (see later). In September 1833 a Mr Hammerstein, appointed on a temporary basis, would not agree to a permanent appointment. Peter Scott once again took on the teaching of the French class as part of his other language teaching, thereby stabilising the situation, although it was only after further repeated requests that he was properly paid for this. The French classroom, as a result became unused and for a while from March 1835 permission was granted for its use for choir practice for the Established Church, with the proviso that the Directors hoped that the pupils would also form a class in sacred music. In 1838 the school published a booklet, presumably written by Peter Scott, with exercises for translation into French[23] [Figure 9.2].

The Rev. John Clark, "Black Clark", the arithmetic and writing teacher, and for a while also teaching Latin, resigned in 1833 through ill health.[24] Clark had previously turned down a retirement package, but this time was given the sum of £30, together with his current salary. He was a native of Inverness and had been the teacher in the Academy for eighteen years. He had been brought before the Synod of Moray in 1818 on a charge of fornication, and this lead to a mass of legal paperwork.[25] The case was thrown out by the General Assembly, with Inverness Presbytery ordered to expunge its record on the matter. At one stage it was claimed that Clark taught a class of 223, although Adam's 1835 report lists the highest number as 216 in the first half of 1819, just before the death of James Wills. It was two years after the death of Wills that the Rev. Clark formally took over responsibility for the teaching of book-keeping. Class numbers had declined to under 30 a session by 1824, but then suddenly rose to 95, before falling off again until Clark's resignation. There had also been a number of unsatisfactory examination reports. His dispute with Adam in 1821 was mentioned in Chapter 7.

The pending report of the committee, examining the management of the Academy, caused the next appointment to be on a temporary basis, but James Falconer's appointment (see Chapter 8) was a fairly successful one.[26]

Numbers in the writing and arithmetic class rose from around 40 to over 180 immediately following his appointment (he had previously been teaching privately in the Town). Falconer was ill for a short period prior to the 1835 examinations, and again in 1837, when he asked for an assistant due to the size of his class, which had reached 145. This was agreed to as long as the assistant's post was not regarded as permanent. In his first year he was given £25 for teaching the French class and in 1835 a further £30 for his services, at which time his post was made permanent. His classroom was also enlarged, presumably by moving the partition walls on the upper floor of the building.

Isabel Anderson recalls that Falconer lived at Island Bank and used to drive to the Academy in his little phaeton (an open four-wheeled carriage).[27] She says he was the terror of careless and disobedient boys, "to whom he freely administered severe floggings, although to studious pupils he was particularly kind, never stinting praise and encouragement".

Financing the School in the 1810's, the 1820's and the 1830's
The Directors had tried to do something about the lack of proper financial control, when in early 1812 they examined the accounts since 1804. Sixteen pages of accounts appear in the minutes book covering that period. Details of repairs are also entered, as well as the income from the executors of the Castlehill Estate, from whom they were still waiting for the final dividend. Both the Town and the Commissioners of Supply were in arrears with their subscriptions, the Town by only £20, but the County by several years. (The Commissioners did pay arrears of £100 in 1813 and a further £80 in 1815.) In 1823 the Commissioners made their usual appointments to the Board of Directors, but declined to pay the usual £20. By 1844 the Directors were trying to get the Commissioners to resume payment.

In 1813 there had been sufficient surplus funds for £1000 to be available for loan on heritable security. Glengarry applied for the loan,[28] but it seems it was granted to George Inglis of Kingsmills. That year a John Noble in Demerara (on the north coast of South America) sent a bill of exchange for £114 11s to cover the cost of the education and boarding of his son at the Academy.[29] He was to be placed "as a boarder with one of the masters or any other genteel boarding house". The father was concerned as to whether his son had arrived safely in Inverness, but this did happen as the son's name appears in the prize list several times over the next three years or so. Noble's subscription of 10 guineas [£10 10s] was one of those collected by Phineas Mackintosh, who returned to Inverness from the Caribbean in 1814. Mackintosh had collected a total of £285 12s in Demerara, including his own subscription of 50 guineas [£52 10s], continuing the link with the West Indies and the Caribbean which had started with the initial funding of the school.

The Glengarry controversy of 1820 led to the deposit of £900 in the British Linen Bank following the annual meeting that year, and by the time of the annual accounts the following May this had increased to £1000. This was loaned on a personal bond to Alex. McKenzie of Hilton and John McKenzie of Farr, who held the bond only until the start of 1826. Interest rates generally fell during 1823 and the early part of 1824. As a result the Directors were forced to reduce rates to 4% on the various sums of money which were then on loan. At the same time the Rev. John Clark and Peter Villemer were asking for increased salaries and a decrease in the fees, presumably to attract more pupils to their classes. The Directors in their usual way refused the salary increase, but said that the teachers could reduce the fees if they wanted to![30] Further appeals for salary increases from various members of staff took place in January 1827, but were yet again rejected by the Directors.

The 1825 annual meeting looked at ways of raising more money, and consideration was given to laying out £2000 on heritable security if this yielded at least twice the existing interest. Nothing had been settled by the time of the 1828 annual meeting. It was not until 1829 that the Mason Lodges of Inverness offered to take the money on heritable security for land in Church Street.[31] This was the first offer that had been received for the money. At the same time it was noted that Fraser of Torbreck had two personal bonds, totalling £450, but his property was for sale. The Directors called on him to grant security or else they would demand payment. He was at that time in Tunbridge Wells, from whence he sought a delay in payment until Martinmas (November), a request that was granted. By the summer Provost Grant announced that the Town magistrates would pay up the bond of £1400, taken out in 1793, which had yielded £70 a year to the Academy for many years,[32] and the bond was finally discharged on 11th November 1829.[33]

That year (1829) Inglis of Kingsmills demanded a lower interest rate, and it was agreed to restrict the interest to 4% in line with other loans. At long last some of the money due from Lewis Cuthbert's estate of Castlehill was paid at a rate of 12s. 6d in the £, yielding £266 7 8d, less expenses, out of the £340 due. This was a fairly poor return after so many years of delay. The final dividend of £75 18 7d was not paid until 1842. The £2000 held in a bank account was giving a return of only 2%, and it was agreed to move this money into public funds at 3½% interest as soon as the stock was opened for purchase. This happened in the opening days of 1831.

Administering the school in the 1810's, 1820's and 1830's
In 1814 consideration was given to adopting the Lancastrian system of education,[34] as used in the High School of Edinburgh and elsewhere, and a report indicated that it saved on staffing and speeded up learning. Joseph Lancaster, the founder of the system, lectured in Inverness about his system during 1815.[35] Although the Directors adopted the report, no further action seems to have been taken on this proposal, as it seems it was more suited to a more elementary level of education.

Holiday dates were changed yet again in 1818 when the staff petitioned the

134

Directors for a delay in the start of the summer holiday until mid-June when it is warmer, and allowed "rural recreation and sea bathing". This was agreed. In 1828 the examinations were moved to early August, with the holiday thereafter until the end of September, to cover the harvest, the visit of the Circuit Court and the Northern Meeting (a social gathering for the middle and upper classes). This really marks the start of a single-session year, rather than the two six-month sessions that had operated since the opening of the school in 1792. The teachers had found great difficulty in getting pupils to attend at the start of sessions, and hoped this scheme would help.

A table attached to the 1821 report lists the average emoluments of the teachers.[36] The Rector was the third most highly paid member of staff, with emoluments of £158 15s (but he also had a rent-free house); the highest paid was the Latin teacher (based on Campbell's earnings) with £234 8s, followed by the writing and arithmetic teacher (Urquhart) with £177 12s. However the class fees, which formed a major part of the emoluments, were frequently changed. This report also proposed the abolition of the Rector's fee of 2s 6d per pupil, with the introduction of a matriculation fee of 1s per session and an annual increase in his salary of £25 to compensate him.

The Directors administered the examinations each year, but in some years so few Directors turned up that this proved difficult. A committee reported in December 1823 on how more Directors might be encouraged to participate.[37] The key points were:
1. the examination would be conducted in one day
2. the clergy would be asked to attend
3. there would be three committees, each of three people, with a clergyman leading each one
4. the Chairman would contact members in advance to ensure that they were available
5. a superintending committee would be appointed annually to visit classes at least once a month.
These points were accepted, other than arranging for the Secretary to write to members in advance rather than the Chairman making contact. The letters were to be sent by post.

Building works frequently required attention. A decision was taken in May 1811 to build a house for the janitor,[38] but, although it is not recorded that it was built, in 1813 the vents [?= chimneys] required adjustment. In 1812 is was agreed that the janitor could have grass for a cow, and a piece of ground for a garden to the north of the Rector's garden. Metal entrance gates for the school, to replace the wooden ones, were purchased in 1813 at a cost of £32 10s for the pair from John Fraser, a local blacksmith.

At the annual meeting in May 1821 various modifications and additions were proposed for the main building, and a plan was prepared by John Clark, presumably this time "Red Clark", the drawing teacher. Early in 1822 these plans were considered along with an estimate.[39] It was agreed that an architect, a Mr Elliot, would produce an alternative plan if he came north that year as expected. The minutes are then silent on any progress, and it must be assumed the scheme was dropped. The next mention of work on the building, apart from routine maintenance, is the provision of water spouts on the roof in early 1828, at a cost of £48 8 5d. A water closet was provided for the girls in 1829 at a cost of £4 11s, but the boys seemed to have to make do with buckets, which were frequently in need of repair. The wooden belfry, built in 1794 and repaired in the 1820's, had by 1832 proved too expensive to maintain, and it was then demolished and a new one built attached to the janitor's house.

In his 1830 report Adam pointed out that the floor of the arithmetic classroom was sinking as a result of a brick partition built across it, and this was getting progressively worse. He also requested a supply of river water to stop the annoyance of some of the pupils going from house to house for drinking water; a supply of gas would also be useful for evening lectures. This coincided with the development of supplies of both of these utilities through the Town towards the end of the 1820's. Gas was available in the Town at the end of 1826, and the water supply, delivered from a tank at the present-day junction of Culduthel Road and Old Edinburgh Road, became available in September 1829. The matter of the partition wall was referred to a committee to act as necessary, and a plumber was paid in 1832 for introducing water into the building, although the minutes say nothing about any action with regard to the gas supplies.

Apart from the ongoing issue of the poor quality of Rector's house (which lay to the south of the school building), the Academy also had to deal with problems associated with the house immediately to the north of the school, owned by Mrs Jane Cooper (specifically identified on Wood's map [see Figure 8.1]). For much of the time Arthur Cooper, a writer [= solicitor], was a Director of the school, and was presumably her son, rather than her husband, as she was the houseowner. Two issues appear. One of them was that the house threw out its dirty water and there was no proper ditch to take this away, leading to a foul smell in the Latin classroom. The other issue was that there was no proper wall between the properties. Although Cooper, in 1811, did offer to build a wall, it was built for only part of the length of the boundary, and the rest was filled with a pailing [= fence]. In 1822 another letter, this time from Adam, concerned some action of Cooper's, but the Directors did not record what this was and simply decided to inform Cooper of the contents of the letter. This was probably again to do with dirty water.

By 1830 Peter Scott was complaining about the end of the Academy building being polluted by waste water from Cooper's house, and as Cooper was present he agreed to get the offending drain covered.[40] Mrs Cooper asked for the wall to be completed in 1832, and the Directors agreed to this as long as she paid one third of the cost and stopped throwing the dirty water onto the

Academy grounds! She had been living in the house for twenty-three years. Two years later the Directors did relent (in the presence of Cooper himself) and they agreed to pay the full costs of the wall, on the grounds that she had spent a lot of money on repairing the pailing fence which had been damaged by the pupils and by cattle.[41] A wall to the south of the grounds in 1830 had cost a further £56.

Edwards, who had taken over as Chairman from Gilzean on his retirement in 1833, himself resigned in 1837, and was replaced by Affleck Fraser of Culduthel. For the first time a payment was made to the Secretary, Robert Smith, of £10 for each of the last two years. A year later William Colquhoun, the Sheriff Substitute, was appointed Chairman, and the Secretary's fee became 10 guineas (£10 10s). Col. Mackintosh of Farr donated £100 to the Academy funds in 1839, and thus he and his male heirs, became Directors in perpetuity.

School life under Adam
An account of a pupil's timetable in 1815 has come to light in the Fraser of Reelig Papers, in the form of a letter written by George John Fraser, aged 15, to one of his elder brothers who was a civil servant with the East India Company in Calcutta. Part of the letter reads:[42]

Inverness 24 March 1815

Dear Aleck
A rainy day and a cold has prevented my going to the Academy today and I think my time cannot be better employed, than in writing to you.

... I go to the academy at nine, and repeat greek grammar till ten, when I go to the writing and arithmetick and continue at it, till twelve, then comes French till one, play till two & arithmetick again, till three, and I read Terence till four. In the evening I write French and Latin versions [= translations] and read some interesting book such as Sullys memoirs or Shakespears plays. You will see by this that I am not very hard wrought, but probably I shall have to make up for it if I go south this summer ...

He then moved to a small school in England for more education, before also going to India where he joined the army. A note at the end of the letter in his mother's hand says:

I fear you will think this but a poor specimen of George's writing – either as to matter or manner.

George Fraser did not take mathematics, and therefore would not have been taught by Adam himself, but his teachers would have been William Allerdyce for English, either James Wills or James Simpson for writing and arithmetic, either Alexander Campbell or Rev. John "Black" Clark for Latin, and Pierre Villemer for French.

Ancient geography was added to the curriculum in late 1820, when roller maps were acquired at a cost of £3 9 6d, but this teaching, presumably by the classics teachers, was not to interfere with the Rector's geography class. Kennedy describes how the classics class was organised around 1830:[43]

There were some five or six classes in different stages of progress, and one teacher managed them all, the number of pupils being between fifty and sixty. Class after class was called up, the different classes learning their lessons in the different parts of the well-sized room till their turn should come. The plan answered well – better than would have been expected, and better than it would have been but for the character and management of the teacher. The monitorial system, though not in a formal manner, was adopted.

My teacher during those years was Mr. Peter Scott ... in many respects a model teacher. His look could not be considered attractive. He was tall; his face was strongly marked by smallpox; he walked with a stoop, and walked very fast. He was one of the most punctual and diligent of men. ... His temper was kindly and patient. I do not think he had a tawse. He had a cane, but I do not remember him applying it with any severity, except twice or thrice, when it was amply deserved. He was never impatient with a boy, however slow or dull, who seemed desirous to do well. He was ever encouraging those who did well to do better. ... We read Cæsar and other great generals. We read Cæsar's "Commentaries," Sallust's "Jugurtha," and Livy's "History" with an intelligence and interest far beyond that which mere words would give us.

Mr. Scott was a great reader... He got up for his class a small library, containing such books as Bruce's "Travels," Mungo Park's "Travels," and Cook's "Voyages," which are so interesting to young readers. ... I got then a taste for reading which has never left me. ... Mr. S.'s principal defect as a teacher was, I think, his assisting us too much. I have often thought we should have been better scholars had we been left to plod on as we best could, unaided by anyone, in trying to translate a difficult passage.

Donations of books were made from time to time. Sir John Macgregor Murray of Larnich and Balquhidder in 1810 presented a volume of Ossian's poems – then accepted as genuine early Celtic literature, but now regarded as the work of James Macpherson of Kingussie in the 1750's. A further copy, in two volumes, seems to have been donated through Raigmore in 1820 by Murray, this time given as "of Lanrack Castle", but presumably the same person. In 1813 George Inglis of Kingsmills donated the first twenty numbers of Dr Thornton's *Illustrations of the Linnean System of Botany* and the Directors agreed to purchase the rest of the volumes as they were published, and to bind them properly, even though it was to cost them £40 plus the cost of the binding. At the end of that year Mackintosh of Raigmore gifted a set of the twenty-nine parts of the *The Edinburgh Encyclopædia*, edited by Dr Brewster, to which Nimmo had contributed several articles.

Carmichael, the recently appointed classics teacher, was given charge of the library books following the annual meeting in 1821. Repairs were needed for the bookcases, and an inventory of the books was drawn up.[44] A further gift of the Gaelic books from the estate of Alexander Maclaurin, an Edinburgh stabler, was received with thanks in December 1825, even though Gaelic was no longer a subject on the curriculum. Following Carmichael's departure for Edinburgh, Adam seems to have resumed control of the library, and there are several statements requiring him to lodge the books in the correct cupboards and produce a list of the holdings, but this never seems to have been done.

The Central School, Inverness's third school after the Academy and Raining's Charity School, was opened in the summer of 1821, but this was not seen by the Academy Directors as any sort of threat, as its education would be restricted to the more basic subjects, taught to those who were unlikely to move on to the Academy, and probably could not afford the fees they would be required to pay. The fourth school, at the Merkinch, opened in 1829.

The Orations

The orations, which had developed from the Latin orations in the Grammar School, were held most years until the 1850's. Although no programme of the event survives until 1837, the accounts associated with the entertainments which followed the 1813 and 1814 orations survive.[45] These entertainments were at that time held in Bennet's Hotel (on the site of the present Ramada Jarvis (formerly the Caledonian) Hotel in Church Street), and the 1813 bill is headed "Young Gentlemen of the Academy". The event seems to have been somewhat riotous, as in both years six bottles of port wine and six of sherry were consumed, along with a large quantity of fruit. The 1813 event also led to the breakage of nine glasses, for which the Directors had to pay 1s 6d, out of a total bill of over £6.

In the early 1820's a letter in the *Inverness Courier*, written under a pseudonym, was concerned about the possibility that there would be no orations that year.[46] However there is evidence in the minutes of most of the annual meetings in the 1820's of preparations for the orations, to be followed by a ball in the evening. There must have been a gap round about 1830 as the *Courier* examination report in August 1832 was pleased to say that the orations had now resumed, after being "disused for some years". This gap is confirmed in the 1834 report on the state of the school. This report also noted that the preparation was often rushed and carried out by the Latin teacher. Mr Calvert, a professor of elocution in King's College, Aberdeen, was employed in 1834 and 1835 to prepare the orations, but Peter Scott, the classics teacher, organised the 1836 event as Calvert did not come to Inverness that year.

The programme of the 1837 event survives, as do two from the 1850's [Figure 9.3]. The Directors' Minutes for the summer of 1837 record the payment of £1 for the band which performed at that event. Following the 1838 examination the Directors agreed to dine at 5 p.m. in the Caledonian Hotel at their own expense, but Academy funds would pay for the guests including any members of the presbytery from outside Inverness and for those teachers who wished to attend. The cost of these guests was £2 14s.[47]

The Prizes and the Medals

A relatively modern transcript of the prize lists, starting in 1813, also allows some individual pupils' names to be identified,[48] often with their place of residence. There are some addresses given such as "Upper Canada", "Demerara", "Rotterdam" and "India", as well as addresses throughout the Highlands, not just in the Inverness area. Although the vast majority of names are of boys, some of whom became quite famous, there are some girls' names amongst the list, including a Miss Isabella Suter, who gained the prizes in both the geography, and the arithmetic and writing, classes in December 1813. Girls were most likely to attend these, and the French, classes, rather than classics or mathematics, although as time went on girls' names appear more frequently in all classes. By the 1828 examination there were 74 boys and 49 girls on the school roll.

The prize fund was generally £10 or ten guineas (£10 10s), but from time to time the Directors agreed to increase this to £12, with the proviso that if numbers in certain classes were very small, no prize would be awarded. A decision was taken in 1821 to buy the prize books alternately from the two Inverness booksellers. A number of prize books from the 1830's have found their way back to the Academy, especially those awarded to a family called Black. Amongst them is an all-time classic, *The Natural History of Selbourne*, by the Rev. Gilbert White (published 1833). Few of the titles, or their modern equivalents, would be found at any modern-day prize-giving:[49]
- anon.: *Travels in Europe and Asia* (published 1831)
- Christian Milne: *Simple Poems on Simple Subjects* (1805)
- Jacob Ruddiman: *Tales and Sketches* (1828)
- Richard Magnall: *Historical and Miscellaneous Questions for the Use of Young People* (1834)

Separate prizes for Scottish and English history appear from the 1838 prize list onwards, as previously there was only a prize for English History. The 1839 list includes prizes for ornamental writing, for elocution and for the best class monitor. By this date girls' classes (or the "young ladies' division") are being listed separately in a number of subjects, and significant numbers of girls seem to have been in attendance at the school. Staff also awarded prizes and medals over and above those awarded by the Directors. Two medals or tokens, one for English from 1821 or soon thereafter, and another, an undated Latin medal with the number 'XXXII' from around the same period, survive[50] [Figure 9.4].

Various lists of the Raigmore medallists (see Chapter 8) also exist separately[51] and the winners' names are also recorded on the honours boards still on display in the present building of the Royal Academy. The first of these boards was agreed to in 1836.[52] The silver medal winner for mathematics in December 1814 was James Davidson, son of Matthew Davidson, the resident engineer at Clachnaharry on the Caledonian Canal. He should also have gained the gold medal for classics the following summer, but, under Raigmore's rules for the award of the medal, a person could only receive one medal during their time at the Academy. The winner two years earlier had been his brother, John.

The award in 1820 to William Gordon of Dundee was challenged by Simon Chisholm of Fort Augustus, but the minutes say that the examiners' decision stood, although the prize list states that the medal was awarded to Chisholm. In 1827 the gold medallist was Edward Strathearn Gordon, later Lord Gordon of Drumearn. He rose to become an Advocate, the Solicitor-General for Scotland, and then in 1867 Lord Advocate under Disraeli (see Chapter 12). In 1828 the contest for the gold medal was so close that an extra examination had to be arranged to separate the top two candidates in classics. In 1831 the winner was James Kennedy, a section of whose autobiography was quoted above.

The medallist for 1833, Matthew Campbell, gained fame (or perhaps notoriety) in 1849 at the time of the collapse of the old stone bridge over the River Ness during a flood. Isabel Anderson tells the story:[53]

> ... the last person who had crossed the stone bridge was a sailor, named Matthew Campbell, who had gained the gold medal for Classics in Inverness Royal Academy in 1833. Up to the last moment he had been indefatigable in his exertions, going to and fro across the bridge to assist the poor people in the Green *[on the west side of the river]* in removing, and he had barely reached the northern bank when the whole structure disappeared.

Apart from the collapse of the bridge, major flooding took place and many people, especially the poor, were made homeless. Some versions of the story suggest that Campbell was "two sheets in the wind" at the time of this event which took place in the early hours of the morning.[54]

In 1837 the silver medallist for mathematics was George Macandrew, whose mathematics notebook for session 1835-36 survives[55] [Figure 9.5]. There was a dispute as to whether Macandrew should have received the gold medal rather than the silver one under the terms of the gift of the medal by Raigmore, and this is recorded in Adam's register for that year.[56] A letter from Adam to the Directors in the previous August had raised with the Directors the possibility of awarding the gold medal in alternate years for mathematics and classics, as Raigmore's original proposal was that there would be alternate awards every six months. Since 1828, with the start of the summer holiday not being until early August, there had been only one annual prize list, with the silver medal being awarded for mathematics, and the gold medal for classics. The Directors decided at that time to continue to award the gold medal to the classics class, and it was given to Duncan Macbean. Alternate awards for the two subjects were not introduced until 1841, after Adam's departure.

Macandrew's father did give notice of a motion for the subsequent meeting of the Directors on this topic, but the minutes book does not record any discussion. Macandrew, the son, went on to serve with distinction in the British Army in India, rising to the rank of Lieutenant-General. Some of his memorabilia from his army days are housed in Inverness Museum. The last gold medal to be awarded whilst Adam was Rector, that for 1839, was to Alexander Falconer, son of James Falconer, the writing and arithmetic teacher. The earliest medal known to survive, and also now in Inverness Museum, is that awarded in 1840 to A. Penrose Hay, later to be Town Chamberlain of Inverness (see Chapter 12).

Church attendance

The 1820's mark a period when the control by the church over Academy matters begins to decline somewhat. The policy that pupils must attend church with their teachers started to be eased in 1822 when the Directors suggested that parents or guardians could take their own children to church, as long as the pupils could prove they were there. The rest were to go with the teachers, and censors from amongst the pupils would record attendance. The janitor would also attend. The Sunday evening meeting to review the sermons of the day had fallen into disuse, and by that time there was no examination in religious knowledge, although by the 1830's this was once again tested at the annual examination.

Two years later it was reported that the teachers had without authority given up going to church in procession, and once again the rule was restated that both pupils and staff must process to church, unless the parents had specifically sought exemption. At the start of the following year (1825) staff were reminded that they must arrive in school on time and attend prayers. This reminder was issued after frequent late-coming was recorded in a log that had been kept during visits by the inspection committee over the previous few months. Peter Scott was the only teacher whom they found to be regular and punctual.

Compulsory church attendance was abandoned in 1830,[57] but two pews were to be kept for pupils who otherwise would not have seats, presumably including those boarded out in the Town to attend the Academy. Only fifteen years earlier the ministers representing the Presbytery of Inverness were stating that the masters should be attending church twice on Sundays.

Day to day life

Many minor matters concerning the pupils and staff passed through the minutes. In 1812 a wright [= joiner] was instructed to put up pins [= coat pegs] in the Latin classroom for the pupils' hats. The pupils themselves organised a Juvenile Society, which met in the school, but in June 1812 the Directors ordered their meetings to be suspended until they handed in their regulations. A Literary Debating Society (possibly adult rather than pupil) was permitted in 1837, as long as the teacher whose room was being used agreed to remain responsible. New gowns for the staff in 1812 had cost three guineas (£3 3s) each, and teachers were frequently reminded to wear them when in the Academy. The apparent theft of the gown belonging to "Black Clark" in 1824 led to its replacement, along with the supply of a new gown for Pierre Villemer.

In 1834 a dancing master, a Mr Goldie, sought the use of the empty French classroom for two weeks for his lessons, but this was denied. However at the next meeting of the Directors it was agreed that 15 free tickets for a series of astronomy lectures were to be given to the pupils, and the following year £10 was spent on tickets for "Mr Shier's practical lectures on Chemistry".

Kennedy, writing more than fifty years later, recounts something of play and activities for Academy pupils:[58]

... We had a pleasant park, twice the size of the present park, with no wall dividing it as is now the case in the diminished park, and there we had an abundance of room for our games – marbles, throwing a ball against a high wall, club and ball, football, and all other sports in which boys find bent for their superfluous energy. Then, I must confess, we had our fights with the boys of other schools in the town, whom we in our conceit called "blackguards," fights carried on with stone-throwing, which ended in boys being hit now and again, and which I now wonder did not end in some being killed. The teachers interfered, and the fights were stopped. I did join in them, though not often, and I was glad when they came to an end...

By the time Kennedy wrote this piece, the Ladies' Institution had been built, and the playground sectioned into areas for boys and girls (see Chapter 12).

Serious illness affected the pupils from time to time. An unspecified epidemic is recorded in March 1812, and in 1822 Dr Matthew Bethune treated venereal disease amongst pupils.[59] Kennedy tells us he contracted smallpox in 1831. In 1832 the Town was seriously affected by cholera, as noted by Adam in his 1835 report.[60] The illness spread to the Town in late August, lasting through to early November. On 8th August Adam had attended a public meeting about the outbreak, when he complained that insufficient information had been distributed before the meeting about the decisions that required to be taken to comply with Government regulations. In early October M. Guiot, the French teacher, was requesting permission to suspend his class so that he could leave Town, and a meeting of Directors was called.[61] There is no minute of such a meeting to grant him permission, but later press advertisements say that Peter Scott would conduct the class during Guiot's absence from Inverness.[62] Guiot did not return to Inverness, but his resignation is not recorded until the following summer, as there was no meeting of the Directors in the interim. Scott was later paid for his work with the class from October to July.

There is no record of how many, if any, of the pupils of the Academy were affected or died, but there were 553 cases of cholera in the Town, with 175 deaths,[63] so it is likely that some of those affected were pupils. From the newspaper reports, we learn that the "old Academy" – the former Grammar School building – was used as the cholera hospital, despite its nearness to three of the main churches and a densely populated area in the closes and old buildings of Church Street. The disease reappeared in the Town briefly in 1834, and another serious outbreak occurred in 1849, with 112 deaths, including that of Dr. John Nicol [Figure 9.6], who had served for many years as one of the Academy's Directors, and who was so disliked by Adam.

Teenage vandalism was also a fact of life in the 1820's. A report in the *Inverness Courier* in 1827 records petty thefts and "most wanton and malicious acts of annoyance"[64] by damaging fences, stealing clothes off washing lines, stealing some sheets of music from a house, and:

> [a]nother night, they entered the Garden of Mr Adam, Rector of the Academy, and in the most wanton manner, cut and destroyed many of the fruit trees and bushes.

The final act mentioned was the theft of barley straw and turnips from a farm at Drummond. Whether these acts of vandalism were carried out by Academy pupils is not known.

As was a custom at the time, the windows of the school were illuminated to celebrate national events. A carpenter was paid £6 8 2d for the illuminations following the peace with France in 1814 – clearly very elaborate illuminations. The windows were illuminated again in March 1831 for the second reading of the Reform Bill which scraped through Parliament by a single vote, to the delight of many of the inhabitants of Inverness. This bill was to give the vote to any man who owned property worth at least £10 or leased land worth at least £50. The House of Lords rejected the bill that October, but six months later relented. The bill finally passed through Parliament, and on 22nd May 1832, a crowd of many thousand assembled in the Academy Park, probably the largest open space available in the Town, to welcome the reforms and to hear speeches.[65]

In 1831, the Highland Society, the Inverness branch of which had been founded in 1815, requested the use of the Academy Park for a livestock show. This was agreed by the Directors, with the use of the buildings if required. The following May a letter of thanks from the Duke of Buccleuch and Queensberry, on behalf of the Society, was received. This show is of course the forerunner of the present Royal Highland Show, now based outside Edinburgh. The grounds were again used for the show in 1839 and in several years in the following decades.

Two other matters require mention, namely the Mackintosh of Farr Fund, and the proposed union with the Dr. Bell's Trust Fund, but these will be covered in Chapter 10.

Chapter 10
Capt. Mackintosh, Dr. Bell and the Deans of Guild

The 1840's and 1850's saw attempts to bring money from two local educational endowments, the Mackintosh Farr Fund and the Bell's Fund, under the control of the Academy, but these attempts failed (and the funds were not merged until 1887). This failure caused the Directors even greater financial problems through crippling legal costs. It is now necessary to look at the origins of both of these funds, although parts of their operation are only loosely linked to the operation of Inverness Royal Academy. Arguments over who was the *real* Dean of Guild, and if the Town and County should pay their traditional shares of the cost of running the school, did not help the Directors either.

The Mackintosh Farr Fund
As has been explained in earlier chapters, many Highland sons (especially second and later sons) decided to try to find their fortune in foreign lands. This was especially true in the second half of the eighteenth century. The West Indies and India were the two places which attracted most interest from people in the Inverness area, although North America and Australia attracted attention from Scots in other parts of the country, as has been shown in books such as Tom Devine's *Scotland's Empire*.[1] The East India Company had been closed to Scots prior to the Union of the Parliaments in 1707, but thereafter Scots penetrated this trading company to an amazing degree, far above the relative proportion of Scots within the British population of roughly one in ten (as it was at that time), and in some cases Scots were virtually in total control of parts of the Company's activities in India and on the coast of China.

One person who earned a fortune from this trade was Captain William Mackintosh, whose will was to cause so much strife and discontent in the nineteenth century. Mackintosh, born in about 1744 and educated in Fortrose Academy, worked his way up the ranks as a seaman, sailing mainly to the West Indies and to India.[2] He first became a captain in 1783, and in 1789 took charge of the East Indiaman *Hindostan*, sailing twice from Britain to China. For the second of these voyages, the ship was chartered to Lord George Macartney on a special embassy [= mission] to the Emperor of China in an effort to open up trade with the Chinese, but the efforts proved fruitless.[3] This ship was sold to the Admiralty in 1795 and replaced in 1796 by a new *Hindostan*, a very substantial ship for its time. Mackintosh was captain of this new ship on his third voyage to the Far East, sailing to Bombay and China in March 1797 and returning to Britain in October 1798. Both of the ships are illustrated in paintings and prints by artists such as Nicholas Pocock and Thomas Luny[4] [Figure 10.1a-b].

As was the custom at the time, the East India Company allowed the captain some space on the ship to trade on his own account. The value of such goods, according to one estimate, might approach £10 000, and it is from this money that Mackintosh would have made his fortune. Mackintosh's will, replacing an earlier one or ones, was written at sea in April 1797 on the third voyage. It was written following the "imprudent conduct" of his brother John, who was heavily in debt, "and of another person, to whom I had intended, and had bequeathed very considerable legacies".[5] Considering that Mackintosh gave away several legacies of £5 000 and one of £10 000, his wealth, by the standards of the day, was considerable, at about £40 000.

After cutting off some of his relations from any money, he made the Chief Mate of his ship one of his executors. The Will then goes on:

... it is my express Will that £5000 be vested in Trust with the Magistrates of Inverness for the time being, the interest of which sum is to be appropriated to the education of *five* boys in succession, to be selected – first, from the descendants of the Family of Farr; next, to those of Dalmigavie; and thirdly, to those of the House of Kylachy, or their nearest relations, in the above order of consanguinity, but always of the name of Mackintosh; and it may be hoped that some of these boys, if they succeed in life (which this gives them a fair chance for), will follow the example, to keep up a respectable though declining clan. It is to be remembered that they are to be educated at the Academy lately established in that town; but if the Trustees think it advisable, on discovering marks of genius, to send any of the boys to an University, they are not restricted from doing it. The said sum of £5000, as soon as it may be expedient, *to be invested in lands* in the country; and perhaps it might not be improper to paste up a copy of this bequest in some part of the Academy, which probably would stamp an impression, and stimulate similar acts of liberality. ...

The italics appear in the print version of the will, but it is unlikely that this emphasis was in the original manuscript version.

It is not the will which caused so much difficulty, but some of the six codicils which were added over the following six years. The first says that Mackintosh had made £10 000 from that third voyage, but he cut out the Chief Mate as a beneficiary, being dissatisfied with his conduct. The second codicil adjusted the amount to be paid to his friends and relatives, and then adjusted the sum for education to £10 000, although a Mrs Rae was to get the interest from that money until she died, and thereafter the full interest would be applied to the boys by being vested in lands; in the meantime any surplus from his will could be used for the education of the boys. Codicil 4 cut Mrs Rae out of the will, and the £10 000 was to be immediately used for education.

During 1801 Mackintosh was back in Scotland and met his relatives. He then made various other adjustments to their legacies. It seems that Mackintosh had retired from seafaring on his return to Britain at the end of 1798, and Codicil 6 indicates that he was ill during the early part of 1803. He died in June 1803, soon after his former ship was wrecked on the sands off Margate on 11th January, as illustrated by an aquatint print in the collection of the National Maritime Museum[6] [Figure 10.1b]. Legal proceedings in the Court of Chancery held up any pay-out until 1816, and a few years later an Edinburgh accountant was brought in to examine the somewhat doubtful accounts for legal services of Alexander Mundell, the London solicitor handling the legacy.[7] Further legal action between James Mackintosh (a half-brother), the residual legatee, and the Magistrates of Inverness, started in 1817. An action of multiple poinding (an action against a group of people) was raised seeking to get access to the money, with a host of memorials (statements to the court) being produced. In both 1818 and 1821, the Lord Ordinary produced an interlocutor (a temporary opinion, pending submission of all the evidence). The Magistrates then petitioned for a review of part of this latter judgement as it concerned how the boys were to be selected.[8] The arguments went on, and legal fees multiplied, until a final judgement in 1825, which was broadly in favour of the magistrates and which sorted out the order in which the boys were to be selected. It also established that the fund was an educational endowment, not a fund for charitable purposes.

Further difficulty over the interpretation of the Will led to the opinion of Counsel being sought in 1834, 1841 and 1842. The 1841 opinion required the Trustees to keep a family tree of all the descendants of the four families to determine eligibility. Other points at issue included whether education could take place at schools other than the Royal Academy, and what would happen if a family, descended from one of the branches of the family, changed its name to Mackintosh to allow a claim to be submitted.

Meanwhile, the funds which the Trustees now controlled were, as required, invested in land, particularly in the area of Merkinch, now part of Inverness, but at that stage on the north-west edge of the Town, and at Seafield in the Longman. From these investments, the Fund was to make considerable sums of money over the years, particularly when house-building started to develop in the Merkinch later in the century.

The first pupils funded under the scheme entered the Academy in 1820, following the decision in Chancery, which had allowed an advertisement in the Inverness papers in March 1818. Various records survive of the pupils who benefited from the legacy. One of the pupils, however, did not fully appreciate the education that he was receiving. In June 1829 Matthew Adam had to write to the Provost (as Chairman of the Trustees of the fund) about the behaviour of one Duncan Mackintosh, whom he had put out of his mathematics class for insubordination:[9]

> When I was entering the back door of the Academy yesterday at 10 o'clock A.M. followed by Alexander Mackintosh, also one of the Bursars, a large stone (I suppose about a lb [pound] weight), thrown from the neighbourhood of the Ball-wall, struck the ground with great force almost at my heels; upon which Alexr. Mackintosh complained to me, that one of the boys had thrown a stone at him. After an investigation, & threatening to punish another student, who was accused of throwing the stone, I was at length informed by those who saw it, that it was Duncan Mackintosh who threw the stone. Duncan Mackintosh then admitted that he had thrown it; but, when desired, refused to hold out his hand to receive any punishment with the taws [belt], for this offence, & insisted that I should first punish every boy in the Academy, who had on any previous occasion thrown a stone. On

some previous occasions I found this boy to be refractory, he having sometimes made very impertinent & contemptuous answers, when checked for offenses committed by him in the Classroom. On one occasion, when he answered contemptuously, & refused to hold out his hand to receive punishment with the taws, I whipped him on the shoulders & head, rather than allow him to escape punishment, upon which he loudly threatened me with a complaint to the Trustees of the Fund & forthwith carried his complaint to Mr Ross the Secretary.

As with so many of these glimpses of school life, there is no record of the end of the story, as the relevant minutes book is missing.

Another problem includes concern about the irregular attendance of some of the Mackintosh Farr Fund bursars in 1836,[10] and the magistrates were to be informed (even though some of them were the same people as the Directors!). When Adam was involved in the conflict with the Directors which led to his resignation, he was required to provide a list of the bursars he had taught since 1826.

In 1843 the supervision committee refused the magistrates, as trustees of the Mackintosh Farr Fund, permission to visit the 22 pupils then being educated in the school. A special general meeting was called in protest,[11] at which the byelaws and regulations were examined. The supervision committee was ordered to afford every facility for the magistrates to visit these boys during class hours as they saw fit.

The early minutes books of the Fund are missing,[12] so it is only from 1861 that full details of the operation of the committee are available. At this point some of the Trustees visited the houses where the bursars were living. One bursar was told that if his homework did not improve he would be removed from his own home to a house where he was better supervised. Other reports indicate that bursars were removed from one unsatisfactory boarding house and lodged with the Rector of the time to ensure proper accommodation.

It is interesting to note that Mackintosh was educated at Fortrose Academy, and not in Inverness. In 2006, following restoration, it was possible to hang in the present school building (rather than "paste up", as he requested) a restored copy of the relevant parts of his will [Figure 10.2].

The Bell's Fund
Dr. Andrew Bell was born in St. Andrews (Fife) on 27th March 1753, the second son of a local magistrate who made his living as a barber, wigmaker and watchmaker. At University, Bell distinguished himself in mathematics and natural philosophy. In 1774 he emigrated to Virginia where he tutored, and dealt in currency and tobacco. Back in Britain in 1781, he took orders in the Church of England. Six years later he emigrated to Madras (India) where he secured an army chaplaincy and five deputy chaplaincies. He was soon running the Military Male Orphan Asylum, where, as he could not get teachers, he used a ten-year old to teach the alphabet class. This led some years later to the development of the monitorial system of teaching, often

known as the Madras system. This in turn gave its name to certain schools, such as Madras Academy in his home town of St. Andrews, a school which originally used the system in the form promoted by Bell.

Bell returned to Britain in 1797 with a pension of £200 a year from the East India Company, by which time he had accumulated £26 000. He set about promoting his system for teaching, and, in 1811, under the patronage of Prince Rupert, a society was established, called "The National Society for Promoting the Education of the Poor in the Principles of the Established Church throughout England and Wales", and the first Central School was opened in London in 1812. Bell died in Cheltenham in 1832, and is interred in Westminster Abbey.[13]

The year before his death, Bell informed Provost Robertson of Inverness that one-twelfth of a sum of £120 000 deposited on trust with officials in St. Andrews was available for use in Inverness. This led to the establishment of the Bell Educational Trust in Inverness, and £10 000 of Bank annuities was transferred which gave a capital of £8 800. Progress towards opening a school was slow, and it was not until March 1837 that much happened, when a report recommended several schools be established in Inverness on the Madras system. It was agreed to confer about transferring the Central School (opened in 1821, originally in Queen Street) and Merkinch school (opened in 1829, originally in Madras Street) to the control of the Bell Trustees, and consideration was also given to amalgamation with the Academy, a topic first raised in April 1835, in a motion proposed by Dr Nicol.[14] Amalgamation was also supported, along with a reform in the operation of the Academy, in an open letter from Joseph Mitchell, the civil engineer, to the Directors and Town Councillors, published in the same month.[15] The Central and Merkinch schools were taken over by the Bell Fund Trustees, but the suggestion for amalgamation with the Academy, although agreed at the Academy Directors' annual meeting in 1836, fell through.

However, the Bell Trustees suggested that the site of the Academy Rector's house and garden be considered for building the new "principal seminary" for the Bell Trust (it will be remembered that the house was in a poor state and was at that time occupied by a tenant). In the end, the site chosen was much bigger, and probably the same one as had at one stage been bought for the Academy: what we now know as Farraline Park. The building was erected and opened in September 1841 as a fee-paying school. The Incorporated Trades refused to attend the opening on the grounds that they felt that the fees were too high for tradesmen's children. The fine building, with its Doric architecture, which is currently in use as the Inverness Public Library, cost almost £1800 to erect, slightly less than the cost of the Academy, some fifty years earlier.

Plans for amalgamation of the Funds
A long article about the Bell's Fund appeared in the *Inverness Courier* in the

autumn of 1839[16] and the first thoughts on amalgamating both this fund and the Mackintosh Farr Fund with the Academy funds were made in April 1841. The Directors' annual meeting in May set up a committee, which met some weeks later with the Mackintosh Farr Fund Trustees, when general agreement was reached, but once again discussions moved very slowly. The next major step did not take place until 1848, shortly after the time when James Steele of the Bell's School became Rector of the Academy (see Chapter 11). A committee meeting on 21st February felt the time was ripe to investigate the three funds, and a scheme to amalgamate them was proposed by the Rev. Mr Macdonald, on behalf of the Mackintosh Farr Trustees and the Academy Directors. The Academy Directors met on 7th March, and, after discussion, passed the matter to the standing committee to consider and report back, although this was opposed by Mr James Suter, jnr., a local wine merchant, who also opposed various other schemes over a period of years. The nature of his dissent was not entered into the minutes.

The standing committee found that the Academy funds would allow them to keep to their part of the arrangement, and by 21st March a scheme had been proposed. The united income was claimed to be £1369 5 1d, after allowing for all anticipated expenditure, from which would be deducted the interest on the £10 000 earmarked for the education of boys under the Mackintosh Farr Trust fund. This allowed nearly £900 to be available to establish a collegiate institution in a suitable building, mainly paid for from the value of land. The report states:[17]

> The value of the grounds and buildings of the Academy and of the Bell's Institution is not computed. Should the proposed buildings be erected in conjunction with Bell's Institution, sufficient ground together with the Academy buildings may be sold to assist if not entirely to erect these buildings. Should it be resolved to raise the College in another locality the value of the two buildings and their grounds would be sufficient for the purpose.
>
> The proposed amalgamation will include:
> 1. The Central and Merkinch Schools for the education of the poorer classes. They are capable of accommodating between 700 & 800 children and the rates of charge may be considered as merely nominal.
> 2. An Elementary School for the better classes, and
> 3. A College, if possible with the power of granting degrees, but at least with the right of insisting that its alumni shall after having passed the course of education be entertained on trial for degrees at the Universities of Edinburgh or Glasgow.
>
> On this scheme, every class of individuals is provided with education suited to their requirements.

This collegiate scheme was originally the idea of Sheriff Colquhoun, recently appointed as Chairman of the Directors of the Academy, and an influential person in local affairs at the time. Mention was also made that the government should be approached to assist with funding.

In a sense this was an attempt to set up a sort of University or Higher Education College in Inverness, as there was also talk of Schools of Divinity and Medicine, as well as training for Gaelic-speaking students studying for the ministry (something the General Assembly of the Church of Scotland had repeatedly urged). The Directors asked for any members who might be going to London in the near future to state when they would be there, so that a deputation could be arranged to lobby the Government. Suter, although approving of the deputation to the Government, once again dissented, "for the same reasons that he had already stated".

The annual meeting at the beginning of May appointed the deputation, and gave its members their instructions. No funds were available for the deputation, but it was hoped that the costs could come out of the funds granted by the government. Various documents were printed, of which only some have survived,[18] including a leaflet setting out the project, which states:

> ... Inverness is the central point of the Counties of Caithness, Sutherland, Ross, Cromarty, Inverness, Nairn, and Moray, being one-third of the surface of Scotland, and containing a population of 281,838 persons.

> The University of Aberdeen is the nearest to this central point, at a distance, however, of upwards of a hundred miles; and the King's College of that town was erected for the use of the Northern Highlands – how inappropriately placed, at least for the present demands of the North of Scotland, is apparent. ...

> The pecuniary assistance required is not large; a mere trifle compared with that which Government had lately bestowed on Irish and English education. The Northern population has always been distinguished for its orderly conduct, and for the limited demands which it has ventured to make upon the resources of Government. The foundation of such an Institution would raise the character not alone of this town and neighbourhood, but of the North generally. ...

It was claimed that the building that had been erected for the Bell's School was unsuitable for the monitorial type of education that Bell had anticipated. The five memoranda outlined each part of the scheme. The Directors' Minutes never actually stated how the scheme progressed at Parliament, but it clearly failed to attract the necessary support. The annual meeting in May 1849 was forced into paying the accounts associated with the promotion of the scheme, as no government money was forthcoming. Despite the attempt at amalgamation, the Farraline Park school remained with the Bell's Trust until 1887, when amalgamation did take place with the Academy, although only for just over a year, at which point it was transferred to the control of the Burgh School Board.

The 1850 Mackintosh Farr Fund Bill
The Mackintosh Fund Trustees however decided to persevere with amalgamation with the Academy funds, and later that same year the Trustees gave notice of their intention to apply for an Act of Parliament to this end.[19] Cosmo Innes, an advocate, had reported favourably on the legal implications of such an amalgamation, although locally Allan MacLean (solicitor) lodged dissent from the proposals, to be followed by Dean of Guild Shaw, who was both an Academy Director and a Trustee of the Mackintosh Farr Fund. Part of this protest dealt with whether or not illegitimate sons of

the clan could benefit from the money.

The "Notice of Intention to apply for a Bill", dated 13th November 1849, was printed in various newspapers, and a 'war' started in Inverness between those who were fully in favour and a significant number of people mainly by the name of Mackintosh, but led by MacLean and Shaw, who were opposed. This debate was carried out through the local newspapers (the *Inverness Advertiser* had started publication by this date, following the demise of the *Inverness Journal* in early 1849), and also through memorials [= statements] and protests produced by both sides. A minister and a doctor, both of the name of Mackintosh, but living in the Aberdeen area, placed an advertisement in the newspapers seeking support for a campaign of opposition. This opposition led to a meeting which took place on 24th January in the Union Hotel in the Town, at which Alexander Mackintosh, a local baker and one of the first bursars on the fund, was appointed Chairman.

The meeting started about an hour late, due to an argument as to whether the meeting was a public one, or confined to interested parties. Speeches were made by MacLean, and by other prominent citizens, but there were none by the heads of the various parts of the clan, as they were generally in favour of the Bill. Another of the speakers was a John Mackintosh, the schoolmaster at Daviot. After a long debate, the meeting became a private one for about 60 people, and a series of motions opposing the Bill were passed, and these were then published in the local papers.[20]

MacLean protested to the Town Council, and this was answered by a document in the name of the Council.[21] MacLean, supported by Shaw, also raised the matter at the Academy Directors' meeting on 30th January. In general, the *Courier* supported the Bill, but the *Advertiser* changed sides as time went on, particularly with regard to the use of public money to finance the progress of the Bill. One of the *Courier's* editorial articles became an offprint or reprint, presumably at the request of The Mackintosh of Mackintosh, amongst whose papers it survives, as he supported the scheme.[22]

The Bill itself was drawn up by April 1850, and a loan of £500 was required to finance the legal costs, although MacLean once again opposed this, seconded by Mackintosh of Raigmore. A booklet was produced at about this time with the text of the Will, and chronicling the legal steps and pronouncements up to that date.[23] A petition was presented to the Town Council on 16th May, signed by a good number of members of the clan opposed to the proposed Bill.[24] However, Col. Mackintosh of Farr successfully moved a motion to let the Bill proceed, by 8 votes to 4 with one abstention.

In late July the proposed Bill, with some amendments, came before a House of Lords Committee consisting of the Earl of Shaftesbury, the Earl of Eglinton and Lord Colchester, and both Inverness newspapers employed special correspondents to record the debate.[25] Four days were used to examine the Bill, with cross-examination of witnesses from both sides of the argument. Various side issues got mixed up, including the issue over the two Deans of Guild and which of them was entitled to be the Academy Director (see below), and also an argument as to whether the Academy was in decline, through lack of finance. There was debate as to whether the sums of money claimed to be available were overstated. The main arguments presented against the Bill were that the members of the Clan Mackintosh would suffer, even with the safeguards which had been built in to maintain a proportion of the money for the sole use of supporting the bursars.

After a short adjournment, the Lordships really sealed the fate of the Bill by deciding:

1. The committee are of the opinion that no sum of money should be contributed out of the Mackintosh Farr Fund for the purposes of the Academy.

2. The committee are of the opinion that the clauses relating to the management, audit, and supervision, of the Mackintosh Farr Fund, and the admission of bursars, except in so far as such clauses direct any sum of money to be paid to the Directors of the Academy, should be allowed.

The meeting of the Committee was then adjourned until the following day for the promoters of the Bill to decide their course of action, but there was no option other than to withdraw the Bill and think again, as the main element of it had been rejected by the Law Lords.

The opponents of the Bill celebrated their success with a grand dinner at the start of September, with about 120 people present in the Union Hotel.[26] The Rev. Mr Clark, the First Minister of Inverness, and one of the people who had appeared before the House of Lords Committee, spoke for an hour and a half, claiming the defeat of the Bill was the triumph of right over wrong. There was disorder when one of the party tried to toast the Chief of the Clan Mackintosh, who was not present and did not support the opposition to the Bill. Some of those present refused to drink this toast and remained seated. The event lasted until midnight, but some of those present did not depart for a long while after that time!

The financial arguments over the expenses incurred by both sides rumbled on for many months.[27] The Law Lords had declined to apportion costs for the section of the Bill they refused to accept, which was the main part, and both sides had to find funds to pay their own costs. The new council elections in November brought about a change of position amongst the magistrates, with most of them now opposed to the move to amalgamate the funds. These new magistrates attempted to recover the money from the Mackintosh Farr funds, but by the time a bond had been drawn up to cover an overdraft from the bank, Col. Mackintosh of Farr had obtained an interdict to prevent any of the Fund being used for this purpose. Dr. William Welsh Forbes, one of those opposing the Bill who had travelled to London, was attacked for the size of his expenses claim, which he then attempted to justify in a letter to the

Courier. The arguments as to who would pay ended up in the Court of Session, when one of the judges was Lord Cockburn, who, only ten years or so earlier, had been helping select the Rector of the Academy. The final cost associated with the abortive Bill was over £1700, and this was not fully settled until August 1853 with a compromise on payments. Peace between the Academy Directors and the Mackintosh Farr Trustees was declared in March 1853, when the two sides held a joint dinner at the Muirtown Hotel, when "a very harmonious and social evening was passed".[28]

Additional bursars on the Fund were called for in August 1851, in an attempt to use some of the money now available, and further applications were invited in later years. From early 1852, the Trustees employed the Secretary of the Spalding Club, an Aberdeen-based club then actively involved with antiquarian matters and publishing old documents, to produce a family tree for the Mackintosh Clan. This had still not been completed in 1861, following at least one change in compiler, and at this point the Trustees decided the task was impossible and it had already cost them a fortune. No further work was to be done meantime, or seems ever to have been done.

There were no further legal moves until the Mackintosh Farr Fund Act was passed in 1862[29] which properly established the legal rights under which the Trustees could hold land, and also established the principle that anyone related to somebody who had benefited from the fund could then legitimately apply for assistance, even if, as was claimed, some of the earlier claims were from people who were not properly descended from the heads of the four families named in the original will (the illegitimate element mentioned above). This Bill produced only limited objections from a small number of members of the Clan, and these were in the end overruled in the House of Commons. The total cost of the measure was about £1200. The Trustees then appointed the Rector of the Academy to supervise the bursars, for which he received an annual fee of £15.

The argument over the Deans of Guild
The Academy Directors also got embroiled in another matter, although it was not really of its own making. Due to a change in the law, there were now two Deans of Guild in Inverness, one appointed by the Town Council, and the other appointed, as he traditionally had been, by the trade guilds themselves. Under the Academy Charter, the Dean of Guild was *ex officio* one of the Directors, so the question was: which Dean of Guild was entitled to the seat on the Board of Directors?

This situation had come about by consequence of the Burgh Reform Act of 1833, when there was a change in the law on the appointment of Deans of Guild, following the gentrification of the medieval guild system during the eighteenth and early nineteenth centuries. Both Deans of Guild had appeared at Directors' meetings for some years, and there had been motions against one or other of them taking part in votes, especially in 1836. A note of suspension and interdict was granted against the Dean of the Merchants' Guild in 1843,[30] although the Guildry had won an action of their own a couple of years previously. In the end the parties settled out of court, and the later Court of Session papers show the money that was wasted, such as legal expenses of £18 6 3d, and a tax of £7 10 1d, all of which had to be paid by the Academy.

The battle with the Town and County, and other financial issues
The serious shortage of funds, brought about by very few new subscriptions being obtained, and crises in the financial markets from time to time, caused the Directors to search for additional sources of funding. One possible source of money was the sale of the painting of *The Holy Family*, claimed to be by Sassoferrato, gifted by James Clark in his Will (Chapter 6). This matter was raised several times, with "Civis", who was a very active writer to the *Inverness Journal* at this point, claiming that if it was sold there would be no more bequests to the school. This controversy will be further dealt with in Chapter 13. Consideration was given to removing the salaries held by the English and commercial teachers (Johnson and Falconer), but it was decided not to act on this. A report by the Secretary for the annual meeting in May 1844 showed a projected deficit of £231 for the forthcoming year.

£600 of the £2000 financial bond with the Masons for their building (on the site which is now occupied by the Ramada Jarvis (Caledonian) Hotel) was paid up in 1841, with the balance to remain invested with the Masons on the security of the building until 1853. The final dividend due from the winding up of Lewis Cuthbert's estate at Castlehill was not paid until 1842, after a delay of almost 50 years. A bond on Fairfield estate was paid up in 1843, and offered up for loan. In the end the money was put into Bank of Scotland stock, as nobody could be induced to borrow it at a better rate of interest. The Directors even took issue with the newspaper proprietors with a view to a reduction in the cost of advertising of the examination report and prize list. In the same year, payment of a voluntary levy for Poor Relief was turned down on the grounds of the insufficiency of the Academy funds.

From late 1841, the Directors looked at the possibility of feuing part of the Academy Park, on the grounds that there was more than enough land for a playground – it should be remembered [see Figure 8.1] that the land purchased for the school building stretched into the area which today comprises the railway yards and part of the Longman industrial estate. The staff indicated that only one-third of the land was actually required as a playground. There were doubts as to whether feuing was legal, but Alexander Ross, who was later to make his mark as an architect of great significance in Inverness, prepared a plan in early 1843, and the tenant of the former Rector's house was warned that he might lose the tenancy. Further legal points were raised, and a sub-committee reported, with no decision being taken by the Directors. Once again the debate spilled over into the pages of the local newspapers. One letter from "Alumnus" was opposed to the feuing on the grounds that the Academy boys might resort to the streets and "mingle with boys of lower order, thereby getting their principles undermined and destroyed ...".[31]

As part of further proposals on feuing, it was suggested in 1852 to allow enough space for three staff houses, which would be rented by deduction of salary at 7% of the cost of building the houses. The great size of the Academy lands is shown by the fact that at one time a flock of sheep was kept on it, and they were put into a fank during playhours. In 1852, Sgt. Keith, the janitor, said he would not keep any more sheep and so did not need the fank, but he wanted extra garden land for growing potatoes, a request which was granted. Some land was offered for feu in 1858, but no offers were received, and this idea seems to have been dropped.

It had been discovered that the titles to the whole property had never been transferred from the key officials in the Council to the Academy Directors when the Charter had been granted in 1793, so the necessary conveyancing steps had to be put in place in 1845, although it was decided that infeftment (legal possession) was not required at this point. This did happen in two stages in 1855 and 1861, due to the taking over of parts of the Academy property for use by the railway company (Chapter 11).

However the key financial issues were about the grant previously paid by Inverness Burgh (as a continuation of the salaries paid to the former Grammar School teachers), and the payment which for many years had been voted annually by the Commissioners of Supply from County funds. The grant from the Town had last been paid in August 1833, just after the date when Gilzean had retired as Treasurer, but in 1843 the Directors raised the matter with the Town Council (some of these being the same people) with a view to the resumption of this payment. There was division in the ranks of the Council, and eventually a sub-committee was elected to meet with the Directors. Before long, however, the Directors issued a summons against the Council for the money.

By early 1845 it was decided to compromise, and it was agreed to restart payment at Whitsun 1845, with the arrears of £560 secured either by a heritable bond at 2% interest or by an appropriate annuity.[32] Even this agreement did not please some of the Directors. "Civis", the letter-writer, protested strongly against this settlement, using information in the 1834 report, written by Dr Nicol, to show that the doctor had changed sides over the matter, and was now the instigator of securing the money.[33] The writer went on to claim that the school fees were far too high, and a significant reduction would encourage far more pupils to attend, and so increase the income, without the need for the Town money. A week later there was a further letter from "Civis" on a related topic (see Chapter 11). The compromise finally passed the Directors on 31st January 1845, following a motion two weeks earlier proposed by Mackintosh of Farr, rather than Dr

Nicol who was also a member of the Council.

The grant by the Commissioners of Supply had ceased in 1822, and this was noted in May 1844, but the motion raised at a Commissioners' meeting by the Provost of Inverness was not allowed, as a financial matter like this should, the chairman ruled, have been dealt with earlier in the meeting. The Provost felt that if the Commissioners were annually appointing six Directors, they had a moral obligation to make payment. The County meeting in May 1846 did remit the matter to the finance committee to report in October, but nothing seems to have happened. In the following May the matter was raised again, but again no definite decision was taken, with the general view being that the grant should not be paid and that the Commissioners should cease to appoint Directors. The matter was raised yet again at the County meeting in 1847, but matters were taken no further, and the Commissioners of Supply continued making their annual appointments, without payment, right through to the change of management of the Academy in 1887.

Attempts were also made to attract funds from the Government, and these included in 1846 discussions with The Chisholm about holding a meeting in London with a view to asking for a grant from the Privy Council. It was soon clear that no money was likely to be forthcoming from this source, and an attempt was made to gain additional funds from new subscriptions. A small number were obtained, such as Mr Henry Baillie (yr.) of Tarradale, the M.P. for Inverness-shire, who paid his £50 in September 1847. It was even suggested that subscriptions could be paid by instalments, although no such payments seem to have been made. Negotiations over amalgamation with the Mackintosh Farr and the Dr. Bell's Trust funds, and the proposal to set up a college in Inverness, then took precedence over attempts to get extra subscriptions.

Fees were also a recurring problem, as it is clear from various evidence that the Academy's fees were amongst the highest, if not the highest, of similar schools in Scotland. A campaign had been waged through the local newspapers over a period of time that they should be reduced, but it was not until the start of 1845 that the Directors took the matter seriously. Bailie Allan Maclean dissented from one resolution, and demanded that all fees must be reduced, and that David Gray's successor as Rector (Chapter 11) should not be guaranteed any more than £80 in salary. However, Maclean did not find a seconder, nor did he find a seconder at that year's annual meeting when he raised a motion to reduce both the mathematics and geography class fees.

A sub-committee was appointed to review fees in 1849. In a report of the dinner which followed the prizegiving that year, the *Inverness Courier* claimed that the numbers of pupils had decreased, but James Steele, the Rector at that time, challenged this in a letter to the newspaper saying that he had checked the registers as far back as 1825, and numbers were currently at their highest, with any problems with the school not being the result of the high fees.[34] The level of fees was mentioned by several of those interviewed by the House of Lords Committee in the summer of 1850. In the end, fees were reduced and the new rates implemented from the start of the 1853-54 session.

Following the appointment of George Robertson as Rector in 1862, numbers attending the Academy did improve, bringing urgently-needed funds. Financial matters did not fully sort themselves out until 1887, when the Royal Commission which had introduced the Educational Endowments (Scotland) Act in 1882, finally produced the scheme for those endowments which related to Inverness Burgh and County (see Chapter 13). This brought together not just the Academy, the Mackintosh Farr and the Bell's Trust funds, but a range of other endowments that were then available locally. Even this settlement was far from simple, as at this point the Directors became aware of fraud by the then-deceased clerk to the Mackintosh Farr Trustees.

Chapter 11
The school itself in the financially lean years

Following the departure of Adam in 1839, the next decade or so brought about a more stable time as far as the staff and teaching were concerned, although the situation was more uncertain in the late 1850's, with many changes of staff. Some wise decisions on the appointment of Rectors helped considerably in this stability.

Replacing Adam as Rector

It is quite clear from the proceedings in Parliament in connection with the abortive 1850 Mackintosh Farr Parliamentary Bill that in 1839 the Directors were basically buying off Adam to get rid of him, and were eventually happy to pay almost any price. Roughly concurrent with his departure, the Directors introduced new Rules and Regulations,[1] which included the provision that all new staff (including the Rector) were to be appointed on a year by year basis, and could be dismissed for misconduct or inefficiency without any payment unless the Directors decided otherwise. These regulations also introduced the idea of a seven-person Standing (or Supervision) Committee to deal with the day-to-day running of the school.

To select the new Rector, the Directors invited Lords James Moncreiff and Henry Cockburn to choose the successful candidate, in this case from a short leet of four. The successful applicant was Professor David Gray, who had returned to Scotland having been Professor of Mathematics at King's College, Fredericton, New Brunswick. He was guaranteed a minimum income of £250 a year for his first two years (exclusive of the income from any popular lectures in the evenings for the public),[2] and £50 was spent on improving the apparatus, much of which was certainly still the items bought by James Weir. Gray's appointment turned out to be a very satisfactory one as we shall see. However, funds were at such a low level that in December 1841, Gray offered to forgo £40 of his guaranteed salary of £250, to bring it down to the level achieved by Adam in the 1830's, for which Gray was thanked by the Directors. At that point the Directors were still trying to sort out Adam's annuity.

At Gray's departure in 1845 the Directors used the same method to appoint Peter Wilson, who moved from being Professor of Mathematics at the Andersonian University, Glasgow (now the University of Strathclyde). Lord Cockburn, in his well-known book *Circuit Journeys,* shows a little of the operation of the leading citizens of Inverness in his account of Wilson's appointment:[3]

> On that next day (Wednesday the 16th *[April 1845]*) Moncreiff and I were honoured by a grand academic banquet. For above half a century Inverness has been so distracted by local dissension, that when the directors of their *Royal* Academy had to elect a Rector about seven years ago, the only thing they could agree upon was a resolution that they could agree about nothing, and therefore

they concurred in a request that we two would elect for them. We did so, and got a capital man, Mr Gray, who was promoted last spring to the Professorship of Natural Philosophy at Aberdeen. On this vacancy they found that they were as discordant as ever, and they had just the sense to repeat their application to us. We again acted, and think that we have got them another good Rector. For all which we were requested to inspect the school, which we did, and also to submit to be banqueted and complimented, which we did also. So at four we sat down at a long table, with other forty or fifty, in the museum *[main hall]* of the Academy. The table was gorgeous with cold meat and spring flowers, and there was no want of ice or champagne. The chairman of the directors drank us and the Queen. Moncreiff replied. I asked for a holiday for the boys. And at five it was all over. A very well managed affair.

Cockburn had a special interest in education, and was one of the figures behind the founding of the Edinburgh Academy, so he did have some idea what he was doing. There was criticism in the local press, in the form of the usual letter under a pseudonym, that the public were excluded from the visitation. The cost of the meal for 32 people was £21 6s, of which the Directors agreed to pay about half, and left the poor hotel proprietor to pursue the individual Directors for their personal contributions!

Gray's arrival as Rector soon led to a rapid improvement in the standard of education at the Academy, and the first examination report in the following July expressed great satisfaction with his work.[4] Very little appears in the minutes about Gray, presumably as there were no crises of the type that had beset Adam's time as Rector. In July 1841, the *Inverness Courier* comments on the "greatly increased efficiency" of the school, and some months later they were again full of praise:[5]

INVERNESS ACADEMY PUPILS. – We have had frequent occasion of late to speak of the good name and success which our Northern seminary has been earning for itself in our immediate neighbourhood. We have this week recorded some very pleasing facts, which show that its fame is outstanding to a distance, through the character and attainment of its pupils. We have given, as usual, to-day, the names of the successful competitors for the bursaries annually granted at King's College, Aberdeen, after a very strict examination; and, it will be observed, that *no less than four bursaries* have been carried off by pupils of the Inverness Academy, three of them having been gained by boys who have just left the Academy classes. This success of the Inverness pupils, which we believe to be unprecedented, is highly honourable, and must be gratifying both to pupils and masters; and we earnestly trust that our institution will long retain the useful character it is now assuming.

In this bursary list, in fourth place, appeared Alexander Penrose Hay, who, later in the 19th century, was to become Inverness Town Chamberlain, and the Secretary and Treasurer of the Academy Directors.

Gray obviously introduced, or persuaded the Directors to introduce, changes. One of these was to invite academics to conduct the annual exam, rather than using the local ministers and others. Another was updating the curriculum of the classes he taught. In 1844 the report of the examinations included a brief outline of his syllabus:

• Geography Class: geography, astronomy, physical and political

geography (the textbook used was Thomson's *Geography*)
- Junior maths: geometry and algebra
- Senior mathematics: revision, plane trigonometry, geometry of solids; spherical trigonometry
- Senior mathematics advanced (first year of this course): theory of equations, more trigonometry, analytical geometry, differential calculus
- Natural philosophy: hydrostatics, pneumatics, heat

The following year Gray resigned to take up the appointment of Professor of Natural Philosophy at Marischal College in Aberdeen. The Academy supervision committee expressed very high satisfaction with his work, and claimed that the school had risen in public esteem after his appointment.[6] A dinner was held in the Caledonian Hotel to mark his departure, at which Sherif Colquhoun, the Chairman of the Directors since 1841, was the main speaker.[7] (Peter Wilson, who had by this time arrived in Inverness and was present at the dinner, was also toasted.) Gray had married in early January 1842 in Edinburgh, and had at least one child, a son, born in September 1843. He worked in Aberdeen until his death in February 1856, at the relatively early age of 45, from gastric fever and diarrhoea.

In a letter to the *Inverness Courier*, "Civis" suggested to the Directors that Cockburn and Moncreiff be invited to nominate Gray's successor, and, apparently fairly seriously, suggested that Dr Nicol, who was interested in the subject, should use phrenology (the study of the shape of the brain) to select the best candidate.[8] Peter Wilson was appointed in April 1845, but he was only offered a guaranteed minimum salary of £200 in his first year. It is virtually impossible to establish exactly what either Gray or Wilson earned, as so much of their emoluments was made up from fees which they collected directly from the pupils. Wilson took a house in Ness Bank, in which he took boarders. Promptly after his arrival, he opened a class in geography and astronomy for young ladies. By the autumn he was offering lectures for adults on the atmosphere, and a class was opened in the school for practical mathematics and engineering. Electromagnetism appeared for the first time in the classwork. Also introduced in 1847 was a ladies' class for "Readings in Science".

Wilson's tenure as Rector of the Academy lasted just over two years, at which point he returned to Glasgow, before becoming Rector of Tain Academy and rescuing that school from decline. He died in 1854, also at the relatively early age of 48, of inflammation of the brain. So both Wilson and Gray died within two years of each other.

The other staff in the 1840's
Peter Scott, who had joined the staff in 1824 as teacher of classics, continued to serve the school right through this period, and finally became Rector after James Steele and Robert Harper had served their terms. Scott too took in boarders from amongst the pupils, but was nearly lost to

Inverness when he applied firstly for the Rectorship of Perth Academy in 1829,[9] and later, in 1843, for a mastership at the High School of Edinburgh.[10] The English classes continued to be taught by George Johnson who had been appointed during Adam's tenure as Rector. He remained in post until the autumn of 1851, when he was allowed to retire on an annual pension of £37, at the time that Robert Harper was appointed as Rector. This was agreed despite Bailie Maclean objecting on financial grounds and the grounds that Johnson was still able and fit to teach.

James Falconer continued to serve as commercial teacher, that is teaching basic arithmetic and book-keeping skills, but he was ill for part of 1840. However his work at this stage seems to have satisfied the Directors. His class numbers had increased from less than 20 in 1833 to 146 in 1843, and so he then asked for an assistant. At the meeting on 7th July where this was discussed[11] a motion was brought forward that his services should be dispensed with as he had had a letter published in the *Inverness Journal* which had displeased the Directors. The letter itself is not available, as no copy of the *Journal* for 1843 survives in Inverness for consultation today. The letter was published after he had waited five weeks for a reply to the request he had sent to the Directors. The Directors seemed able to react rapidly when their authority was questioned, but not at other times.

Accusations were bandied about, concerning his claimed excessive absence (which turned out to be four days in the previous session), employing assistants without authority, and inflicting corporal punishment without reference to the Rector. The following day there was a row at the adjourned Directors' Meeting, and the sub-committee who had prepared a report on the matter all resigned. This meeting included further arguments about which Dean of Guild was entitled to vote, and if the Chairman had a casting vote, but in the end Falconer was only reprimanded and cautioned. However, the magistrates who were *ex officio* Directors of the Academy had their own meeting at which they passed several resolutions, some critical of Colquhoun, the Chairman, and matters began to calm down. At a meeting on the 22nd July, there were further resignations from the supervision committee which the meeting refused to accept, and the same people were then promptly re-elected. In the end the matter seems to have been swept under the carpet, as several of the accusations seem to have been grossly exaggerated.

The matter seems to have been quickly forgotten, as in the 1844 annual report, the examiners were "more than satisfied; we were positively delighted" with Falconer's work. It was Falconer who replied to the toast of "The Teachers of the Academy" at the dinner for the departure of Prof. Gray, and in November 1847 he called a meeting of all teachers in and around Inverness, which led to the formation of a local branch of the recently-established Educational Institute of Scotland (the EIS), a major teachers' organisation which is still very active today. He continued teaching in the

Academy until the end of 1863, at times with classes even greater than 146, although he did propose to retire in 1852, perhaps through a health problem. An issue over his disciplining of a girl also occupied the Directors in the summer of 1853. He was again ill for part of 1855, but was only allowed to take leave of absence if he found his own substitute.

Appointed at the same time as Gray was a Pole by the name of Proszkowski (although alternative spellings exist), to teach French and German. He seems to have been something of a character, and Isabel Anderson says about him:[12]

> A Pole of the name of Proszkowski at one time taught languages in the Academy, and was such an eccentric character that he was the source of never-ending amusement to his pupils. Some of them, indeed, made game of him to his face, and his name came to be corrupted first into "Prince o' Whisky", and latterly into "Cask o' Whisky", by which they not only designated him when absent, but boldly saluted him when called up to repeat their lessons in school.

In the early days he seems to have been appointed without salary, simply receiving the class fees, but even in his first session the Directors agreed to give him a donation of £20, as they were very satisfied with his work. In the following years he received £30. He remained on the staff until 1844, when his pupils presented him with a silver stuff-box, and others gave him a purse of sovereigns to the value of 40 guineas [£42], which is more than the annual grants he had received (exclusive of class fees) in lieu of salary. He gave as his reason for leaving that he wished to see his child.[13] Peter Scott once again taught French without salary until the appointment of Donald Mackenzie in 1846 without salary, as the Directors were trying, without success, to find someone who could teach both French and drawing.

The janitor, Thomas Urquhart, was on a yearly contract, and he was persuaded to depart in August 1842, so that a new person could be employed who would superintend in the playground and teach gymnastics, at a guaranteed minimum income of £20 a year. This dismissal brought a furious letter in the *Inverness Journal*,[14] as Urquhart had been employed by the school for sixteen years and was currently the assistant Psalmodist in the (Old) High Church. His wife had died in 1840, and there was a large family. The letter writer, "A Parent", claimed that the person to be employed was a pensioner of diminutive stature who had earned a living selling or circulating newspapers in Edinburgh (and by implication was not a suitable person for this job). In contrast with the modern attitude, the writer clearly had little time for gymnastics:

> Many parents have insuperable objections to gymnastics, as from their violence and excitement, they have often proved fatal to young persons, and prefer the equally effectual and safer games of bowls, fives, shinty, etc.

James Brown was appointed as the replacement janitor, although nothing is recorded about his teaching of gymnastics. He stayed in post until May 1850, when he was commended for his work. Having taken a public-house licence he was not thought suitable for further employment as a janitor. His successor was Sgt. John Keith, elected from a leet of sixteen.

School Life in the 1840's and early 1850's

If the information in the Directors' Minutes Book about the staff is fairly limited, information about the school life is relatively plentiful in the pages of the local newspapers and books of the time. Pupil enrolments in session 1841-42 were about 170, of whom about 160 were attending at the time of the annual meeting in May. By May 1845 enrolments had reached 224, of whom 194 were attending. The following year the figures were 251 and 217, and numbers stayed at around these figures until about 1850, when they started to fall off again, reaching a low of 151 in 1853.[15] It seems that the higher classes were often the best supported, probably as there was no other institution locally that could provide such courses, unlike the courses in the more elementary branches of education.

From early 1841 it was decided that pupils' addresses should be recorded, and if there were no natural guardians the Directors said they would direct where a pupil was to stay to ensure his proper education. Unfortunately the registers where this information would have been recorded have not survived, or were never compiled, for the years before 1862.

At this period there is the beginning of a move to educate the 'young ladies' separately from the boys,[16] which was to bring about the opening of a separate "Ladies' Institution" in 1865. From autumn 1846 this separation amounted to girls' classes being regarded as private classes, rather than part of the course of instruction provided by the school. The idea of introducing a sort of timetable – the 'hour system' of tuition – was raised by staff in April 1847, and got the support of the Directors. This involved the teacher having in class only those he was currently teaching. The other pupils would be set work the previous day, to be completed by the time of the lesson. When first mooted, Johnson (English) dissented from this idea, but within a month he gave his approval to the scheme.

A decision was taken to alter the summer holidays so that, from summer 1848 the school was to close at the end of June, reopening some six or seven weeks later. For some reason this did not happen, and the summer holiday continued to start in mid or late July for the next twelve years. From the appointment of Robert Harper as Rector in 1851 he was required to examine the classes on Saturday mornings, instead of the two hours' holiday on that day. In return, Wednesday was to become a half day.

John Fraser, in his *Reminiscences of Inverness*, records one event of significance in the life of the school in February 1840:[17]

> We will now enter the Royal Academy Park. These young people you see romping about are the pupils, it being their noon play hour. You will observe that they seem highly elated today, the reason being, as I happen to know, that they have just received a letter from the Marquis of Normandy in acknowledgement of their letter to the young Queen *[Victoria]* on the occasion of her marriage. The epistle was

signed in the name of the scholars by Masters A. Penrose Hay and Angus B. Reach *[son of the Academy Treasurer]*. You take my word, many of these bright youths will yet make their mark in their country's history.

Graffiti artists amongst the pupils were nothing new in the 1840's. Following a report that James Steele, the Rector at the time, was unable to trace the culprits who had been writing on the walls of the school, the Directors decided that:[18]

> ... the Teachers shall assemble their classes this day and intimate to them that any of the boys who confess having been guilty of this practice will be forgiven on condition of their not repeating the offence and having the walls whitewashed at their own expense, but should no confession or discovery be made in this way the meeting instruct the Rector and Teachers as a punishment to insist on the students attending their classes on Saturdays as well as on the other week days.

In March 1849 three boys were suspended, although the offence has not been recorded. The Directors supported the suspension, but agreed that the boys could be reinstated if they apologised.[19] In neither case has the result of the disciplinary action been recorded. This second incident did lead to changes in the rules on discipline, with the Rector and staff being given authority to suspend pupils, as long as a report was made to the Chairman of the Supervision Committee with the least possible delay. The Directors could then expel, if thought appropriate. Corporal punishment was also authorised if administered the following day.

During most of the 1840's an Academy ball was held every Christmas, and surplus funds were in some years paid to the Northern Infirmary fund. One newspaper report reads:[20]

> ACADEMY BALL. – The annual ball given by students of the Academy to the inhabitants of the town, took place in the Northern Meeting Rooms, on Thursday evening. This is, generally, one of the best attended assemblies of the kind that the place produces: but the present had never been surpassed on any former occasion. Indeed, the brilliant assemblage of youth and beauty that the scene presented we have seldom seen equalled; and the unalloyed pleasure and satisfaction that seemed to reign on all hands was evinced by none more than the youthful hosts themselves, who were thickly scattered throughout the ball-room, and whose behaviour and arrangements met with the warmest expressions of approval. ... We ought to add that Mr Scott, the classical teacher, was, as usual, master of the ceremonies, and kept his numerous groups in excellent order.

The 1845 event is reported to have gone on from 8 p.m. until after 4 a.m.! The ball did not seem to find favour with Steele, and after his first year in post it does not seem to have taken place. In session 1851-52, under Robert Harper's rectorship, it was announced that the event would be held on the Queen's birthday, but there is no report that this happened.

The orations, at the end of the examinations in July, still proved very popular, although in 1841 it was agreed to dispense with the services of a band for the event, which had cost 1 guinea [£1 1s] that year. The orations seem to have ceased after 1842, but the Directors were before long keen to restart this event, perhaps due to the publicity which the school gained from it. It seems also to have been a major social event for the ladies of the Town. The orations restarted in 1850, with music provided by the band of the 13th Regiment from Fort George.

Original programmes from 1851 and 1853 survive [see Figure 9.3], with the details of the recitations in various other years recorded in the prizegiving reports in the *Inverness Courier*. The 1853 event included vocal music for the first time, finishing with a solo rendering of *Rule Britannia*. Two of those giving orations that year seem, judging by their names, to have been the sons of members of staff. Adults who were not parents were asked to pay for admission in 1859, but there were no orations in 1860 and 1862, with only a limited programme from some younger pupils in 1861.

In 1852 there is mention for the first time of printed papers for the mathematics examinations, to be externally marked. This was the end of Harper's first year, and presumably was being done as one of the changes he was introducing. Nevertheless there is mention in the local newspapers of a large attendance of the public at the examinations, perhaps due to the staff changes the previous summer, so the other subjects seem to have retained the oral examinations which had taken place annually since the school was set up.

The examinations, orations and prizegiving were at first followed by a dinner. The Directors did at least save money for the Academy by paying for their own meal at 7s. each, but they paid from Academy funds the cost of the meals for the staff and for those who had conducted the examinations. This dinner was probably the only 'perk' which the staff were granted in the year. In 1846 it was decided not to pay for guests in future years, a decision that seems to have been overturned or ignored soon afterwards.

It was also decided in 1841, after some previous complaints, that the Raigmore Medal would be given alternately for mathematics and classics. Following Raigmore's death in January 1846 at the age of 74, there was concern that the medal would lapse, but when the Directors started to enquire from Raigmore's son, the estate factor assured them that the son had already given orders for the medals to be made. Other prizes were purchased from money allowed by the Directors, which round about 1850 was normally £8 a year, but later reduced. In the hope that subscriptions could be obtained to cover the costs of the prizes the Directors decided not to pay this sum after the 1851 prizegiving. Alex. Matheson of Ardross, the local County M.P., did agree to donate three guineas [£3 3s] annually for a prize, which later became a medal, but other subscriptions were not forthcoming and the money from Academy funds was restored for the 1852 ceremony. In 1853, both Matheson and the Inverness Burghs M.P., Henry Baillie, donated money for prizes for, respectively, an English essay and an English narrative illustrating geographical knowledge.

The gold medal winner in 1851, was Hugh Clark who later became a

Surgeon in the Bengal Army. Whilst in India he collected plants, and his herbarium is now to be found in Inverness Museum. Sadly Clark died at the early age of about 40 in 1876. During his time in the school, he was probably awarded more prizes than any previous pupil had been given.

Another series of items which have survived the years are three school notebooks of an Alexander Mackintosh of Farr, son of Col. Mackintosh who preserved the Nimmo sketch. Dating from 1852 or later, these volumes are in the Highland Folk Museum collection.[21] Two are for classics and largely English history (the history of Edward I and II and the Crusades, including Edward's involvement in deciding between Robert Bruce and John Balliol as King of Scotland); the third is of drawings, including a sketch of *Raigmore*, one of the two original Inverness railway engines [Figure 11.1], dating from late 1855 or perhaps 1856 when the railway opened. Alexander died in 1853, aged 14, and so it may have been drawn by another member of the family.

Various items were gifted to the school and to the museum (which was still housed in the Academy hall). In 1841 Falconer of Lentran gifted what was thought to be two, but turned out to be three, drawings of fortifications drawn by his son (a former pupil) who had fallen at the Fort of Kudjuck in Upper Scinde, India, earlier that year. A collection of coins, which were Treasure Trove from various sites around Scotland, were added to the Museum in April 1847, but in 1861 some of the coins had been given to a jeweller as they could easily be shaken out of the box. The coins were recovered and a new lock was fitted to the box.

The Rectors and other staff from around 1850

Following Wilson's departure in the summer of 1847, the Directors decided to appoint James Steele, who was at that point the Rector of the Bell's Institution in Inverness. Clearly he was known locally and this affected their decision to appoint immediately, rather than advertise the job more widely. His appointment was subject to the 1840 regulations of an appointment on a year by year basis. The salary was to be £100 exclusive of fees. Steele's appointment may well have been a ploy to ease the proposed amalgamation with the Bell's Trust fund, as the plans for this (mentioned in Chapter 10) were drawn up the following spring.

Within months there were problems as Steele had an involvement with a business partner in a boarding school at Stoneyfield (on the edge of the Town), from which he could not immediately withdraw. Steele's explanations apparently satisfied the Directors as long as his teaching in this school ended by 1st July of the following year. He was thereafter not allowed to advertise a general arithmetic class which would interfere in any way with Falconer's arithmetic class. There was a further issue in November 1849 about some comments Steele had made, following which he had made some form of verbal apology. He was interviewed and the results of this meeting were not regarded as satisfactory. The Directors agreed to terminate his employment the following May unless the "absurd and ungentlemanly" epithets were withdrawn.

His appointment was discussed in January 1850,[22] but under the heading of the results of the proposed Mackintosh Farr Bill, which would require him not to be re-employed. An amendment, with two dissentions, did allow him to continue in employment until the end of the session. In the end, the withdrawal of the Bill allowed Steele to be re-employed for a further year, and whatever had upset the Directors the previous November seems to have been forgotten about. Steele submitted his own resignation in May 1851, to take effect from the end of the session.

Isabel Anderson has provided some comments on Steele:[23]

[Mr Steel [sic]] was considered to teach geography in a more masterly, enthusiastic manner than it had been taught in Inverness before. His geographical class for young ladies was a very large one, and all of them, from the youngest to the oldest, were eager pupils, and looked forward to the daily lesson as a great treat. During the earlier period of Mr Steel's connection with the Academy, he taught mathematics to several girls, together with the boys, and there were two young ladies of powerful abilities who so distinguished themselves as mathematicians that either of them was considered to have a higher claim to the gold medal than any of the boys. It was Mr Steel's wish that it should be bestowed on one of them, but there was an idea among the powers in authority that it should be awarded only to one of the sterner sex, and so, to the Rector's disappointment, the honour was not permitted to be the portion of either of the young ladies.

Soon after this Steele was studying medicine, before practising in Wishaw, near Glasgow.

The appointment as Rector of Peter Scott, already on the staff and well-known for his many years of service to the school, was suggested as soon as Steele had intimated his resignation, but matters were held over for some weeks. Following advertisements in *The Times*, *The North British Advertiser* and *The Edinburgh Advertiser* twenty-one people applied. One of the applicants was Peter Wilson, the previous Rector, but his application was withdrawn when the Directors of Tain Academy increased his salary and persuaded him to remain there. Consideration of the Inverness appointment was further delayed following an argument over whether the notice calling the meeting gave enough information that the election of a Rector was to take place.[24]

Scott was not appointed as Rector for another two years. The new Rector was Robert Harper who had studied at Corpus Christi College, Cambridge, where he gained a B.A. in 1850 as 15th Wrangler (an Honours grading), before becoming an assistant tutor at Putney College. Bailie Maclean dissented from Harper's appointment on the grounds he was only 27 at the time of election.[25] Having failed to advertise the post correctly in terms of their bye-laws, it was decided to appoint him at the pleasure of the Directors, rather than for three years. The matter was to be raised the following May at the Annual Meeting, but at that time he was only reappointed for a further year. At the Directors' meeting following his appointment, it was agreed that Harper would appoint his own assistant for the "minor branches" of English, and this would allow Johnson to retire. This person would get no salary, simply the class fees. Harper appointed John Scott Hoppett, who seems to have been his friend. For over nine years he had been a classics and mathematics teacher at Failand Lodge School near Bristol.

From the middle of the 1840's the Directors had been trying to find a teacher qualified to teach both French and drawing, but no such person could be found. Some temporary staff were allowed to teach in the Academy without salary for a while, including, for drawing, Alexander MacInnes, who had carried out repairs to the painting of the *Holy Family* for the Directors. Finally James Glen was appointed in 1845. He served until 1851, resigning to return to Glasgow. The replacement was someone whose work is still known today, P. A. Jastrzebski (with various spellings), who had worked on line drawings of Pictish Stones in Angus.[26] Alexander Mackintosh, whose drawing book was mentioned above, must have been one of Jastrzebski's pupils, as the book is dated 1852, although apparently with material added later.

After just over a year Jastrzebski left and Glen was persuaded to return to his old job, again without a salary, which he did not get paid until 1863. Sadly soon after this he became ill, then infirm, and a temporary teacher had to take over. Again Isabel Anderson comments on him:[27]

> At a later date than Mr Hamilton, Mr James Glen was drawing master in the Academy, and also had a private class at his lodgings, on Church Street. He was devoted to his art, and his good nature and patience were proverbial. His pupils have erected a monument at Tomnahurich to the memory of this shy, gentle, and single-minded little man.

The John Guy Hamilton mentioned here seems to have been one of the temporary staff, as his name only appears in Adam's 1835 staff list. He was without any fingers or toes, and his pencil or brush had to be strapped to the stump which served as his thumb, but this apparently did not affect his art in any way, and he is reputed to have produced beautiful views of local scenery.

Heinrich Schaefer (in various spellings) came to teach French and German from Musselburgh Academy at the start of the 1851-52 session, at a salary of £20 annually for three years. Mackenzie's unsalaried services were dispensed with after about five years, and he moved his classes to another school in the Town. Like Jastrzebski, Schaefer stayed in Inverness only until the autumn of 1852, when he moved to Perth Academy.

As a result of all these changes, the staff at the start of the 1851-52 session, when Harper took up his appointment, was very different from the previous session, with Peter Scott (classics) and James Falconer (book-keeping) the only teachers who continued to serve the school.

Harper only stayed in Inverness for just over eighteen months, before moving to Dudley Grammar School, near Birmingham, as second master, rising during 1854 to be headmaster. His friend, Hoppett, followed him there at the end of summer 1854, to take over as second master. As Hoppett did not have a salary in Inverness, receiving only class fees, it is likely that there was a considerable financial inducement in this move. One legacy which Harper did leave in Inverness was the establishment of a school cricket club, for which he sought, after his departure, his personal expenses of nearly £10. The Directors refused this on the grounds that they were not liable for these expenses after his resignation. This is the first specific mention in the Directors' Minutes of sport for the pupils.

Shortly after he left, Harper asked for a testimonial, which was not granted, although a copy of this minute was sent to him:[28]

> The Directors of the Inverness Royal Academy considered themselves fortunate in being offered the services of Mr Robert Harper who had obtained so distinguished a place on the Mathematical tripos at Cambridge at taking his degree. Mr Harper entered upon the duties of Rector of the Academy, and applied himself with earnestness to efforts for the amendment of the curriculum. Mr Harper had been accustomed to scholastic forms not in practice in this part of the country, and having received the offer of an appointment at Dudley of greater value, and otherwise more in accordance with his views in life, he had not an opportunity of sufficiently testing in this Academy his mode of teaching, of which the Directors had formed high anticipations from Mr Harper's previous character. Mr Harper even during his short occupation of office had secured the kind feeling and affection of his pupils, and the personal regards of the Directors.

Peter Scott as Rector, and his staff

Peter Scott, a member of staff since 1824, was appointed without any advertisement as Harper's replacement, the post for which he had been suggested eighteen months earlier. As a result, the Rector was a classics teacher for the first time in the Academy's history, as all the previous nine appointees had been, at least in part, mathematics or science teachers. Scott is also the first Rector of whom we have a photograph [Figure 11.2].

His salary as Rector was 50 guineas [£52 10s], but his Rector's appointment was on a year to year basis whilst he still held his classics job *ad vitam aut culpam* (= for life if not guilty). He would also have to continue to teach French until the end of the session, as Schaefer had not been replaced. Scott was sufficiently popular that on his appointment it was decided to hold a public dinner in his honour. This took place on 22nd February 1853 in the Caledonian Hotel. The *Inverness Courier* reported on the event and the associated speeches, including one by Colquhoun, the Chairman. The report ran over nearly three columns of the paper.[29] Scott continued to provide boarding for some pupils.

The examination report at the end of Scott's first year as Rector is fuller than many of the previous ones, and from it we can get a good view of the whole curriculum of the school [Table 11.1]. It is interesting to note that one of the examiners that year was Bishop Robert Eden, who had come to Inverness from Essex, after his appointment as Bishop of Moray and Ross in the Scottish Episcopal Church in 1851. He was to figure in the early 1860's as an important spokesman for educational change in the Academy.

Rector's class: Phœdrus, Caesar, Ovid, Virgil, Horace, Livy, Xenophon
   (*Anabasis*), Demosthenes (two speeches), 20th book of the *Iliad*
Rector's French class: Molière and Racine
Mathematics: highest class: algebra (simple and quadratic equations, arithmetical
   and geometrical progression), Books 1-6, 11 and 12 of Euclid, about 50
   propositions from statics;
2nd class on 5 books;
junior class on 1st book (but had read 2nd and 3rd books)
Geography: mathematical, physical and local, including solar system, earth,
   moon, atmosphere, day and night, seasons, earth's surface, proportion and
   configuration of land and water, tides, currents, principles of climate, winds,
   clouds, rains, hail and snow, dew and fog, races of men, religions, governments,
   education, distributions of animals and plants, elements of geology, Europe
   more particularly, England, Scotland and Ireland minutely
English literature: more advanced: historical, social and literary views of the
   different ages and periods from Anglo-Saxon to modern times
Commercial class: writing, a complete course in arithmetic and book-keeping
English class: two senior classes: histories of England and Scotland, elocution,
   grammar (syntax, prosody, parsing);
third class: elementary history and grammar;
fourth class: reading and spelling
Drawing class: specimens in crayons and water colours

Table 11.1: The 1853 Curriculum (from *Directors' Minutes*, 25th July 1853)

At the same time as Scott was appointed as Rector, John Mackay, a native of Inverness, was appointed to fill the mathematics post vacated by Harper, and he was also to teach geography, on a salary of £35 excluding fees. Mackay also got permission to erect a "gymnastic establishment" at a cost not exceeding £5, in which he would personally superintend exercises. He resigned in the summer of 1855, to continue his studies, to be replaced in September 1855 by Rev. Gordon Lillie of Aberdeen, a person who was strongly recommended by Gray (the former Rector), now at Marischal College in that city. Only five months later Lillie was to write his former professor's obituary in the *Inverness Courier*.[30] He continued in post until the end of the 1861-62 session, when he took up an appointment with the Colonial Committee of the Church of Scotland in Demerara (now part of Guyana in South America). In turn he was replaced by William Eadie, who was later to become Rector.

Hoppett's replacement as English teacher in autumn 1854 was David Hay from Madras College, St. Andrews, but he only stayed until November 1857, when he resigned for a ministry in the United Presbyterian Church, dying very soon thereafter. His replacement was George Leslie, who took up his appointment around the start of 1858. He too only stayed in post until March 1860 when he resigned to take up an appointment as Headmaster of an Academy in Glasgow. An interim appointment followed until the appointment of Dr. John Patterson, who had been Principal and Headmaster of Malta Protestant College, but was at that time living in Glasgow. After he arrived in Inverness, Patterson advertised heavily for boarders, as well as offering private lessons in French, German and Italian. Patterson became unwell with a pulmonary illness in December 1861, and had to resign early the following year, with an interim appointment to cover the classes.

A Professor Karl Fröbel, who was then living in Foyers, took over German teaching without a salary in the early summer of 1853, but no appointment was then made for French. Fröbel also held private French, German and mathematics classes, and the *Inverness Courier* reported that his wife would take conversation classes for young ladies.[31] He did take over the French teaching in the Academy after the summer holiday, assisted by his wife, and remained in post until April 1859. A Mrs Ollendorf took over languages teaching that autumn, the first time the Academy had employed a woman, other than the assistance from Mrs Fröbel.

School life under Scott

An early event of Scott's time as Rector was the establishment of a singing class, in which over seventy were enrolled by the time of one press report, and another report says about 50 were attending an evening class in vocal music and about half of that number were taking instrumental instruction. Herr Fröbel seems to have been not only a linguist, but able to teach the singing class. He also opened an evening class in psalmody in the spring of 1855.

Scott restarted the Academy Ball at Christmas 1853, but now in the Academy's own hall. The event brought another glowing report from the editor of the *Inverness Courier* about the pleasantness of the evening.[32] The report concludes:

> One of the adjoining classrooms, adorned with the drawings of Mr Glen's pupils, was converted into a lounging-room, and in the other Mr Macdonald of the Peacock spread his choicest Christmas stores. The Hall itself was decorated with evergreens and well lighted, one of the chandeliers being of a somewhat novel character – a deer's head with jets of gas springing from its horns, a contrivance made by Mr T. Mackenzie, brassfounder here. The orchestra was under the conduct of Mr Moir, and was very efficient.

In the session 1854-55, the ball was held early in the New Year, with attendance from officers of the 80th Regiment, then stationed at Fort George, having recently returned from India. From the 1856-57 session the ball was held after the orations in July. By this point the Directors' dinner had been discontinued.

A new activity in 1854 was a school outing on the Queen's birthday. The school hired a tug-boat on the Caledonian Canal and about 100 pupils, with staff and some parents, sailed to Fort Augustus, where the fort was examined and a picnic held.

> In the open square within the fort the young folks struck up a dance, and before quitting the place they sung the National Anthem very cordially and harmoniously together.

The singing class also performed some national songs.[33]

On the corresponding day in 1855:[34]

> ... all the pupils of the Royal Academy, accompanied by the Rector and masters, held a "pic-nic" among the woods and rocks above the romantic little village of Kilmuir *[in the Black Isle]*.

A less passive schoolboy activity was reported the following January:[35]

> **School Boy Battles.** – The boys attending the Royal Academy and the Farraline Park Institution have been resuming their snow-ball feuds since the fall of snow. Yesterday they had a pitched battle in the Academy Park – the boys of Bell's School having stormed the walls and carried the war to the very gates of the Academy. The times are surely changed; in days of yore, the Academy boys were more than a match for all the schools in the town put together! On this occasion the police made a timely interference.

The 1854 prizegiving had an award of two silver medals paid for by Old Boys of the school, which were awarded in drawing and music; the Burgh M.P.'s prize was awarded for a written description of the USA, whereas the County Member's prize was for an essay, to be handed in after the holiday, on the poet Cowper. The two leading pupils in classics were so close that an extra test had to be set to these two pupils before the award of the Raigmore medal.

The supervision committee which had operated since 1840, to deal with the general running of the school, was scrapped in 1855, with a decision to hold quarterly meetings, and additional meetings as required.[36] A visitation committee seems however to have been retained. At the same meeting the summer holiday was changed to start even later in July, with school resuming on the "first lawful day after 22nd September", i.e. not on a Sunday. This was to allow for the Northern Meeting, the major social event of the year in Inverness, to be concluded, before school reopened.

An unusual disciplinary matter was dealt with at the annual meeting in 1857.[37] Four pupils had been suspended a couple of weeks earlier. One of the fathers, who was a solicitor, complained that his son had been bullied, but after enquiry the Directors concluded that the charges were theft and association with prostitutes in a brothel. Amongst the witnesses was the Superintendent of Police. The result of the enquiry showed that the instigator was actually the solicitor's son. He and three others were not to be readmitted to the school, and a fifth boy, who had been inveigled into the brothel, would be readmitted after suitable contrition. Two of those expelled were bursars on the Mackintosh Farr Fund, and the Trustees were informed.

The timing of the summer holiday was changed yet again in 1860 when the exams were moved to the Thursday and Friday before the fast day preparatory to the summer communion. This meant that the holiday now started in late June, and the school reopened about the second week in August, six weeks after the closing date.

The buildings, the land and the Charter
Some small work was done in the early 1840's to upgrade the main Academy building, with minor repairs to water spouts and chimney heads. A water closet for the girls was built in the summer of 1847. Roof repairs and repairs to gates, the girls' WC and to the janitor's house were required in the summer of 1850. The flagstones of the staircase passage or lobby were repaired at the end of 1850, but, as was the case for most other repairs, with the comment "at the lowest possible expense". In 1853 Peter Scott was allowed up to £10 for new desks and for a stove. Further repairs, as required with any building, were carried out over the subsequent years, although it was clear that the building was beginning to show its age.

The Academy still owned the house that had been vacated by Adam in the 1830's, and various repairs had to be carried out on it. In 1850 the tenant offered to build a garden dyke at his own expense, as long as he was reimbursed if he did not remain as tenant for the following twelve years. The matter was handed to the supervision committee to report, but the result is not known. More repairs were required during the 1850's, until the house was demolished during the railway developments in the early 1860's. The other house which the Directors owned was that for the janitor, and gas was installed in this house in 1855. This eventually passed into railway ownership, with the Academy renting it back in and after 1862.

Classroom equipment needed to be replaced in 1856, with a new globe, and maps of the Classical world and of Britain. Repairs were needed to the science apparatus. A request from Hay (English) for a new blackboard was delayed, and there is no evidence that it was ever provided. Following the death in Aberdeen of Gray, the former Rector, his philosophical (scientific) apparatus was offered for sale, and the Directors agreed to spend £15, with the Mechanics Institute paying the lion's share of the cost.

The very large numbers in the English class meant that classes were held in the hall, but an attempt to modify the official classroom in 1859 was rejected by the tradesman on the grounds of safety, presumably of a structural type. In the following year a scheme was worked out. That same year a letter from a parent complained about the lack of WCs for pupils, and the filthy state of the privies. This matter was held over until negotiations with the railway company were complete, but the janitor was ordered to keep them as clean as possible.

Coal money had for many years been collected from the pupils, but in 1850, after problems with not enough money being taken in, the Directors agreed to pay this themselves. The collection of the janitor's fees also caused problems. At the time of the appointment of Harper, it was agreed that these would be paid direct to the Rector who would issue a receipt. A decision in 1852 meant that any staff who admitted pupils without having made this payment would find themselves personally liable. Even this arrangement did not work and a sub-committee set up at the annual meeting in 1853 recommended changes to the system of paying the janitor, with the abolition of the janitor's fee after the end of that session. From the start of the 1856-57 session the coal money was collected by the addition of 3d to the fees for each of the first three quarters of the session.

Falconer complained about being allowed only a single fire in his room, and, perhaps because of his illnesses in previous years, it was agreed he could have two in very severe weather. This was at a time when his class numbers were over 160, and he was requesting an assistant. This help was granted if he paid the costs himself, as the Directors said they could not find the money. His class numbers reached 181 in 1858, whilst those in Leslie's English class were 175, with similar numbers the following session. It is unlikely that all these pupils attended at the same time, due to the 'hour system' of teaching, introduced some years earlier.

From 1855 use of the Academy Park was allowed during the holiday for cricket for both a local club and a team from the local Militia, but it was mentioned that bleaching or washing of clothes was not permitted during school hours. The Northern Meeting had failed to pay for the use of the ground in 1853, and in 1855 it was decided that the Park could only be used if they paid their debts, as well as pay for the current year's use. A compromise was later reached on the payments. Around 1860 the land was used as a drill ground for the Volunteer Company. The Farmers' Society also used the Park in certain years for their show, on the understanding that all damage was made good.

A bazaar in aid of the Ragged School was held in the school building during the summer vacation in both 1856 and 1858, with the reopening of the school being delayed a week to accommodate the 1858 bazaar. The Scottish Temperance League held a dance in the Park in October 1859 for the 78th Regiment of Foot (The Ross-shire Buffs, Duke of Albany's Regiment), who had recently returned from the relief of Lucknow in India.

Sheriff Colquhoun had resigned as Chairman of the Directors at the annual meeting in 1857, as he was to leave Inverness, to be replaced by Affleck Fraser, the oldest surviving Director and a former Chairman. It was known that Fraser would not be able to fully carry out the job, but would be more of a figurehead, so the Rev. Dr. Macdonald became Vice-Chairman. Fraser served until May 1860, when Andrew Matheson, the Burgh M.P., was appointed, even though it was known that he would not be able to attend many of the meetings. Macdonald continued as Vice-Chairman. Robert Smith, a local solicitor, had been appointed as Secretary and Treasurer in

1841, with a salary of £25 4s, and he continued to serve throughout this period.

The sum of £1400, which had been the balance of the investment with the Mason Lodge in their property, was paid up during 1853, with most of the money being put into Bank of Scotland stock. The continued financial problems led Colquhoun to propose some amendments to the Charter in that year, but his suggestions depended on recruiting another ten life Directors on payment of £20 each. Nothing came of this scheme, perhaps as the Directors were aware of the proposals by the railway company that were soon forthcoming.

In 1861 some long-overdue changes in staff conditions were brought into effect. The notice that teachers were required to give was reduced from three months to six weeks, and appointments were to be for twelve months from any convenient date. The previous scheme required appointments and renewals to be made at the annual meeting in May, shortly before the end of a session. Staff appointed in the summer would not have their appointments confirmed until the following May.

The coming of the Railway
The first moves to bring a railway to Inverness had taken place during 1845. At the start of January 1846 two projected companies, the Perth and Inverness Company, and the Inverness and Elgin Company, served notice on the Academy Directors about building a terminus next door to the Academy.[38] This followed on from three proposals made the previous year to link Inverness with the south by rail, but all of these schemes fell through as the finance was not forthcoming by the time the powers obtained from Parliament expired seven years later.

A new scheme was launched in 1853, and Parliamentary notices were served on the Directors with regard to a much more restricted scheme for an Inverness and Nairn Railway,[39] with Joseph Mitchell, the civil engineer, playing a key role in the proposals. The Directors agreed not to object to the scheme but reserved the right to claim compensation. As the necessary Parliamentary powers had to be obtained during the 1853-54 Parliamentary session, things moved rapidly, with the Bill reaching Parliament in the summer of 1854. The terminus in Inverness was to be close to the Academy ground on Academy Street, to serve the line to Nairn, and the branch to Inverness harbour. The first sod was cut on 21st September 1854 in a field to the east of the Academy Park. There was a grand procession of the Provost and Magistrates, a wide collection of tradesmen, and, in support, most of the schoolchildren of the Town, as a public holiday had been declared.

In March 1855 the Inverness and Nairn Railway Company offered to buy or feu the whole of the Academy land and buildings. The initial offer was one of £2300, with a feu duty of 5% per annum on that sum redeemable on payment within 10 years. Negotiations continued, with the Academy wanting £5000, rather than £2300. The proposals also involved the former Rector's house, and the house that the Academy had built for the janitor in 1811. Some maps of the proposals still exist,[40] and negotiations went on for some weeks before agreement was reached on taking only an angle of land on the south side of the Academy grounds – part of what is now Station Square – at 4s per foot of frontage, redeemable within ten years. As the negotiations had proceeded, it became necessary to complete the infeftment of that part of the Academy land held under feu. The railway company agreed to pay for a boundary wall between their property and the Academy, but the janitor soon claimed that he was suffering from the height of the wall, presumably through loss of sunlight, and he was granted an extra area for his garden. The opening of the railway line took place on 5th November 1855.[41]

Further arrangements were signed in August 1858,[42] but by early 1860 the Inverness and Ross-shire Railway Company was wanting more land, this time to include the janitor's and former Rector's houses. Roof repairs on the janitor's house did have to be paid for, despite its likely take-over by the railway company. Further agreements were made in February and April 1861,[43] and infeftment of that section of land held as burgage was carried out at the end of that year.

At the same time, the Inverness and Aberdeen Junction Railway (which had absorbed the Inverness and Nairn Railway Company by this time) served notice on the Directors about the possible need for additional station accommodation,[44] and the Directors were told that no more land than that required by the Inverness and Ross-shire Railway would be needed for at least two years, and might not be required at all, depending on what happened when the Inverness and Perth Railway opened. The value of the land taken was settled, as with many similar cases throughout the country, by an arbiter, who gave a total value of £1031,[45] and it was decided that the railway company were required to build a new janitor's house and a substantial wall between the Academy and the station. However it was agreed in 1862 to rent back the existing house from the railway company, so that a new one was not needed.

The Directors were probably very glad to receive this money for little effort on their part.

Chapter 12
A period of reform before the 1872 Education Act

The 1st February 1862 was a significant date in the history of the Academy, even though the Directors had no control over the public meeting that took place that day. New educational ideas had begun to permeate into the Highlands, and the meeting led to a variety of changes and reforms, including a new Rector for the Academy, and the building of a Ladies' Institute. That educational change was in the air is hinted at in the extract minute given to Harper in 1853 when he had asked for a testimonial (Chapter 11). The "scholastic forms" which he had brought with him were not in practice in the Highlands, and a certain resistance to change in the attitudes of the Directors may have encouraged him to move south again.

The public meeting and its outcomes
Circulars had been passed round the Town to call a public meeting in the Town House on 1st February 1862 to discuss the future of education in Inverness and in the Academy. Two of the main speakers were Bishop Eden and Sheriff Thomson (the Academy's Vice-chairman).[1] Bishop Eden said that there was a need for the Rector to have much greater control over the running of the school. He also suggested that the fees were far too low, in terms of the value of the education obtained, a very different view from what was being discussed some twenty years earlier. Andrew Matheson, the M.P. for the Inverness Burghs and recently-appointed Chairman of the Directors, also spoke, but said that he had only so recently been appointed that he had not even attended a meeting. Mention was also made by some speakers, including the Bishop, about the need to improve or replace the building.

Perhaps because he was an incomer, or perhaps due to his ideas for development which led to the building of the Scottish Episcopal Cathedral in Inverness (of which the foundation stone was laid in 1866), Bishop Eden became the spokesperson for the meeting. He had already served as a Director of the Academy as a nominee of the Commissioners of Supply from 1857 to 1859, but for the two and a half years prior to the public meeting he had not been a member of the Board. Presumably as a result of his involvement with the meeting, he was once again appointed as a Director in May 1862.

From the public meeting a committee was appointed to take matters further. Six points were identified by this committee, and these were put to the Academy Directors.[2] They were:
1. the Rector should be appointed during the pleasure of the Directors, and he would have the power to nominate and dismiss staff, although the actual appointments would remain with the Directors
2. the salary of the Rector should be not less than £400 a year
3. the fees should be revised, with a view to their increase
4. the fees should be paid into a common fund from which the salaries of

the officers, and their expenses, should be defrayed
5. there should be various additions and improvements to the building
6. females should not be educated at the Academy, and the appointment of the Rector should be carried out by competent people.

Only limited discussion took place at the next meeting of the Directors, but a committee was appointed to take things further. Their initial response was to accept points 1, 2 and 4, but they reserved consideration of the other three points. At a subsequent meeting these further points were accepted, other than the delegation of the appointment of the Rector. At a general meeting of the Directors on 12th March, the committee's decisions were accepted as long as the sum of £1200 was subscribed before 1st May, only to be called in if there was a deficiency in the revenue during the first three years. There is no further mention about this sum and it presumably was not required. Sheriff Thomson and Col. Mackintosh were delegated to speak with Scott (Rector) and Falconer (commercial) about their retirals, should the plan be approved.

By the annual meeting in May, Scott did offer to resign, as he was in poor health.[3] He had asked for a pension of £80 a year, but was granted £75, with one dissension on the grounds that funds would not permit this and it was inadequate anyway. The janitor, Sgt. Keith, had tried to resign the previous year, but had been persuaded to stay on, and it was agreed to let him leave at the same time as Scott. Falconer was also wanting to retire, but he was not allowed to do so until the following spring, by which time the new Rector had his own nominee ready to take over the classes. Alongside this, although not directly affecting the Academy, was the progress through Parliament of the Mackintosh Farr Bill, which became the 1862 Act (see Chapter 10).

The revised powers of the new Rector were agreed a week later[4] and these were:
• the appointment would be during the pleasure of the Directors with a salary of £100 plus fees
• he would teach classics
• he had full power to oversee other classes and must report quarterly to the Directors
• there was the hope of an increased salary if the Academy did well, and then consideration would be given to paying the fees into a central fund
• the Rector would have a say in appointing other staff
This did not totally match the resolutions of the public meeting, but moved someway towards its views. A couple of days later the adjourned general meeting of the Directors agreed to go ahead and advertise the post of Rector. Consideration was also to be given to appointing a new janitor. Some of the interim staff were kept on until the end of the session.

The final examinations, prize giving and ball under Scott's control took place at the end of June 1862. James Kennedy in his autobiography says about Scott:[5]

He became after my day Rector of the Academy, and continued to teach on into old age. I have been told that in his later years he often dozed in his seat, while the boys played all sorts of pranks. He was at his best during my term.

A quote from the Directors' Minutes when Scott's retiral was agreed, was used by Joseph Cook, the person whose interest in early photographs of Inverness has preserved for us his portrait [see Figure 11.2]:

> The directors unite in bearing testimony to the thorough integrity of Mr Scott's character – the modesty which, from aversion to anything like ostentatious display, often veiled his superior qualities as a teacher and scholar, and to the good taste with which he conducted the studies of a long succession of more advanced pupils in the language and literature of Greece and Rome.

He had served the school since 1824, but only enjoyed his pension for some eighteen months.

Isabel Anderson records the character of Sgt. Keith:[6]

> Keith, the "janitor," a tall old soldier – the terror of unruly boys - used to stand at the hall door on these occasions *[the lectures]*, to look at the tickets of admission and conduct the ladies to their seats. When boys were kept in after school hours, for not having learnt their lessons correctly, and felt the pangs of hunger by five o'clock, they used to try to elude the surveillance of Keith, by letting down a long string with a penny attached to the end of it from one of the upper windows, as a signal to the passers by that a couple of rolls or "cookies" were wanted. Walter Sim, the town porter, was often on the look-out for one of those signals, and securely fastened the rolls to the end of the string, where they often dangled for some time, the boys being afraid to draw them up while Keith was on the watch. Keith was also librarian in the old library in connection with the Mechanics' Institution, which was then situated on Bridge Street, and he used to chat familiarly with every one who came for books, and to give his candid opinion of all the Inverness people.

Falconer eventually retired at Christmas 1863, on a pension of £100 a year, with a present from the pupils of a silver ink stand. A dance followed the presentation, with the Militia Band providing the music.[7] Falconer died in 1876, aged 81, and is commemorated by an obelisk in the Old High Churchyard in Inverness. In 1858 two of his sons had founded the Falcon Iron Works after which Falcon Square in the City Centre is now named. Their father seems also to have been involved in the ironworks project. In a sense, the departure of Scott, Falconer and Keith marked the end of an era for the Royal Academy.

The appointment of George Robertson

The appointment of the new janitor was relatively easy, and Andrew Dallas, a tailor, was appointed in July 1862, with a salary of £16 plus the house and two loads of coal. The salary was increased the following year to £25 in the light of extra duties. Various discussions took place about the appointment of the Rector as the original twenty-one applications came in, but the post was readvertised, bringing in a further eleven applications. An interim appointment was made to cover the classics classes. Two appointments as Rector were made, but both candidates declined to take up the post offered to them, the second one on the grounds he could not get away from his current job. In September it was agreed, on a motion from Matheson, the M.P., to guarantee £300 for three years to the person appointed. A third advertisement was published. This brought in 39 applicants, and one of them, George Robertson, head classics master of Grange House School, Edinburgh, was interviewed but he subsequently withdrew.

At an adjourned Special General Meeting in November[8] Robertson indicated he was still interested in the appointment on certain conditions which the Directors, with one dissension, did not find too unacceptable. He was a critical scholar of classics and an accomplished writer,[9] and he accepted the appointment in January 1863.[10] His conditions included major repairs and modifications to the building, various changes in staffing and an attempt to get a school of design funded in conjunction with the Government Department of Science and Arts Scheme, established in 1853 and first applied south of the Border.

Alexander Ross, the local architect, reported on the modifications required for the building:
1. the boys' and girls' playgrounds were to be subdivided with separate entrances, new "offices" with proper WCs and drainage, and repairs to gates
2. a covered shed was to be provided for boys of size 50 ft. x 20 ft., on the north wall of the Park
3. the main building was to be cleaned, the street front and woodwork to be painted, and glass repairs carried out with obscured glass in the lower sashes
4. various repairs and improvement to the classrooms and hall were to be carried out; the landing of the stair was to become a cloakroom, and the space under the stairs was to become a WC for staff.

The total cost for this work was estimated to be £550, to be completed by early April if possible, when Robertson hoped to start work in Inverness. In the end, costs were considerably higher, with the carpenter's bill alone being £613. The ball-wall in the playground, built in 1811, had been removed the previous summer. Concurrently, the Railway Company asked if the Directors would renew the financial bond at a lower rate of interest, but it was decided to take the money to pay for the repairs.

As part of the staffing changes there were to be two English teachers, a senior one with a salary of £120 and a junior teacher with a salary of £40. The senior teacher would assist the Rector if required and take charge when the Rector was carrying out inspections. An efficient teacher for modern languages needed to be appointed. This scheme actually saved money on staffing. In the first instance only a single English teacher was actually appointed.

Robertson wrote to the first Directors' Meeting immediately after he started work with a list of what still required to be done, and reminding them that he had only agreed to the appointment on the understanding that changes would take place.[11] Interim changes were needed whilst he assessed the situation. The Directors needed to take fees under their own control in a common fund, with some reorganisation rather than increases, the furnishings needed to be improved (at that time they were in such a poor state that the school would not attract a Government grant), and a prospectus should be introduced (something which was apparently not done until 1884).

By the summer of 1863, the staff was as follows:
    Classics: George Robertson, Rector (also temporarily teaching German)
    English: James Vipond
    Arithmetic and writing: James Falconer (with assistant)
    Mathematics and chemistry: William Eadie
    French: Josué Doine, a graduate of the University of Bordeaux
    Art: James Glen
Other staff noted in the prize list for that year were a Dr. Thomas Aitken who gave lectures in biology, and Sgt.-Major Maclernan [sic] who took drill and calisthenics. Also mentioned were the Officer (janitor), Alex. Dallas, and, as matron (a post never previously mentioned), Mrs Dallas.

For his first end-of-session examinations, Robertson seemed to have invited people whom he would have known from his time in Edinburgh: Professor James Pillans (a key figure in education at that time but who in the end could not come through illness), Dr. Leonhard Schmitz (Rector of the High School of Edinburgh) and Simon Laurie (Secretary to the Education Committee of the Church of Scotland). Schmitz had provided an introduction for Robertson's translation of part of a Roman History, so was obviously known to him. Both Schmitz and Laurie received £3 3s for their services. Public examinations would follow the written examinations and were to be based on them. The orations and prizegiving would conclude the session.

The *Inverness Courier* reports at length on the event[12] as well as commenting on the changes that had taken place such as the subdivision of the playground and the amount of land which had passed to the Railway Company. The Inverness Brass Band (at a cost of £2 2s) had played in the Park in the morning, and in the afternoon they were in one of the classrooms next to the hall. The Provost and Magistrates were ushered in by the Town Officers in full dress, with halberds, etc. It was also noted that the prize-winners had chosen their own prizes. Sheriff Thomson, in his speech, noted the big improvements even in the three months since Robertson had arrived.

Pupil numbers were only at 171 at the time of Robertson's appointment, but soon increased greatly, although falling back once he left [Table 12.1].[13] The figures for 1864 were clearly a major step forward, bringing significantly increased fee income, with much of the increase in numbers being in the senior classes. Robertson also seems to have written up admission registers

	1863	1864	1868
English	104	225	192
Writing and Arithmetic	125	224	176/182
Classics	36	86	93
Mathematics	19	34	37
French	16	73	106
German	8	14	9
Drawing	31	105	103
Book-keeping			10
Music			92
Lectures		60	
Total number of pupils	171	328 (308 attending)	215

Table 12.1: Pupil numbers in 1863, 1864 and 1868

which were backdated to cover the whole of the 1862-63 session,[14] and from this point the school has complete records of admission. In early 1865 both the Rector and the Directors stressed the importance of elementary Latin in the boys' curriculum.

Perhaps due to the changes in the air, two new Directors paid their £50 fee to qualify during this period. One was Dr Welsh Forbes, a former pupil; the other was Charles Waterston, who was soon to be appointed to various subcommittees. Dr Forbes, on the other hand, frequently challenged financial matters, such as the repairs demanded by Robertson as a condition of his appointment, and paying Eadie a salary out of Academy funds. Robert Smith, the solicitor, who was Secretary and Treasurer, paid his £50 in May 1864, to qualify himself as a Director, rather than just an official of the Trust. Soon after this he resigned as Secretary, and was replaced by Penrose Hay (see below).[15]

At the annual meeting in 1863, a sub-committee on management was once again appointed, with full powers to handle teaching, fees, etc., but there was bad news in July when it was discovered that both the Drawing and English classrooms had rotten joists and they both had to be refloored. This pushed the total cost of repairs up to over £900 and the final bill was almost £1300.[16] Insurance cover on the buildings was also significantly increased. A long-standing overdraft was finally paid off in the summer of 1864, when credit was arranged on the security of stock held by the Directors, instead of paying a higher rate of interest on the overdraft.

New bye-laws, based on the discussions following the public meeting in February 1862, were introduced, and these gave Robertson far more power than had been exercised by any Rector since the introduction of the bye-laws in 1840 which replaced some aspects of the Royal Charter. Fixed salaries for the Rector and staff were introduced, and the pupil fees were collected by the Secretary/Treasurer. Some amendments were made to these regulations only three years later, and these set out in much more detail the duties of the Rector, including how many hours he was to teach, and the time to be used to "superintend" the work of the other staff. Daniel Fearon, in his report for the Taunton Commission (see later), saw this as a move to make the Rector very similar to the Headmaster "in the English sense of the word", i.e. in the English 'public' school, like Eton or Harrow. This dominance of the Rector was very much a novelty in Scotland at the time of Robertson's appointment.

Other changes introduced in the early 1860's included telling the Northern Meeting and the Farmers' Society that the Park would no longer be available for their events. The museum was removed, partly into the Mechanics Hall in Bridge Street, and partly into storage in the Old Poor House.

Staffing and school life under Robertson
There was a series of rapid changes in staff after Robertson's appointment. Bishop Eden had written to the *Inverness Courier* in March 1863[17] concerning the appointment of a certificated art master, a post which would attract Government funding, and in the autumn of that year Glen was at last given a salary. Dallas, the recently appointed janitor, died that October, after only fifteen months' service, leading to the appointment of Alexander Cameron, who had to be dismissed the following year for drunkenness. A James Lawrence is mentioned as teaching vocal music, the beginning of a major development in music teaching in the school. Junior English and junior classics appointments were made early in 1864 with Robert Thomson and John Suter respectively, but for a while Eadie had also to take the arithmetic class, vacant as a result of Falconer's retiral.

However some misunderstanding between Robertson and Vipond led to the suspension of Vipond for a week in late January 1864. Robertson himself had to take leave of absence for four weeks for medical reasons just after this, and Suter taught the classics classes during that period. Vipond and Thomson had some disagreement in the spring of 1864, and this led to Thomson's resignation later that year.

An interim writing teacher was not re-employed after the summer when William Reid from Dundee became the new teacher of writing and arithmetic and William Handcock of Manchester took over the junior English post. Vipond resigned with effect from October to set up his own school in Manchester, although an attempt was made by Bishop Eden to get him to stay. Robertson identified Alex. Walker of Kirkcaldy as his replacement, and, as he was able to start the day after he was interviewed, he was appointed with immediate effect. Walker was soon to be advertising private Sanskrit lessons for anyone wishing employment in the Indian Civil Service. Handcock was dismissed after less than six months, but the minutes do not record a reason. His replacement was Frederick Calvert from Edinburgh, who was forced to retire through illness at the end of 1865. James Glen became ill by early 1865 and was also forced to retire, with a small allowance of £20 a year. He died in June of the following year, and is buried in Tomnahurich Cemetery.

The examinations in the summer of 1864 were on similar lines to those of the previous year, with Dr Schmitz and Mr Laurie in attendance. Professor Kelland from Edinburgh examined in mathematics, as Professor Pillans had recently died. The prizegiving, which included both the orations and music from the Highland Light Infantry band, three violinists and a piper, had to be held in the open air as the hall was too small for the event. Cricket seems still to have had a hold in the school, with a report in the local newspaper of two games against a team from Forres Academy, but both games were won by Forres.

In February 1864 an Inverness Academy Club was founded, the first mention of such a venture, although ten years earlier the money for a prize had first been donated by Old Boys. About thirty former pupils attended the inaugural meeting, and A. Penrose Hay [Figure 12.1] was called to the chair. He had been the 1840 Raigmore medallist and was soon to be the Secretary and Treasurer of the Academy. A dinner was held in the Union Hotel on 18th March.[18] No money was made available for prizes that year, but Charles Innes, on behalf of the Club, announced arrangements that would apply from the following year. In a letter to the Directors, the Club suggested that the school should make use of the University of Edinburgh Local Examinations, about to be introduced, and which could be held in centres throughout Scotland. This idea was soon taken up by Robertson, who may well have been considering it already.

In January 1867, the Club's annual dinner was chaired by the 1827 Raigmore medallist and distinguished former pupil, Edward Strathearn Gordon, who was now the Solicitor General under Disraeli. That same year he was given the Freedom of Inverness.[19] After the 1872 Education Act, Gordon was involved with attempts to keep religious education as part of the school curriculum. About sixty former pupils and local dignitaries attended the dinner. As was common at that time all and sundry were toasted, including "The Academy and its Directors", "The Academy and its Teachers", "The former Teachers" (with a reply by James Falconer, the former commercial teacher), "The Prize Boys" and "Old Academy Boys at Home and Abroad". Later in 1867 Strathearn Gordon paid his £50 to become a Director of the Academy.

Financial solvency at last
At the time that Penrose Hay took over as Secretary and Treasurer (in January 1865), the Finance Committee produced a financial statement which

for the first time for many years showed a surplus on both the general and fee accounts, even though the surpluses were only just over £100 and £16 respectively. Changes in designations within education in Scotland led to the division of the school into three sections: ages 5 to 7 as preparatory, ages 7 to 11 as ordinary school, and for ages 11 to 15 a mercantile education was provided, with both classical and modern elements. The committee were also clear that the Rector's decision to introduce the Edinburgh University Local Examinations, in their first year of operation, was correct. Some adjustments in fees were suggested, with those taking the new examination paying extra. Once this change was in place it was felt that the school would be ready for dividing the boys' and girls' classes into separate schools or buildings, with suitable courses introduced for the mid-Victorian young ladies.

In the first year of the University Examinations in 1865, 29 out of the 61 candidates took the examination in Inverness, all the rest sitting the exam in Edinburgh. The results were very satisfactory for Inverness, with eighteen of the successful candidates, including several girls, being from the Royal Academy, the largest number from any one school.[20] The following year, funds were provided by the Academy Club to provide prizes for those who gained honours passes in these examinations. At the start of the following session it was agreed to hold a preliminary examination, so that pupils could be allocated to suitable classes. Prior to this time, pupils were generally enrolled for whatever class they wished, regardless of ability. Classes were to be restricted to thirty, with special classes for those about to enter University.

Enquiries started that autumn about a School of Art under the Government scheme previously mentioned. Formal application to join the scheme was made in October 1869. The Royal Academy became one of only a handful of schools in Scotland to receive this money.

The Ladies' Institution
The first moves in the formation of a separate Ladies' school occurred at a meeting in April 1864, but plans were not produced for another year for a building with four classrooms and a separate room for the Lady Superintendent, at a cost of around £900.[21] The building was largely completed over the summer of 1865, but there was no formal opening ceremony. In August, fees for the various classes were fixed, and these ranged from 12s a quarter for the preparatory class, up to £2 12s 6d for some of the advanced classes.[22] As soon as the building opened, it was realised that it was inadequate, and Ross, the architect, was ordered to produce plans for dressing rooms, WCs and an additional music room, at a cost of nearly £300. A porch was added in the summer of 1867 to try to eliminate draughts. The heating proved inadequate, and the boiler had to be replaced the following year. At the same time three further rooms were built. The final cost, including fittings and fixtures, was around £1830 [Figure 12.2].

The first advertisement for the post of Lady Superintendent produced only one suitable candidate, but she wanted a salary of £150, £50 more than what the Directors were prepared to offer. In the end, the first appointment was that of Miss Helen Haswell, of Moray Park Institution, Edinburgh, but her salary was fixed at £120 per annum. She put in her resignation at the end of the first session, but seems to have withdrawn it again, remaining in post until August 1871, when she was forced to resign through ill-health, although the *Inverness Courier* report says that there were "more inviting prospects elsewhere".[23] The Directors commended her for her high standard of work. Her replacement was a Miss Rose.

Shortly after the opening of the Ladies' Institution a 'senior governess' was appointed[24] as well as some junior governesses. A Miss Laing was thought to be suitable for teaching the Ladies' junior preparatory classes, but not suitable for older girls' classes as she was only slightly older than some of the girls in these classes. The janitor's wife became the 'female attendant' and was given a salary of £40 for these duties.

In addition to the traditional subjects of instruction, other subjects listed in the opening announcement in the local papers were French, German, needlework, wax flower making, and calisthenics. Herr Fleckstein, from Morrison's Academy in Crieff, was appointed as Music Master, as music was to form a key part of the curriculum in the Ladies' Institution. Lessons on the pianoforte were offered at three levels, as well as singing lessons in the English and Italian styles, either in class lessons or individually. Demand for these classes was so high that an additional junior music governess had to be appointed only six months after the Ladies' Institution opened. In 1868 a new piano had to be purchased at a cost of about £30, and an existing one exchanged for a better one at a cost of £18.

Fleckstein was a founding member of the Inverness Choral Union. After two years he moved to Perth Academy, and was replaced by Ernst Kesting from Edinburgh, who was to serve the school until well into the 1890's. He also taught German for part of the time. Miss Georgina MacKid, who had studied at the Conservatoire of Berlin, but was native to Inverness, was appointed as his assistant. She taught the junior German class, presumably having learned the language in Berlin.

The *Inverness Courier* once again was full of praise for the work of the young ladies, and carried reports of the high standard of needlework and art, as well as details of the annual concert, first held in 1867, at the conclusion of the July public examination. Attendance at this event was so great that in and after 1870 the concert was held in the Music Hall in the Town. The newspaper particularly noted in July 1867 that there were now six medals (including two supplied by the Academy Club) available for competition and of these four had been awarded to ladies.

Robertson's resignation
In November 1865 Robertson said that he intended to apply for the

Rectorship of the High School of Edinburgh, and asked for a testimonial which he was given:[25]

> [The Directors] record their high sense of his administrative abilities and their confidence that these, along with his well-known scholarlike acquirements and his great experience as a Classical teacher, fully qualify him to fill the situation of Rector of the High School of Edinburgh in a manner that will be both creditable to himself and of advantage to that Institution.

He either did not actually apply for, or else did not get, the job in Edinburgh, but instead was given a salary increase to £400 per annum and a grant of £100 for his services over the previous year.[26] By May 1866 he had produced a draft of new regulations, ordinances and byelaws for the governing of the Academy, which then passed through the annual meeting. However, Robertson was forced to put in his resignation in July, when it emerged that he was ill, and had been ordered to rest. The High School of Edinburgh is reported as having made changes from summer 1866 in the way it was organised, and these changes closely matched the changes that Robertson had steered through in Inverness.

From later evidence, although Robertson may have been a good administrator, he does not seem to have got on well with the rest of the staff, particularly in his role of overseeing their work. By August, William Eadie, already on the staff, and presumably happy with the changes that had been made in the running of the school, was appointed to the vacant post.[27] Staff relations seem to have improved under Eadie's control. He was to serve the school until his retirement in 1888. During the early part of his tenure, most of the Directors' business seems to have been fairly routine, with changes of staff, payment of accounts and little else of interest. Salaries for all staff were gradually increased after 1869, as the school succeeded in its new role and funds were in a healthier state. Occasional lapses in staff behaviour were generally met with a reprimand, following a promise of no repetition. At the adjourned annual meeting in 1871 the staff were told to be more sparing in the use of corporal punishment. The most significant event that year was probably the trial of Sheriff Thomson, Vice-Chairman of the Directors, who was charged with forgery, although this was not connected with the Academy.[28] Found guilty, he was given five years' penal servitude. His place as Vice-Chairman was taken by Charles Stewart of Brin.

Pupil numbers increased in the early years of Eadie's tenure of office, with the 223 of 1869 rising to 351 and 353 in 1871 and 1872 respectively. Fees were reduced where there was more than one child in a family attending the school. The Academy continued to enter a significant number of candidates for the University Local Examinations, with considerable success. The annual public examination and exhibition of work still attracted considerable space in the *Inverness Courier*, as did the reports of the annual ball at Christmas. The Directors were required to look into an incident in early 1869, when a boy was injured in the arm by a knife, but the result of the enquiries was that the wounding was accidental, caused by reckless behaviour, and the pupil was reprimanded in the presence of all the pupils.[29]

Boys' school:
- First Course: English reading, spelling, dictation, grammar, history and geography – 17/6d a quarter
- Second Course: English reading, spelling, dictation, etymology, elocution, grammar, history and geography – £1 7s a quarter
- Third Course – English, dictation, elocution, grammar, elements of composition. history and geography, writing, arithmetic, Latin, drawing, religious knowledge – £1 15s a quarter
- Fourth Course – English literature, elocution, grammar and composition, history, physical and political geography, writing, arithmetic, Latin, French, drawing, religious knowledge – £2 2s a quarter
- Senior Course – English literature, grammar, analysis and composition, history, physical and political geography, arithmetic, book-keeping, Latin, French, Greek, mathematics, drawing, physics, religious knowledge – £2 7 6d a quarter
- Fees for individual classes – including drill (2s 6d), vocal music (2s 6d); janitor, coal money, etc. (1s 6d)

Ladies' Institution:
- Preparatory course: Junior: English reading, spelling, grammar, geography, calisthenics, needlework, religious knowledge – 12s 6d a quarter; Senior: English grammar and derivation, reading, spelling, dictation, elementary composition, history, geography, elementary science, writing, arithmetic, calisthenics, needlework, religious knowledge – £1 1s a quarter
- Junior Course: English grammar, composition, etymology, dictation, history, geography, elocution, French (one hour daily), writing, arithmetic, calisthenics, needlework, religious knowledge – £1 11 6d a quarter
- Senior course: English literature, grammar and composition, modern history, physical and political geography, elocution, senior French (one hour daily), writing, arithmetic, drawing, calisthenics, needlework, religious knowledge – £2 2s a quarter
- Advanced course: history of the English language and literature, English composition, ancient history, physical and political geography, use of the globes, elocution, French (with conversation), German, writing, book-keeping, arithmetic, drawing, painting, calisthenics, needlework, religious knowledge – £2 12 6d a quarter
- Lessons on Pianoforte: Junior – £1 1s per quarter; Advanced (two lessons weekly from master) – £1 11 6d to pupils of institution, £2 2s to others if space is available
- Lessons in English or Italian Singing – class singing for those attending the course – 5s per quarter; by single lessons to those attending the course – £1 11 6d per quarter
- Fees for groups of two classes; janitor, coal money, etc. – 1s 6d

Table 12.2: Prospectus of work and fees in the Royal Academy, *c.* 1871

The Colebrooke Report (see Chapter 13) provides us with a prospectus for the first time from which it is possible to get an outline of the work of the school in the early 1870's [Table 12.2].[30]

The *Inverness Academical*, the school magazine in the early part of the 20th century, provides an account of some of the staff of this period.[31] Referring almost certainly to the Rev. James Purdie, classics master from 1868 to 1872, the account says:

> ... I recall his voice of thunder and fierce rolling eye. He would have scorned the modern notion that the function of a teacher is to "draw out" the aptitudes of the pupil; his theory was the old-fashioned one, that the pupil's mind is a receptacle (mostly empty) into which the teacher must drive perforce as many facts and figures as it can hold. ... Most of the classical lore that lives in my memory is associated with a flogging; and indeed, it would be curious if it were not so; for we were flogged on principle from day to day. How often have I stood trembling at "Hellgate" (as we termed the door of the classical room), anxiously listening to the far-sounding voice of the master within: and, when the class preceding ours was dismissed, how we envied the parting guests, and queried, with bated breath, as they passed, "Is he wild today?" One scene I can never forget. In an evil hour it fell to my lot to read and translate the line – *Dulce et decorum est pro patria mori*. Alas! my quantities were bad, egregiously bad: for, instead of dwelling sonorously on *decorum*, I gave it a short jerky o – an absurd and irritating mistake to any classical or even musical ear. "*Decorum!*" repeated the master in disgust; "Good Heavens! *decorum!* Come out here, sir! and let me see if I can't drive some notion of euphony into you; decorum indeed. Hold up your hand, sir; lower down, sir; do you hear me? – there now! *Dulce* (whack) *et* (whack) *de* (whack) *cor* (tremendous whack) *um* (whack), and so forth throughout the whole line, emphasising each syllable with a whack. Need I say that this line has become part of my being; that it dwells, and will always dwell, with me: so that, if I should ever be called on to fight for my country I will cheerfully take up arms, and die with these words on my lips. No one can say that a master has lived in vain who could achieve that result by means of Latin and leather.

Despite this pupil's thoughts on Purdie, "a number of his most attached pupils" presented him with a walnut writing desk at the close of the 1870-71 session. George Dunn, who replaced Purdie in 1872, was apparently a very different type of teacher. The writer of this article also comments on William Eadie, two native French teachers, and Samuel Thomson, the English teacher from 1866 until 1883. The article concludes with an account of the snowball fights with the pupils from the Bell's School next door. Both Eadie and Thomson received presentations from pupils during the 1871-72 session, "as a mark of esteem".

State involvement in Education in mid-Victorian Scotland
Prior to Robertson's appointment in 1863, the Royal Academy had been almost completely detached from any involvement with the national policy for education in Scotland, such as it was. The "school in every parish" introduced by the Act of 1696 only applied to rural areas, but education there was neither compulsory nor free. The Scottish Society [originally: The Society in

Scotland] for Propagating Christian Knowledge (the SSPCK), founded in 1709, had helped fill some of the gaps in the Highlands where poverty, distance, and the weather, restricted attendance at the school which was funded by the landowner and supported by fees. Little educational legislation had been passed relevant to the urban situation, and the towns were largely left to their own devices, with cities like Edinburgh having many schools, some with large endowments. Smaller towns struggled to maintain a single school. There was often a mixture of public, private and charitable effort, but parents who wanted it would normally have had little problem in getting at least a basic education for their children.[32]

Wherever the education took place, Inverness included, the Church, in the form of the established Church of Scotland, was not far away. From the 1830's both secular intellectuals and some religious leaders had started to call for a greater involvement in education by the state, and some limited funding was made available from 1834. The Disruption of 1843 did alter the situation, after which time the Free Church set up their own pattern of schools throughout Scotland, including one which was to become at a later date Inverness High School. The Free Church, along with the Roman Catholics and the Episcopalians, were willing to accept grants to assist with building new schools. The Church of Scotland, however, was determined to hang on to its privileged position with regard to schooling. Progress was only possible when religious passion started to die down somewhat, and most of the churches were prepared to surrender their total control over local schools.

A campaign had begun in 1850 to put in place a 'national' system of education, but this really meant 'non-denominational'. A debate arose over the role of religious education in such a system. A supporter of the Free Church, Lord Advocate James Moncreiff (who it will be remembered worked with Lord Cockburn to appoint two Rectors for the Academy), did try to introduce a Scottish education bill in 1854, but it failed through hostility from the Church of Scotland. Several other bills fell in the following fifteen years, despite attempts at compromise. Moncreiff did succeed with a Bill in 1861, which abolished the religious test for burgh and parish schoolmasters but they still had to declare that their teaching would conform to Scripture and the Shorter Catechism. Free Churchmen could now be appointed as schoolmasters, but the parish schools remained Presbyterian in character. Roman Catholic and Episcopalian teachers had no place in the burgh and parish school systems.

As the Academy was clearly providing education for the middle classes, it ruled itself out from the grants introduced primarily for educating the children of those who supported themselves by manual labour. In 1862 the various grant regulations had been brought together to form a 'Revised Code', and the grants payable depended on results, determined by the attendance register and an annual inspection, based on the 'three Rs' – reading, writing and arithmetic – organised at six standards.

This code met with serious objections in Scotland, as it was partly based on the report of the Newcastle Commission which only reported on English education. There was no provision for recognising 'higher subjects', the ones which would qualify a pupil to enter University, probably at about age 16. At first the Code was not to apply to Scotland, but the failure of one of Moncreiff's Bills in 1862 led to the introduction of the Code in 1864, to be partly suspended only three months later. This controversy led to the establishment that year of a Royal Commission headed by the Duke of Argyll – the famous Argyll Commission – a body which was to have a major influence on Scottish education.

The Reports leading to the 1872 Education Act

Argyll, an active politician rather than a detached aristocrat, had Liberal views, similar to Moncreiff (who was also a member of the Commission), and extensive enquiries by the Commissioners provided information on the situation throughout most of Scotland. Educationalists, clergymen and interested laymen were all interviewed, statistics produced and special reports written, one of which is relevant to our topic, the one on burgh and middle class schools.[33] The term 'secondary' was coming into use, to replace the term 'middle-class', but it was to mean a type of education suited to the middle classes and their career aspirations, rather than a sector which followed on from an elementary or 'primary' scheme and intended for all.

The main report of the Commission, published in 1867, had identified that there were adequate elementary school places but had said that they felt that the quality varied very considerably. A Board of Education was required, and amongst its duties would be advising the Committee of Council on the allocation of grants. A national system of non-denominational education was proposed, with a doubling of the number of teachers to cope with some of the proposed new schools, which were to be run by school committees with local rating powers. No mention was made of religious instruction other than there should be a 'conscience clause' for those parents who objected to a basically Presbyterian form of religious instruction.

Daniel Fearon's visit for the Taunton Commission

Prior to the Argyll Commission's work, another enquiry was to involve the Academy. In January 1866 Robertson had met in London with the Secretary of the *Schools Inquiry Commission for England*, and as a result, the Academy was selected as one of the sixteen Scottish schools for inspection and enquiry, as part of a comparison between secondary education in the two countries. In terms of the actual report of the Commission, the Taunton Report of 1868, the main emphasis was on enquiry, rather than inspection, but the *Inverness Courier* was sure that the school "should have nothing to fear" from the inspection.[34] The newspaper failed to pick up the point that this was fact-finding for an English report, not applicable in Scotland.

The school was visited in mid-June 1866 by Daniel Fearon, an English school inspector, and from his report we get an interesting insight into the operation of the Academy. He noted that, under the changes in rules and regulations made in 1863, the Rector had been made "supreme", rather than operating in a system where all the masters were at the same level. He found that some of the "subordinate masters" had very strong feelings against the Rector (Robertson), and there had been many changes of staff in the last few years. The numbers of pupils were declining, perhaps due to the increase of 30% in the fees the previous session. Some of those pupils who had left the Academy had moved to the High School. The 1866 amendments to the bye-laws had only been in place for six weeks at the time of his visit, so he was unable to assess their effect on the operation of the school. It was also to be the final months of George Robertson's term of office, although Fearon would not have known that.

Fearon attended various classes, but was not impressed by much of what he saw, with the teaching showing "much less energy, vigour, and skill than I had generally observed in Scotland". He was concerned that neither Latin nor mathematics was included in the girls' curriculum. Music, he felt was "most judiciously made an extra", with large numbers involved, even though, once married, he thought that these girls would never touch the piano or sing a note again. However, the teaching of mathematics in the boys' school, and of music in the girls' school, he found very good:[35]

> ... The girls were well taught in harmony, and showed a sound elementary acquaintance with the grammar of music. And as regards their playing, the energy and force of will possessed by the master [Herr Fleckstein] had produced a most rare and happy result, one which I seldom found attained even in the best English girls' schools, viz., that the girls almost all took up good classical music, instead of showy and trashy pieces. A considerable quantity of Mozart and Beethoven was played to me in good time and very correctly. This is as much as one can expect from young girls. ...

Fearon administered some tests that he had used in various schools that he had visited and found the girls very backward in arithmetic, although he had seen worse work in some London schools. He also identified the nature of the pupils attending the two Inverness secondary schools [Table 12.3].[36]

The average annual school fees for 1866 were calculated, and this shows that the Academy had the highest average fee in Scotland of about £5 16s, apart from the High School of Edimburgh which had an average fee of £10 3s. The lowest figure was at Hamilton Grammar School, with an average fee of just over £1 5s.

As a result of the level of fees, many burgh schools and schools such as the Royal Academy (with a type of mixed Burgh management and independence through the Charter) excluded the poorest classes. The comparison in Table 12.3 between the Academy and the High School (still under Free Church control) is interesting in this respect, where scholarships allowed those from the working classes to attend. The richest often already sent their children to

	Royal Academy	Inverness High School
Landed proprietors	0	0
Professional men	41 (17.3%)	26 (7.3%)
1st-class merchants, wholesale traders, etc.	16 (6.8%)	0
Large Farmers, superior employers, managers, etc.	64 (27%)	n.a.
2nd-class merchants, superior retail traders, etc.	56 (23.6%)	100 (28.1%)
Inferior retail traders, small farmers, clerks, etc.	52 (21.9%)	150 (42.1%)
Artisans, labourers, mechanics	8 (3.3%)	80 (22.5%)
TOTAL	237	356

Table 12.3: Parental occupations of pupils attending Inverness Secondary Schools

the English type of 'public' school, which is, of course, totally private.

A table supplied by Fearon, based on information from the last ten boys and ten girls to enrol in the Academy prior to his visit, lists the distances that pupils travelled to school. An innkeeper's daughter, aged 14, is described as living 'distant' and lodging in Town, as was an innkeeper's son, aged 12 (probably a brother and sister). The sons of a clergyman and an excise officer travelled daily by train eight and eighteen miles respectively. The other sixteen pupils lived either in town or within a mile of the town.

The visit of Alexander Sellar for the Argyll Commission
In their report for the Argyll Commission, Thomas Harvey and Alexander Sellar, the two assistant commissioners, looked at a much wider range of Scottish burgh schools, reporting on fifty-nine, generally finding them to be secondary schools because of the level which could be reached in the various subjects. The age of the pupils in such secondary schools might be from as young as six or seven up to about sixteen, often including a significant number of girls. It was Sellar who visited the Royal Academy for two days in April 1867, only ten months after Fearon's visit.

The gender segregation system, introduced a couple of years previously in the Royal Academy, was commended by the report, as at this time mixed education was regarded, as we saw from the report of the public meeting in 1862, as inappropriate by especially the upper middle class. The Commissioners say in their report:[37]

The arrangement of the Inverness Academy is upon this principle [separate buildings for boys and girls], and seemed to meet what is wanted in a Burgh school more completely than any other system arrived at in any other school. At this school the boys and girls never meet. The girls have their own class-room, under the supervision of a lady-superintendent; but they have the advantage of being taught by qualified masters, and on the same system as boys. The tone both in the boys and girls' school struck us as being decidedly higher that what it is in many, indeed in most, of the schools which we visited, and it appeared to us to be desirable that similar arrangements might with advantage be more universal.

Nevertheless the full Argyll Commission thought, as had Fearon a year earlier, that this position was rather cautious.[38]

Sellar, after summarising the history, constitution and buildings of the Academy,[39] describes the financial arrangements, including a list of the salaries of the Rector and other staff, amounting to £1250 a year. Fee lists are given, along with details of the "course of instruction", similar to that in the Colebrooke Report given in Table 12.2 above, although this was written some four years later. 215 pupils were on the role, of whom 197 were in attendance at the time of the visit. Visits in the boys' school were made to classes in arithmetic, two for Latin and one for Greek, to an English class (although the teacher was ill), and to French.

If Fearon's earlier report is to be believed, standards had improved since Eadie had replaced Robertson as Rector. Sellar comments in his conclusion:[40]

... it is very clear that the school has greatly improved during the last year under the change of rector and masters, and both masters and scholars appear desirous of doing their best. With the exception of girls' arithmetic, the whole work of the school is creditable, and the tone throughout appears to be very good. Under the present *régime* there is every reason to suppose that the Academy will return to the good position from which it is said to have fallen under the management of the late rector.

When Argyll himself introduced an Education Bill in 1869, consideration was given to it at a public meeting in the Town in April.[41] After amendment the Bill was returned to the House of Lords on the last day of the session, and so fell with other uncompleted business. The English Education Act followed in 1870, allowing no time for a Scottish measure. In February 1871 the Directors appointed a sub-committee to consider the new Scottish Bill.[42] There was also public opposition to parts of this Bill, when a group of prominent citizens asked the Provost to call a meeting of those who wanted both Bible education included in the curriculum, and a Scottish Education Board in Edinburgh. For various reasons this Bill failed to pass through Parliament, but a new one was promoted the following year.

Many, but not all, of Argyll's proposals made their way into the 1872 Bill which, by the time it became an Act, introduced compulsory education until the age of thirteen.[43] However the legislation was mainly about what we would now call 'Primary' education – it said and did nothing about the 'higher subjects' which today we would regard as part of secondary education, other than to create a new category of 'higher-class schools', which were defined as those mainly giving 'instruction in Latin, Greek, modern languages, mathematics, natural science, and generally in the higher branches of knowledge'. These schools were free of the provisions of the Revised Code, but in consequence received no state aid nor school board rate income. They were entirely dependent on fees, and sometimes endowments.

It is now necessary to consider the Directors' response to this proposed measure.

Chapter 13
From opting out to the reform of the Endowments

As soon as the draft of the 1872 Bill was published, the Directors expressed strong opposition to inclusion in the legislation of the Academy as a Burgh school, and their actions and the force of their arguments ensured that Inverness Royal Academy was one of four proposed 'higher-class schools' in Scotland which were in the end excluded from the legislation. It was to be another fourteen years before the report of the Endowments Commission brought any change to the Inverness scene.

Opposition to the 1872 Education Bill

England had passed an important Education Act in 1870, and from that point it was resolved that Scotland would need separate legislation. A Scottish Bill had been introduced in 1871 by Lord Advocate George Young, but for a variety of reasons it did not pass through Parliament. A second Bill, introduced at the start of 1872, had a very stormy passage.

The Directors first considered the matter at their meeting on 16th March 1872, and their main objection to the Bill was that the Royal Academy was not a Burgh school. The Secretary was instructed to produce a statement on the objects and constitution of the Academy which would include reference to the Royal Charter. Once again the Directors were very happy to play whichever side of the game suited them at the time – thirty years earlier, they were keen to prove they *were* a Burgh school, so that they could insist on payment of the traditional contributions towards the teacher's salaries, from the Town Council, and from the Commissioners of Supply.

On 19th April the statement was almost ready and it was agreed that it would be circulated to the Town Council, the Mackintosh Farr Trustees, the Convenor of the County, and the Presbyteries, with the request for petitions to be sent to the House of Commons to have the Academy removed from Schedule C of the Bill, the schedule which listed the proposed 'higher-class' schools. Following a brief history of the school, and an explanation of the current management and staffing, the statement goes on to say:[1]

... [The Academy's] management has all along commanded a feeling of satisfaction on the part of the public.

The Magistrates form a very small numerical proportion of the general body of Directors. The Town contributes a sum of £81 yearly towards the general expenses of the Institution, but there is no school salary levied on the inhabitants.

Inverness is largely supplied with excellent schools, which afford ample instruction in the more elementary branches of education usually taught in burgh and parochial schools, and these are numerously attended by the children of the lower classes.

This chartered Academy does not represent the usual idea of a Burgh School. The salaries in the case of a Burgh School are wholly defrayed from the Burgh Funds, or by the rates levied on the inhabitants, while in the Academy the salaries and expenses were, and are, mainly drawn from a fund contributed by the whole North of Scotland, and by individuals in all parts of the world. The object of the Burgh Schools was the instruction of the youth of the immediate neighbourhood in some of the elementary branches of education, while that of the Academy was to amend the faults and defects of the system of education pursued in the North of Scotland, and to give the benefit of a classical and scientific education to the youth, not only of the Burgh of Inverness, but of all the Northern Counties. Burgh Schools are under the sole patronage and direction of Town Councils; the Academy was placed under the charge of a numerous body of Directors, of whom the Magistrates formed only a small part.

In Burgh Schools it is believed, that the clergy had, as in Parish Schools, a right to visitation and examination, but in the Academy they are represented only by the Moderator of the Presbytery of Inverness, and even his qualification was obtained through the payment of £50 by the Presbytery towards the fund of the Academy.

The Directors, as well as the general community, are desirous that the management of the Institution should not be interfered with, and would regard its transfer to such a Board as is contemplated by the bill now before Parliament as a great calamity to the educational interest of the North of Scotland.

This opposition, including some comments which were rather 'economical with the truth', paid off, and the Royal Academy was removed from Schedule C, along with the High School of Dundee, Greenock Academy and Madras College (St. Andrews). The decision was probably the right one, as transfer to the Burgh would not have brought any financial advantage, and possibly even have handicapped the school through lack of funding.

When the 1872 Act was finally passed, compulsory education from age 5 to age 13 was introduced, but this attracted remarkably little comment. School boards were also to be established for every burgh and parish, elected exclusively by ratepayers, and these Boards would take over all existing burgh and parish schools, and be entitled to levy rates, and to borrow money to build their own schools; they would also take over any schools that religious groups wished to transfer to them. The establishment of a Board of Education, based in Edinburgh, was forced into the Bill by critics, originally for three years, to supervise the transition to the new scheme. There was also to be a 'Scotch Education Department' [sic] in London controlled by the Privy Council. No financial provision was made in the Act to support those burgh schools across Scotland which became 'higher-class schools'.

National concern about endowed schools led to the establishment in the same year of the Colebrooke Commission to enquire into all Scottish Endowed Schools and Hospitals (with 'hospital' here meaning a residential school for those in special need, such as orphans or children with parents of very limited means). Sir Edward Colebrooke surveyed all Scottish endowments, and the Academy's submission gives us a further snapshot of the school round around the end of 1872.[2] At that time the Academy staff was nine males and three females, along with the calisthenics (physical exercise) instructor. Eadie, the Rector, was the only member of staff taking boarders and he had eleven, but Samuel Thomson, the English teacher, was about to do the same. It was claimed that the school could accommodate about 250 boys and 180 girls, but there were only 170 boys and 130 girls attending, with ages ranging from six or seven up to nearly sixteen. A sort of prospectus, signed by Penrose Hay, Secretary and Treasurer, was also included, but it does not seem to have been published as a separate document.

Colebrooke in his final report in 1875, recommended further legislation. The Secretary of this Commission was Simon Laurie, who was one of the examiners for the Academy in 1863 and 1864. Some of the material from this report was used by James Grant in his important book on the Burgh Schools of Scotland, published in 1876.[3]

A change of heart
Meanwhile the Inverness Burgh School Board, set up under the 1872 Act, had been busy providing new buildings for both the Merkinch and Central Schools, and planning the opening of a new school at Clachnaharry. The new Merkinch building was opened in February 1877 and the Central building was ready the following month. In September 1878 the foundation stone was laid for a new building for the High School (the building which is now used by the Crown School), now under School Board control rather than the control of the Free Church. As a private venture, the Inverness Collegiate School had laid the foundation stone of its building in May 1876, the building which is now the old part of the Highland Council headquarters and faces Ardross Street. This school had been operating since 1873 in temporary premises nearby.

The views of the Directors began to change once it was seen that the School Board was able to run the local elementary schools satisfactorily. In April 1875 Charles Waterston, a banker, gave notice that, at the annual meeting at the start of May, he would move a motion that the Academy be transferred to the School Board. Two of the Directors did oppose this action, but only to allow further consideration of the terms of the transfer.[4] The *Inverness Courier* seemed to be in favour of this move,[5] and The Mackintosh was enquiring about progress with a letter to Penrose Hay, for which the reply survives.[6] A meeting was held with the School Board on 27th August, and a memorial was submitted to Counsel to enquire about the legal position of the sale of the Academy assets.[7] The response from Counsel was not helpful, suggesting that a private Act of Parliament would be required to permit this transfer and sale. As a result the matter was dropped.

1878 saw two Acts of Parliament, one which eased the financial restrictions on higher-class schools (but this did not affect the Academy), and the other which set up a Royal Commission on endowments, headed by Lord

Moncreiff. This Commission had the power to revise endowment schemes, but only with the agreement of the parties. The annual meeting that year had seen a motion from Donald Davidson, another banker, that if this Bill became an Act during the ensuing year, the standing committee was to examine its provisions.

A letter writer to the *Inverness Courier*, 'D.D.', saw the need for a further endowment of perhaps £5000 over the next three to five years,[8] and the newspaper itself once again supported transfer.[9] The Burgh School Board started discussions in April 1879 about taking over both the Academy and the Bell's School, and there was the first of several debates as to whether the Academy should keep after transfer what we would now call a Primary Department. Replies to questions sent to the High School of Dundee, and Perth and Greenock Academies all suggested this should be retained. A further valuation of the buildings in May 1879 by architect Alexander Ross (who was to become well-known for his design of Inverness Cathedral) gave the value at £7500 (which was no change from his 1875 valuation), although it might cost £9000 or so to replace the complete school, and this sum, or more, might be realised if the building and land were sold commercially.

Henry Craik, as the very influential head of the Scotch Education Department, did open a file on the possible transfer, but whatever papers this file might have contained are no longer there, other than a single sheet of paper, dated 27th January 1880, suggesting the need to consider the minute of the Burgh meeting on the subject, when a scheme came from the Home Office.[10] A public meeting was held in the Town on 14th January 1880, to discuss the issue of transfer, but it was poorly attended. Charles Innes, Chairman of the Burgh School Board, and also an Academy Director, moved a motion that the transfer should take place, but in the end the meeting was adjourned until 10th February, when a further meeting would consider the whole issue of education in Inverness.

At the adjourned meeting, the Music Hall was crowded,[11] and Innes' motion was approved by a large majority. A committee of twenty members was suggested, five members of the Town Council (representing the Bell's Trustees), five Directors of the Royal Academy, five members of the Burgh School Board, and five others to represent the outside public, with Provost William Mackintosh as Convenor, and Roderick Scott as Clerk. Various letter-writers filled the columns of the *Courier*. Things did not go according to plan, as the Directors, at their meeting on 19th February, disagreed as to whether they should appoint members, and in the end, by six votes to four, it was agreed not to make any appointments.[12] Some days later the Bell's Trustees also decided to make no appointments, and at a meeting on 3rd March of both the School Board and public members of the proposed joint committee, it was realised that no committee could exist, and this situation would require to be announced at the public meeting scheduled for 8th March. As parliamentary elections took place at the end of that month, the matter seems to have disappeared from public concern.

Opinion of Counsel was sought again in early 1882, but this was about an idea to increase the number of Directors by appointing Parent Directors on payment of £10.[13] The opinion was favourable, but nothing could be done that year as it was claimed that, as the matter had not been raised at the preparatory meeting prior to the annual meeting, it could not be discussed. This decision was made after a vote of five to four.[14] As a result the matter was not raised again until the following year's annual meeting, when it was approved.[15] However, no Parent Directors seem to have been appointed and no such payments seem to have been received.

The effects of the 1882 Act
A significant change in the legislation was made with the establishment in 1882 of a further Endowments Commission under Lord Balfour of Burleigh. This Commission had compulsory powers, although it took seven years for it to complete its work throughout Scotland. An advertisement appeared in many newspapers in early November of that year, stating that, under Section 22 of the Act, directors of endowments could submit their own schemes for consideration, failing which the Commissioners would act on their own. The *Courier* once again gave its support for transferring the Academy to the control of the School Board.

The local School Board had just produced a statement about local education[16] stating that they considered there was adequate provision for elementary education, but that they were unable to provide higher education, and the nearest provision under public control was in Aberdeen. It must be remembered that 'higher-class schools' could not be a burden on the rates. A part of the report also listed all the local schools [Table 13.1].

Public: High School, Central School, Merkinch School, Clachnaharry School
Endowed: Royal Academy (with its own funds and the *quasi*-private Mackintosh Farr Fund), Farraline Park School (Dr Bell's Trust)
Adventure: Northern Counties Collegiate School
Private: Miss Leith's Kindergarten
Denominational: High Church School (discontinued, but the endowments remained), Roman Catholic School, Raining School (partly maintained by endowments and partly by SPCK), Cathedral Boys' School, Bishop Eden's Girls' School
Table 13.1: Schedule of Schools in Inverness in 1882

In December 1882, the Academy Directors decided it would be wise to propose a scheme to the Commissioners under the Act.[17] The resolution was to be communicated to the Provost as Chairman of both the Dr Bell's Trustees and the Mackintosh Farr Fund. A special committee meeting in January 1883 with some of the Dr Bell's trustees set out their joint position:[18]

I. That all the Educational Endowments be under the administration of one corporate body for the promotion of secondary education.
II. That in the rearrangement of these Endowments the following objects should be kept in view –
   1. The additional Endowment of the Royal Academy so as to secure that a first class secondary education be provided.
   2. The providing of bursaries of which the majority should be restricted to competition by children from the Board Schools or otherwise, so as to furnish a secondary education free of charge to poorer children.
   3. The provision of bursaries by which scholars of promise may be enabled to attend the University.
III. That in the providing of bursaries the following points shall be kept in view –
   1. Retaining the names of Donors of Endowments by calling certain bursaries after their names.
   2. Providing for the carrying out of the original design of the Donors in so far as at present advisable or possible.

A first draft of the submission was considered at the end of January, although at this stage the Mackintosh Farr Trustees were unwilling to get involved with the submission of a scheme, and did not want the property or funds handed over to the new body.[19] During the following six weeks all three of the main bodies (the Academy, the Dr. Bell's Trustees and the Mackintosh Farr Trustees) considered the draft submission, and by 3rd March the Mackintosh Farr Trustees did approve of the scheme with some reservations.

The final version was prepared in March and a special meeting of the Academy Directors approved the scheme to bring together not just these three funds but various others:[20]
   1.   the Royal Academy Endowments (from 1788)
   2.   the Mackintosh Farr Fund (1816)
   3.   the Denoon Bequest (1802)
   4.   the (Hector) Fraser Bequest (1812)
   5.   the Forbes Bequest (1882)
   6.   the Ettles Bequest (1863)
   7.   the Bell Bequest of Egmore (1831)
   8.   the Raining Bequest (1724)
   9.   Colin Davidson's Bequest (1870) – education of a boy for one year at a Free Church Institution [note: the High School was no longer controlled by the Free Church]
   10. (Murdoch) Logan's Bequest (1849) – education of a boy, named Logan or Paterson, or relative of the Trustor at any school
   11. The Laird of Mackintosh Bequest (1740) – maintenance of two boys, one a Mackintosh or member of the Clan Chattan, the other of the name of Duff, at Raining's School or any other charity school where taught gratis – under the control of the Kirk Session

12. (George) Duncan's Bequest (1715) – for six poor boys under the age of 14, at any school and providing clothes and books – under control of the Kirk Session

The Forbes Bequest (see later) was to cause problems, as bequests made within the previous few years were excluded from the provisions of the Act unless the executors agreed they should be included. At this stage the Academy had only just been advised of the terms of the bequest, and nobody had yet benefited from its provisions.

Meetings of the other key parties in late March and early April finally approved the proposals, although the Mackintosh Farr Trustees were still not happy that some of their money would be used for the benefit of the Academy.[21] Finally a conference of all the parties agreed to submit the statement and the various minutes to the secretary of the Endowments Commission. Nothing further happened for over a year, presumably as the number of schemes submitted from around Scotland delayed any immediate response.

Meeting the Educational Endowment Commissioners
As part of a tour of Scotland, the Educational Endowments Commissioners came to Inverness from 25th to 27th September 1884, with Balfour of Burleigh himself, the Earl of Elgin, Sir Thomas Boyd and Mr Ramsay, M.P., appearing. The first day and a half was taken up by evidence about endowments from places outside Inverness, and the evidence on the Royal Academy position was taken on the afternoon of the second day. All three of the main bodies had met and prepared their positions with further statements.[22] The Academy was represented by Duncan Forbes of Culloden (Chairman), James Anderson (solicitor), Rev. Mr Robson and Penrose Hay (Secretary).

From the evidence it appears that the total income of the Academy in the previous year was fee income of £1760 (of which only £1569 was collected), and endowment income of £171 4s, although the expenditure was around £2100. As a result it was not possible to offer any bursaries for competition. It was felt that the management body was too large, and a committee of nine was suggested, appointed to reflect the fact that 27% of the pupils came from "suburbs" outside the town, and 18% came in by train daily or else lodged in the town during term-time. The Directors suggested that, as the costs of running the Dr. Bell's School were much higher than the other elementary schools in the Town, this money would of greater benefit to the Town by providing bursaries at the Academy. This event saw the first serious attempt to make the case for a new Academy building, something that was not to materialise for another eleven years.

The thorny issue of the Mackintosh Farr Fund also came up again, especially with regard to who was eligible to benefit from the money, and whether the surplus could be used for promoting secondary education. The first part of the third day of evidence looked at this fund, when the Provost, representing the Trustees, suggested that about a quarter of the income might be used for supplementing the salaries of the teachers at the Academy, in return for some representation on the governing body of the Academy. In the evidence given it was stated that there had been no direct male succession in Clan Chattan (the Mackintoshes) for 150 years, and eighteen out of the twenty-one officers fighting for the clan at the Battle of Culloden in 1746 had been killed. There was disagreement amongst the trustees as to whether or not the fund was an Inverness endowment.

The Burgh School Board also put forward their favoured scheme for the Academy as a school for secondary education, with all available funds at the disposal of the governors. Brief discussion also took place over some of the other funds listed above.

The draft scheme was published in April of the following year (1885), and following discussion some amendments were suggested. The scheme was submitted to the Scotch Education Department [SED] in June for comment, but as a result of a last-minute objection the scheme was not published until April 1886, at which point the details had to lie on the Table of the House of Commons for two months. As Parliament was dissolved before the two-month period was completed, the matter had to await the next session of Parliament. At the last possible moment Charles Fraser-Mackintosh, previously the M.P. for the Inverness Burghs, but now the M.P. representing Inverness-shire, handed in a petition signed by 100 members of the Mackintosh clan, objecting to the use of the money for any purpose other than for members of the clan. Progress then stalled until February 1887, when the Secretary to the Directors was ordered to write to Mr Robert Finlay, the replacement M.P. for the Inverness Burghs (later to be Lord Chancellor), to oppose Fraser-Mackintosh's motion. Both the Academy and the Burgh School Board produced statements,[23] appealing for the Scheme to be passed, and stating that the objections were from a very small number of members of the Mackintosh clan. The Scheme was finally laid on the Table of the House on 28th February 1887, and after debate Fraser-Mackintosh withdrew his motion, clearing the way for progress. The final move took place on 25th April, when the proposed Scheme was again debated, with Fraser-Mackintosh attempting to move rejection of the Scheme as far as the Mackintosh Farr provisions were concerned. However this move was defeated by 151 votes to 25. The Scheme received Royal Approval on 13th May 1887, and two months later this action brought to an end a scheme of management that had existed with little change since the establishment of the Academy 95 years earlier.

The final version of the Scheme,[24] with sixty clauses, set up a new body to be called "The Directors of the Royal Academy and Governors of the Inverness Educational Trust", and brought together all the funds except the Forbes Fund (which had been bequeathed very recently), and established the new governing body of nine members, three elected by the Town, three by the Burgh School Board, and three by the Commissioners of Supply to represent the Inverness County interests. Various bursaries and free scholarships, including some for university or college, were to be introduced. The Mackintosh Farr Fund was to be brought under the control of this new body, although its accounting was to be kept separate. The issue as to direct descent from the heads of the four clans was fudged, as, where definite information as to genealogy was not available, the Scheme allowed bursaries to be given to relatives of those who had already benefited.

The Ettles Bursaries, the Forbes Fund, and the 'Sassoferrato' Painting

The Ettles Bursary and Trust Fund have significance to the Academy. Anna and Mary Ettles were sisters who lived in Church Street. The sisters had established a University bursary in 1863, which was open to competition every four years by those who had been resident in Inverness for at least five years and had attended the Academy for at least three years. Anna had died first, and Mary during her lifetime arranged for £1000 to be invested to form a trust fund[25] for the running of:

> an annual course of lectures by a learned & qualified person who may be one of the said Trustees themselves on Literature, Philosophy or Science to be delivered in the Inverness Royal Academy or other convenient place in Inverness if sufficient accommodation cannot be got in the Academy Buildings and which all Teachers and Students in the said Academy at the time shall be entitled to attend free of charge, and to which other persons may be admitted either free of charge or on payment of such charges as the said Trustees may from time to time fix and which charges if made shall be annually used for carrying out the purposes of the Trust, ...

Before her death in 1872 Mary requested that Dr Donald Macdonald, the First Minister of Inverness, be invited to give the first series of lectures. These took place over the winter of 1873-74 on "Sketches on the History and Literature of Scottish Philosophy", and similar courses of lectures were held for many years, covering a wide range of philosophical and scientific topics. Speakers in the twentieth century included Sir Ernest Shackleton (in 1910) and Captain Amundsen (in 1912). In the late twentieth century, as the value of the fund declined, it was incorporated into the Provost Smith Memorial Fund, and to a minor extent carried out the wishes of the Ettles sisters, although the Academy connection was lost. In the first decade of the twenty-first century the outstanding money was handed over to Eden Court Theatre, and the fund closed.

In the summer of 1881, the Directors were advised about a trust deed from Dr George F. Forbes, sometime Surgeon Major in Her Majesty's Bombay Army, for £4000, to provide for the education of three or more boys of the name of Forbes, for two years at the Academy and three years at an Aberdeen College. However a clause in the deed allowed for his sister, Mrs Margaret Tuach, to get the interest from the money during her lifetime as long as she "refrains from the vice of intemperance, and lives at least twelve miles from Inverness". Following the death of this sister in March 1882, the money became available in the form of a bond for land in Haddingtonshire [East Lothian]. The first bursars were appointed in the autumn of 1883.

One of the final acts of the Directors before the 1887 change of management structure was to pass the oil painting of *The Holy Family* to the Town Council for safe keeping. It will be remembered (Chapters 6 and 10), that this painting had been gifted to the Directors in 1801 in the will of James Clark. After the abortive attempt to sell the painting in 1868, it was rehung in the Drawing classroom of the Ladies' Institution, where it was thought it was less likely to be damaged than if it were hanging in the main hall. Despite this, the painting was damaged in 1882[26] and a further attempt was made to find a better place to hang it.

At the annual general meeting on 1st May 1886, it was agreed that the Secretary would approach the Town Council to see if the picture could be hung in the new Town Hall, which had been opened in January 1882. This was agreed to with the following minute:[27]

> Read letter from Mr Hay, Secretary to the Academy Directors, dated third instant, asking permission to place the oil painting of the "Holy Family", belonging to the Directors, in the Town Hall. The Council agreed to grant permission to the Directors to place the painting in the Town Hall for custoday *[sic]* in a situation to be fixed by the Improvements Committee.

There is no record that has been traced of further discussion on the subject, and it appears that the picture is still hanging in the Town House at the request of the Directors of the Academy.

School life in the 1870's and 1880's

Little of note occurred in the life of the Academy at this time. The number of pupils slipped from about 320 in 1872 to about 200 in 1876, but then picked up again.

In 1875 Professor Black of Aberdeen was asked to conduct the annual external examination, as William Eadie, the Rector, did not know him (too many examinations in the past were in effect a 'pat on the back' for the Rector). The examination was to be conducted in the same way as in the 'Higher-class Schools' established under the 1872 Act. Black's report was generally satisfactory, although he felt that more pupils should go on to University. His fee was £10 10/- [£10.50], and Black continued to inspect the Academy annually until 1879, when he was very slow in producing his report. The following year he was invited again to report, but in the end it was done by Professor Geddes, who continued to examine for a few years. Most of the examiners' reports appear in the pages of the *Inverness Courier*, although some of them seem to be rather lacking in criticism.

The public examination, largely to view the art and needlework exhibits, which the outside examiner frequently admitted he was not competent to judge, continued annually on the last day of the session, prior to the orations and prizegiving. Newspaper articles always reported on the work, and the needlework exhibits frequently receiving great praise, especially after the appointment of Miss Grace Middleton as the teacher of needlework, following her transfer from the High School in 1882. The traditional orations gradually changed into more of a concert, although the Ladies' Institution also held what was called a music examination, such as those held in 1880, 1881 and 1883 [Figure 13.1],[28] which lasted about two hours according to the press report. The event was held in the Music Hall, then off Union Street, except in 1889 when a fire in an adjacent property had damaged the building a matter of days before the scheduled event, and the prizegiving and concert took place in the Town Hall.

The first class photograph that survives dates from session 1877-78, with a picture of the senior English class with their teacher, Samuel Thomson [Figure 13.2].[29] However he and his junior colleague in the English department, Andrew Wilson, were both seen drunk in July 1879, and were reprimanded, as this was a first offence,[30] with the warning that they would be dismissed without notice if it happened again. Thomson was again accused of drunkenness the following autumn, but there was confusion as to whether there was sufficient evidence to act. In the end he was persuaded to resign from the end of the 1882-83 session, after about 18 years on the staff.

George Cumming Gray, a pupil in session 1880-81, mentions both English teachers in some reminiscences which appeared in the *Inverness Courier* in 1940.[31] Thomson, known as "Sammy", always wore a silk hat and double-breasted jacket of dark material, but managed, according to Gray, to inculcate a love of good literature and elocution amongst the pupils. Wilson, or "Wilkie" out of his hearing, was, according to Gray, an excellent teacher, and is remembered for his tawse, which he kept handy in his coat-tail pocket, and which provided "a mighty incentive to study". He apparently had a habit of saying "Avoid talk" whether or not the pupils were whispering amongst themselves. Both Thomson and Wilson could be persuaded to spend the lesson before the Christmas holidays and before examination day telling the class a story that managed to exactly fill the hour's lesson.

Also mentioned by Gray is Thomas Cockburn, who was to become a much-beloved teacher. He started as a classics teacher in December 1879, although under Rector W. J. Watson he was also to teach English, German and Hebrew. Cockburn is still remembered in the Academy by a special collection in the School Library (see Chapter 18). In his younger days he had briefly tried to tutor Robert Louis Stevenson in Latin without any success, due to Stevenson being too ready to talk and read his own manuscripts.[32] Known as 'Cobey' to the pupils, Cockburn served thirty years on the Academy staff, before retiring in 1909, at a relatively early age, to Edinburgh where he continued his love of languages, becoming an expert in Sanskrit, Icelandic and various Indian languages, although he admitted defeat with Hungarian. He learned Gaelic during his time in Inverness. He probably knew well over forty languages, despite only ever having left Scotland once, a journey from his native Duns in the Borders to Northumberland. He died in 1947, aged 95, and the tributes in *The Scotsman* were led by a famous former pupil, The Very Rev. Professor John Baillie.[33]

Herr Waack, the German teacher, was remembered for his capable playing of the violoncello at local music events. French was also taught by a native of the language, a Monsieur Baillod. The teaching of Pitman's shorthand was introduced in session 1876-77, probably by George Easton, the commercial teacher, who wrote in a beautiful hand himself, whilst encouraging the pupils to follow suit. William Eadie, the Rector, still taught mathematics using slates, although the writing with Easton was done in copybooks.

Another teacher, who, although part-time, made a significant contribution to the Academy was W. Stewart Roddie, first appointed as teacher of sol-fa music notation in August 1883. Roddie also served in various other schools, as well as leading a local church choir and various singing groups in the Town. His appointment was in addition to that of Herr Kesting, who had taught music since 1867. From the summer after his appointment, Roddie introduced "Grand Floral Concerts" in the Music Hall, which was decked with flowers and greenery. The early events were mainly for the girls, but later included a significant number of boys. Large numbers of parents and others attended, and some performances had to be repeated to allow all those who wished to attend to do so. The first such performance was *The Flower Queen*, by Root, but within two years Roddie was writing his own material, with a performance of *The Hermit's Cell* in 1886. That same year the boys' singing class performed *John Bull and his Trades*. Later performances included his versions of a Robin Hood story and of *Sleeping Beauty*. Eventually these events migrated from the Academy to the Junior Choral Society, and so involved a wider range of local young people.

The Lady Superintendent in 1881, Mary Anne Fraser, appealed for an increase in her salary up to the level that her predecessors had received.[34] It was to be over a year before her salary was increased to £120.[35] Other members of staff frequently requested increases, especially the female members, who would always receive lower salaries than the males, as was normal at that time. The first printed prospectus was produced in 1884, but no copy of this edition has survived, although copies of almost all later editions are available.

Sport begins to appear as an extracurricular activity, and occasional references to football matches start to appear in the pages of the *Inverness Courier* from 1882. From the recorded scores it seems that the game was hardly football as is known today. Cricket games are also mentioned from time to time, and by the 1890's football, in the modern sense of the word, seems to have become popular in the Town, with the boys asking the Directors to find a proper pitch where they could play, rather than in the playground behind the original Academy building.

Snowball fights also get a mention in any reminiscences of the period, including another article of "Memories" which appeared in a school magazine early in the twentieth century.[36] Fighting between the boys also seems to have been quite common, usually broken up by the approach of the "jannie" [janitor]:

> ... How slowly and reluctantly he used to advance up the Park to put a stop to a battle royal, to the distant sounds of which he had turned, as long as he dared, being a soldier and a fighter of fame himself, a deaf yet anxious ear. Then at the first whisper of his coming, erstwhile foes would be hoisted by eager hands over the high wall and under the wire netting, long ago loosened by by-gone generations for just such an emergency as this; over, I say, the high wall and the higher netting which separated us from the hallowed precincts of the girls' playground.

The janitor was probably Sgt. Hugh Macleod, late Seaforth Highlanders, although it may have been either his predecessor or his successor, both of whom had army service.

With the introduction of the new Inverness Endowments Scheme in the summer of 1887, the old order for the Academy, based on the Royal Charter, passed away, and the new Board of Management took over, although the Academy was not really yet a public school in the Scottish meaning of the word 'public'. The new Trustees asked the existing Directors to continue the day-to-day running of the Academy for the first few months, whilst they established themselves as an effective committee. Soon the school would be celebrating its centenary and starting to construct a new building.

Chapter 14
The approaching centenary and the new building

The Board of Directors had served the school for ninety-five years in its original form. However change had come – a new Rector was to be appointed, there was talk of a new building to replace the original one, and, almost unnoticed, the centenary of the opening of the Academy approached.

A new beginning

The first meeting of the new Board of Directors and Governors took place on 11th July 1887, when the Provost of Inverness, Henry Cockburn Macandrew, was elected to the chair. Within the next month the draft regulations and standing orders were drawn up,[1] and it was agreed that the posts of clerk and factor would be advertised. Within a further week Robert Hay, a solicitor, was appointed as clerk, and Hugh Fraser, a writer (solicitor) and W.S., became the factor, but had to produce a guarantee of £1500 for his actions. It was agreed that Bell's School would be continued under the Board's management for the next year, subject to the approval of the Scotch Education Department [SED], in the hope that by the following year some arrangement would have been made with the Inverness Burgh School Board for them to take over the school and its building.

The new scheme allowed the Directors to dismiss all the staff and appoint a new Rector. It was known that Eadie wanted to retire. The staff were all re-employed but on three month's notice. The advertisement for the new Rector, at a salary of £300 and a capitation grant to be arranged, brought 75 applications, including Eadie, applying for his own job, as no arrangements were yet in place for a pension. From this list three candidates were interviewed on 24th November, but no appointment was actually made until the state of the funds was better known. When the finances had been checked, it was felt that Eadie could get a retiring allowance of £100 for up to ten years, again subject to SED permission, which was granted. This allowed him to withdraw his application for his own job. Early in 1889, a testimonial fund was started for him, following letters in the *Courier*,[2] and over the next two years the sum of 60 guineas [£63] was collected, and sent on to Eadie who by this time was living in Dollar.[3]

One of the candidates on the short leet for the post of Rector tried to push for an early decision, and was promptly taken off the list. George Bruce, at the age of 29, of Gordon's College, Aberdeen, was invited to take up the post after Christmas, but after discussion at the Board meeting on 13th December it was agreed that he could start on 13th February 1888.[4] His salary was fixed at £300, the minimum allowed under the scheme, with a capitation payment of 10s [50p] for each pupil over 150 on the roll. Bruce accepted the job a few days later. The provisions of the new scheme provided for the Rector to appoint all the staff, so all the existing staff were given notice. Bruce was given permission to advertise for a mathematics master to continue the teaching that Eadie did, and by early February John Wilson Reid, one of those who had actually applied for appointment as Rector, was appointed.

Very soon after his appointment Bruce, in the company of the Town Provost, had visited various Higher-Class schools in Scotland to establish how they operated. These were George Heriot's and George Watson's in Edinburgh, the Heriot-Watt College (then a trades training institution in Edinburgh), Edinburgh Ladies' College (better known today as The Mary Erskine School), Glasgow Academy for Boys, Kelvinside Academy, The High School of Dundee, Harris Academy (Dundee) and four public schools. This list shows a distinct emphasis on 'private' fee-paying schools, which in part still matched the role of the Royal Academy in Inverness.

His report was brought before the Directors in June, but even before then Bruce had introduced changes, as outlined in the *Courier* in May.[5] He himself took over the teaching of the senior English classes in both the boys' and girls' schools (which, it will be remembered, were in separate buildings), as well as the boys' Greek class; new classes in physics, chemistry and elementary French were introduced for the boys; special preparation was made for girls to enter the Edinburgh Local Examinations (which became an important route for girls who were interested in becoming teachers or other professional jobs deemed suitable for women); and the boys had drill and the girls calisthenics as an integral part of the timetable. For the girls a 'tennis green' was prepared.

Staff numbers were reduced, and, after repeated protests from the public about their high level, a reduced scale of fees was agreed in the hope that numbers would increase to make up the reduced income per pupil. Primary education was now available free of charge for all who wished, following the full implementation of the 1872 Education Act, and many were hoping that secondary education would also become free. According to the sheet listing class fees for session 1888-89, the numbers attending the Academy at the start of the 1888 summer holiday were 95 boys and 64 girls, spread across the age groups, just above the level at which Bruce was to receive capitation payments.

By August of 1888 Bruce had appointed new staff, which included someone whose name is still known in Inverness – Pierre Delavault – as his illustrations of Old Inverness are still in demand [see Figure 2.2 for his painting of the former Grammar School]. Delavault was to serve on the staff and run evening classes in art until his fairly sudden illness and death in the early days of 1907.[6] Cockburn continued as classics teacher, and was to be commended by the School inspector in the summer of 1889 as one of the best teachers that he had ever seen.[7] Inspection reports remained good, although in 1890 the inspector said that the teachers were not sufficiently valued, and their salaries should be increased. Some increases were paid the following year.

Following a motion by one of the Directors, the Rector and the Directors' Education Committee were asked to report on the use of books that used the words 'England' or 'English' when it should have read 'Britain' or 'British'. In the end the Rector was allowed to use his discretion as to the books to be used. There was also a row about whether or not the Directors should consider the religious affiliation of those applying for appointments. Forbes of Culloden raised the issue, despite strong protests from the Chairman (Sir Henry Macandrew), but in the end the proposed staff were found to be Protestant, and thus were appointed.[8] This seems to be the only time when this matter came to the fore. There were also debates as to how far, and from what age, boys and girls should be taught separately, and whether the lunch break in winter should be one hour or only half an hour. It was proposed that during a shorter break hot lunches could be provided by a local confectioner.

The new session in September 1888, the first new session after Bruce was appointed, opened with an organ and piano recital in the Ladies' Institution by the school music staff and the Cathedral organist (the organ was probably an American organ or harmonium). A dancing teacher was appointed, and there was consideration of the appointment of a dressmaking teacher. Funds were still so tight that requests to introduce the new scheme for bursaries and free scholarships had to be turned down for a couple of years, despite a question on the subject being asked in the House of Commons.[9] The scheme was introduced in a limited way in 1890. Funds could not even be found to enter pupils for the recently introduced Leaving Certificate examinations, and some pupils paid their own entry fees of 2s 6d per subject in 1889.

The revised scheme for the Forbes Fund, bequeathed in 1881, was brought into operation in 1890, and bursaries became available both in the school and at Aberdeen University, with the university bursaries awarded after a competitive examination along the lines of the Aberdeen University competitions. Over half of the first part of the examination were papers in Latin, Greek, and mathematics (included fractions and proportions, simple algebraic equations and the first three books of Euclidian geometry). The second part of the examination provided a choice between translations from English to Latin, more advanced mathematics, and some combination of papers in Latin, French, German, chemistry and biology. When the scheme was first advertised, none of the potential candidates was a pupil at the Academy, and their parents were advised to enrol them immediately if the child was to sit the examination.

Approaching the Centenary
The period around the time of the centenary in 1892 was marred by two problems. One was the possibility that the former clerk and factor had misappropriated funds from the Mackintosh Farr endowment, and the other was that the new Board of Directors lost faith in Bruce. Work did start on planning the new school building.

The Directors struggled to establish what the Factor, Mr Alexander Simpson, had done with some of the Mackintosh Farr funds, as some relevant documents could not be traced. In 1888 there were debts of £2286, some of which had been paid by Simpson's brother, as the former factor had since died. The main cause seems to have been the misappropriation of rents and feus from some of the larger farms owned by the Mackintosh Farr Fund. The sums in question had not been paid into the bank account, causing it to be overdrawn. Legal opinion had to be sought as to whether the Directors were personally liable for the debts, and, if so, to what extent. The SED also got involved. By 1891 it was agreed to pay off the debts in yearly instalments from revenue, and at least one potential Mackintosh Farr bursar had to be turned down due to the restricted funds that were available. Meanwhile all the necessary day-to-day issues to do with ownership of land by the Trust had to be dealt with, including legal charters, the clearing of blocked sluices, and the Railway Company wanting to purchase further land.

The Directors seem to have made no reference to the centenary, and it was left to Bruce, as Rector, to try to engender some interest. A school magazine, *The Academical*, was issued for the first time in February 1892,[10] with a cover design by Pierre Delavault [Figure 14.1], but it was described as "essentially a masters' magazine", with very little input from pupils. The magazine was to run until Bruce's departure in June 1894. The first issue contained an article by Thomas Cockburn recalling his brief attempt in his earlier years to tutor Robert Louis Stevenson. The December 1892 issue included a coloured insert of art work by Pierre Delavault. The March 1893 edition, at the time when construction on the new school was just about to start, contained a reprint of an "Ode on erecting an Academy at Inverness", which had first appeared in the *European Magazine* in April 1793.

In March 1892 'Ian', probably Bruce himself, appealed for suggestions as to how to celebrate the centenary. By the April meeting of the Academy Board Bruce had written to them suggesting that armorial bearings for the school should be designed:[11]

I have sketched out a design, after careful consideration of the history of the foundation and progress of the school. In arranging and selecting quarterings, I have been struck by the prominent part played all along by the Mackintosh family in founding and maintaining the Academy. After it received the Royal Charter in 1792 *[incorrect date]*, a substantial Endowment Fund was raised mainly through the efforts of the then Mackintosh of Raigmore. William Mackintosh was Provost of the burgh in the year of foundation, 1792; and, I believe, lent the dignity of his office as Chief Magistrate to promote the scheme and help his fellow-clansman of Raigmore. In 1810 *[incorrect date]* Captain William Mackintosh of Farr bequeathed to the Academy a large sum of money, which is well known under the name of the Mackintosh Farr Fund. Lastly, we have two gentlemen of the same honourable name on the Board of Governors in this year of grace 1892. For these reasons, I have quartered on the shield in the enclosed sketch the oared ship which is an integral part of the Arms of Mackintosh of that Ilk. In the first quarter I have placed the lion rampant of Scotland; in the second the facade of a Greek temple, foreshadowing the new Academy; in the third, an open book, with the key to

213

knowledge across its pages, indicating the object of our existence. The whole is surmounted by a Royal Crown, as befits a Royal Corporation; and the motto proposed is, *Labore et virtute*, "By labour and by virtue." This crest might appear on our medals, prizes, certificates, and such like rewards and documents. It might have to be sanctioned by the Lyon King of Arms, if adopted."

The Directors approved the project, and a sub-committee was appointed to carry out arrangements for the centenary. A letter in the *Courier* supported the proposal,[12] and suggested that the Rector and the Secretary should write a history of the school, but this came to nothing. Another letter claimed that Bruce's suggestions for the coat of arms were heraldically wrong. Mr G. H. Gall, an architect in Aberdeen, redrew the coat of arms for a fee of three guineas [£3 3s], with the final version agreed in June 1892 [Figure 14.2]. *The Academical* carried a feature in the November 1892 edition:

The new Coat of Arms for this institution, as designed by Mr G. H. Gall, architect, shows a saltire or St Andrews Cross on a blue field surmounted by an open book - meaning that they represent a Scottish seat of learning. On either side of the saltire are a camel's head and an elephant's head, respectively to show, heraldicly [sic], that the seat is in the burgh of Inverness; in the base is the crest of the Mackintoshes - a cat salient - to commemorate the interest taken by that family in the foundation of the institution. The title "Royal" is indicated by an imperial crown above the saltire, and below the arms is the motto, suggested by the rector, "Labore et Virtute." In future, all the class books and papers will bear the new academy arms, and all documents will be authenticated by a corresponding seal.

The machine to emboss the seal, which cost £4 5s, is still in occasional use in the school today. It was not until 1933 that the final sentence of Bruce's letter was put into effect, when the School was threatened with legal action by the Lord Lyon King of Arms if the arms were not properly matriculated (see Chapter 17).

Typewriting was introduced as part of the commercial course in 1892 when two new typewriters were purchased. Instruction was only to be for those aged over 14, and it was to be regarded as an 'extra' subject, with an additional fee of 5s per quarter to be paid. Fraser-Mackintosh, the local antiquarian, and at that point the local Member of Parliament, presented a centenary medal for mathematics.[13] When the pupils requested a football pitch, permission was given to use the site of the new school as long as a teacher or janitor was present during games.

1892 also saw the revival of the Christmas 'At Home' in the school hall, suitably decorated. It took the form of a ceilidh, although that word was not in use at the time.The *Courier* report ended with these words:[14]

The programme of music and interval for tea and talk having been successfully carried through, the younger pupils retired, while the seniors prolonged the evening with an additional hour's dancing. The entertainment proved a most agreeable one, all the performers acquitting themselves excellently, the Christy Minstrel item affording much amusement. Some of the character dresses of the young ladies were very prettily designed and extremely becoming. The old

customs of the Academy bid fair to be resuscitated.
The cantatas directed by W. S. Roddie, and performed in the Music Hall, continued, with that performed in 1893 being *Beauty and the Beast*, and in 1894 *Dangerland*. Photographs of some of the productions are in the Christmas 1893 edition of *The Academical*.

Another new Rector
With the plans of a new school building starting to be realised, the Directors were keen to increase the numbers of pupils and so bring in more money through fees. At their meeting in early 1893, it was revealed that fee income was actually declining,[15] and the Rector was asked to explain why this was happening. In his report later in the month he suggested that it might be possible to obtain money from a Government scheme for Aid to Secondary Education, and the Directors' Education sub-committee proposed a scheme for fifty free bursaries, which would attract Government money. The scheme came into effect from the start of the following session, with those with merit certificates from their own schools not being specifically examined. 26 young people took the first exam, with two others exempt. One of the first batch of pupils to benefit was Evan Barron, later well known as the editor of the *Inverness Courier*. He was to become very involved with the Academy Old Boys' Club and he started to write the suggested history of the Academy (see Chapters 15 and 16).

From 1891 the school was also involved with a national scheme promoted by the Department of Science and Art in London to instruct for, and conduct exams in, various subjects, through evening classes. It was necessary to improve the artificial lighting in the school for this to happen. John Reid (mathematics), Pierre Delavault (art) and Charles Greaves (commercial subjects) were involved in the teaching, but one of the early examinations was deemed invalid as none of the local organising committee was present at the time the examination was conducted.

Although there was some disagreement amongst their number, by March 1893 the Directors were inviting Bruce to resign.[16] Partly due to more provision of free education in other schools in the community, the speed at which pupil numbers were increasing was not fast enough to bring in enough money to run the school efficiently. However, the following month the decision to dismiss Bruce was rescinded. Then, in June 1893, came a fairly critical examination report from two of Her Majesty's Inspectors, neither of whom had inspected the school previously. The report was suppressed. Bruce, in his response to the Directors, complained that one of the Inspectors seemed biased against the Academy, and that there were errors in the French examination which he had set.[17] He also said that the same Inspector flourished an umbrella over a girl's head when she was attempting to answer a question.

Discussions also took place in the autumn of 1893 on the future of secondary education in Inverness.[18] A conference of all interested parties was held in the Town, from which the Academy felt that being an efficient secondary school was the way forward, with the primary department being closed if necessary. It was claimed at that point that there were 170 paying scholars and 130 free scholars. The planned new school would accommodate 400, so there was room for a further 100 scholars paying £5 a year. The corresponding report to the Town Council suggested the strengthening of technical education in the Town, although not necessarily all under one roof. The details of this debate, which included a considerable number of letters to the local press, fall outwith the scope of this history, but there was a motion in 1894 to discontinue the primary department of the Academy as soon as funds permitted. That year the Burgh School Board agreed to centralise secondary education for pupils who did not attend the Academy. This was put into effect in the old Raining's School building, under the control of the High School, and was to be free.

The call to Bruce to resign as Rector was renewed in early 1894, and he was told that if he did not resign, his appointment would terminate at the end of the session. A special general meeting was held on 8th May, at which Bruce spoke and gave explanations about teaching, management and attendance.[19] As required under the regulations, his dismissal was confirmed at another meeting on 25th May. The *Courier* gives some clue as to the problems when it said he was conscientious and hardworking, but had not been as successful as had been hoped. The first known photograph of the staff was taken round about this time, if the listed names are correct [Figure 14.3].

Bruce appealed for more time, and support for his retention, for at least another year until the new school building was fully operational, came from a significant body of parents. A parents' deputation spoke at a Directors' meeting, but it was to no avail. Following the meeting on 13th June, the unsatisfactory Inspectors' report from the previous summer was released to the press. Pupil numbers had fallen from 259 last session to 208 this session. The pupils hissed at some of the Directors when they came on to the platform at the annual entertainment and prizegiving.

Bruce ceased to be Rector from the end of the session that summer, but was given six months' salary instead of the three to which he was entitled. At least Bruce was able to leave following a more satisfactory Inspectors' report than he had received the previous year, even though the same two HMIs carried out the inspection. At his farewell following the prizegiving, Bruce received an inscribed writing desk and various volumes of literature from the pupils, and he shook hands with every one of them as they left. He was to stay in Inverness for some years, taking over the running of the New Glenmoriston College for young ladies in a house in Culduthel Road. Thereafter he emigrated to Canada to farm, dying in 1947, aged 90.

Seven or eight candidates came forward for the vacant post of Rector, from which a short leet of four was selected. The selected candidates came from

George Watson's College and Daniel Stewart's College (both in Edinburgh), Kelvinside Academy (Glasgow), and Glasgow Academy. The four candidates were given Bruce's recent report to the Directors and asked to comment.[20] After a recess of one and a half hours for them to study the report, they were then interviewed. When it came to the vote, William J. Watson from Kelvinside Academy was appointed on the casting vote of the Chairman, with Thomas Adams from George Watson's College being unsuccessful. Watson, who was born in Strathconnon although largely educated in Aberdeen and Oxford, was the first native Gaelic speaker to be appointed as Rector of the Academy, although his University degree was in classics. He was aged 30 at the time of his appointment.

It was soon agreed that fees would be reduced with effect from the following session, by which time the new building would be in use. One of the Directors moved that secondary education at the Academy should be free, but he got no seconder for his motion,[21] but the number of free scholarships was doubled from 50 to 100. Later in the month it was agreed that an immediate reduction of fees would be made, rather than wait to the following session. Fees were reduced from £6 to £4 per annum for the Middle School and from £8 to £5 for the Upper School. Soon Watson persuaded the Directors that boys and girls should be educated together.

The new school building
Immediately the new management scheme was in place in 1887, negotiations proceeded with the Inverness Burgh School Board over the transfer of Bell's School, which the Academy Directors did not see as having anything to do with them, other than for the value of its assets. The transfer scheme required them to get rid of this school within a year if possible. The Directors wanted £4000 for the building, but the School Board was only willing to pay £3000 – in the end an offer of £3500 was accepted in July 1888, with dissent from Forbes of Culloden.[22] The deal was finally signed in November[23] and included the furniture and plenishments [= equipment and furnishings], even though these were not included in the original offer.

This money was essential to the Directors so that planning for the new school building could be started. Various inspectors' reports over the previous ten years or so had commented on the poor facilities available in the existing Academy Street building. In the early summer of 1888 various alternative sites were examined. The Prudential Heritable Property Trust offered a site at the Crown (not the site eventually used). A site at Haugh Park was examined, but the suggested price of £3600 was regarded as far too high and preliminary enquiries were to be made about an offer of £2500. The old building was offered for sale but by the deadline in August no offers were received. The following summer the Town Council was enquiring if the building was still for sale, and at what price. It was agreed that £7000 would be asked, as long as the Academy could retain possession of it until the new school was ready. This negotiation did not proceed.

Little happened to expedite the new building for another two years, as the finances had still not stabilised after the new management structure was introduced. Some minor repairs and improvements were made in the existing building, but major work was impossible. Then in September 1891 the Treasurer was able to make this statement:[24]

... After the most anxious consideration, the Reporter is of opinion (1) that the Trust is now in a position, without financial risk, to face the expense of building a new Academy; and (2) that the want of suitable and sufficient accommodation is a financial loss to the Trust, a loss to the Town, and a hindrance to the proper working of the Scheme.

Reported by

HUGH FRASER, *Treasurer.*

James Anderson, a solicitor, and one of the representatives appointed by Inverness County, pushed matters forward through October with special meetings, reports, and site visits. Sites at Broadstone and Damfield were visited, and in the following month sites at Viewfield and Maryfield were also inspected. The Viewfield site, apparently just west of the present site of Porterfield Prison, was regarded as too small, although financial negotiations did take place early in 1892. Correspondents and editorials in the local newspapers also brought the matter to public attention. One *Courier* editorial provides some background:[25]

The Site of the New Academy – We understand that, in the matter of selection of a site for the New Academy, things are practically in the same position as they were left by the recent meeting of the Academy Board, when the offer of a site adjacent to Viewhill House was allowed to stand over, and a committee appointed to examine the other sites offered or suggested. The Governors meet again in a few days and there is a possibility that a new site may be selected. At all events, it is stated that an offer will be considered in respect to a piece of ground on the north side of Midmills Road, just beyond the opening into Victoria Circus. The ground is finely situated and is, we believe, of more than sufficient extent. It would be more particularly defined as lying between Midmills Road, Victoria Circus, Lovat Road and Cawdor Road. A line of cottages separates this site from Midmills Road, and it is only a stone throw, in a north-easterly direction from the High School. No steps have, of course, yet been taken as to the site, but it appears to be regarded as a suitable one by several of the Governors, and if the terms offered by the owners of the land, the Prudential Heritable Property Trust, are moderately reasonable, the site is likely to be favourably considered.

In the end the site selected was somewhat west of that defined in the newspaper article. The land then on offer excluded a strip of land adjacent to Stephen's Street, which would later become the front entrance to the school, but which the Prudential Company had wanted to retain, probably for house building. Negotiations with the Prudential Company proceeded through the spring of 1892, and, at a special committee meeting in May, matters started to conclude with an offer for the whole area of land south of Crown House for £22 10s an acre, with the boundaries going right to Stephen's Street and Midmills Road, and with entry at the legal term date of Whitsun 1892. James Anderson chose to dissent from this decision, but the grounds of his dissent were not recorded.[26]

Ross and Macbeth, the architects retained by the Directors, estimated the cost of a school for 500 pupils (even though actual numbers of pupils were far below this figure at that time), to include some provision for technical education, at £7000, with an extra £1000 for laying out the grounds and building boundary walls.[27] Clause 26 of the endowments scheme required the new school to be built and fitted out for under £10000, and this in the end was not quite achieved, even though attempts were made to keep down the costs. Final agreement went through the Directors' Meeting on 9th June. The following day the *Courier* had this to say in its editorial comment:[28]

> The Governors are, we believe, fully alive to the requirements of the present day in relation to that matter *[providing a school for secondary and higher education]*, and, as they are gentlemen of taste and public spirit, they will also allow the architects sufficient margin to design a building which will be a structural thing of beauty and a public ornament for many a year to come. The site – the Crown ground at the upper end of Stephen's Brae – is a highly satisfactory one from most points of view. We confess to a leaning towards the place originally chosen at Viewhill, but there is a good deal of resemblance between the one place and the other. Either would be vastly superior to the present dingy, barrack-looking building, which might have been profitably abandoned years ago. Still, for old Academy boys – and despite chances and changes, there are a good many left in Clachnacuddin – the ancient edifice will always have happy memories.

There was argument as to what the architects' fees should be, and Alexander Ross did to some extent modify his fees. Debate in January 1893 realised that it was impossible to build a suitable school within the costs – some money could be saved by omitting certain wings, and having a central hall as a gymnasium, and giving certain rooms removable partitions so that one teacher could supervise more than one class. (Some of these partitions remained in place (although fixed) until the 1970's.) In the end the plan was scaled back to accommodate 350, or perhaps 400, pupils at a cost of £7550, including furniture, walls, gates and heating and ventilation equipment. The plans were first published in *The Academical*, the recently established school magazine, but they are so heavily reduced, and the printing methods of the day were so basic, that it is difficult to determine the detail, although the main structure is clear enough[29] [Figure 14.4].

Eventually by April 1893 the Directors were able to examine the estimates for the various trades, and although Anderson had previously had reservations about the whole project, he now proposed the motion to accept the seven offers which totalled £8767 15s 6d – already well over the costs that had been previously been stated. A few weeks later the plans passed through the Dean of Guild, something which had only become a requirement a few years previously.

Work seems to have started immediately, but it was then realised that the Grand Master Mason of Scotland, the Earl of Haddington, was to visit

Inverness, and so a ceremony for the laying of the foundation stone was arranged for 27th June 1893 at 3 p.m. Mr Roddie trained up a choir to sing a Masonic hymn. The foundation stone would contain a copper plate with the names of the Directors and officials, the architect and the contractors; specimens of the current coins up to the value of a sovereign; the four last newspapers published in the Burgh, a school prospectus, and copies of *The Academical* which included the plans.

The Highland Volunteer Artillery Band was engaged (for a sum not to exceed £4), and the police were to attend. In the presence of the Town officials, and members of the Burgh School Board, a procession assembled in the Town and proceeded to the site. Local photographers took photographs of the event, two of which by a Mr Cooper survive in the school archive[30] [Figure 14.5]. After the ceremony, a cake and wine reception was arranged in the Town Hall, something which was to cause problems later when the SED questioned this expenditure as a legitimate item in the costs of the new school. Just as with the opening of the first Academies in the 1790's, Fortrose had beaten Inverness in constructing their new Academy, as the foundation stone of their new building had been laid in August 1890, and the building opened in March 1892.

It was only towards the end of 1893 that the old school building in Academy Street was once again offered for sale, and the Directors agreed that the building should be put up for public roup with an upset price of £7500, the figure which Ross, the architect, had put on the building several times,[31] although it was later reduced to £7000. Newspaper advertisements appeared in February 1894, and on the 16th March the only, and therefore successful, bid was that from Macrae and Dick, the firm that still survives in Inverness today as a motorcar sales and repair business, but at that stage was a coaching and posting business. It is possible that the only known photograph of the school building before conversion [see Figure 4.2] dates from this time.

Meanwhile work proceeded on the new building, although at times progress seems to have been rather slow. Furniture was costed in January 1895, and very soon plans were made for the opening of the new building, even though there was no accommodation on site for the janitor, and would not be until 1900. It had been a particularly snowy winter, and early February had seen a particularly heavy frost. The toilets in the old building became frozen, forcing the premature closure of the old building and a short school holiday, while furniture and other items were moved. The opening was fixed for Monday 25th February, with due ceremony, even though the toilets at the new building were not ready either, and the architect was told to make temporary arrangements.

As usual for a major Inverness event the *Courier*, without the aid of photographs, painted 'word pictures' of the new building:[32]
The new institution is, from an architectural point of view, a pleasant contrast to its

predecessor. Its erection has entailed an expenditure by the Academy Board of £10,000; and designed by Messrs Ross & Macbeth, it has every appearance externally and internally, of answering the many purposes of a modern educational institution. Facing Stephen's Brae, the new building stands within its own grounds, and forms a fine level stretch of about 5½ acres. The structure has a very handsome appearance and is designed in the Elizabethan style of architecture, having two spacious flats. Entrance is by a broad flight of steps which leads into the outer hall, at the end of which a corridor runs along the breadth of the building, separating the front block from the main portion of the school. To the front there are rooms for the rector and other teachers. The large central hall, measuring 70 by 30 feet, occupies the centre of the floor, and is excellently adapted for examinations, science classes, and entertainments. The hall is overlooked by side galleries to which admission is gained by broad flights of stairs. On the ground floor on either side are the ordinary class-rooms. The gallery stairs give access to the science laboratory and lecture rooms on the right wing, and to the art and modelling rooms on the left wing, all on the upper floor. The rooms for the teaching of modern languages, needlework, cookery and domestic economy, and senior and junior music, and in the front of the first floor. All these rooms are large, lofty, and well ventilated.

Poor weather caused the abandonment of a proposed 'grand academic procession' from Academy Street to the new site in the Crown District. The Rev. C. V. A. MacEchern many years later described how the pupils did move from the old building to the new one:[33]

.... The entire school marched in disorderly array up to the NEW ACADEMY on the Crown land. The juniors carried flags and the seniors kept replying in their own way to the jeers and rude remarks from the boys going to the High School. At anyrate, the big boys were proud of their school blazers. That was something which the boys of the rival school must have envied.

At the new school we had the same staff. I remember best Miss Brown, the head of the juniors; Miss Middleton and Miss Kennedy; and among the masters Mr Cockburn, Mr Reid, Mr Greaves, M. Delavault and, of course, Mr W. S. Roddie, the Father of Inverness music. Mr Watson, the rector, made Monday morning a nightmare, for that was the day when he came and took our Latin class.

The re-opening of the school in the new building in the Crown district brought to a close over 103 years of use of the original building in Academy Street, and this was soon put to other uses. The Ladies' School, to the rear of the old building, was demolished so that Macrae and Dick could build workshops and stables for the horses. By October 1895 they were able to move into their new premises, reached through the lane on the right of the 1792 building.

The original school was converted into shops, including a 'steam bakery', later to be known by many older Invernessians as Burnett's Tea Rooms and shop:[34]

THE TRANSFORMATION OF THE OLD ACADEMY. – The plans of the steam bakery and other buildings which are to take the place of the Academy block in Academy Street have been laid before the Dean of Guild Court. The old block is to be only partially demolished. The plans show four large and handsome shops on the ground floor, one of which will be utilised for the business of the Bakery company, while in the rear is to be erected a building in which the bakery will be carried on. Four large ovens are to be put in and the latest machinery is to be introduced for the rapid production of bread. The new block will have a fine frontage. The upper flat will be let as offices.

Chapter 15
Moving from independent school to School Board school

Although the new building was a vast improvement on the previous one, the Royal Academy was only to survive another twelve years as an independent school with its own Board of Directors. Early in the twentieth century the financial situation was such that the Directors were forced to agree terms with the Inverness Burgh School Board for the management of the school, although an Act of Parliament was required to permit this change to take place.

The volume of the Directors' Minutes, covering the period from June 1901 until September 1904 is missing and so it is only possible to get information about their meetings between these dates from the reports that appeared in the *Inverness Courier*.

Administering the school in its new building

In February 1895, when pupils moved in, work was still incomplete at what was to become known to generations of Academy pupils as the Midmills Building. It was over a year before the boundary walls were built, partly due to a contractor defaulting on the work, and this led to a legal dispute over payment. Final payments for the whole contract were not made until early in 1897.

For the first few years at Midmills the janitor had the use of a rented house nearby. A janitor's house was constructed in 1899/1900 to the north-east of the main school building at a cost of almost £435. As other funds were not available, a curious financial arrangement was put in place, involving granting a feu to the Rector. Due to an administrative oversight this arrangement ran on until 1983, several years after the school had moved to Culduthel.

The Directors had been greatly affected by the sudden death, just weeks after the opening of the new building, of Robert Hay, their Secretary, who had been appointed at the time of the establishment of the new board in 1887. His replacement was William Anderson, a local solicitor. Sir Henry Cockburn Macandrew, the Chairman since 1887, died three years later.

Financial matters took up a lot of the Directors' time in the autumn of 1896. Fees had to be increased, with fees in class 1 in the lower school rising from 15s [75p] a quarter to £1, while those for class VI in the upper school rose from 25s [£1.25] to £2 a quarter. There were some reductions for parents with several children attending the Academy. Music and typewriting were charged extra: piano or violin instruction was 21s [£1.05] a quarter for juniors and 31s 6d [£1.57½] for seniors, whereas typewriting was 5s [25p] a quarter.

In 1897 the auditor for the Scotch Education Department complained about the overspend on the construction of the building, and the Directors were forced to repay this sum to capital as soon as possible to allow the bursary scheme to be fully introduced. However grants approaching £200 a year were earned by the teaching of Science and Art, under the Government scheme to encourage the teaching of these subjects. The Secretary of the Department of Science and Art was not happy that their grant money was used to pay salaries, and requested that the Directors consider paying fixed salaries to these members of staff, possibly supplemented by some of the grant.

A lot of time was also taken up with administering the Mackintosh Farr Trust lands. Land at Seafield was required by the Highland Railway Company for railway extensions, and negotiations on this were protracted. In the end the Directors were paid more than £10 000 for over 30 acres of land. The money was invested.[1] Various farming tenants also took up Directors' time with matters about repairs and maintenance, and there are frequent references to feu duty issues relating to housing on land owned by the Fund in the Merkinch.

There was an enquiry from the Public Health Committee of the Burgh about building a tramway to the Longman across Trust Fund property, for the disposal of rubbish for the Cleansing Department at a new site.[2] This scheme seems to have fallen through, as does a scheme for a light railway from Inverness to Lochend (at the north-eastern end of Loch Ness) which would have partly crossed Trust land. This would have been part of a much more ambitious scheme which never came about to build a direct rail route to Glasgow along the Great Glen.

There were only some 215 pupils attending the school at the time of the move in 1895 (a number reflecting the average of the previous few years), but this rose within months to 255. This number included 60 free scholars under the Inverness County scheme, together with eight free scholars under the Academy's own scheme, and the children of nine teachers. During 1896, schemes were drawn up to increase the number of bursaries, to help make income approach expenditure.[3] The following year a boy called Mackintosh Smith was denied a bursary from the Mackintosh Farr fund as a result of his surname, but he was eventually given a free scholarship to cover his education for two years. The Rector of Dingwall Academy was employed for several years to set and mark the bursary competition examination papers.

By the end of the century the numbers of pupils enrolled were around 320 to 350, generally with rather more girls than boys. However actual attendance (excluding absence through illness, etc.) was rather less than this, being only about 250.[4] In the new century numbers declined somewhat. At 30th June 1902 the actual numbers on the role were:

| Boys under 12: 49 | Girls under 12: 44 | Total under 12: 93 |
| Boys over 12: 98 | Girls over 12: 78 | Total over 12: 176 |

making a total role of 269 pupils. The corresponding figure in 1907 was 229, but with an average attendance figure of only just over 200.

Life in the new school building
Prior to the move to the new building there had been a threefold structure of preparatory school (average age seven to ten), middle school (10 to 13), and upper school where there had been a choice between a classical or commercial curriculum. The classical curriculum was primarily aimed at those who intended continuing studies at a university, whilst the commercial curriculum covered subjects useful for those going into business. At the time of the opening of the new building the school was reorganised into a lower department and an upper department, with six classes in each section. The age of transfer was about 11, although this almost immediately moved up to 12, in line with the new ages being introduced for entry to university (mentioned below).

The hours of work in the upper school were 9 a.m. until 12.10 p.m. and from 1.15 p.m. until 4 p.m., with a short break in each half day. The first class in the lower school did not meet until 9.45 a.m. and all lower school classes were dismissed at 3.20 p.m. A change in local train times in the autumn of 1900 led to the hours being changed for a while to 9.30 a.m. until 4.30 p.m. The following year the Rector was involved in discussion with the railway company over the timing of the trains on the winter schedule. The prospectus for session 1899-1900 contains the timetable for the Upper School [Figure 15.1], but this was not repeated in subsequent editions. Classes were then meeting from 9 a.m. until 12 noon and 1 p.m. until 4 p.m.

An extra week's holiday was granted to pupils to celebrate Queen Victoria's Diamond Jubilee in 1897. As part of the celebrations, a children's procession started at the Academy and proceeded to the Victoria Park (west of the river) where sports were held. Lengthy closures due to epidemics feature several times. Measles struck in 1896, and again in November 1900, when a further outbreak affected the whole Town. This closure lasted three weeks.

A further closure in spring 1904 was due to an outbreak of scarlet fever, and this led to the abandonment of the spring holiday to make up for lost teaching time. A measles epidemic reoccurred in May 1905 when at one point, according to the school log book, the attendance in the lower school (Primary school) was only 54%. Epidemics of mumps also seriously affected attendance from time to time.

Official holidays were granted on a regular basis for major events, such as the Northern Meeting (in September), harvest thanksgiving (which could be as late as December) and the sacramental fast days. The school bell, originally presented by Hector Fraser, Rector of the Grammar School (see Chapter 2), made its way from Academy Street to the Crown in early 1896, where it remained in use until the end of the transfer of the Academy to Culduthel in 1979.

Soon after moving into the new building, the Rector (Wm. J. Watson) proposed some staffing changes, which included replacing both a Primary teacher and the modern languages teacher, as well as changes in the staffing for music and art. That spring there was the annual inspection by Her Majesty's Inspectors. The 1896 HMI report was very favourable: "The Royal Academy is in a very efficient state at present under Mr Watson, and the excellent staff by which he is assisted". Slates for written work were finally abandoned in the junior English class in session 1904-05 following criticism from the school inspectors.

Some notable staff were employed at that time. Their names can be found from printed staff lists starting in November 1898, as well as from the annual prospectus.[5] Thomas Cockburn continued to serve as classics teacher, Charles Greaves for commercial subjects and Pierre Delavault for art. Most of the staff (including the Rector) were employed to teach for 26 to 30 hours a week, although Ern(e)st Kesting, the music teacher since 1867, only worked 7 hours a week, but with a salary similar to some staff who taught for 30 hours. He was awarded a pension when he was forced to retire at the start of 1898. His replacement received roughly a third of his predecessor's salary for 10 hours' work a week. M. Delavault taught for 13 hours a week,[6] and was to issue his *Pictures of Old Inverness*, by which he is still remembered, in 1903.[7] He died suddenly early in 1907, following a short illness. During his stay in Inverness, he became a naturalised British subject.

Watson, as a native speaker himself, introduced weekly Gaelic classes from 1903, with about 12 to 15 scholars that year. The Directors agreed to approach the Scotch Education Department about setting a paper in Gaelic which would count towards the Leaving Certificate. The SED said that there were grave difficulties in establishing such an examination and suggested that the subject be included in the evening class programme. The Directors gave Watson permission to pursue any form of action he thought appropriate in a quest to establish the subject. By January 1907 the SED was prepared to consider the matter again and the Rector was authorised to conduct discussions with them. A subject introduced for boys around the same time was instruction in metal work, which was carried out in the Burgh School Board's Training Centre. This was in addition to woodwork classes which had been running since about 1900.

W. Stewart Roddie continued to produce his cantatas each March or April. As he was a keen sportsman, having won a "Blue" at Oxford for shot put, the Rector organised school sports meetings in June 1895 and 1896 at the Northern Meeting Park [Figure 15.2]. A note of the proposed 1898 event is one of the first entries in the first volume of the School log book, but there is no press report of the results, suggesting it was not held, nor is there mention of an event in any subsequent year. A cricket club was also started with the Rector as President, Mr Forsyth (modern languages) as Secretary and Mr Cockburn (classics) as Treasurer. All boys over the age of 10 were expected to join at a cost of 1s 6d a year, unless their parents asked for them to be excused. In about 1890 a debating society had been launched, and the minutes books, covering the period from 1902 until 1907, survive in the Academy archive.

The official school log books, completed by the Rector, start in 1898,[8] but early entries are few and far between. The very first entry concerns a truant, and a few months later a parent was requesting that her daughter discontinue Geometry and Algebra:

> She did not understand anything of it. Examined the girl at 4 p.m., found a fair foundation up to and including Factors, and requested her to try examination tomorrow....

Other entries in the first year include investigating accidents and theft of a packet of sweets from the cloakroom, as a result of which a girl was withdrawn from attendance, although later readmitted. Class III complained in a letter to the Rector that they had not been allowed to use a football for which they had paid through their membership of the school Athletic Club. This was a case of bullying by older boys, a matter which was apparently sorted out by the Rector. More petty theft features in 1902 and cheating in an examination during 1903. Smoking by pupils is also mentioned from time to time.

Frequenting ice cream parlours in the Town whilst playing truant is also recorded. A copy letter from the Rector, dated 1907, reads as follows:

> Dear Sir, I expelled .... this morning. He played truant again on Tuesday afternoon and the whole of Wednesday, partly in the Free Library, partly in an ice cream saloon in Eastgate. He had given me his written pledge that he wd. not enter one of these saloons so long as he remained a pupil of the Academy. The morning he brought the enclosed note. I need not say that I am sorry to have had to resort to this step in the interests of the Academy ...

In the ice cream parlour the pupil had been taught to play billiards at a cost of 8d an hour or 2d a game. His parents had been giving him 2d a day for sweets, but this had now been stopped. As a result of this case the Rector made all boys in the upper school (excluding Class I) sign a promise not to smoke cigarettes or enter an ice cream parlour so long as they were pupils in the school. A couple of months later a boy in class IV was expelled for playing truant, frequenting an ice cream parlour, producing a false or forged absence note, and lying.

For most years from 1899 until 1909, the school log books lists the work covered in the different classes, but mainly by naming the textbook used. In the summer of 1896 138 subject passes for the Leaving Certificate were earned, compared with only 115 the previous session.[9] This was regarded as very satisfactory particularly as there had been the outbreak of measles during the session. By the following year the number of passes was 154.[10] From 1890 a new pattern of university entry was introduced, as part of a package of university reform in Scotland. Students now enrolled at age 17 or

18, two or three years older than previously, having sat an entrance examination. The ordinary and honours degrees, following three or four years' study respectively, gradually became the norm.

From session 1890-91, significant numbers of girls attending the Academy entered for the LLA qualification (Lady Literate in Arts) in an extra (thirteenth) year of attendance. Until 1890, women had not been allowed to enrol in Scottish universities so the LLA qualification had been introduced in the late 1870's by two of the universities to cater for their needs. Attendance at a university was not required to obtain the LLA, and so relevant courses could be taught anywhere, and self-study was even possible. The qualification lasted until 1920, eventually becoming a seven-subject degree-level diploma. The take-up of university places by women was initially very slow, and the LLA provided an alternative route for those who could benefit by higher education.

Watson married in the summer of 1906, and, at the closing ceremony in late June, the teachers and pupils presented him with a revolving bookcase and a pair of silver candlesticks. His new wife was to present the prizes at the 1907 closing ceremony.

The Old Boys' Club and the Former Pupils
A meeting in the new school building in March 1897 led to the formation of an Old Boys' Club, the first official grouping of Old Boys for thirty years.[11] An Academy Club for former pupils had previously existed from 1864 to 1867 (see Chapter 12). Although the names of the President and Vice-President of the new Club are not known today, that of the first Secretary and Treasurer certainly is. This person was Evan M. Barron, who was to become editor of the *Inverness Courier*.

An athletics section was set up, with plans for gymnastics, football and cycling, to take place alongside fortnightly meetings for debates. One of the early cycle meetings took members to Dalcross.[12] A picnic was held at Darnaway Castle, with the Academicals travelling by train.[13] By 1899 the Old Boys' Club were financing a medal for the annual prizegiving, and from the following year an annual dance or supper (sometimes both) was held between Christmas and the New Year. In 1902 the Club took over the grounds of the Inverness Tennis Club in Bishop's Road, and the club was run by the Academicals until about 1924.

The first formal Club dinner took place just after the new year in 1905.[14] The Rector was guest of the evening, and he was toasted by Evan Barron, who pointed out that within the previous five years, under Watson's leadership, a pupil had won the prestigious Ferguson scholarship in Mental Philosophy, and the Hutton prize at Aberdeen University had been won twice by former Academy pupils. Barron suggested an honour board on the school wall. Peter J. Anderson was unable to attend the dinner, but in September of that year he supplied a list of former school medallists with biographical information. He was to be the guest of honour at the dinner held in December 1906, when Provost Arthur Ross, Chairman of the Directors, promised to bring up at their next meeting the issue of getting a board inscribed with the names of the medallists. The tentative list was published in the *Courier* in two parts,[15] and the board was in place by the time of the dinner in December 1907. From the prospectus issued in the summer of 1889 lists of the successes of former pupils are noted. Former pupils in Edinburgh started their own dinner and reports of the first two such events appear in the *Courier*.[16]

At the 1906 dinner Evan Barron, as a trained historian, was requested to start preparation of a history of the Academy, and the Directors soon granted him permission to get access to the various records he would need. However, although some subscriptions were forthcoming to finance the venture, the scheme was never completed and fell by the wayside during the First World War (see Chapter 16).

Transfer to the School Board
From early in the twentieth century there was severe concern about the lack of money to run the Academy effectively and to administer the bursary scheme properly. By May 1903, the Rev. Mr Connell, a member of both the Burgh School Board and the Academy Directors, suggested to the Directors that the Academy should amalgamate with the secondary school run by Inverness Burgh School Board, namely the High School.[17] It was realised that an Act of Parliament would be required to bring about this change. Against this idea, it was pointed out that many of the members of the Burgh School Board were clergymen and not businessmen, and this meant that there was a lack of financial expertise on that Board to manage a school system effectively. There were also issues about the social standing of the two schools, with the Academy primarily serving the needs of the middle class (who could afford to pay relatively high fees), and the High School (where fees had only recently been abolished) serving the working class. This pattern permeated Inverness education to some extent right through to the development of comprehensive education in the 1970's.

At that point the proposal to hold a joint conference was defeated at the Directors' Meeting by four votes to three. Six months later it was agreed to hold a conference between the two bodies, and this was held on 8th December 1903.[18] It was known that there was overlapping between the secondary departments in the Academy and in the High School, but Sheriff J. P. Grant of Rothiemurchus, a County representative on the Academy Board, objected to the Academy coming under the control of the Burgh School Board which was only funded by Burgh ratepayers. He felt that the County pupils would be at a disadvantage. It was expected that a Scottish Education Bill would be laid before Parliament soon, and it was agreed that all sides in the discussions would keep a watch on the progress of the Bill when it was tabled. The Act was not passed until 1908, but even then it did not really relate to the situation in Inverness. The main change in the administration of local schools in Scotland, bringing in proper County Education Authorities, did not pass through Parliament until 1918.

The Chairman of the Directors (James Anderson) together with the Law Agent met with the Chairman of the Scotch Education Department in London in May 1905 and some changes in the existing arrangements were suggested. Discussion continued throughout 1906, even though Anderson died at the beginning of that year, having been a Director since 1887. In September 1906 the Rev. Mr Connell proposed another motion, which was passed, to hold a further conference with the School Board.[19] There was some objection to this proposal, particularly from Sheriff Grant who was still concerned that, as nearly half of the Academy pupils resided outwith the Burgh, their interests would not be properly represented if the Academy was controlled by the Burgh School Board.

The Burgh School Board also agreed to the conference, and Connell moved at both committees that the main business to be discussed should be:
1. how to obtain additional funds for the maintenance of the Academy and for bursaries;
and
2. how to make the Academy more widely useful for the Burgh and County of Inverness.

The meeting was held on 7th November when Connell, seconded by Bailie John S. Fraser, moved that the Academy be controlled by the Burgh School Board. The Rev. Mr Gavin Lang moved an amendment, seconded by Donald Macdonald, that implied that doing so would seriously disadvantage pupils who attended from the County. However, the original motion was accepted by eight votes to two, the two dissenting voices being Rev. Mr Lang and Mr Donald Macdonald. It had been agreed previously that the resolutions of the conference were not binding on either side.

At the next meeting of the Burgh School Board there was a row when Kenneth Macdonald moved an amendment that the report of the joint meeting be not adopted and the School Board "decline to become a party to the attempt now being made by their representatives on the Academy Board to divert the Academy endowments to the sole use of the Burgh of Inverness". This was seconded by Lang. Nevertheless the original motion was carried by four votes to two, with one abstention. A pamphlet was later published to promote Macdonald's case against the transfer.[20] Letter writers to the *Courier* were also active.

At a special meeting of the Directors on 28th November, Bailie Fraser moved that the SED be asked for permission to apply to the Court of Session for an alteration of the management scheme to allow the transfer. This was opposed by Sheriff Grant of Rothiemurchus, again acting on behalf of the County of Inverness, saying that, as none of the endowments had come from the Burgh, the transfer should not happen. Provost Ross, as Chairman, managed to establish a committee to look for common ground between the factions, and a meeting did take place producing a compromise which was acceptable to all but two of the members of the various committees, Rev. Gavin Lang and ex-Bailie Donald Macdonald:[21]

1. That the buildings of the Academy and its endowments, subject to the following provisions, be handed over to the Burgh School Board to maintain the said Academy as it is at present maintained under the Scheme.

2. That the income of all funds available for Bursaries tenable at the Academy be divided into three equal shares, one share to be allocated amongst pupils attending the Royal Academy, one share among pupils attended State-aided schools within the Burgh, and one among pupils attending State-aided schools in the County, the selection of candidates in the first two cases to be in the hands of the Burgh School Board, and in the case of the remaining share, of the County Council, all Bursaries being tenable at the Royal Academy only.

3. That no child be selected to a Bursary unless found by examination to be qualified to benefit from the course of education provided at the Academy, and unless the selecting body is satisfied that the child nominated intends to take full advantage of the course.

4. That in the event of the full number of qualified candidates not being found either by the School Board or the County Council, the other body shall have the right to the vacant Bursaries if they present qualified candidates.

5. The Mackintosh Farr Fund Bursaries shall be allotted, in the first place, to duly qualified candidates under the existing Scheme, but on the failure of qualified candidates the Bursaries shall be thrown open under Section 2 of this Minute.

The *Inverness Courier* rejoiced that a solution had been found:[22]

THE ROYAL ACADEMY – Satisfaction will be felt in the community that the Governors of the Academy have come to an agreement. There are still two dissentients, but as most of the members of the Board are consenting parties, the arrangements will no doubt be carried into effect. The Academy is to be handed over to the School Board, to be carried on as a fee-paying school under the authorised Scheme, with certain modifications. Provision is made to retain bursaries for qualified applicants from the county. Sheriff Grant was so far satisfied that he seconded the proposal, and Mr William Anderson concurred. As representatives from the County Council, however, they desire to have the sanction of that body. The proposal has to be approved by the Education Department and the Court of Session, but we may assume that no formidable obstacles exist. It is satisfactory to find that difficulties have been amicably settled, and the hope may be entertained that the Academy will have a prosperous career under the new management.

The final details were sorted out in January 1907 after another protest from Lang and Macdonald who then left the meeting.[23] The scheme was then submitted to the SED who suggested some further amendments. There was also an issue concerning the appointment of assistant teachers, as under the existing scheme the Rector had powers to make these appointments for the Academy, but the Burgh School Board made the equivalent appointments in the schools that they controlled. The legal processes proceeded through the early part of that year, and advice from Counsel was that the changes should be brought about by means of a Provisional Order, rather than by application to the Court of Session. By May, Parliamentary procedures were advancing and on 15th August 1907 the Secretary of State for Scotland signed the order with the draft of the Bill. This went through Parliament without discussion, receiving Royal Assent on 28th August.[24] The total cost of the Provisional Order was £491 10s 6d, which was taken from the capital account with the intention of repayment as soon as possible.[25]

Apart from the transfer of control to the Burgh School Board, the Order provided for a Primary Department to be maintained only if it could be self-supporting or was required to support the Secondary Department. Fees could be charged and the Rector was fully responsible for the organisation and discipline of the school, although the School Board was given the power to appoint staff. Details of the bursaries to be awarded, the operation of the Mackintosh Farr Fund, and of the Forbes Fund, were set out.

In the summer of 1907 the heads of both the Academy and the High School produced statements for the School Board about the operation of their schools. The buildings for both schools were in the Crown district, with the High School occupying the building now used by the Crown Primary School, only yards from the Royal Academy. The High School had been using this building since 1880.

The Qualifying Examination had recently been introduced for pupils at about age 12, to identify those who were suitable for a full secondary education. Mr H. A. Braine, headmaster of the High School, proposed that his school moved to a scheme, which was then under national discussion, of elementary, intermediate and secondary schools, where the intermediate school provided, in effect, the first three years of a secondary education with a certificate at the end of it. This scheme was formally introduced in Scotland following the 1908 Education Act. Braine proposed that his school should present for the intermediate certificate, and when awarded, suitable pupils would move to the Academy to study for the Leaving Certificate. Much of his statement was concerned with maximising the income to his own school from grants, as different funding levels were provided for the different levels of course. Many pupils did not intend to complete the three years of the course for the intermediate certificate, and separate supplementary courses were provided for them, with many leaving after the first or second year of such a course.[26]

Watson, for the Academy, gave an outline of the state of his school at that time. Pupils were prepared for the Intermediate Certificate, the Leaving

Certificate and the University Preliminary Examinations. There was a staff of 14, including one visiting teacher, for a pupil population of about 210 of whom slightly over half were over age twelve. Thirteen pupils had gained the Intermediate certificate the previous summer and four the Leaving Certificate, which from 1902 was a group award certificate, rather than one where passes were recorded by individual subjects.[27] It was now used as a standard for entering professions that did not require a university degree, and gradually became a replacement for the University entrance examinations. Forty pupils had moved on to Scottish Universities last session. The school had recently been recognised as a centre for training Junior Students, aged 15 to 18, under the first step of the revised method of training future teachers that was just being introduced.

The Academy received grants from the SED based on the number of pupils over 12 years of age, and other grants for the teaching of specific subjects, namely science, drawing, practical geometry and the subject which these days is called home economics. Watson wanted to have all the potential Junior Students attending the Academy, unlike Braine who wanted to retain some in his own school, presumably largely so that it could receive the relevant grant money. Watson suggested all supplementary course pupils would attend the High School, thus eliminating overlap. As presented by Watson, the argument was much more on educational grounds, although the details of the grants he would earn were set out in detail.

The Burgh School Board were more inclined to Watson's views, and these were then implemented. The Governors were asked to continue to run the Academy until the end of 1907 while the Burgh School Board put in place their own management scheme. A number of pupils attending the High School who had gained Intermediate Certificates were transferred to the Academy and some of the pupil-teachers (under the scheme being discontinued) who were being taught in the High School started to attend the Academy for their 'literary' studies, whilst continuing to attend the High School for their practical studies.

The change of management meant that Kenneth Macdonald had to resign as a Burgh School Board member as he was the Secretary to the Directors of the Academy and the Governors of the Inverness Educational Trust. He was then appointed as the Treasurer and Factor of both the Academy and the Mackintosh Farr Fund at a salary of £190. Macdonald, despite his initial opposition to the transfer, had been the person, as law agent to the Academy Directors, who had drafted the Provisional Order and seen it through the legal process.

The final recorded meeting of the Academy Board of Directors took place on 23rd December 1907, when it was agreed to pay certain outstanding accounts, and thereafter Inverness Royal Academy ceased to be an independent school, and became fully under the control of the local authority.

This ended just over 115 years as an independent school. Many schools in other parts of Scotland, which had had a similar history to the Royal Academy, also lost their independence between the 1872 and the 1918 Education Acts. These include Bellahouston Academy, bought out by the local School Board in 1885, and Allan Glen's School which was transferred in 1912 to the Glasgow School Board. James Gillespie's School in Edinburgh lost its independence in 1908 after which it was controlled by the local School Board.

Chapter 16
The Academy under Inverness Burgh School Board

From the date from which the school came under the control of the Burgh School Board at the start of 1908 the development of Inverness Royal Academy becomes quite similar to that of many other Scottish schools, although there are still interesting stories to tell and some memorable events to record. Wm. J. Watson was to remain in post as Rector for only a further eighteen months, to be followed by Gilbert Watson and then George Morrison, who both made their mark in education during and following their time as Rectors of the Royal Academy. One further change in administration was yet to come across Scotland, and that was the transfer in 1918 of all responsibility for education to specially-elected County Committees, which in the 1930's became part of the County Councils.

Administering and developing the Academy

Much of material in the records of the Burgh School Board in the period leading up to and over the First World War is routine, and has a more general remit than just affecting the Academy, including matters such as staff salaries which were now paid monthly rather than quarterly. However, a management committee for the Academy was appointed for taking day to day decisions, and the usual matters over management of the Mackintosh Farr lands, such as fences, leaking buildings and flooding, required attention.

Enrolment at the Academy increased. Pupil numbers in 1910 were 350 (only once reached in the previous twenty years) and by 1912 numbers had reached 425 – 173 in the Lower [Primary] School, and 252 in the Upper School (including the Junior Students), for an official capacity of 350. Extra staff were needed and there was pressure on space. Numbers were to rise even further over the First World War years. The Burgh School Board, to ensure maximum income, started pursuing the parents of pupils whose fees were overdue. One local hotelier was very displeased to receive a small debts summons. After three years of requests, from 1911 the Rector had some clerical assistance, a post initially shared with the High School.

The pressure on space especially in science led, before the outbreak of the First World War, to the provision of a new building, running along Midmills Road, to house science and art, and also providing a gymnasium. Planning was set in motion in 1910, and tenders were accepted in November 1911.[1] An agreement was worked out whereby the High School (which at this stage was still located close by) would share some staff and the new accommodation with the Academy. The new building was officially opened in January 1913 by J. Annan Bryce, M.P., with a large attendance of local dignitaries.[2] Several photographs of the classrooms survive from about the time of the opening [Figure 16.1 a-c], and these images show that little was to change in these rooms between their opening and the time the Royal Academy moved to its new site in 1979.

There were four science laboratories on the ground floor, along with the gymnasium. The art rooms were on the first floor along with a science lecture room, much later converted for use as a music room. Toilets and cloakrooms were also included. The total cost was something like £8000, towards which the Scotch Education Department provided a grant of £2500. The balance was shared between the ratepayers of Inverness Town and the County of Inverness. Shortly after its opening the Continuation Classes in science and art (held in the evening for those who had left school) were moved from the High School to the Academy to take advantage of the new facilities. It was not long though before there were problems with a section of the roof, probably due to a design fault. The rooms in the main building formerly used as laboratories and as an art room were converted to general classroom use.

Staffing

Thomas Cockburn retired (although well below retiring age) in the summer of 1908 after twenty-nine years' service to the Academy, to pursue his interest in languages in other ways. He had been appointed to teach English, but Watson had persuaded him to teach German, and sometimes Latin and Greek. He was to move to Edinburgh, where he died in 1947, but he was not forgotten, and a special collection was established in the School Library in 1956 in his memory (see Chapter 18).

Watson, the Rector, moved on in the summer of 1909, having made a most significant contribution to the quality of education on offer in Inverness. The Burgh School Board noted his contribution as follows:[3]

> While the Board feel a sincere pleasure on Mr Watson's promotion they experience a keen sense of regret in the severance of the pleasant connection existing between him and them, and on the transfer of his conspicuous abilities from the Educational system. Under his capable management the Academy has improved upon the high position which it always occupied as an Educational Institution, and by his ability as a scholar and a student of Celtic Literature and Traditions Mr Watson has added further distinction to the Academy and the community in which it is situated. The Board will always watch with interest the progress of Mr Watson's career in the world of Education and Literature.

He moved on to become Rector of Edinburgh's Royal High School at probably twice the salary he earned in Inverness, and in 1914 he became Professor of Celtic at Edinburgh University. His time as Rector in Inverness had seen him produce a number of books, the most significant of which was *The Place Names of Ross and Cromarty*, produced in 1904, the production of which was aided by one of the Academy staff and some of the pupils.[4] More works were to follow, including Watson's major work, *The History of Celtic Place-Names of Scotland*.[5] He was also the Honorary Secretary of the Gaelic Society of Inverness for 44 years, and at various times Secretary and President of the Inverness Field Club. Watson was to die in 1948 at the age of 83. Numerous lengthy obituaries were published throughout the Celtic World.[6] He is buried in Tomnahurich Cemetery, as he regarded Inverness as his "spiritual home".

There were twenty-six applications for the vacant post of Rector, and the successful applicant, aged only 27 (two years younger than Wm. J. Watson had been when he was appointed) was Gilbert Watson, also a graduate of Oxford University, and prior to that a pupil of the Royal High School in Edinburgh. He was only to stay as Rector for little over a year, at which point he was 'headhunted' for an appointment as one of His Majesty's Inspectors of Schools, rising to become a Senior Chief Inspector of Schools. He lived to be over 102 years old, and was sent a congratulatory message from the Rector of the time on his 100th birthday, to which his reply survives in the Academy archive.

Gilbert Watson's replacement was required, as traditional, to be a classics graduate, and there were thirty-one applicants. The successful candidate was George Morrison, who had been classics master at Robert Gordon's School in Aberdeen where several of his pupils had won prestigious bursaries and awards. He was to serve until after the end of the First World War, at which point he returned to Robert Gordon's as headmaster of their secondary school, having previously narrowly missed appointment as Director of Education for Aberdeen County and as Rector of the Royal High School in Edinburgh. He served in Aberdeen until 1933, soon after which he became the Member of Parliament for the Scottish Universities, continuing to serve until 1945. He died in 1956, aged 86.

In February 1911 J. Wilson Reid, who had been appointed as mathematics teacher in 1888 and had twice applied to become the Academy's Rector, died on his way home for lunch. He fell off his bicycle when it swerved and he was to die shortly afterwards. His replacement was appointed despite a comment at the Burgh School Board meeting that the person's Aberdeen accent was unintelligible in Inverness! W. Stewart Roddie, the singing teacher, was injured in a cycle accident, and as a result was unable to take a leading part in the Inverness celebrations for the coronation of King George V that summer. Having been a member of staff since 1883, he was eventually persuaded to retire, aged 67, at Christmas 1912, when he was given a superannuation payment. He died in 1931, aged 85.

Another teacher of the time whose name is still mentioned today in Inverness was Donald Dallas, a local Highland Games competitor and entertainer, who was employed part-time to teach physical education. A former pupil remembers him thus:[7]

> ... Now thoughts roam to the teaching staff, and I willingly risk a charge of non-academic bias by putting in first place the truly unforgettable Donald Dallas. The school was served by many devoted teachers but none more endearing than "Dan". He had come into my ken on the theatre stage, acting as Dugald Cratur in an amateur production of Rob Roy MacGregor. "Dan" dominated the gymnasium wearing such unorthodox if not outrageous garb as Harris tweed plus-fours, the very aspect of which brought out a lather of perspiration in the boys before the exercises started. Dan was a loveable if peculiarly laughable figure who would devote the last few minutes of the period to cooling off and an anecdote. He told

how he climbed Ben Wyvis and got back to Dingwall in a day. His tale once began with a warning never to tackle a "Munro" on a full stomach, and ended with a smile of triumph after his latest exploit. "Yes! I set off after only a light breakfast and went up Ben Wyvis like deer!"
He retired from teaching in 1935 after an illness.

At the end of 1912, at the same time as the school was preparing to open the new accommodation, the School Board set in motion the dismissal of a teacher, largely on the grounds of poor class discipline and insubordination to the Rector. He had been appointed in 1908. The teacher concerned contested his dismissal and an interim interdict was temporarily served on the School Board, although it was then withdrawn. An appeal by the teacher to a later Board meeting failed.[8]

From about 1912 more women seem to have been appointed to posts in the secondary school, whereas previously most such appointments were for the junior classes. This became more significant following the outbreak of war in 1914, when many men who would have applied were not available through military service. As was normal at the time, the salaries of the women were below those paid to men doing comparable work. Women were still expected to resign if they were about to marry. In June 1912 there were 95 applications for one job as an assistant mistress in the Junior Department of the school.[9] In 1917 the role of Lady Superintendent was defined to include superintendence of the Junior Students and the significant number of girls who lived in lodgings in the Town.

School Life and the Development of Sport
An annual excursion for senior pupils took place under the control of Wm. J. Watson, and in June 1908 about 100 pupils went by train to the Black Rock of Novar where there were a picnic and games, as well as some educational work on local geology and history.[10] An art teacher also took pupils into the country, to sketch from nature. The art course for a while included work on Celtic art forms, something commended by His Majesty's Inspector.[11] Concerts and similar events were held from time to time, with the proceeds from some of them going to the School library fund, and in one case, following a local tragedy, to an Ardersier fishing disaster fund. Special holidays were granted for the funeral of King Edward VII and the coronation of George V. Installations of a new Rector also seemed to merit a half-holiday. Each Christmas there seems to have been an "At Home", held in the school, the forerunner of the present-day Christmas Dance.

Prizegivings continued each June, usually associated with exhibitions of art and needlework, to be much admired by parents and friends of the school. P. J. Anderson (who was at this stage Librarian at King's College, Aberdeen) together with his sister, Isabel, set up a essay prize. In its first year (1913) there were 32 entries from Academy and High School pupils at a standard much higher than had been expected. After some discussion, the topic for the essays became "The History and Topography of Inverness, Town and

County", with prizes at three levels. Peter J. Anderson died in May 1926, and a plaque in his memory is now to be found at the entrance to Aberdeen University Library. In his will he paid for a stained-glass window in memory of Ewan Maclachlan (see Chapter 8), and also for the treatment of the carved oak screen in the University Chapel.

Jas. Coats, the thread manufacturers in Paisley, presented a library of 100 volumes to the school in November 1911. This company was to become well known for its donations of books to schools across Scotland. Under Morrison, a school magazine reappeared in Autumn 1911, something which had not happened since the departure of Bruce in 1894. The new publication, called *The Inverness Academical*, appeared termly until Spring 1913. Thereafter it only appeared twice during the First World War, as War Service Numbers, and the final edition, in December 1921, carried the Roll of Honour, a description of the War Memorial, reports of the opening ceremonies for the War Memorial and the School Hostel (see Chapter 17), and a long article, taken from his talk to the Inverness Field Club, by Evan Barron, on the history of education in Inverness up to the opening of the Academy in 1792.[12]

The Autumn 1912 edition of the magazine had included as an insert part of a specimen chapter of Barron's proposed history of the Academy. At that time, this was a standard method of advertising a forthcoming book, and was intended to seek subscriptions to give some idea of the size of the print run. Some subscriptions were received, but nothing further seems to have been published, although some of Barron's notes have survived, partly in the Academy archive, partly in the Highland Council archive.

School sports seem to have resumed at some point in the first decade of the twentieth century, but they were held within the school grounds and attracted less mention in the local press than the events run by Wm. J. Watson in 1895 and 1896. Various sports reports appear in local newspapers concerning Academy teams. For boys the cricket club seems to have continued throughout this period. Football also starts to feature as a School sport, and all boys over 10 were expected to join the both the football and cricket clubs. Girls played hockey in winter and cricket in summer. A miniature rifle club was established by some of the senior pupils in 1911. This developed sufficiently quickly that by the following year Lt. Hamilton Leigh of Culloden House, a local shooting enthusiast, part-financed a trip to the National Rifle Championships at Bisley, a visit which was repeated in 1913 but thereafter abandoned due to the outbreak of War.[13] In both years the Academy was the only Scottish school to take part, achieving good results overall. Leigh was also to present two miniature rifles to the Club.[14]

The Academicals' tennis club in Bishop's Road went from strength to strength each summer, not just with tennis but also with fund-raising events such as cake and candy stalls to finance improvements. The Academicals also had an active hockey club. The Old Boys' Club dinners continued in most years.

An Old Girls' Club was established in 1912. In Edinburgh there were further reunions of former pupils, with the signed attendance list for one event being held in the Edinburgh University Library.[15]

The First World War

Reopening for the new session in August 1914 was delayed as the building was occupied by the military following the outbreak of the First World War. The Chief Constable requested the availability of 24 local Boy Scouts (many of whom would be pupils either at the Academy or the High School) for duty, during which time it was hoped that they would be exempted from attendance at school. However the Scotch Education Department said that only actual school attendance would qualify for grant aid, and so this idea was dropped.

Although the troops moved out of the school building fairly soon, they were billeted in the Crown Church Hall over the road. A request was made for the use of the toilets, etc., in the Science and Art School, and this was arranged by setting up a barricade separating them from the part of the building used for school purposes. The School Board expected costs such as water to be paid. This arrangement lasted until late 1915.

A. R. Forsyth (modern languages teacher) was immediately called up for military service, as was the janitor, Sgt. A. H. Watson. The School Board were able to continue Forsyth on full pay for a while, as it was not necessary to replace him. He was to serve in charge of a supply column. It was not long before two other male staff were called up to serve in the War. In April 1915 the Burgh School Board agreed that commissioned officers would receive half pay, and other ranks would have their Army pay made up to their normal salary.[16] By 1916 an initial roll of honour was being prepared, which was published in the *Inverness Courier*, asking for corrections,[17] before a final version appeared in the school magazine, *The Inverness Academical*.[18] A further War Number of the Magazine appeared the following year with another roll of honour.[19]

The Old Girls' Club held fund-raising events such as concerts and then ran entertainments for the troops. Whist drives were held at the Cameron Barracks in Inverness at which ladies were instructed to "bring your own sugar". The pupils agreed to donate part of their prize money towards comforts for the Troops, and in addition raised other money and collected clothing. In 1915 certificates were presented to the prize-winners, rather than books. In June the staff and pupils organised a fete in aid of the Camerons' Comforts Fund and the Academy War Fund. Fund raising continued throughout the year, and by late 1917 over £2000 had been raised towards War Savings. Over the winter of 1916-1917 the school day was shortened due to lighting restrictions which by then had come into force. Waste paper was collected through the school from May 1917, and that summer a party of senior boys were involved with wood cutting for war purposes at Carr Bridge, under Charles Greaves (science teacher), with the School Janitor, now demobbed, in charge of cooking and messing. In 1919 the school was offered relics from the First World War, including a captured German rifle, and a trench mortar. However, these were in the end declined, as inappropriate for a school.

At the end of December 1914 a significant staff appointment was made when W. Crampton Smith, from Keith Grammar School, was appointed as principal teacher of mathematics from the 49 applicants.[20] He took up appointment in March 1915 on a salary of £250, and was later to serve as Rector for nearly a quarter of a century, having briefly served as acting Rector during the later part of 1918 during a period when Morrison was ill. Crampton Smith was very active in the community, being involved with the Crown Church, where in 1916 he was to start a Boy Scout Troop which survives to the present day with only a short gap.

In May 1916 the pupils were engaged in a 'celebration' to mark the tercentenary of Shakespeare's death, and this included the planting of a memorial tree. Six months later there was a celebration for the centenary of the birth of John Curwen, the proponent of the tonic sol-fa system of musical notation, and of his son, also John, who had just died. Much of the singing in the school would have been taught by this method at that time. Pupil numbers reached 513 by September 1918, which was a record. Some classes had 40 pupils when the maximum permitted number was only 30. Numbers rose even higher that session and by the time of the prizegiving they had reached 528, of whom 143 were new pupils. Inspection reports, despite some minor criticisms and problems caused by the War, continued to indicate a high level of achievement in the Academy.

Morrison had his salary increased in 1915 to £450 and then to £500, as it was felt that he was paid less than Rectors of comparable schools.[21] The Rector requested that the status of geography be upgraded, as it was now much more significant in the curriculum, but the Burgh School Board decided it was not possible to appoint a principal teacher in the subject due to the ongoing war,[22] although an assistant teacher specialising in the subject was appointed. It was to be after the end of the Second World War before a principal teacher of geography was appointed. Technical subjects continued to be taught to Academy pupils at the Technical School in Church Street. Classes for boys were in wood and metalwork and for girls in various aspects of domestic science, such as needlework, cookery and laundry work.

Miss Grace Middleton (needlework/domestic economy) and her sister had for many years been accommodating a few girls as boarders in their own house in Victoria Terrace. During the War, Hugh Robson (classics) started using his house in Muirfield Road for boy pupil boarders, and he was to run this venture successfully for many years. From these beginnings the separate girls' and boys' hostels were to develop (see Chapters 17 and 18).

Discussion had started in the press in 1913 over the need for hostels to accommodate pupils from the County attending school in Inverness, a cause which was to be taken up by the Old Boys' Club. The County Education Committee started discussing the issue of providing a hostel in December 1915. In June 1918 Evan Barron and Hugh Robson organised a meeting in the Academy gymnasium to put forward proposals for a permanent War Memorial on the walls of the School and for a school hostel. At that stage 77 pupils were in lodgings in the Town. A subscription list was started, and lists of subscribers appear regularly in the columns of the *Courier*. Various fund-raising events were held, including a bowling tournament and a clock-golf competition. A major "Victory Fair" was held in aid of the War Memorial Fund on 20th and 21st June 1919, and this was to raise £1036. The hostel was to open in 1921 (see Chapter 17).

The 1918 Education Act
A new Education Bill for Scotland was published in December 1917, and passed through Parliament the following year. The Act officially raised the school-leaving age to 15 (although this did not happen in practice until 1945). Various proposals for the new education authorities were put forward, and the original intention was that they should be part of the County Councils and the large Burgh Councils. There was too much opposition to this and the compromise was to have them as separately-elected bodies. Other opponents of the Act had wanted the authorities to serve areas other than the counties, but this idea was also rejected. An interesting, but minor, clause in the Act changed the name of the Education Department from 'Scotch' to 'Scottish' Education Department, a change which had been long sought after.

One of the problems that Scotland had faced was that there had been too many school boards. A total of 947 School Boards were now reduced to 38 new Education Authorities. The initial elections took place in April 1919, and Inverness County Education Authority held its first meeting towards the end of that month. The final meeting of the Burgh School Board took place in May. Just over a decade later, the Education Authorities across Scotland were to be amalgamated with the County Councils, exactly what the Government had wanted when framing the 1918 Act.

Chapter 17
The 1920's, the Depression and another War

In the early part of the period between the two World Wars Crampton Smith was appointed as Rector, and this period also saw the opening of the War Memorial Hostel for girls attending the Academy. In 1925 a new Primary School building was added and soon after this the playing fields were developed. The girls' hostel later moved into the building previously used as a private boys' hostel. A new boys' hostel was opened, and this was later to be taken over by the Education Authority. The school acquired an official Coat of Arms. There were several significant staff appointments but the Second World War brought staffing problems. Crampton Smith, after a period when he served on various national committees, retired as Rector early in 1944.

The War Memorial and the Girls' Hostel[1]
Up to 1916, Inverness College, a private school based on English 'public' school lines, had occupied the buildings in Ardross Street at the corner with Glenurquhart Road, now the older section of Highland Council's headquarters. The failure of that school in the early part of the First World War was caused by financial and staffing difficulties. After that date, part of the building had been used by the Admiralty. By July 1919 Evan Barron was in contact with the County Education Authority enquiring as to whether, if the Old Boys' Club acquired that building for use as a War Memorial hostel, the Authority would run it, whilst allowing Club members to serve as trustees on the management committee.[2] The replies from the Authority were favourable.

Subscriptions received up to that date for a War Memorial were insufficient, so Evan Barron and Hugh Robson had to appeal in October 1919 for further donations to reach the sum of £4000 that was required by early the following month.[3] Only £2500 had been subscribed, but some Inverness College shares, owned by local people, many of whom were former pupils themselves, could be added to this, leaving a deficit of not more than £1000. A School Board sub-committee met with the trustees in late October and the terms were drawn up, and these included these points:
1. the Education Authority would maintain and run the building as a hostel
2. the unbuilt ground around the hostel would remain as a playing field unless the trustees agreed otherwise
3. the Authority would relieve the Trustees of all financial responsibilities
4. the Authority would allow at least three representatives of the Trustees to be on the Management Committee, one of these being the Rector.

Some surplus equipment was purchased from the Admiralty at Invergordon, a temporary caretaker was employed, and by April 1921 a matron and her assistant were being appointed. Expenses of over £2000 were necessary to open the building, and matters were in place for the hostel to open at the end of August 1921, although some tenants of parts of the building had to be persuaded to leave over the next year or so. The first matron, soon to be renamed as warden, was Miss Isabella Paterson, who had been running hostels in Edinburgh although a native of Ross-shire. Discussions were held on which churches the girls should attend, and about the employment of a former pupil as the doctor and medical superintendent. He was soon to report on the inadequate provision of toilets.

Forty-five girls were accommodated in the first session, and around 60 the following session, although some moved into the hostel under protest. For several years the building ran at a loss, bringing comments from the Scottish Education Department (SED) that it must become self-financing as soon as possible. Some income was made by letting the building to the Holiday Fellowship during the summer holiday in 1921, but the request was not granted the following year as there had been some difficulties, being a hostel only designed for girls. The hostel did break even in session 1923/24, but this situation was not to last, with losses in most subsequent years. Also frequent repairs and upgrading were required, suggesting that the project had been underfunded at the outset.

Life in the hostel in the early days was recorded in an interview conducted in 1992 with Robin MacPhee (later Mrs R. Denoon) who was one of the first girls to live in the hostel[4] [Figures 17.1 a-b]:

> There was a big gate with the letters IRAWMH (Inverness Royal Academy War Memorial Hostel) in gold in a semi-circle. We went in through that gate and under the arch. I felt, and I'm sure all the other girls felt, terribly proud because it was a magnificent place, It was just like the boarding schools we had read about. We had dormitories and studies just as they did. I thought it was quite glamorous.
>
> The 61 girls came from far and near. Some came from North and South Uist, Harris and Skye, and we were a little jealous of them because they could speak Gaelic. ... I was from Tomatin only 15 miles away ...
>
> The first dormitory I was in when I went to the hostel consisted of eight beds with enough space in between for a person to get up and get dressed. Each bed had a chest of drawers and a chair beside it. There was a great big wardrobe at the end. Clothes had to be hung in it and nothing had to be lying on the floor. ...
>
> When it was time for high tea, a bell rang and we all went trooping into the great big dining room. We stood behind our chairs until Miss Paterson the Matron came in. She was a big handsome woman from Beauly. She said the Grace, then the maids with their white caps and black and white uniforms came in and served the food to us. You had to watch your manners because the Matron wouldn't put up with any nonsense. We were frightened of her. Some girls grumbled about the food but I thought it was lovely. ...
>
> After our evening meal we spent so many hours studying until bedtime. The big study was at the right hand side at the front for younger girls and the small study was for classes V and VI. We all had lockers on the wall for our books and sat two at a table. ...

At bed time every night I remember that Matron came along to see that everything was tidy and our clothes folded on the chairs beside our beds. "Good night, girls!" "Good night, Miss Paterson!"

Subscriptions were also collected from former pupils for the war memorial boards to be placed in the school. Many editions of the *Inverness Courier* contained the subscription lists. The Memorial Boards [Figure 17.2] were made in oak by William Morris & Company (Westminster) Ltd., and measure 14 feet by 6 feet (about 4.3 metres by 1.8 metres). They were erected on the wall, part-way up the staircase, under the large window at the east end of main school hall. Over 500 former pupils and staff served in the Armed Forces in the First World War; on the central panel are the names of 83 old boys and one member of staff who died, and the side panels have the 420 names of those who served. Along the top and bottom of the boards is the inscription:

"In memory of the Old Boys of Inverness Royal Academy who served in the Great War 1914-1919, this tablet has been erected and an Academy Hostel founded"

The boards were eventually unveiled on 10th October 1921, by Viscount Robert Finlay, Lord Chancellor of England and Wales, but well-known in Inverness as the former M.P. for the Inverness Burghs. Later the same day Viscount Finlay performed the official opening of the girls' hostel, although it had been in use for some weeks by that time. Following the move to the new building at Culduthel between 1977 and 1979, the Memorial Boards were relocated in the corridor adjacent to the school's lecture theatre.

The Boys' Hostel, and the switch of the hostels

For some years Hugh Robson, a classics teacher at the Academy, had been running a private hostel for boys at Nos. 2 and 4 Muirfield Road. However, the number of boys requiring accommodation increased in the early 1920's. In the early summer of 1923 Robson bought the nearby Hedgefield House for the sum of £3750, with the aid of a loan from the Education Authority. The house had been built in 1821, with an extension, designed by George Rhind, a local architect, added in 1846. From 1853 until 1878 the house was occupied by Bishop Robert Eden, Bishop of the Scottish Episcopal Church for the Diocese of Moray and Ross (as it was then called). In 1878 he moved into Eden Court, which had been specifically built as a bishop's palace.

Robson was to run this hostel at Hedgefield for the next eleven years. From 1929 there was discussion about the Education Authority taking over the boys' hostel officially, or subsidising it by a contribution of 5s [25p] a week per boy towards the costs of the bursars who were accommodated there.

By the early 1930's the number of girls who were resident in the Ardross Street building began to fall, as more country buses were available, and some of the girls from the Outer Isles decided to attend Portree High School for their education, rather than come as far as Inverness. From 1933 there was discussion about moving the girls' hostel to Hedgefield, to allow the County Council to take over as their administrative headquarters the building that would be vacated. Their offices up to that point had been dispersed over several locations. The Hostels sub-committee were agreeable to this if the heating at Hedgefield was improved. This would require Robson (who was shortly to retire from his teaching post) to be provided with new accommodation for his boys' hostel. Lack of consultation with the Trustees about this proposed change led to a letter from Evan Barron to the County Council setting out the conditions under which the trustees would agree to the change. The matter went through various committees and by February 1934 the County Council had purchased Hedgefield.

Further discussion led to Robson acquiring Drummond Park in Drummond Road, formerly the residence of Mrs Playne-Smith, as a hostel for the boys. Hedgefield, which was now to be known as the War Memorial Hostel, was formally taken over at Easter 1934, although it was not until 1952 that the arched gateway, mentioned in Robin Denoon's memories, was moved to the Culduthel Road entrance of the new girls' hostel. As a girls' hostel Hedgefield provided for about 36 resident girls. Each summer from 1935 until the outbreak of the Second World War income was made by letting the hostel to the Holiday Fellowship for six or seven weeks each summer. His Majesty's Inspectors visited Hedgefield in June 1938 and were generally satisfied, although commenting on the awkward layout of the basement floor, and on the need to repair the floor between the kitchen and the dining room.

In 1937 discussion started over the purchase by the Education Authority from Mr Robson of Drummond Park, at a cost not exceeding £4000, although the final price, agreed in January 1939,[5] was £4500, with vacant possession at Whitsun 1939, all subject to consent by the SED. This was granted with some provisos. Robson would now run the hostel on behalf of the Education Authority, rather than as a private venture. One advantage of this was that he would no longer be responsible for transporting the younger pupils to and from the school, and for providing bicycles for the older ones.

The purchase of Drummond Park also included the East and West Lodges. West Lodge, although in a very poor state of repair, remained tenanted as it was not required by the hostel, but East Lodge was retained for future hostel use. Hugh Robson and his wife finally bowed out after six years at Drummond Park in the summer of 1940,[6] to be replaced by Mr and Mrs Leslie Frewin.

The Primary Department extension

Inverness Burgh Schools Management Committee agreed in principle in October 1920 to build a new Primary department to accommodate 200 pupils.[7] The original idea was a two-storey block of eight classrooms behind the north end of the Academy main building. Based on the sketch plans at the start of 1922 the extension was expected to cost between £10 500 and

£13 500. In the end a loan of £10 030 was required to build a one-storey extension which ran along the north side of the school grounds, only partly linked to the main building, at effectively the same cost as the main building thirty years earlier. Tenders were sought in the early summer of 1924, after a row with the SED over the quality of the wood to be used for the lining of the corridors and classrooms, and for the doors.

Seven classrooms, each capable of seating 40 pupils, were set along a central corridor. A staffroom and toilet accommodation were provided. At the far end of the corridor was a large hall, for "drill" [physical education], assemblies and events, which unlike the halls of many older schools, could be directly ventilated from outside. The classrooms and the hall all had pitch-pine dados. Heating was by means of a low-pressure hot water system and electric lighting was provided from the start. Pupil toilets were provided at the back of the building.

The formal opening of the primary department extension was on 2nd December 1925. The ceremony was performed by Dr George Macdonald, Secretary of the SED, using a gold key.[8] In his speech he noted that the Academy, under Crampton Smith, had introduced a wide variety of courses, with less dependence on the study of Latin and Greek. He appealed for greater study of the English language, and thought it likely that art and domestic subjects would develop. As for physical training, Dr Macdonald felt that indoor work was not enough, and that open-air exercise and organised games were essential in the curriculum. There was a need for better provision of playing fields for developing physical education.

The Playing Fields and the Pavilion
When the Academy first opened at Midmills, there was a considerable area of land behind the building. However with the building first of the Science and Art block, opened in 1913, and then the Primary School wing (just mentioned), by 1925 there was inadequate land for playing fields for a growing school. Although there was provision of playing fields around the girls' hostel, the Burgh School Management Committee started in late 1924 to look at provision of playing fields for boys. By early the following year it was decided to feu a field at the foot of Victoria Drive (now the north end of the site of Millburn Academy) from the Kirk Session who owned the land. Negotiations continued through 1927, and the feu charter was recorded in April 1928. Following ground preparation, the new playing field was ready for use in the autumn of 1930, and the first school sports day to be held there was held in the summer of 1931. Pitches were available for association football and for rugby, but the school shinty team still had to make use of the pitch at the Bught for their home games.

No pavilion was available on the site, but by the summer of 1936 plans were in hand to construct one, at a cost of over £2000. Funding came from the school endowments and from fund raising. An appeal for donations went out through the *School Magazine* in December 1937. A sale of work in September 1938, opened by Lord Lovat, raised £300[9] which it was hoped could be used for extras, rather than the actual cost of construction. The new pavilion [Figure 17.3] was formally opened at a special event on 28th October 1938 by Major J. E. McConnell, Secretary of the Northern Regional Committee for National Fitness. At the time of its opening there was a national campaign for improving the fitness of the general population, hence the choice of guest. After the ceremony, football, rugby and girls' hockey matches were played. Other sports promoted by the school at this stage were shinty, cricket, tennis, badminton, rifle shooting and swimming. The pavilion served the school until the Royal Academy moved to Culduthel between 1977 and 1979.

Managing the School

Pressure on space in the school grew with the start of the 1919/20 session, and by September 1919 the Rector, George Morrison, declared the school to be overcrowded. Some temporary classrooms were provided. By October 1923 pupil numbers had reached 680 and were over 750 by 1927, with nearly 250 in the Primary and 550 in the Secondary Department. From session 1922/23, some music classes had to be held in the Crown Church halls across Midmills Road. A significant development was the agreement to end fees in the Post-Intermediate Department, i.e. the upper end of the Secondary School, and this took effect from the start of the 1920/21 session.

In the summer of 1920 Morrison returned to his old school in Aberdeen as Headmaster. From the twenty-four applicants for the Inverness job, a short leet of six, and then of three, was agreed. One of those on the leet was Crampton Smith who had been on the Academy staff for the previous five years as Second Master and Principal Teacher of Mathematics. He was appointed as Rector at a salary of £800, rising by £25 per annum, to £850, taking up duty at the end of August.

Miss Grace Middleton resigned in the summer of 1923, after 41 years' service to the school. However this resignation was brought about through a serious illness, although she was able to take advantage of her retirement until 1943. A subscription list was drawn up, which produced the sum of over £150.[10] The second master who was also head of classics, Alex. Duthie, appointed in 1922, was given a financial inducement to stay at the Royal Academy rather than transfer to a new job in Portree.[11] Something seems to have gone wrong in the next few years, as his classics department was criticised in 1927 by His Majesty's Inspector, the former Academy Rector, Gilbert Watson, and Duthie was given a final warning about the standard of the work in December 1931.

Charles Greaves, who had been appointed as the school's commercial teacher but under Wm. J. Watson had changed to teaching science, retired in the summer of 1930 after forty years' service. He had also been a keen sportsman, laying out the first sports field for the school. He was presented with a wallet, embossed with the school crest, enclosing a significant sum of money, and he was to be the chief guest at the Old Boys' Club dinner in April 1931,[12] in the presence of the former Rector, Wm. J. Watson, by then Professor Watson. Andrew H. Watson, who had been the school janitor since 1894, died in April 1935 after a period of illness, having served for 41 years under five different Rectors.[13] He had started work in the original Academy building in Academy Street, some ten months before it was closed. His health had deteriorated during the 1930's, with absence from duty becoming more frequent. Donald Dallas, the physical education instructor, became unwell during 1936, and was forced to resign that autumn. A formal presentation was made to him in the summer of 1938.[14]

From the early 1920's the increasing pupil numbers led to the appointment of extra teachers, including the first appointment for many years of a teacher of Gaelic. The teaching of Gaelic was soon expanded with the upgrading of the teacher to principal teacher status. From 1930 the subject was taught from the third year of Secondary education, rather than from the fourth year as had been the case previously. In September 1924 a major appointment to the English department was that of Donald John Macdonald, known to generations of pupils as 'D. J.' (see Chapter 18). In 1929 he became head of the English Department, and subsequent inspection reports suggest that standards in his department started to improve thereafter. 'Jake' Johnston was appointed to the Art Department in 1925, where he was to serve until retirement in 1968, becoming Principal Teacher in 1930, when he replaced James A. L. Kennedy, who had served the Town schools and then the Academy since 1894. Ellis Stuart, who was to serve the school for around forty years, took up his post in October 1936, soon becoming Principal Teacher of French. During the Second World War he worked behind enemy lines for MI5. Many other staff, too many to record here, served the school for long periods of time, throughout the early part of the twentieth century.[15]

In the first part of 1924 the school and the hostel were hit by serious illness. In January there were fourteen cases of whooping cough in the infant class. For two weeks in February the school was closed on the order of the Medical Officer of Health due to an influenza outbreak. Seventeen cases of scarlet fever in the girls' hostel had to be transferred to the Fever Hospital at Culduthel, but all the affected girls recovered. The matron received an honorarium for her extra work during the outbreak, and special cleaning and distempering were carried out over the Easter holidays. The following spring there was a further scarlet fever outbreak in the hostel, with 45 girls in quarantine, some of whom had to sit their Leaving Certificate examinations in the hostel. Pupil deaths were quite frequent, and in the period from March 1932 to August 1933 the *School Magazine* recorded the deaths of eight pupils from the secondary school. The causes of death included appendicitis, rheumatic fever and an accident in the playground whilst playing football. In 1939 a pupil in the first year of secondary school was drowned in Loch Moy.

The deaths of some serving members of staff are also recorded.

The school log book records frequent visits by His Majesty's Inspectors, and their reports, both for the Primary School and the Secondary School, continue to be generally very complimentary, although often interspersed with comments suggesting possible further improvements. The inspection of physical education only seems to have been reported on from session 1933/34, and this brought criticism as to the state of the floor in the gymnasium and the quality of some of the apparatus. Religious knowledge was examined on a regular basis by local ministers, and they generally seem to have been impressed with the results of their inspection. In their report for session 1938/39 His Majesty's Inspectors were very critical about the state of the playground, the provision of cloakroom accommodation and lack of adequate cycle sheds. They recommended numbered pegs in the cloakrooms and suggested charging a storage fee for bicycles to fund extra racks.

In May 1930 the Inverness County Education Authority was wound up, with the responsibility for educational administration passing to a sub-committee of the County Council, the position that the Government had wanted when framing the Education Bill at the end of the First World War, but had been unable to push through. Around this time there was considerable discussion about the creation of a Technical School in the Town, to provide an alternative form of secondary education for those who were less academically inclined. This was eventually to lead to the construction of a new building for what is now know as Inverness High School on the west side of the river. This opened in December 1936.

The reduction of pupils using the science and art departments (which had been previously shared with the High School) from March 1937 allowed the rooms to be partitioned over the following two years, and for the gym to be reconstructed. The raising of the school leaving age, long planned, was finally set for 1939, and it was realised that a combined technical drawing room and woodwork room was required along with a domestic science room and a dining hall for 200 pupils. The projected cost was £5000,[16] but then it was hoped that space could be found at the new High School building, as the Royal Academy was not to be included in the list of schools affected. These specialist rooms were not fully provided at the Academy until 1960.

The Endowments and the Armorial Bearings
An Endowments Bill was introduced into Parliament in May 1928. The Education Authority considered the proposals and it was left to the Convenor and officials to draw up a response including consideration of any changes that were needed. The Educational Endowments (Scotland) Commission held an enquiry in the second half of 1931.[17] Meetings were held in Inverness in October[18] at which Crampton Smith spoke about the funding of the IRA bursars. The draft of the revised Royal Academy scheme became available

in April 1932, and this proposed a special trust to administer the endowments,[19] but, following discussion and representation from the Old Boys' Club, it was agreed that a sub-committee of the County Council would administer the scheme and that two representatives of the Old Boys' Club would serve on the governing body of the trust, the first two people to serve being Evan Barron and Athole Mackintosh (solicitor).

The schemes covering the Royal Academy endowments and the other Inverness-shire endowments were finally approved by the Privy Council in October 1933. It was to be another three years before the Howden Trust Scheme was also updated.[20] In 1913 Miss Elizabeth Ponton Howden, of Albyn Villa in Inverness, gifted the sum of £400 to Inverness College to be used for medals for deserving pupils. As the College had failed during the First World War (see above), in 1921, by agreement, the scheme had been transferred for the use of the Royal Academy, and still survives today as the Howden Medal prize, awarded to deserving members of the sixth year, often the boy and girl captains. Honours boards in the school list the annual recipients from 1922 [Figure 17.4].

In 1930 consideration was given to the sale of the farms of Seafield, the Citadel, Kessock and Carse, owned by the Mackintosh Farr Fund, and to leasing land at Thornbush Road to the Town Council for housing. The leasing initially fell through as the Town Council considered the feu duty proposed to be too high. However, the following year the Town Council agreed to buy South Kessock Farm from the trust for £1900.[21] In 1933 negotiations were in hand for the sale of Seafield Farm to the Town, and this was completed in October for the sum of £3500. Citadel Farm was sold two years later, again to the Town Council, for £2750.

In late 1932 the Lord Lyon King of Arms wrote to the school about the use of the school coat of arms without it being officially registered in the Public Register of All Arms and Bearings in Scotland. This led to a petition being presented in May 1933, and the award of an amended version of the badge and coat of arms, still in use today[22] [Figure 17.5; see also Figure 14.2]. The cost of matriculation was £19. The design differed only in detail from that which had been in use in the 1920's. The school name disappeared from the top, and the school motto moved from the bottom to the top of the design. The only additional element was, above the shield, the helmet "of befitting degree with a Mantling Azure doubled Argent and on a wreath of their liveries is set for Crest ...". The June 1935 edition of the School Magazine was one of the first documents to use the new version of the crest.

School Life in the 1930's[23]
An account of school life in the early 1930's is provided in a book by Father Anthony (Ian) Ross[24] who moved to the Academy in 1931 at the start of his fourth year of secondary education, having been attending school in Beauly:

The Rector wore a gown, as did the Second Master and the Lady Superintendent who supervised the girls' behaviour. Each new pupil was interviewed by the Rector [Crampton Smith], an Englishman with a science degree from an English University. He frowned on hearing that I wished to learn Greek. 'Do you intend to become a minister?' 'Oh, no!' I answered cheerfully, 'but I like what I've read in translation and want to know more.' ... 'There is enough available in translation. You will have to follow a science course. H'm, mathematics weak I see. In that case it had better be Chemistry with Botany rather than Physics.' So it was settled for the next two years. ...

At the Academy, each year was divided into three streams, A, B and C. Pupils studying Art, or Domestic Science, or Commercial Subjects, were in C as a matter of course. Division between A and B streams depended on ability, and it was possible for someone in a B stream to join an A stream for a subject in which he or she was particularly good, although that did not happen very often. All those in the A stream were regarded as potential university candidates; some of those in the B stream might be in that category, but as exceptions to the average in their stream. There were no attempts to push any of us towards university if we had other plans for the future, as several already had as early as their fourth year.

Another account of life in the school is provided by Alex Cameron of Ardersier who was much the same age as Ian Ross, but joined the school at the start of his first year of secondary education in 1930, having been awarded a bursary to the Royal Academy. In an on-line account of his life, Cameron recalls travelling by "puggy" (a small train) from home to school each day. He recalls part of his school day as follows:[25]

For the first two years at the Academy I used to take sandwiches and a flask of tea with me for lunch. No school meals in those days! With others like me, lunch was eaten in the boys' cloakroom sitting on the central heating pipes (wonderful in winter!). ... At 11 a.m. each day we were 'allowed out' for a break and run about in the playground. When one had a spare penny it was customary to join all the others who were equally lucky and run down Stephen's Brae to a baker's shop where the most delicious cream doughnuts were made. I remember 'drooling' as I watched the lengths of dough being placed in a pan of sizzling hot fat (as is still done with chips!) and waited until one by one they were deemed ready by the baker. ... I can still feel the taste in my mouth! ...

[After a medical examination, a doctor ordered him to] have a 'proper meal' at 'dinner time'. So my dear mum had to arrange for me to go to Melvins the Bakers at the foot of the Raining Stairs on Castle Street. About two dozen pupils filled the restaurant each day and enjoyed a three course meal. Wednesday was the shop half holiday and as a result (for reasons unknown to me) we were always offered two helpings of delicious apple charlotte on Thursdays! On Friday we had to pay the bill for our week's lunches – five shillings! ...

Alex Cameron also describes some of his teachers, including Alex Duthie (who was the author of several Latin textbooks used in schools throughout the country), Donald Dallas, Leslie Frewin and also D. J. Macdonald, with whom in later life he was to become a personal friend. Cameron was also the only boy in a small class taught German by Miss Jeannie Cruickshank, another well-remembered teacher from that period.

Concerts and dramatic performances were a regular feature of the Academy at this period. In summer 1931 excerpts from *Riders to the Sea* (J. M. Synge) and *Hiawatha* (Coleridge-Taylor) were performed, and in 1932 part of *Land of Heart's Desire* (Yeats) was included in a concert [Figure 17.6]. In September 1937 the "Biennial Dramatic Entertainment" took place in the Empire Theatre, with a programme of short plays interspersed with choral items, one of the plays having been written by some former pupils who had recently left school. The annual Ettles lecture, to which over 300 pupils and 60 staff and friends would get free admission, continued with speakers such as George Mallory (talking about Everest), Randolph Churchill (Winston Churchill's son), and in 1935 Lt.-Col. Stewart Roddie, son of the school's former music teacher. Roddie spoke about Germany, as he had been a member of the Allied Control Commission overseeing disarmament in that country after the First World War.[26]

An art exhibition continued to feature at prizegiving time. Christmas brought a concert and an "At Home":[27]

> The senior classes of Inverness Royal Academy held their annual "At Home" in the school on Wednesday evening. The gay and happy gathering included in addition to the members of the teaching staff, many of those connected with education in Inverness, and former pupils of the school. The school hall was transformed by a charming decorative scheme, carried out by the pupils of the Art Department, and the shaded lights and myriads of multi-coloured streamers imparted a gaiety that effectively cloaked the normal austerity of the hall.

A school magazine, now called *Inverness Royal Academy School Magazine*, was restarted in April 1925, and this was to run until just after the outbreak of the Second World War, appearing at first monthly, but soon settling at three issues a year. All but one of the issues were printed; the December 1931 issue had to be duplicated due to financial difficulties. To raise funds, the Magazine committee organised a dance in the school, with tickets priced at 3s. [15p], held at the time of the publication of the next issue. Alongside the usual collection of pupils' prose and poetry, occasionally in Gaelic, the magazine records active teams in a variety of sports, including rugby football, association football, hockey and shinty, all in winter, and cricket in summer. From the middle of 1926 photographs of the teams begin to appear, along with photographs of the two sixth-year classes. From the late 1930's a "Junior Section", featuring work from the Primary School, appeared.

The annual sports took place each year in June. Tennis became available for all Academy girls at Hedgefield in the summer of 1934 and badminton followed later that year. A debating society also started that year, and its minutes books, covering the period up to 1969, survive in the school archive, although the society itself did not operate continuously. The rifle club was restarted in the autumn of 1926, after a lapse of a couple of years. In the revived inter-school sports in 1927, the Academy won two of the three trophies available for competition. In the late 1930's there was talk of introducing the prefect system, then becoming common in other similar schools, but this did not happen at the Academy until after the appointment of D. J. Macdonald as Rector in 1944.

A party under Miss Lucy Cruickshank, French and Lady Superintendent, visited Paris in April 1931, something which must have been regarded as a major adventure for young people at that time.[28] A further visit took place in 1935. Charles Mitchell (Principal Teacher of Mathematics) ran a camp at Carr Bridge in July 1931, using a site provided by the Boys' Brigade. It was sufficiently successful that further camps were held until at least 1934.[29] In 1933 and 1934 pupils from the Academy joined many other schools when they sailed on *S.S. Neuralia* to Norway and the Baltic Sea.[30] For some years in the period before the Second World War the school also "adopted" a merchant navy ship, and followed its progress.

A Girl Guide Company, the 3rd Company, was active in the school from around 1923 until the early 1940's [Figure 17.7], in the early days under Miss Mary Roy (geography) as Captain, and with, from 1927 to 1932, Miss Jessie Horne (art) as Lieutenant. Their 1927 summer camp was held at Rosemarkie in the Black Isle, and in 1929 the camp was beside Loch Meikle in Glenurquhart. A Brownie Pack was formed in 1929, but it does not seem to have lasted for any length of time. After a period with no Captain, the Guide Company was led by Miss Marshall, and by Miss Ola Campbell (until summer 1938) and Miss Chrissie Ferguson (from autumn 1938). The Company received their new Colours in February 1939. In 1937 one of the Academy girls was selected to attend the coronation of King George VI, and another attended an international Guide Camp held at Blair Atholl in Perthshire. Another Girl Guide, not necessarily from the Academy Company, attended an international camp in Hungary in July 1939, returning home only a matter of weeks before the outbreak of War. Both girls reported on their visits in the *School Magazine.*

Money from the Education Authority for the award of books as prizes had been stopped after 1932, due to the financial crisis of the time, but some payments restarted in 1936. In June 1937, shortly before the retiral of Murdo Morrison, Director of Education for Inverness-shire, the boys at Drummond Park made a presentation to him of a lamp as a token of their esteem and affection, as well as for the personal interest he had taken in them. Three days later he was to receive a fountain pen from the girls at Hedgefield. Mr Morrison was the guest of honour at the school prizegiving the following June.

Fetes, often in aid of sports funds, took place from time to time, but on the day of the fete in September 1935, due to be held at Hedgefield Hostel and to be opened by Lady Hermione Cameron of Lochiel, the weather was so poor that it had to be transferred indoors to the Academy. It raised £60, partly to provide a radio set for the girls' hostel, with much of the rest going to the school fund. This fete was soon followed by a concert in the Empire Theatre in Academy Street.

A minor fire in the school roof in December 1924 brought about a half-day's holiday for the pupils.[31] Regular holidays included the local Fast Days, the Harvest Festival and at the time of the Northern Meeting in September. Skating holidays also feature when the weather obliged. The visit to Inverness of the Prince of Wales in June 1931 brought a day's holiday. In 1935 the school closed for a day to celebrate King George V's jubilee. About 300 pupils attended the cinema to see the film *Royal Cavalcade*, and the following day each pupil received a box of chocolates and a souvenir medal. Pupils were allowed an extended lunch-hour to witness the proclamation of Edward VIII as King, following George V's death in January 1936. Four days later the whole school was closed for the funeral. For the Coronation of King George VI in May 1937 pupils were presented with a Coronation medal and a box of chocolates. Primary pupils were also given a flag, the gift of a former pupil, and post-Intermediate pupils got a copy of the Town Council's souvenir programme. Sports were held in the afternoon at the Bught Park.

In May 1938, the newspaper *The Glasgow Herald* published a illustrated feature about the school, in a series "Famous Scottish Schools".[32] The same year the period length was reduced from forty-five minutes to forty minutes, and extra periods at the end of the day for some pupils were abolished. Closing time became 4 p.m. each day for all pupils.

Former Pupils and the Old Boys' Club
The Old Boys' Club continued to be very active through the late 1920's and 1930's, holding regular dinners and a Christmas dance. Evan Barron continued to be a key figure. Sport figured prominently, both within the club and as semi-independent Academicals teams. In a magazine article in 1929, Barron described how the school took its colours of blue and gold:[33]

> ... The original colours were a combination of dark blue and light blue, and first came into use 40 years ago. Some years later the Academy Football Club entered a team for the Junior Football Cup and jerseys of the Academy colours were ordered for the eleven. On the morning of the first match these had not arrived, and as colours, of course, were necessary, the town was searched for jerseys in which the team could appear. In those distant days colours of any kind were not so easy to obtain as they are now, and eventually the Club had no option but to invest in eleven jerseys of a rather crude dark blue and an equally crude yellow or gold. When the team appeared on the field decked out in these, their appearance so delighted the spectators that they were promptly dubbed "the Wasps". The colours thus accidentally acquired remained, in less crude pigments, the football colours, and gradually ousted the real school colours, the dark and light blue, until they became the recognised insignia of the Academy. The Old Boys' Club, however, which was founded in 1896, remained faithful to the old colours, but now they have decided to incorporate with them the gold of the present school colours, and so unite the old and the new.

Apart from football, the Old Boys' Club and the Academicals had teams playing cricket and hockey and ran a badminton club. In early 1929 two members of the Academicals' hockey club played as members of the Scottish Men's Hockey team against England, one of them scoring a goal. Both had previously been selected to play for Scotland but not at the same time. The tennis club continued in Bishop's Road; golf was added as a sport in the early 1930's, with the Kinmount Cup being open for competition when it was presented shortly before the outbreak of the Second World War by John Kinmount, S.S.C., of Edinburgh. In 1933 an Old Girls' hockey club was established.

The first formal dinner of the Club after the First World War was held in April 1931 with Charles Greaves as chief guest (mentioned above). News of former pupils becomes more frequent in the *School Magazine* from about 1929. One former pupil who became well-known, was Elizabeth Mackintosh, author and playwright, using the pen-names of Josephine Tey for her detective novels and, for her plays, Gordon Daviot, from her place of residence as a child at Daviot, just south of Inverness. She contributed a crossword to the March 1939 edition of the *School Magazine*.

Amongst the obituaries is that of Jack Birnie, a noted golfer, who died in January 1930. A key member was lost in January 1931 with the death of David Macdonald, who had served as the Club Secretary for many years. Club Rooms in Church Street were acquired for a short period in 1934. By the following year the Club was trying to assist former pupils gain employment at a time of economic downturn.

The Second World War and another change of Rector
During 1938, the talk of possible war increased. Nationally preparations were put in hand. During the political crisis in September that year, air-raid trenches were dug at the Royal Academy. Some members of staff were briefly absent attending military training courses. In 1939 the School log book records that the school was closed from 1st to 11th September to allow staff to make arrangements to receive evacuees. Pupils from Edinburgh, Glasgow and other parts of Scotland soon arrived, along with a number from south of the Border, especially from London.[34] Over 90 evacuee pupils were enrolled in session 1939/40, although some of them stayed for only a matter of months. Numbers in subsequent sessions were lower, with about 50 in session 1940/41, 25 the following session, and only a handful each year in and after session 1942/43. Partly due to the number of evacuees (16 in the Primary Department and 34 in the Secondary Department) the school role had reached 827 in October 1941.[35]

Various members of staff were soon called up for military service, requiring replacement temporary staff to be appointed. Other staff took on duties in the Town such as gas identification officer, air-raid wardens, members of the Observer Corps and billeting officers. Older pupils were also involved as stretcher party members and messengers, and some became part of the Home Guard. Senior pupils also acted as temporary postmen over Christmas

1940. Miss Maude Yule (later Mrs Maude Anderson) (science) became resident mistress at Hedgefield Hostel. The scheme for religious instruction was changed, and two honorary chaplains were appointed to the school.

Lewis Owen, who had been the music teacher since 1912, died in October 1940. Over the years choirs which he had trained won many competitions at local festivals. His place was taken some months later by another person who was to serve the school over many years, Laurence Rogers. Under the age limit rules, Miss Kathleen Kennedy, who for thirty years had been head of the Primary Department, retired in 1942, as did, after twenty years' service, Mr Duthie, second master and Head of Classics. Mr Duthie's second son had been killed in action in late 1941. Later that same year Miss Mary Roy retired from her post as teacher of geography. All three had their services acknowledged in the inspection report for session 1941/42, one of the few times when these reports specifically named members of staff.

The school bell fell silent for the duration of the War. Blackout curtains were fitted in certain rooms, used by senior pupils after the younger ones were dismissed at 3.20 p.m. School over the darkest winter period started at 9.30 a.m. instead of 9 a.m. The toilets in the Science block were once again requisitioned by the Armed Services billeted in the Crown Church halls, and access to the main school blocked off. From near the start of the Second World War, some of the surplus land at Drummond Park Hostel was let for use as a nursery garden. At the school, night-time fire watching started in March 1941, with senior pupils and a member of staff on duty.[36] The school gates were removed as part of the drive to provide metal for the War effort. An "alert" occurred during a Leaving Certificate examination in March 1941, but caused no problem, and a further "alert" took place a week later. In September the Town Council discussed with the school the provision of a rest centre in the event of a serious bombardment of Inverness from the air. However Inverness was never directly attacked by German aircraft.

The Academy was brought into the free milk scheme. The school meal provision at the Crown School, in the building vacated by Inverness High School in 1936, was extended to the Academy from the start of the 1943/44 school session. The serious shortage of farm labourers meant that the Academy closed for four weeks in each October from 1943 to 1945 to allow pupils to assist with the potato harvest; the summer holiday had been greatly shortened to allow this to happen. At Drummond Park Hostel Mr Frewin invested in some hens and feedstuffs which allowed the hostel to have a supply of fresh eggs during wartime rationing.

The number of boy residents at Drummond Park increased, requiring adjustments to the sanitary arrangements. There was also a need for additional help at the hostel to allow Mr and Mrs Frewin to have one night a week off duty. Both hostels required the provision of new air-raid shelters, to supplement and replace the existing provision. In the summer of 1942 Miss

Paterson was forced to resign through ill-health as Matron at Hedgefield, after 21 years' service. She was given a superannuation payment, and as a leaving present she received a silver tea service, an electric fire and a cheque. Her replacement was a lady from Portree.

Fund-raising for war charities was impressive. In January 1940 a concert was held in the Empire Theatre in aid of War charities. In "War Weapons Week" in 1941 over £1000 was collected, whilst the following year, in "Navy Week", the total came to £926. Pupils in the summer of 1940 were involved with a forestry camp at Tomnacross, involving both boys and girls, with the boys working at felling and brashing, while the girls seem to have been involved in road and bridge making (not very successfully, according to the *School Magazine* report!).

Academic results continued to improve under Crampton Smith, with a record number of 69 Leaving Certificates gained in the summer of 1940. Prizes, except for special and endowed prizes, were discontinued from the autumn of 1940. A couple of years later it was not possible to present medals, and book prizes were substituted. After the last regular edition in December 1939 until the *Memorial Magazine* was published in 1947, the *Magazine* managed only one edition, in December 1940. The Academy Guide Company lost both its Captain and Lieutenant to National Service at the outbreak of war, and, although carried on for a while under temporary leadership, the Company seems not to have survived very far beyond 1940. The December 1940 *Magazine* records the war service of many former pupils up to that date.

A collection of Gaelic books was presented to the school in September 1940 by the Minister of the Free North Church, Rev. Kenneth Cameron, M.A. In the summer of 1942, the school Charter, which had been presumed lost, was found in the safe of the late Clerk to the School Management Committee. The Education Committee agreed that it would be returned to the school to be in the care of the Rector. It was lodged in the school safe until restored at the time of the School bicentenary in 1992, and is now on permanent display in the school [see Figure 5.2].

Crampton Smith continued to serve on various national committees for education, and in February 1940 attended the official opening of St Andrew's House in Edinburgh by King George VI and Queen Elizabeth. During the summer of 1943, Smith gave early intimation of his intention to retire, and this allowed the selection procedure to take place during the autumn. His retirement date was at the end of January 1944. The school's *Magazine* in 1947 recorded his service as follows:[37]

> Mr Smith was a brilliant teacher of Mathematics, and to his headship of the School he brought all the clarity of mind and standards of precision and finish which made him a success in the classroom. ... In the wider field of education lay perhaps his chief interest after the Academy. During his whole tenure of office he played a big part in the work of the Educational Institute of Scotland. As Convener of its Reconstruction Committee he was chiefly responsible for the production of its

massive report on Educational Reform. ... His last big undertaking was membership of the Secretary of State's Advisory Council on Education from 1943 to 1946. Two honours came to him for these services to education, the degree of F.E.I.S. from the Institute and in 1938 the O.B.E. from the King.

Crampton Smth's replacement as Rector was to be Donald John Macdonald, who, as noted above, was appointed to the staff in 1924, and had become second master in the summer of 1942. With another internal appointment, 'Jake' Mowat filled the vacant post of principal teacher of English.

Chapter 18
The final third of a century at Midmills

From 1944 until 1962, the Royal Academy was overseen by perhaps the most highly regarded of all the Rectors who have served the school, D. J. Macdonald. 'DJ' was to introduce a number of significant reforms, such as the prefect system. He was to be followed as Rector by W. S. Macdonald until 1971 and then by Ian Fraser. Further extensions to the building at Midmills were opened in both 1960 and 1973, but in summer 1977 the school started the move to a new site on the southern edge of the Town, at Culduthel, a move completed two years later.

'DJ' as Rector

Donald John Macdonald, 'DJ' as he was known to many Inverness people, served as Rector for more than eighteen years. He was selected for the job from 47 applicants, having been originally appointed to the school as an assistant teacher of English in 1924, becoming Principal Teacher of his department in 1929 and Second Master in 1942. He was born at Lochcarron in Wester Ross, and was a fluent Gaelic speaker and scholar. Part of his installation as Rector was conducted in Gaelic. Sadly his wife, a former pupil of the Academy, died in 1961, and for a variety of reasons DJ decided to retire as Rector with effect from January 1962. The Royal Academy was the only school in which DJ was to serve as a teacher. His retirement was marked with a variety of presentations, and a special dinner provided by the Former Pupils' Club.

The school's *Memorial Magazine* in 1947 recalls a story from his first year as a teacher. He was attending the annual Ettles Lecture, to which free admission was provided for Academy staff and pupils. "He was about to select a seat when he was confronted by a senior lady member of staff, who was acting as a marshall. Where, she enquired, did he suppose he was going? – he ought to know they were staff seats – pupils must go elsewhere."

Dr. Macdonald made a number of changes in the administration of the school, the first of which was to introduce the prefect system to the school, and framed photographs of each year's prefects are to be found in the school archive. The annual installation of the prefects was completed in an impressive ceremony. He also introduced individual record cards for the pupils, rather than record all information in a central marks register. School "houses" were introduced in 1945, using local place-names which were Abertarff, Dunain, Farr, and Raigmore. These house groups were used especially in sports competitions until the early 1970's. Following the award of an honorary degree of LL.D. from Aberdeen University in 1957, the staff presented DJ with a lectern Bible.[1]

During his time as Rector the primary department of the school was phased out, something which he regretted, but he was still in office at the time of the opening of the extension in 1960 which included a proper assembly hall, soon equipped with an organ to accompany the hymn sung at morning assembly. DJ is also remembered by the quality of his oratory. He served on many committees both during his time in office and following his retirement (see Appendix 2). In 1992 he was able to attend, at the age of 92, and just a year before his death, the bicentenary celebrations of the Royal Academy, when he met the Earl of Inverness (see Chapter 19).

The school develops[2]
The first eighteen months of DJ's tenure of the office of Rector saw the final phases of the Second World War. In June 1944 the school raised about £1700 for "Salute the Soldier" week, through a bring and buy sale, games evenings, an auction sale, etc. After the summer, until 1945, the secondary department was still opening three weeks before the primary department to allow secondary pupils to take part in the annual potato harvest in October and November. Due to lighting restrictions and the retention of summer time through the winter, the primary department opened later in the morning in the darkest months. In the early days of 1945, severe weather caused flooding on the main stair and in the hall from snow-melt which could not run away due to blocked rhones. A few weeks later, during severe frost, the boiler at the playing fields burst.

The end of the War in May 1945 brought pupils two days of holiday for the 'Victory in Europe' celebrations. A further two days' holiday came for secondary pupils in August for the 'Victory in Japan' celebrations, with another day for all pupils in early September for the final celebration of the end of war. Three members of staff who had served in the Forces returned to duty in the school. Some of the trappings of war had disappeared with the removal of sandbags from the main hall in October 1944. The brick baffles protecting the junior school door and windows were not removed until early 1946 and Anderson shelters in the playground survived until late that year. Gates and railings around the school, removed for the War effort, started to reappear in 1948.

The final chapters of the story of the Second World War started with the publication in the summer of 1947 of the *Memorial Magazine*, which listed the Roll of Honour. The sixty-five former pupils who had served and died in the War, a rather shorter list than that from the First World War, were recorded on the Second World War Memorial tablets erected in the main hall. These were designed by C. J. Buchanan of the Art Department. The original gates had been removed to aid the War effort, so the Old Boys' Club offered to provide memorial gates with the two front corner entrances on the continuation of Stephen's Street being combined into a single central entrance. In May 1950 the Education Committee accepted the offer without discussion, and the gates were formally opened in November 1954[3] [Figure 18.1].

In January 1947 the Education Committee started the provision of school meals, as required under the 1945 Education (Scotland) Act, but as there was no suitable space available in the Academy, pupils taking lunch had to cross the road to an annexe of the Crown School, a situation that continued until the opening of the new hall and canteen area in 1960. Prizes were reintroduced in 1947, but the award of medals could not be restarted due to metal shortages, and book prizes were substituted. In 1954 the return of the 1922 Howden Medals by the holders of these awards allowed a token medal presentation. The severe winter at the start of 1947 caused major plumbing problems in the junior school building. The main school heating system started to fail and it had to be upgraded in the early 1950's at a cost of well over £1000. At the same time, dry rot in the roof trusses of the main hall and elsewhere cost £850 to repair, and at one stage the end wall of the main hall had to be demolished during term-time.

From the start of the 1948/49 session all pupils in the secondary department got free education. Fees had to be abolished under the 1945 Act, as there was no alternative secondary school in the Town providing an academic education. Fees had already been discontinued at the upper end of the secondary department in 1920. The loss to the Education Authority in fee income was reckoned at about £2700 per annum. Books and stationery were also to be provided free. 1949 also saw the length of the school year extended to 400 attendances (200 days) in place of the traditional 385. The same year the transfer of the teaching of commercial subjects to the High School led to this subject being dropped from the Academy curriculum.

It is impossible to record all the significant appointments to the staff over the years, but one which should be mentioned is that of William (Bill) Murray as head of Physical Education from early in 1951. In his time on the staff until 1977 he was to make a major impression on sport, school dances, and much else. In 1953 he introduced sports colours, in the form of yellow braid, on school blazers.

In the mid-1950's, it was anticipated that numbers in the secondary department would rise from 600 to 800 by 1962, requiring up to seven more classrooms. The decision was taken in June 1955 to progressively close the primary department.[4] However the homecraft and handicraft rooms would be retained. Those pupils completing the primary department who were not deemed suitable for an academic course were thereafter transferred to the High School.[5] Fees in the primary department continued to be levied until that department had been phased out by the summer of 1961 [Figure 18.2]. In its final two years, due to redevelopment of the primary wing, primary classes were transferred to the Crown School annexe, across Midmills Road.

A number of special items of equipment were purchased from endowments in the period after the War, such as an epidiascope (for projecting a printed page onto a screen), and a marquee for use on sports days. The sale of some surplus chemistry equipment allowed the purchase of a slide projector and some filmstrips. A 16 mm silent film projector was provided from the profits of a concert. Blackouts were soon provided in certain rooms to allow the development of the use of audio-visual aids. A rotary ink duplicator replaced a much older flatbed model. To supplement the school fund a scheme was started whereby pupils for many years contributed one (old-style) penny a week, which, according to the school magazine, would raise about £90 a year if every pupil contributed. A major sale in June 1950 raised a further £730.

As a result of the abolition of fees in the secondary department, money previously used for bursaries could be redirected to other purposes. One of the early proposals was for "wireless receiving equipment", i.e. radios, to be installed, but this was not permitted by the Scottish Education Department, but electric gramophones were purchased. The radios were provided from a different source of funding the following year. In 1952 money was provided from the endowments to fit out Room 1 (later Room 36), next to the Rector's office in the main school, as a library, but it was not long before it was realised that this room was too small for its intended purpose. The need in 1961 to provide a fire screen around the ground floor and gallery of the internal hall in the main building led to the library being returned to the main hall [Figure 18.3].

Soon it was necessary to amend the Endowments scheme, and discussions between 1952 to 1955[6] led to a public enquiry in Inverness in September 1955.[7] The SED would not agree to the initial revised plan,[8] but further discussions over several years led to a new plan being agreed late in 1959, and this was signed in February 1960, with the scheme coming into effect in May 1961.[9] Due to the availability of free education for all, and now that the Education Authority had full responsibility for running the school hostels, only about half the available endowed money was being spent each year. The new scheme allowed a wider range of spending, and a variety of the smaller funds, including some prize and medal funds and the Howden Trust Fund, were taken fully into the Academy Endowments. There was also provision for the proportions of the money allocated under different heads of the scheme to be adjusted without the need for the provision of a completely new scheme.

Between 1947 and 1949 the deaths of several former members of staff were recorded. Thomas Cockburn, who died in October 1947, had first been appointed as a classics teacher in 1879 (see Chapter 13), but had retired to pursue his other interests in 1909. He was to be commemorated in the Cockburn Library. Following letters in *The Scotsman* and *The Inverness Courier*, a memorial fund was started and in November 1956 the library of some 700 volumes, mainly for sixth form use, was presented to the school by Evan Barron, on behalf of those who had subscribed to the fund. This library, with a plaque, which was originally placed in Cockburn's own classroom, is still in existence. The books act as a supplement to the main school library, and contain many volumes of special local interest to Inverness and the Highlands, some of which are difficult to obtain elsewhere.

Also to die a couple of months later was Charles Greaves, who was appointed in 1890 as the commercial teacher, but later he changed to science teaching (see Chapter 17). He had retired in 1930. In March 1948 Prof. W. J. Watson, the former Rector (see Chapter 15 *et seq.*), died. These three former members of staff were probably the last links with the original Academy building in Academy Street, as all of them had started their career at the Academy in that building. Crampton Smith, also a former Rector, died at the end of November 1949. Hugh Robson, who had been so active in establishing the boys' hostel, originally as a private venture, died in 1956.

School life
A lectern cloth embroidered with the school coat of arms was made and gifted to the school in 1947 by Gladys Fairie, formerly Gladys Yule, a member of the Art Department, who had had left the staff at the time of her marriage. School colours were introduced onto school blazers from 1953. Cycle shelters were planned in 1954, but the SED regarded the construction costs as being far too high, but in the end the original plan was adhered to. The annual "At Home" event took place each December [Figure 18.4], evolving through time into a Christmas dance. Concerts were also held from time to time, and ceilidh performers and a school choir appeared on BBC radio broadcasts. Various choirs achieved success in the local musical festival, including the mixed voice choir, who in 1952 fell through the platform on which they were performing!

Sports clubs continued despite the problems of transport to away fixtures during and after the war, and their successes and failures are too numerous to list in detail here.[10] Large numbers of photographs of the teams are found in the school archive, some even covering the War years. Sports photographs appear in the school magazines from 1957.

Many new clubs and societies were started under DJ's rectorship, one of the most significant of these being the Outdoor Club, started in 1946 by Frank Cunningham, the new Principal Teacher of Geography. Log books in the school's possession record the many hillwalking trips that were carried out. 1949 saw a visit to a ration-free Switzerland. In 1955 the 100th expedition was held. However tragedy was to strike when a pupil was killed in a fall on Stac Polly in April 1962. A Debating Society continued to operate until 1969, and like the Outdoor Club, their log books record their activities over the years. Another long-running club was the school's Country Club, which had been started in 1956 as a junior branch of the Scottish Association of Young Farmers' Clubs, although the programme was somewhat wider than that of many YF clubs. The Country Club, especially under Miss Pat Forbes' guidance, had great success, winning four national speechmaking competitions, but, like the Outdoor Club, did not survive the difficult times in teaching in about 1984.

School visits to foreign parts also developed. Following Outdoor Club visits to Switzerland in 1949 and in 1953, school visits to Germany took place in 1955, 1956 and 1957, mainly under Miss Jeannie Cruickshank's command, and in 1958 parties left for both France and Germany. In 1960 a party left for Switzerland under Mr Alastair Gammie, Miss Pat Forbes and Miss Janet Banks. Thereafter foreign visits became almost an annual event.

Prizegivings were generally held in the Playhouse Cinema. At the 1958 event, at a time when inclusion in mainstream education of pupils with disabilities was unusual, a special prize was awarded to a pupil with cerebral palsy, and this award was greeted with a standing ovation and reports in various newspapers. The next year the Academy featured in two national newspapers in an article about pupils smoking in some of the cafés in the centre of the Town during lunchtime and after school. As usual with this type of article, the story was over-dramatised. School magazines continued to appear after the *Memorial Magazine* in 1947, at first twice-yearly, and then annually. In 1961 the Morris brothers, former pupils of the school, presented a massive trophy to the school for the best magazine article each year.

The Old Boys' Club does not seem to have revived to any extent in the period immediately after the War. Hockey, rugby and golf clubs restarted, but it was 1950 before the main Club was reformed, although Evan Barron, for health reasons, would not continue as President. The Club assisted with the school sale in the summer and restarted their annual dance close to Christmas, with increasing attendance during the early years of the decade. As mentioned above they were to fund-raise for the War Memorial Gates, opened in 1954. After this the club seems to have faded away. In the end, the concept was reborn with the establishment of a Former Pupils' Association in 1965 (see below).

The Hostels
Drummond Park and Hedgefield Hostels each continued to provide a home for pupils from outside Inverness who required residential accommodation to pursue their education. Both hostels had their problems. Shortage of linen and towels at the end of the War lead to a decision that pupils would have to provide their own towels, and a later resolution of the Education Committee was that cotton sheeting would be purchased and made into sheets by pupils during their sewing classes. Other equipment was purchased from Government surplus supplies.

Hedgefield was used at holiday periods for various training courses for leaders of youth organisations and Church groups, bringing in a small profit. The field at Hedgefield was let for horse-grazing. Eventually, in 1951 through the efforts of the Old Boys' Club, the arch over the gateway at County Buildings in Ardross Street, which had recorded the use of that building as the original War Memorial Hostel, was moved to Hedgefield. The annual "At

Home", held shortly before Christmas, was the hostel girls' social event of the year. An unusual honour was the award of the British Empire Medal in 1958 to Miss Elizabeth Campbell, who had been matron at Hedgefield Hostel since 1942, having previously been working in the hostels at Portree and Fort William.

A fire in Drummond Park in April 1946 caused serious damage in one dormitory, five stores and a garage. The cost of repairs amounted to £1300, and further money was spent on the provision of "fire appliances", presumably fire extinguishers. Some of the extensive land was let as a nursery garden, although the burn that ran through the grounds flooded several times. The West Lodge, which had been declared unfit for human habitation before the Second World War, was considered for upgrading, but this was found to be too expensive, so it was sold, and later demolished. A diary written by one of the hostel pupils in the period from 1956 to 1958 exists in the Highland Council Archive.[11] One incident that is recorded is the appearance in a local newspaper of a false advertisement for an assistant janitor for the school, which had been placed by some pupils. In 1962 Leslie Frewin and his wife retired as wardens after a service of twenty-two years, to be replaced by Mr and Mrs Malcolm Cumming.

There was pressure on accommodation at both hostels from 1948, partly due to the need to provide accommodation for some pupils attending the Technical High School. An extension at Drummond Park, built in the early 1950's, was originally to cost £9600, but when plans were drawn up the cost was nearly £24 000. The extension was opened in August 1955, providing a number of 4-bedded rooms and some accommodation for housemasters who would assist the warden in the supervision of the boy pupils, who now numbered up to 50. Accommodation was also provided for the domestic staff. A new kitchen was installed and oil-fired central heating provided. A major extension was added to Hedgefield in 1961/62, at a cost of about £59 000, providing smaller bedrooms for the girls, as had been done at Drummond Park.

Although not directly linked to the school, a number of girls attending the Academy were resident in a hostel run by Roman Catholic nuns at Hill Park in Culduthel Road, close to Hedgefield. This building was extensively damaged by fire one night in June 1959. One nun and one of the girls were injured.

Playing Fields
The playing field at Millburn was used for sheep grazing during the summer holiday period, and this continued until well after the end of the War. The growth of the school also led to pressure on the provision at Millburn. Plans were put forward in 1947/48 for an extension southwards onto farm land, and, although this was in conformity with Town's planning proposals, it was later decided not to proceed. This is the land that was used to build Millburn Junior Secondary School, officially opened in November 1961, although with

the rebuilding of that school, by then Millburn Academy, in 2008, the school building now stands on part of what was the Royal Academy playing fields, and the extension southwards has become playing fields.

Each year in June the Academy held a sports meeting, normally on a Wednesday afternoon, which coincided with the half-day closing of many shops and some business premises, a practice which was common at that time. This arrangement meant that many parents would attend. Until its condition deteriorated too much, the marquee (purchased in 1947) was pitched and afternoon teas were served. Sadly, as always happens even in June, some sports days were just too wet, and some events had to be postponed. Eventually a telephone was provided at the field, allowing the groundsman to keep in contact with the main school, and also for use following the occasional accident. An equipment hut was also provided in 1957.

The 1960's extension
The gradual closure of the primary department, which was completed in 1961, was concurrent with the planning and building of the fourth extension to the school to the east of the main building. This enclosed an area that became known as the quadrangle. The plans were approved by the SED in late 1957, subject to a reduction in the size of the stage, at an estimated cost of just under £120 000, but within months the tenders, which did include various alterations to classrooms elsewhere in the school, had reached £128 000. Construction work was started late in 1958, and the building was ready for full occupation at the start of the 1960/61 session, although some parts had come into use during the previous session. A new oil-fired heating boiler for the whole school was installed, thus saving Alex. Munro, the janitor, hours of work stoking boilers and removing ashes. Teething problems with the system included the break-up of the concrete floor of the new boilerhouse due to the heat.

On the ground floor the main accommodation provided a large assembly hall, with a canteen and kitchen attached. A sliding partition separated the hall from the canteen, so that for morning assembly and other large events the whole area could be used. A technical workshop (the first proper provision for this subject that the school had had) was provided, and Allan Beattie became the first qualified teacher to teach that subject. He will be long remembered for the items of special furniture for the school and its Outdoor Centre, which he made so robustly that it was almost impossible to damage them. The rest of the new accommodation included a science laboratory and toilets, cloakrooms, a staffroom (which became the male staffroom), a medical inspection room and associated storage. Over the new entrance, facing Midmills Road, a second storey provided four classrooms, of which two were allocated to history teaching and the other two to geography classes. Even this extension was to prove inadequate and it was not long before further accommodation was required.

From the school endowments, the assembly hall was soon provided with an electric organ, which saw daily use accompanying the hymns sung at assembly. During the 1960's and 1970's, the stage, which was well equipped with lighting gantries and sound equipment, saw various school productions, the first of which in 1963 was *Papageno*, an adaptation of Mozart's *Magic Flute*. This was followed in subsequent years by Gilbert and Sullivan's *Iolathe* and the double bill of *Trial by Jury* and *HMS Pinafore*. Later productions included *The Chiltern Hundreds*, *Time and the Conways* and *Macbeth*. Several pupils who were to make a name for themselves in the entertainment and theatrical world attended the school in the late 1960's and early 1970's. These included Janis Kelly, Harry Nicol and John Doyle. A little later Jimmy Chisholm was another pupil who was to follow a stage career.

Later, the stage also provided a 'home' for the first television set and video-cassette recorder purchased for the school. Classes were taken to the stage to view programmes. It would only be after the move to Culduthel from 1977 that transportable televisions sets and video-cassette recorders would allow programmes to be shown in classrooms.

A new Rector
W. S. Macdonald, no relation of D. J. Macdonald, was appointed as Rector with effect from January 1962. A native of Caithness, he had three honours degrees, and a Distinguished Service Cross for his wartime work (see Appendix 2). He served the school until 1971, when he returned to his native Caithness, and took a mature student's divinity course at Glasgow University. He was soon elected as a councillor for part of Caithness, and visited Brussels on business in connection with the European Economic Community (as it was then named), before his death in 1978.

The school roll was increasing, and by 1967 it was approaching 1000. Many new staff appointments were required. Two temporary classrooms had to be provided in 1963, one as a general classroom and one as a science laboratory, and these were located to the north of the 1960 extension, towards Crown Avenue. A third hut was added shortly afterwards. The 1911 extension was discovered to have a roof that was too heavy for the walls, and urgent remedial work had to be carried out.

The 'Highers', the key examination for senior pupils taken in the fifth and sixth years, were moved in 1962 from their traditional time in March to the month of May. The final school term, after Easter, for many sixth year pupils had become a waste of time, and the requirements of the examination system meant that pupils could not leave school, otherwise they would not receive their Leaving Certificate. All sorts of activities were introduced to fill this time [Figure 18.5], but it was still a time of frustration for those moving on to University or into employment. It was not until the summer of 1967 that senior pupils could leave immediately after the conclusion of their examinations. In 1969 the school celebrated the work of Miss Mary McGill, who had served as School Secretary for 47 years. The previous year 'Jake' Mowat retired from his post as head of English which he had held since 1944.

Foreign visits at this time included a twinning with St. Valéry in France, a town which has particular links with Inverness as the Highland Division was captured here during the Second World War, in June 1940. The Outdoor Club visited the Lake District, Northern Ireland and Norway, as well as organising more local hill-climbs. There were visits to Switzerland, under James (Jimmy) Johnstone, the recently-appointed head of geography. In the mid-1960's the geography department held field excursions to Carbisdale Castle Youth Hostel, in the extreme north of Ross-shire. In 1966 survey work was carried out for the recently-established Highlands and Islands Development Board (later modified into Highlands and Islands Enterprise). From 1969 geography visits were to Skye. Several parties visited the Pitlochry Festival Theatre, and the Edinburgh International Festival. Parties also took part in cruises to the Mediterranean, the Baltic, and elsewhere, on board SS Uganda, a schools cruise ship.

In 1962, the school took part for the first time in the radio quiz-show Top of the Form, but only reached the second round [Figure 18.6]. The second attempt in 1970, in the television version of the show, proved much more successful, with the Academy team becoming runners-up against a team drawn from Salisbury's boys' and girls' Grammar Schools. The Academy team went on to become winners of Transworld Top Team, earning an Owl of Wisdom as a trophy.

Other quiz teams did well in road safety quizzes and the inter-schools Gaelic quiz competitions. Carol concerts and concerts of religious music were held in local churches. Some of these concerts were held in conjunction with the choir from the Fort Augustus Abbey School. Academy choirs took part in two editions on BBC TV of both Songs of Praise, and A Service for Schools. Brass musical instrument instruction in school time first appeared in the curriculum in 1968.

The school magazines record a wide range of activities ranging from the birth of a folk club in 1965 and a chess club the following year, to school-to-university conferences. "The Future of the Highlands" was the title of a 1965 event, with key speakers from the Highlands and Islands Development Board, the Crofters' Commission, and industry. In 1967 a conference on sport was held in the school, with pupils from all Inverness-shire secondary schools attending. Sport continued actively, and magazine reports include those for golf, badminton and cross-country running, as well as mention of the more traditional rugby, hockey, shinty and football teams. Saturday skiing started in 1963, and curling joined the list of school sports in 1970.

A Former Pupils' Association was established in early 1965, replacing the Old Boys' Club, and it pursued an active programme of social activities, including car treasure hunts and formal dinners. An Edinburgh branch was also formed, with visits, talks and dinners, and this lasted until the late 1970's. At the same time as the Association was founded, the school noted the death of Evan Barron, who had done so much for the previous Old Boys' Club. An early President of the new Association was Jimmy Johnstone, a former pupil, but now, as mentioned above, a member of staff. He had quickly become the school's careers master and later served as Depute Rector. The Association continued to be active until the end of the 1970's, but thereafter, apart from activity round about the time of the Bicentenary in 1992, few meetings took place, and the Association was formally wound up in 1998.

Junior High and Senior High Schools
In 1966, a fundamental change in the position of the Royal Academy was brought about when it was agreed by Inverness-shire Education Committee that Millburn Junior Secondary School (as it then was) and the Academy would work together, with Millburn taking all pupils for their first two years of secondary education. At the end of that time, those thought suitable of taking an academic course would move to the Academy, and other pupils would complete their education at Millburn. This brought about a junior and senior High School arrangement. The Secretary of State accepted this, although he indicated that in the long term Inverness should move to a fully comprehensive system, something which would not be introduced for another decade.[12]

The scheme came into effect in August 1971, but only after a campaign in the press by the Academy's Rector and staff, as well as parents, highlighting the apparent lack of parental consultation. Attempts at the Education Committee meetings to delay the introduction of this scheme were unsuccessful. There would be a temporary reduction in the roll of the Academy (which was over 850), as there was to be no first-year intake. Within two years the roll was below 700 pupils. Even so a further extension was immediately planned with a two-storey prefabricated CLASP construction adjacent to the huts on the north side of the school. This was built during 1972 and 1973, containing biology laboratories, technical rooms, a homecraft room, a commercial room and a language laboratory. The move of the Biology department into the new extension allowed the development of the Art department on the upper floor of the 1911 building. The provision of these new rooms allowed a more wide-ranging group of courses than had been previously possible, to allow for the extended third year intake from the start of the 1973/74 session. From that session the overall roll of the school started to increase again.

Computing entered the school curriculum in a very minor way in the early 1970's with a group attending a course in Aberdeen, in the days when one computer occupied a large room. For the next few years it was possible to encode material in Inverness, send the information to Aberdeen, and a couple of weeks later, the printouts would be returned. Another trust fund became available to the Academy in 1972 when the Forbes Meteorological Trust, originally gifted in 1881 by the widow of Arthur Forbes of Culloden to the School Board of Inverness, came under the control of the Education

Authority who decided that it could be used by the Academy. The accumulated income was used to purchase a weather station for the school, housed in the quadrangle during the remaining years at Midmills, and thereafter at Culduthel.

In 1972 the Academy took over the old primary school at Bunoich in Fort Augustus as an outdoor centre, and for the next fifteen to twenty years gradual conversion and development took place to allow the buildings to accommodate up to thirty-two pupils and four staff [Figure 18.7]. Workparties, led by various members of staff, cleaned and painted the building and erected bunks designed and built in the school's technical department by Allan Beattie, Principal Teacher of Technical Subjects. From the summer of 1993 class groups and groups like the Outdoor Club used the facilities, which were also available to youth organisations and other schools on request. However, circumstances from the middle of the 1980's gradually led to very limited use, with many staff unwilling to lead parties and stay in what was very basic accommodation. The use of the building was finally given up in 2001.

Discussion started about the closure of some of the school hostels in the Highlands due to the provision of all-through schools on the west coast and in the islands, areas which had been served up to then by Inverness schools. By the start of the session in 1977 there were only 21 girls and 26 boys requiring accommodation in Inverness, with Hedgefield having space for 74 pupils. Despite some objections to having a mixed-gender hostel, amalgamation went ahead from that date,[14] with Drummond Park becoming a hostel for those attending Inverness College, until its final closure in 1987. At the same time Hedgefield Hostel closed its doors for the last time for school pupils, with only about 10 or 12 pupils left in residence. It too became a hostel for Inverness College, closing in May 2002. Eventually the building and land (apart from a section used for the Mackenzie and Woodlands Centres) was sold to a developer, but none of the money realised by the sale came back to the original Trustees, namely the Academy's Former Pupils' Association (as successors to the Old Boys' Club), or to the school.

Another Rector
Ian Fraser was appointed Rector in April 1971, taking up his appointment after the summer holiday. He was to lead the school through the move to Culduthel and through the Bicentenary celebrations in 1992. Mr Fraser came to Inverness from Waid Academy in Fife, having previously taught in Stirling and Elgin (see Appendix 2). An early task he had to face was to control the implementation of the move of more-academic third-year pupils from Millburn School to the Academy. This required the introduction of suitable courses for all abilities, as well as overseeing the opening of the latest extension to the building.

The tradition of school prizegivings taking place in the Playhouse Cinema

271

came to an end in 1972, following the arson attack in which the cinema was completely burned down. Subsequent prizegivings took place in the school hall. That summer, Miss J. E. ('Jess') Thomson, a former pupil, retired after 40 years of service in teaching classics. The following summer Ellis Stuart retired, having served in the modern languages department, albeit with a break for War Service in the Intelligence Corps, since 1936. For his final twenty years he served as head of department. In 1975 Alex. Munro retired after serving as the school's janitor for 28 years.

Musical activity was revived in session 1972/73 with a performance of *Amahl and the Night Vistors* by Menotti, and Mozart's *Ave Verum* was rendered at an Easter Service. At Christmas 1974 Gilbert and Sullivan's light opera *The Gondoliers* was performed, although Christmas 1975 only saw a concert with mince pies. Quiz teams achieved good results, on the radio in Gaelic, on European topics and in a *Sunday Post* quiz. A school minibus first became available, after a long period of fund-raising, at the end of 1972. First Aid classes for staff were started in 1974, and ran for several years.

The *Magazine* continued to record the successes, and some failures, of school sports teams in a wide variety of sports. Several editions from the 1970's contained supplements featuring excellent art work, mainly from senior pupils. Annual publication ceased with the move to Culduthel, as the amount of staff time required to produce it, even with a pupil committee doing much of the work, could not be found. The next edition did not appear until 1980.

1972 had seen the first steps in the acquisition by the Education Authority of land at Culduthel for the construction of a completely new secondary school building (see Chapter 19). Planning for the new school started in earnest in January 1973, with staff preparing outlines for new courses for a fully comprehensive intake. The SED gave their permission in principle for a first phase of the building to be constructed, starting in 1974/1975, although work on the playing fields started immediately.[15] With the reform of local government administration in 1975, oversight of the planning of the school changed from Inverness-shire County Council to Highland Regional Council. Additional responsibility allowances became payable to promoted staff in advance of the move. The first that many pupils saw of the new building was a photograph in the 1976 magazine of the steel girders of the new school, with the title 'Phase 1 – New Zoo'. The following year, in an edition published just after the new building was opened, the cover illustration featured both old and new buildings.

In August 1977 the new building at Culduthel became available at a cost of over £2 million, and over the next two sessions, originally intended to be three sessions, the building at Midmills saw less and less use, until it was decided to close it for Royal Academy use at the end of the 1978/79 session. Thereafter the building became the temporary home of Culloden Academy, a completely new school, which eventually moved into its own building at Culloden in 1982. The Crown Primary School also made brief use of the building in 1984 while their own building was upgraded. Subsequently the Midmills building became part of Inverness College, and housed various departments that could not be accommodated at the main building in the Longman in Inverness. In 2011 the former use of the Midmills building by the Academy was commemorated by the unveiling of a plaque funded by Inverness City Heritage Trust.

Chapter 19
The Culduthel Years

On 24th August 1977 Inverness Royal Academy opened its doors on its third site since its foundation in 1792. Then very much on the edge of the Town, and surrounded on three sides by farmland and on the fourth by the woodland around Culduthel Hospital, it was a very different location from the two previous sites, being on the edge of the city. The school grounds were divided, and still are, by the Inverness to Inverarnie Road, and they are now bounded on the south by the Inverness Southern Distributor road. The total area is over 11 hectares (more than 27 acres). A main water supply for the Town had to be re-routed as it crossed the construction site, and there were issues about the size of the sewer available to serve such a large development.

Work on the playing fields was started in late 1974, to allow two full growing seasons before they would be used by pupils. The contract for this was given to Sportsworks, Ltd. Two houses for janitors and a pavilion were also included in the playing field area, across the public road from the main school building.

During 1975 work had started on levelling the land for the main building, and at an early date a construction vehicle broke through the cover-slab of a Bronze-Age cist, located (as far as can be ascertained) in the present main car park area. This grave turned out to be of great significance, and the reconstructed beaker or pot that was recovered from it is now on display in the National Museums Scotland in Edinburgh.

Even before the building was opened there was a story about a school 'ghost' in one of the stair wells,[1] and this story has resurfaced from time to time, presumably linked to the grave find. The Culduthel area has proved to be very important archaeologically, as another grave site had been located in the 1930's to the west on Culduthel Farm. Major excavations around 2005, across the Southern Distributor road, located evidence of a large Iron-Age community, complete with iron smelters [see Appendix 4 for further details of the archaeology of the Culduthel area].

In initial discussions in 1972 it had been suggested that a swimming pool be included in the project, and Inverness Town Council was asked if they would be prepared to assist so that the pool would become a community resource. However a letter in September 1973 from the SED said that approval could not be given at that stage for such a project, and the matter was dropped. It was agreed that a games hall would be included in the physical recreation provision, rather than a gymnasium with youth and community facilities.[2] It is not clear from the surviving correspondence if the original idea was that there should be two gymnasia, one of which was dropped from the plan to provide the games hall. One gymnasium was built, along with a dance studio, in a largely self-contained unit which includes the games hall.

The main construction company for the building, dealing with design, consulting engineering and quantity surveying, was Lesser Construction, Ltd., a company that had not previously worked in the Highlands. The original cost for the tender was just under £1.9M out of a total expenditure on the project of almost £3m.[3] The new building was basically a steel frame, with a flat roof. Although opened for pupils in August 1977, the official opening was carried out on 20th April 1978 by Dr. D. J. Macdonald, the former Rector.[4]

In the days before energy conservation became an issue, little insulation was included in the walls, and this soon had to be installed where there was a cavity wall thick enough to take it. The flat roof also started to leak. Originally a second phase of construction, west of the present main building and south of the dining hall, was planned to start almost immediately, but educational expenditure reductions and revised projections of the school roll soon caused this to be postponed, and later abandoned.

In 1981, the Former Pupils' Association asked for the War Memorial gates to be moved from Midmills to Culduthel. However Midmills had become a listed building, and as the FPs declined to finance the removal, it was agreed that the gates would remain at Midmills, with a plaque erected to explain their significance.[5] This plaque was never installed, although the school crests were removed from the gates and are now displayed on the railings in the library at Culduthel. After a long delay the school bell was removed from the belfry at Midmills, and eventually through the efforts of Allan Beattie (Principal Teacher of Technical Subjects) was housed in the display case currently outside the Rector's office. The bell had started its life at the Grammar School in the late 1700's (see Chapter 2).

Accommodation at Culduthel
Although some work kept contractors on site for a while, the building was opened to house first, second and third year secondary pupils, with the second and third year pupils who lived in the new catchment area moving from Millburn Secondary School (as it was then called), along with many of their teachers. With only three of the six years of a secondary school using the Culduthel building, the school lacked the influence of the senior pupils, who were still being taught at Midmills. It was very difficult to arrange joint events, as the two buildings were nearly two miles apart. Highland Regional Council supplied the school with an old minibus, and one of the janitors was almost permanently employed transporting, from one building to the other, staff who either had no car or chose not to use it. A complex timetable was established with 35-minute class periods, staggered by 15 or 20 minutes, to allow staff to travel, but frequently minor delays *en route*, or problems with the minibus, caused teachers not to be in class at the start of the period.

Some staff were unhappy with the prospect of teaching mixed-ability classes, as in their previous career they had only taught academic pupils. Careful timetabling allowed some who were close to retirement to remain at Midmills; others found the transition very difficult. The staff who were transferred from Millburn Secondary School had the advantage of having taught some of the second and third-year pupils during their first and second years at that school. The Rector and his depute also had to arrange that, as far as possible at any given time, the two of them were in different buildings.

Within a year of the opening, the Rector, Ian Fraser, was writing to the Education Committee about the problems of operating on the split site.[6] After considerable pressure on the Committee and a press campaign by staff and parents,[7] it was agreed that staffing for the split-site school would be six teachers (7%) above the 'Red Book' standard as laid down by the SED,[8] and urgent consideration would be given to operating on only one site. The Director of Education was required to produce a report for the next meeting of the Education Committee setting out the way forward, on the assumption that this would happen as soon as possible.

At that meeting it was shown that the Academy roll would probably fall from 1360 to 1169 by session 1985/86.[9] There were 1050 places available at Culduthel and 650 at Midmills (including the temporary classrooms) at that point. It was agreed that the nucleus of a new Culloden Academy would be established at Midmills, whilst Culloden's permanent building was constructed at a new site in the developing community.

The only solution for the Royal Academy that could be ready in time would be to erect twelve demountable units on the playing field immediately to the south of the main building, thereby accommodating the whole school, with these being available from the start of the following session in August 1979. The cost of this was estimated at £109 700, soon increased to £121 700, and this included the transfer of a science laboratory from Lochaber High School. Part of one of these units was later destroyed by fire.

The Midmills building closed its doors for Academy senior pupils in July 1979, with the remaining pupils, moving into their sixth year, transferring to Culduthel. This caused much less pressure for staff, and a simplified timetable, with 40-minute periods, was introduced.

Pressure on secondary accommodation in Inverness would only be eased when a new school at Charleston, on the west side of the river and canal, became available several years later. Then the numbers of pupils at the Royal Academy did fall significantly and by 1990 they were between 750 and 800, even though the number of pupils continuing education beyond the statutory leaving age was well above the national average. Around one-third of all leavers went on to some form of higher or further education. Staff numbers settled at around 60 full-time equivalent members.

Life at Culduthel

After a gap of twelve years, a school prospectus was reintroduced in 1977 for the opening of the new building. However until about 1990, remarkably little of the day to day life of the school at Culduthel is recorded in the school archive or in the Education Committee minutes. The school magazine, which became somewhat irregular in appearance, and the Rector's annual reports, record the departure of some long-serving members of staff such as James Johnstone (Depute Rector), Maude Anderson (*née* Yule) (physics) and Janet Banks (mathematics).

Some special events organised by the school included musical performances such as *The Wizard of Oz* in 1989, with *Grease* being performed the following year. Occasional foreign visits included visits to France and Iceland, and ski trips were arranged in conjunction with other Highland schools. The Duke of Edinburgh's Award Scheme proved popular, with significant numbers of senior pupils taking part in at least one of the stages. Teams and individuals recorded many successes in a wide range of sport disciplines. The school's "spaghetti bridge-builders" had repeated successes in various national engineering design competitions. Fund-raising provided money for the school itself, through annual fetes and sponsored walks, to finance the running and replacement of the minibus and to help subsidise sporting activities. Large sums of money were also raised for local charities, such as the Highland Hospice. In session 1990-91 almost £3800 was raised by the school for good causes. Christmas dances and fund-raising discos took place in the much larger space of the new games hall, compared with the assembly hall at Midmills.

During the late 1980's and early 1990's various changes, such as the introduction of Standard Grade courses to replace Ordinary Grade courses, took place in line with national policy. The 5-14 Development programme, introduced around 1990, affected courses in the first two years of the Secondary School. SCOTVEC modules were introduced for pupils in S5 and S6. The philosophy behind these, and various other, curricular changes falls outside the scope of this book. A Principal Teacher of Computing was appointed in session 1991/92. The Technical Department of former years became Craft, Design and Technology, which involved a change from learning activities by rote to a problem-solving approach. In 1992 modules on law were introduced by the Business Studies and Economics department for senior pupils. Work experience weeks were introduced for all fourth-year pupils, to give them some idea of what might face them on leaving school.

In accordance with national guidelines, an Academy School Board was elected in 1990, to represent parents' views and interests in the running of the school. Following discussion at the School Board and comments from parents, school sweatshirts and T-shirts were introduced for the first time in 1992, and soon started to replace as official uniform the traditional blazer and school tie, which were by that date little worn, having been replaced for many pupils by fashion and leisure garments. A Parent-Teacher association was established in the same session, and this group organised social events, and provided careers and course information evenings. School newsletters started to be produced in 1990, and these record activities such as visits by touring concert parties, discos, and community service projects. When a third computing room was brought into use, the newsletter noted "The Growth of Computing".

The Bicentenary
In 1992, Inverness Royal Academy reached its 200th year. This was celebrated in a much more active way than had been the case at the centenary. The events were mainly held close to the end of the summer term, as the actual date of the bicentenary fell during the school summer holiday. The highlight was a Royal visit from Prince Andrew, Earl of Inverness, whose ancestor, George III, had issued the Royal Charter in 1793. The bicentenary provided the school with a major opportunity to present itself to the public on its new site, and considerable press and media coverage brought the event to a wide public.[10]

Restoration and framing of the Charter with the attached Grand Seal of Scotland (see Chapter 5), was carried out by a specialist firm in Central Scotland, funded by a grant from the Inverness Town Common Good Fund. At a ceremony in April 1992 the Charter was returned to the school by Provost Alan Sellar, as his last public duty before retiring from office. A commemorative plaque, funded by Inverness Chamber of Commerce, was installed on the corner of the original Royal Academy building in Academy Street [Figure 19.1]. This was later to disappear and a replacement, funded by the Inverness City Heritage Trust, was erected in 2010.

A staff committee had been established in the autumn of 1990 and it drew up a programme of events which included open afternoons, a music evening, sports, art and music competitions, and a fete and sale. Jimmie Macgregor, a well-known TV and radio personality of the time, gave a lecture about the West Highland Way. This took place under the auspices of the Provost William Smith Trust Fund, which in 1986 had absorbed the Ettles Trust Fund for lectures (see Chapter 13). Former pupils were contacted and provided reminiscences of their time in the school, and these were later bound together for future reference. Glass and porcelain ornaments with the special bicentenary logo were offered for sale and a postal first-day cover was available locally with a special Royal Mail franking. A folio of document reproductions and short articles was produced, as no proper history of the school could be prepared in the time available.

An adventure trip to the Ardèche region of France was held in May. After the summer holiday a 'Young Musician' competition was held, with sponsorship by the Rotary Club of Loch Ness. The winner was a girl pianist from Shetland who used her prize to assist with the costs of attending music tuition in Switzerland.

The Royal Visit took place on Friday 26th June. After formal introductions, including one to Dr. D. J. Macdonald, the former Rector, and then aged 92, the Earl of Inverness unveiled a commemorative plaque in the front foyer [Figure 19.2] and signed the visitors' book. A short musical performance took place in the theatre, and this was followed by a tour of the historical exhibition in the Library, where the Prince saw the restored Charter. However his attention was drawn to a handbell which had 'mysteriously' disappeared from his former school, Gordonstoun, after an Academy rugby trip in 1956, and had never been returned. This story was picked up by several of the newspapers covering the event. Following a viewing of an art exhibition and the presentation of various awards, the final stop was on the sports field to see some events in a junior sports day. The presentation of a pair of whisky glasses was, at the last minute, changed to a Caithness Glass paperweight, as the Prince does not drink alcohol.

A year after the celebrations, after 22 years of service (sixteen of these at Culduthel) Ian Fraser retired as Rector in the summer of 1993. He had seen through a period which included industrial action by some teachers, underfunding, and a whole variety of curricular and methodology changes. In an interview published in the local press[11] he commented that the role of the head teacher was changing to one where the work was primarily management rather than educational issues, and teachers were not trained for this. More pupils were staying on into the fifth and sixth years, requiring a wider range of courses. Mr Fraser's departure from the school was marked by a special concert held in the school's lecture theatre, which included the performance of a pipe tune, *Fraser's Farewell to Inverness Royal Academy*, specially composed by Alasdair McAffer, the school's piping tutor.

Chapter 20
Epilogue (and the future)

It seems appropriate, for the present, to close this history of Inverness Royal Academy at the time of the bicentenary. Although about twenty years will have passed between that event and the publication of this book, and much has been added to the school's story, it is better for there to be a much longer period of reflection before passing judgement or comment on recent events. In some ways the more recent history has less to tell, as the school is now one of many state secondary schools throughout Scotland which follow much the same policies and direction. As a result, it is only the special events that set one school significantly apart from another, even though tradition can form part of the equation.

Certainly there have been significant events, such as the visit by Tony Blair during his time as Prime Minister. Prince Edward has visited the school twice in connection with the Duke of Edinburgh Award Scheme. Two further rectors have served the Academy. Ian Fraser was replaced in 1993 by John Considine who was the twenty-first Rector of the Academy, and he in his turn was replaced in 2010 by Alastair McKinlay. In 1999 a Special Needs unit was opened in a permanent extension to the main building, and a sensory room within that unit was added in 2003. The Millennium was celebrated with a construction of a mosaic representing the tree of learning, installed on an outside wall of the present building, where it can be seen by those who visit the school. Devolved School Management means that the school has more control over priorities for expenditure on matters including to some extent staffing.

Inspections by Her Majesty's Inspectors of Schools have always been very satisfactory, although suggesting some areas for improvement as these reports always do. Examination results at Higher Grade and other levels have continued to improve in most years, with occasional upsets and statistical 'blips'. Expeditions to countries such as the Gambia for voluntary work now regularly feature as part of the extra-curricular provision for older pupils, alongside ski trips, art study weeks, and similar events. A space exhibition was a highlight for younger pupils in 1997. Sport has continued to have a high profile, and many pupils, far too numerous to even start to list, have achieved major success in their chosen discipline.

Since about 1990 there has been significant development of housing within the school's catchment area. At the time of completion of this book there is talk of a major upgrade to the facilities at the school, possibly involving a complete rebuild on the present site, to accommodate the large number of potential pupils who occupy the housing that has appeared since about 2005 on the hillside to the south of the school. Certainly the school cannot accommodate them without some major expansion. Repairs and maintenance have been more limited than has been required, although roof repairs have eliminated most of the leaks.

Vast numbers of pupils now support the school by taking part in an enormous range of activities, including sport, public speaking, art and music events. The range of sports has increased significantly, from mainly football, rugby, hockey, golf and some athletics, to include American football, cheerleading, roller hockey, trampolining and much else, with most activities available to both girls and boys. Music instructors cover many stringed instruments, piano, brass, woodwind and piping, as well as percussion.

Developments in computer technology and minor changes in the curriculum have proceeded through recent years. The installation of the 'smart board' has seen the decline of the traditional 'blackboard' or even 'whiteboard' in many classrooms. With the opening of the Gaelic-medium primary school, Bun-sgoil Ghàidhlig Inbhir Nis, on a site close to the Academy, provision for secondary education in Gaelic now takes place in the Royal Academy. The first pupils to receive part of their secondary education in that language came to the school in session 2007/08. A shortage of secondary teachers who are fluent in Gaelic means that not all subjects will be taught through the medium of Gaelic for many years.

So what has been achieved in the first two centuries of the Royal Academy's history? Certainly the school has been at times a trailblazer in the north of Scotland, but equally there have been very rocky periods in its history with bad management, some poor Rectors and repeated financial crises. From being the only significant school in the Town, educating pupils from age 6 or so up to 15 or so, the Academy is now one of five roughly equivalent secondary schools providing education from age 12 to age 18 for those living in the city and its surroundings. The need for these extra secondary schools has been brought about by the vast increase in the local population, particularly in the second half of the twentieth century. The Academy has ceased to make any provision for what we now call Primary education, covering roughly ages 5 to 12. Several local primary schools feed their oldest pupils into the Academy, mainly from within the southern part of the city of Inverness, but some of them coming by bus each day from rural areas in the hills to the south, such as Foyers and Whitebridge.

The Academy has also ceased to function as a centre for pupils from the wider world, as it did in its early days, with pupils from Jamaica and other parts of the West Indies, North America, India and other parts of Britain, especially the Highlands, mixing with local youth. It has also ceased to serve, as it did for much of the twentieth century, pupils living in the more distant rural parts and in the islands of the former Inverness-shire county. The two hostels which provided accommodation for the pupils are now but memories and, as far as Hedgefield is concerned, a plaque on a gate pillar. The essentially middle-class ethos has gone with, firstly, the abolition of fees and the selective primary school, and, secondly, the requirement for a full secondary education for all who wish to benefit from it, with a minimum of an education to age 16.

The school has provided education for countless thousands of pupils, many of whom have gone on to make their mark in innumerable professions and trades throughout the world, from politicians to forensic archaeologists, to business leaders, professors and scholars, and much else. The jury must remain out on whether it was morally acceptable to benefit in the past from a school that was founded at least in part on money earned in the slave trade. However social values change and this would have been seen in the 1790's as an asset, whereas today's view is that slavery is an unacceptable misuse of human labour.

Two listed buildings, formerly used by the school, and a street that takes its name from the school, allow the enquiring visitor to seek out more of Inverness's local history. Since the bicentenary, the school has developed a proper archive, following initial work by the Highland Council archivist of the time, Robert Steward. The staff and pupils have become much more aware of their school's history, as some of the key illustrations are on permanent display in public areas of the school. The bust of Hector Fraser, the Grammar School rector from the second half of the eighteenth century, faces all pupils who enter the library, recalling another part of the history. His bell, taken from the grammar school, *via* the two previous buildings, is immediately noticed by all who pass through the administration area. Enquiries from former pupils and their relatives now arrive on an almost weekly basis, requiring some degree of research. Academic researchers have also contacted the school in pursuit of information on their research topics.

Sadly in a way one of the elements of the tradition, the teaching of Latin, which was the mainstay of the former Grammar School, is no longer on the curriculum. Nor too are writing and simple arithmetic, but this is more to do with the two-fold structure of modern school education where these subjects belong to the primary school. Even more distant is the Song School of the late Middle Ages. Perhaps one of these days further research will locate documents which will help to fill in the gap in the story from Song School to Grammar School. Certainly writing this book has uncovered much local history that had not previously been noted, and there is certain to be more, as further archives list their holdings on line, making it easier to locate material.

So what of the future? Only time will tell. Perhaps a further chapter or chapters in the history of education in Inverness Royal Academy will be written at the time of the 250th birthday or at the tercentenary, but that will involve a wait until at least 2042 or even 2092!

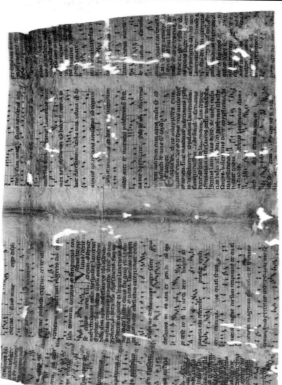

Figure 1.1a: The Inverness Fragments: examples from the music. *Left:* folio 6 from a secular breviary, probably from the 15th century, following Sarum use, showing the Sanctorale for the first half of August. *Right:* part of the processional psalm *Laudate pueri* (Psalm 112 in the Roman Catholic Psalter, Psalm 113 in the Protestant Psalter), set for the Easter Vespers procession. Images used with the permission of the Trustees of the National Library of Scotland

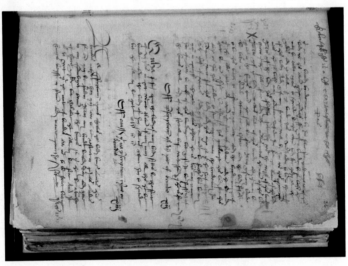

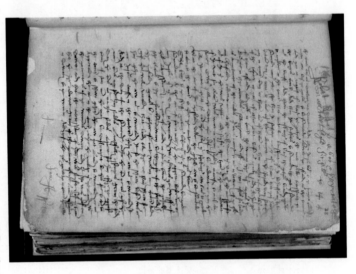

Figure 1.1b: Two pages from *Regiam Majestatem*, the title given to the collection of feudal laws of Scotland, originally drawn up and compiled in the late fourteenth century. The book was much copied, and this is a sixteenth-century manuscript copy. The music fragments shown in Figure 1.1a originally formed part of the binding of this book. In the top margins of the two pages shown here (folios 36 recto and 38 recto) are the seventeenth-century schoolboy graffiti writings, partly in Scots, partly in Latin, with the name of Ronald Ross. The book has now been rebound and heavily conserved. *Images used with the permission of the Trustees of the National Library of Scotland*

284

Figure 2.1: Dr James Fraser, son of the minister of Petty, near Inverness. James was a pupil of Inverness Grammar School, leaving in 1660, aged 15, to study at King's College, Aberdeen, where he graduated with an M.A. in 1664. He became the first secretary of Chelsea Hospital, London, and left donations and legacies to the Inverness Kirk Session Library and to King's College, as well as endowing two bursaries for pupils of Inverness Grammar School to attend King's College. *Image © University of Aberdeen Ref. ABDUA30063*

Figure 2.2: The Dunbar Hospital Building in Church Street, which housed Inverness Grammar School from around 1668 until 1792. The schoolroom was the ground floor room on the right. This illustration is by Pierre Delavault, Art Master of the Royal Academy around the start of the twentieth century.

285

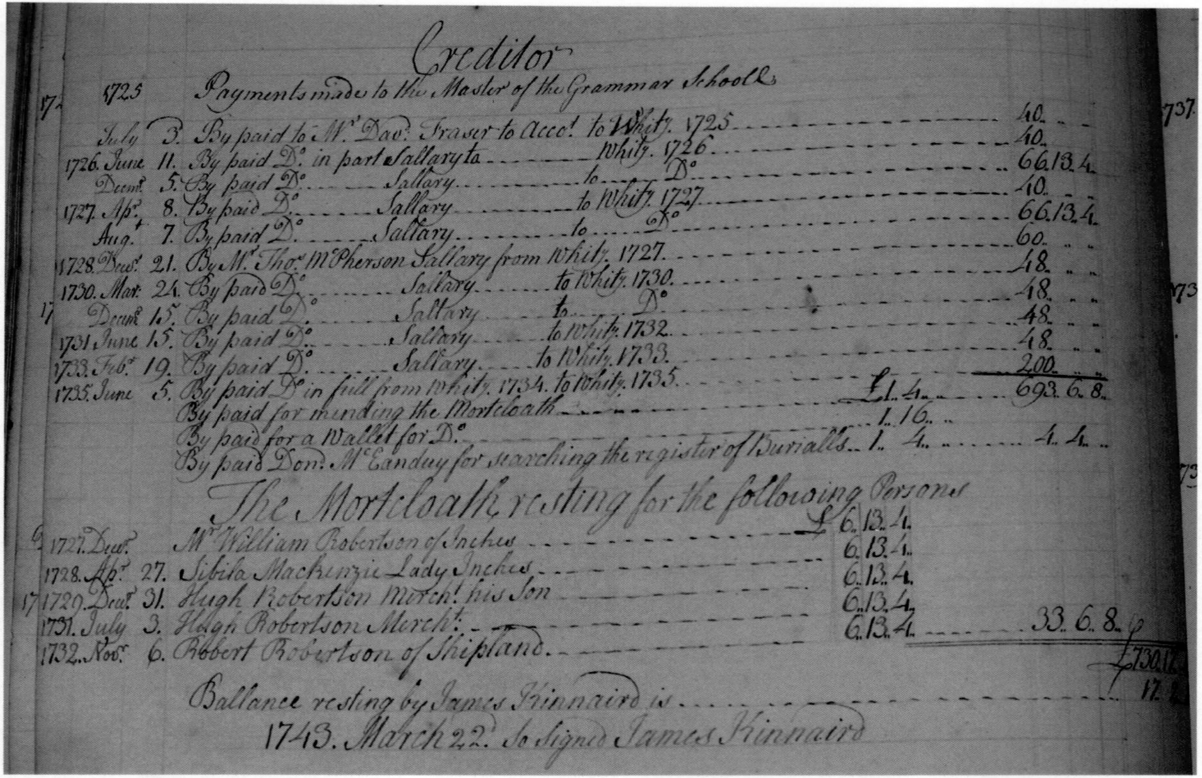

Creditor

1725 Payments made to the Master of the Grammar Schoole

July 3.	By paid to Mr Dav. Fraser to Acco.t to Whity. 1725		40..
1726. June 11.	By paid D.o in part Sallary to Whity. 1726		40..
Decem.r 5.	By paid D.o Sallary to D.o		66.13.4
1727. Ap.l 8.	By paid D.o Sallary to Whity. 1727		40..
Aug.t 7.	By paid D.o Sallary to D.o		66.13.4
1728. Dec.r 21.	By Mr Tho.s McPherson Sallary from Whity. 1727.		60..
1730. Mar. 24.	By paid D.o Sallary to Whity. 1730.		48..
Decem.r 15.	By paid D.o Sallary to D.o		48..
1731. June 15.	By paid D.o Sallary to Whity. 1732.		48..
1733. Feb.r 19.	By paid D.o Sallary to Whity. 1733.		48..
1735. June 5.	By paid D.o in full from Whity. 1734. to Whity. 1735.		200..
		£1. 4..	693. 6. 8.
	By paid for mending the Mortcloath	1. 16..	
	By paid for a Wallet for D.o	1. 4..	4. 4..
	By paid Don. McEanduy for searching the register of Burialls		

The Mortcloath resting for the following Persons

1727. Dec.r	Mr William Robertson of Inches	£ 6. 13. 4.	
1728. Ap.l 27.	Sibila Mackenzie Lady Inches	6. 13. 4.	
1729. Dec.r 31.	Hugh Robertson Merch.t his Son	6. 13. 4.	
1731. July 3.	Hugh Robertson Merch.t	6. 13. 4.	
1732. Nov.r 6.	Robert Robertson of Shipland	6. 13. 4.	33. 6. 8.
			£730.1[illegible]
	Ballance resting by James Kinnaird is		17. [illegible]

1743. March 22. So signed James Kinnaird

Figure 2.3: Part of the Burgh Accounts for Inverness from 1725, showing payments of salary made to the Masters of the Grammar School, firstly David Fraser (until 1727) and then Thomas Macpherson. Payments are in pounds Scots. The lower part of the document shows payments from the mort-cloth money. © *Highland Council Archives*

Figure 2.4 a-b: Hector Fraser, Rector of the Grammar School from 1755-1777. *Left:* the marble bust sculpted by Richard Westmacott. *Right:* the bell presented by Fraser to the Grammar School, and later moved to the Academy buildings, first in Academy Street, then at Midmills, and now in a display case at Culduthel. *Courtesy Am Baile/High Life Highland*

287

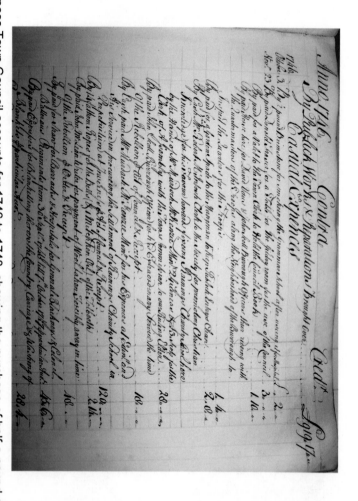

Figure 2.5: Inverness Town Council accounts for 1746 to 1748, showing the purchase of half a pound of brimstone to disinfect the Grammar School building after it had been used as a hospital after the Battle of Culloden. The date of 1746, immediately above the October date, seems to be an error, and should read 1748 (the accounts were made up in two-year periods). An entry for August 1748 on the previous page shows a payment of £133 3s for replacement of the desks, seats and tables after they had been burned while the building was used as a military hospital. Two other entries in this extract show payments in connection with the establishment of the Raining's Charity School in the town, and this did not happen until 1747. © *Highland Council Archives*

Figure 4.1: *(left)* The successful estimate for the wright work (joinery) for the building of Inverness Royal Academy in March 1790. The successful wright was William McDonald. © *National Archives of Scotland*

Figure 4.2: *(below)* The 1792 Academy building in New (Academy) Street, although photographed probably around the time that the school moved to Midmills in 1895.

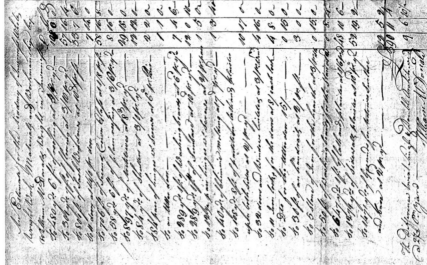

289

Figure 5.1: *(left)* The opening announcement of the Academy which appeared several times in the *Edinburgh Evening Courant* in June 1792.

INVERNESS ACADEMY.

THE INVERNESS ACADEMY will be O-PENED on the 16th day of JULY; under the immediate patronage and direction of a Committee of the Gentlemen of the County, Town, and Presbytery.

In conducting the business of it, the year is to be divided into Two Sessions—The First to begin as above, and to end on the 20th December—The Second to begin on the 5th of January, and to end on the 10th of June.

The course of education will be comprehensive and liberal, as adapted to Civil and Commercial Life; a solid foundation, too, will be laid for the learned professions.

THE FOLLOWING BRANCHES ARE TO BE TAUGHT BY THEIR RESPECTIVE MASTERS:—

First Class, ENGLISH, after the most approved method—by Mr VATCHELL, a native of England.

Second Class, by Mr YOUNG—LATIN and GREEK.—The FRENCH LANGUAGE will also be taught by an able Master.

Third Class, by Mr WILLS—WRITING, ARITHMETIC, and BOOK-KEEPING.

Fourth Class, by Mr DOUGLAS, late of the Marine Academy, Edinburgh—EUCLID's ELEMENTS, with their Application—ALGEBRA, Plane and Spherical Trigonometry, Mensuration of Solids and Surfaces, in all its parts—GEOGRAPHY, with the Use of the Globes—NAVIGATION, with Lunar observations—ARCHITECTURE, Naval, Civil, and Military—Practical GUNNERY, Fortification, Perspective and Drawing.

Fifth Class, by Mr WEIR, the Rector—NATURAL and CIVIL HISTORY, NATURAL PHILOSOPHY, CHEMISTRY, and ASTRONOMY.

In compliance with the desire of the Highland Society of London, a GAELIC CLASS will be opened.

Fees of the 1st Class are to be Six Shillings each Session; of the 2d and 3d Classes, Twelve Shillings; of the 4th Class, One Guinea; of the 5th Class, One Guinea and a Half.—Over and above what is paid to the Masters in the 1st, 2d, 3d, and 4th Classes, each Student shall pay a small sum to the Rector.

Proper INSTRUMENTS will be provided for explaining the practical parts of Mensuration, Geography, and Navigation; and a suitable Apparatus for illustrating the principles of Natural Philosophy and Chemistry.

INVERNESS is well known to be healthy and pleasant, and it is in every respect a most eligible situation for the seat of an Academy.—Board may be had on moderate terms; and the Trustees assure the Public, that the moral conduct and literary improvement of the Young Gentlemen sent thither for their education, will be carefully attended to. As the teaching is to be carried on in Classes, it will be of consequence to Students that they enter at the beginning of the Session.

N.B.—Two of the teachers, Messrs Douglas and Wills, have each of them Accommodation for a Few Boarders.

Figure 5.2: *(below)* The Royal Charter of Inverness Royal Academy, 1793, showing the Great Seal of Scotland, the title page and an inside page. The charter is on vellum. Both the charter and seal were restored and repaired in 1992, through a grant from the Inverness Common Good Fund, and are now suitably framed and displayed in the school.

Figure 6.1: The painting *The Holy Family with the infant St. John*, originally thought to be by Giovanni Battista Salvi de Sassoferrato (1609-1685), was gifted to the Royal Academy as part of the will of James Clark, a native of Inverness, who died in Italy in 1799. The person originally claimed to be the artist, Salvi, is usually known by the town where he was born, namely Sassoferrato. It is now believed that the painting, which is on wood, was painted by an unknown artist of the Central Italian School of Art about a half-a-century earlier. It reached Inverness in 1804, and for many years hung in the original Royal Academy building in Academy Street. The painting was moved to Inverness Town House in 1886, and now hangs at the top of the main staircase. As far as can be determined, it is probably still the property of Inverness Royal Academy. © *Am Baile/High Life Highland*

Figure 7.1: Sketch of Fort George by Alexander Nimmo, dating from either 1805 or 1806, now in the Highland Folk Museum Collection, Kingussie. *Courtesy High Life Highland*

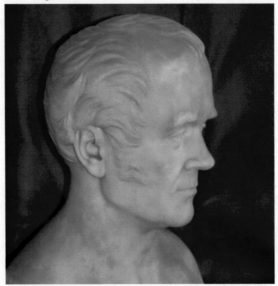

Figure 7.3: Bust of Alexander Nimmo, by John Edwards Jones (1808-1862) in the Royal Dublin Society's premises. *Courtesy Noël Wilkins and Royal Dublin Society*

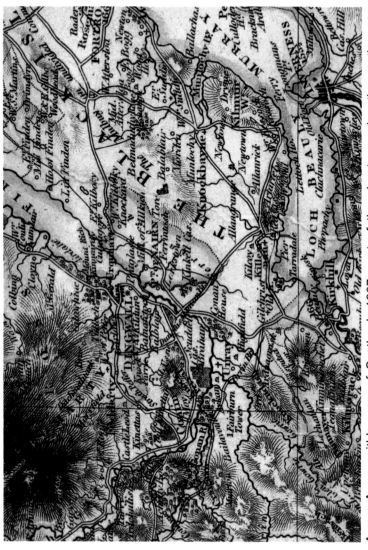

Figure 7.2: Aaron Arrowsmith's map of Scotland, 1807: part of the sheet covering the north-eastern quarter of Scotland. It shows the county boundaries surveyed by Alexander Nimmo in the summer of 1806. Note the detached part of Nairnshire south-east of Dingwall, and a part of the county of Cromarty surrounded by Ross-shire to the north-west of Dingwall. Nimmo did not resolve all the boundary problems: an area north of Beauly is marked 'Disputed moor'. *Image used with the permission of the Trustees of the National Library of Scotland*

293

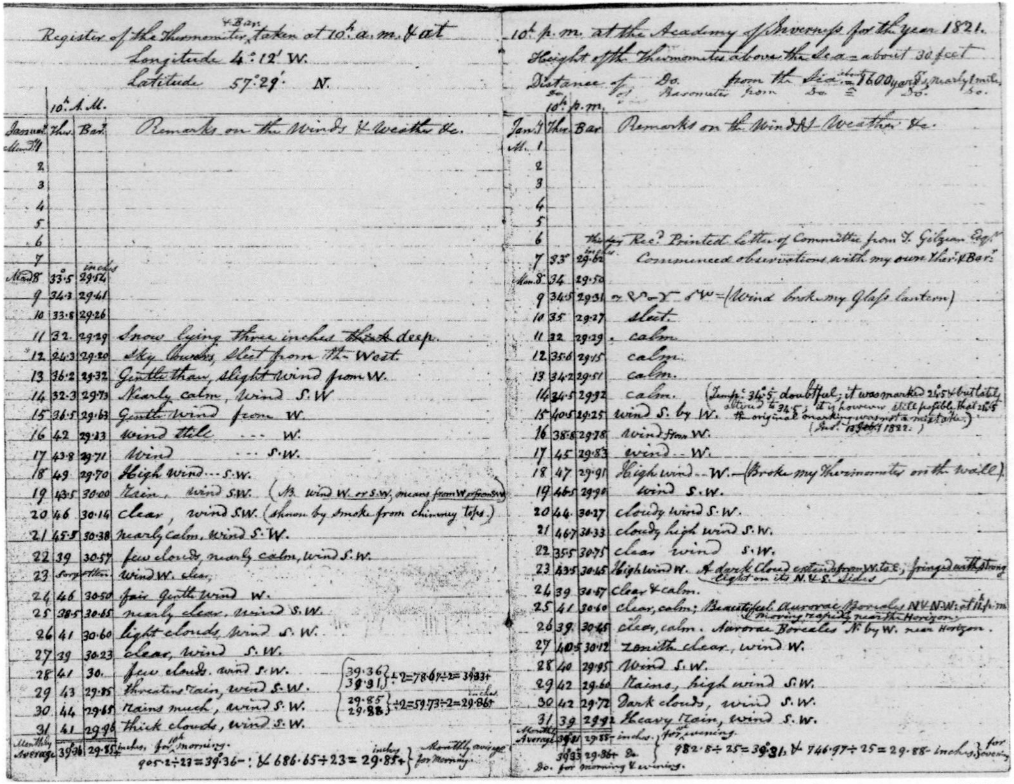

Register of the Thermometer & Bar. taken at 10h. a.m. & at 10h. p.m. at the Academy of Inverness for the year 1821.
Longitude 4° 12' W.
Latitude 57° 29' N.
Height of the Thermometer above the Sea = about 30 feet
Distance of Do. from the Sea about 1600 yards, nearly 1 mile.
Do. of Barometer from Do. Do. Do.

10h. A.M.

January Month	Ther.	Bar.	Remarks on the Winds & Weather &c.
1			
2			
3			
4			
5			
6			
7			
Mon. 8	33·5	29·56 inches	
9	34·3	29·41	
10	33·8	29·26	
11	32·	29·29	Snow lying three inches thick deep.
12	34·3	29·20	Sky Cloudy, Sleet from the West.
13	36·2	29·32	Gentle thaw, slight wind from W.
14	32·3	29·73	Nearly calm, wind S.W
15	36·5	29·63	Gentle wind from W.
16	42	29·23	wind still ... W.
17	43·8	29·71	Wind ... S.W.
18	49	29·70	High wind ... S.W.
19	43·5	30·00	Rain, wind S.W. (N.B. wind W. or S.W. means from W. or from S.W.)
20	46	30·14	clear, wind S.W. (shown by smoke from chimney tops.)
21	45·5	30·38	nearly calm, wind S.W.
22	39	30·57	few clouds, nearly calm, wind S.W.
23	forgotten		Wind W. clear,
24	46	30·50	fair, Gentle wind W.
25	38·5	30·65	nearly clear, wind S.W.
26	41	30·60	light clouds, wind S.W.
27	39	30·23	clear, wind S.W.
28	41	30·	few clouds, wind S.W.
29	43	29·85	threatens rain, wind S.W.
30	44	29·65	rains much, wind S.W.
31	41	29·96	thick clouds, wind S.W.
Monthly Average	39·36	29·85	inches, for 10th morning.

39·36 } 39·91 } ÷ 2 = 78·67 ÷ 2 = 39·33+
29·85 } 29·88 } ÷ 2 = 59·73 ÷ 2 = 29·86+ inches

905·2 ÷ 23 = 39·36 – ; & 686·65 ÷ 23 = 29·85+ inches } Monthly average for Morning.

10h. p.m.

Jan. M.	Ther.	Bar.	Remarks on the Wind and Weather &c.
1			
2			
3			
4			
5			
6			this day Recd. Printed Letter of Committee from T. Gilzean Esqr.
7	33°	29·62 inches	Commenced observations with my own Ther. & Bar.
Mon. 8	34	29·50	
9	34·5	29·31	[illegible] (Wind broke my Glass lantern)
10	35	29·27	Sleet
11	32	29·29	calm
12	35·6	29·15	calm
13	34·2	29·51	calm.
14	34·5	29·92	calm. (Temp. 34·5 doubtful; it was marked 24·5 but lately altered to 34·5; it is however still possible that 24·5 the original marking was not a mistake) (Ind. 13 [illegible] 1822.)
15	40·5	29·25	wind S. by W.
16	38·8	29·78	wind from W.
17	45	29·83	wind – W.
18	47	29·91	High wind – W. – (Broke my Thermometer on the wall)
19	46·5	29·96	wind S.W.
20	44·	30·27	cloudy, wind S.W.
21	46·7	30·33	cloudy, high wind S.W.
22	35·5	30·75	clear, wind S.W.
23	43·5	30·45	High wind W. A dark Cloud extending from W. to E., fringed with strong light on its N. & S. Sides
24	39	30·57	Clear & calm.
25	41	30·60	clear, calm; Beautiful Aurorae Boreales N. & N.W. at 11h. p.m. (moving rapidly near the Horizon)
26	39	30·45	clear, calm. Aurorae Boreales N. by W. near Horizon.
27	40·5	30·12	Zenith clear, wind W.
28	40	29·95	Wind S.W.
29	42	29·60	Rains, high wind S.W.
30	42	29·72	Dark clouds, wind S.W.
31	39	29·92	Heavy Rain, wind S.W.
Monthly Average	39·31	29·88	inches, for evening.
	39·33	29·86+	Do. for morning & evening.

982·8 ÷ 25 = 39·31, & 746·97 ÷ 25 = 29·88 – inches, for evening.

Figure 7.4: The opening pages of Matthew Adam's meteorological observations log, for January 1821, as sent to the Royal Society of Edinburgh, but now owned by the National Library of Scotland. *Image used by permission of the Trustees of the National Library of Scotland*

Figure 8.1: John Wood's plan of Inverness, 1821. Note the Academy buildings and the houses of Thomas Gilzean and Arthur Cooper, close to the Academy, as well as the Ball Wall in the school playground. The "Old Latin School" shows the location of the former Grammar School in the Dunbar Hospital building in Church Street.

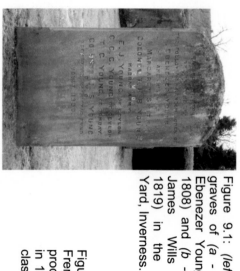

Figure 9.1: (left): The graves of (a - upper) Ebenezer Young (died 1808) and (b - lower) James Wills (died 1819) in the Chapel Yard, Inverness.

Figure 9.2: (right): A French textbook, probably produced by Peter Scott in 1838 for the use of his classes in the Academy.

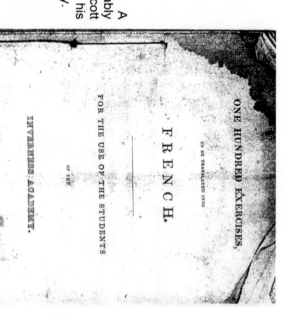

ONE HUNDRED EXERCISES,

TO BE TRANSLATED INTO

F R E N C H.

FOR THE USE OF THE STUDENTS

OF THE

INVERNESS ACADEMY.

INVERNESS:
PRINTED BY ROBERT CARRUTHERS,
BANK BUILDINGS, BANK LANE.

M.DCCC.XXXVIII.

ORATIONS

TO BE DELIVERED

IN THE ACADEMY HALL,

ON

FRIDAY, 28TH JULY, 1837,

TO COMMENCE AT ONE O'CLOCK P.M.

1. Latin Address, by	...	*Master* Duncan M'Bean
2. Adelgitha	...	...	*Alfreck Fraser.*
3. Brutus on the death of Cæsar	...	*William Nicol.*
4. Lochinvar	...	...	*John Hunter.*
5. Hotspur's Account of a Fop	...	*Lawrence Hynd.*
6. Newcastle Apothecary	...	*Charles M'Kay.*
7. Starry Heavens	...	*Summers Hunter.*
8. Destruction of Sennacherib	...	*James Scott.*
9. Quality of Mercy	...	*John Falconer.*
10. Well of St Keyne	...	*Alex. Falconer.*
11. Quarrel of Brutus and Cassius	...	*John Hunter and Charles Mackay.*
12. Hector to Polydamus (Greek)	...	*Duncan M'Bean.*
13. Soldier's dream	...	*John Campbell.*
14. Contest between Nose and Eyes	...	*William M'Rae.*
15. Cæsar to his Soldiers (Latin)	...	*James Cameron.*
16. Drowning Fly	...	*Henry Hunter.*
17. The Gladiator	...	*George Freeman.*
18. Richmond to his Army	...	*Edward Kyle.*
19. Boadicea	...	*David M'Intosh.*
20. Cato on the Immortality of the Soul	*Charles Falconer.*
21. Henry IV. to the Notables (French)	*George Freeman.*
22. Lord Chatham against employing Indians in the American War	*Alex. M'Intosh.*
23. Rhoderic Dhu	...	*Charles M'Kay.*
24. Sir Robert Peel to the Glasgow Students	*Duncan M'Bean.*

INVERNESS : Printed by R. Carruthers.

ORATIONS

To be delivered in the Academy Hall, on

Wednesday, 23d July, 1851,

COMMENCING AT HALF-PAST TWO O'CLOCK P.M.

1. Latin Address—By John Ross.
2. Waterloo—John Ross...*Byron.*
3. Lochinvar—Joseph Hunter....................................*Scott.*
4. Highlander—John Stewart...................................*Campbell.*
5. Song from Waverley—Peter Scott........................*Scott.*
6. Boadicea—John Ferguson......................................*Cowper.*
7. Modern Logic—William Clark...............................*G. Colman.*
8. Death of Nisus and Euryalus—William Turnbull } ...*Virgil.*
9. Bruce's Address—Alexander Gollan........................*Burns.*
10. Brutus and Casius—Hugh Clark and John Ross } ...*Shakespeare.*
11. Address to the Students—Hugh Clark.

ORATIONS

To be Delivered in the Academy Hall, on Tuesday,

the 19th July, 1853.

TO BEGIN AT TWO O'CLOCK AFTERNOON.

1. Latin Address—By William Esson.
2. Cato's Senate—James Ross, Peter Scott, and John Ferguson...*Addison.*
3. Richmond to his Soldiers—Archibald Falconer.....*Shakespeare.*
4. Marcellus to the Mob—Walter Murdell.................*Shakespeare.*
5. Mercy—James Mitchell.
6. Brougham on Negro Slavery—Joseph Hunter.
7. Modern Logic—Ewaler Wilson.
8. Final Triumph of Liberty—William Clark...........*Victor Hugo.*
9. Bruce's Address—Robert Sutherland...................*Burns.*
10. The Soldier's Dream—David Profeit...................*Campbell.*
11. French Oration—John Simpson...........................*Racine.*
12. John Gilpin—William Clark...............................*Cowper.*
13. Coriolanus and Aufidius—Joseph Hunter & James Ross...........................*Thomson & Shakespeare.*
14. Mariners of England—John Forsyth.....................*Campbell.*
15. Rule Britannia—William Turnbull.......................*Thomson.*

297

Figure 9.3 a-c: The programmes for the orations in 1837, 1851 and 1853. The orations were linked with the prizegiving at the end of the session, and sometimes a band was hired to provide music. The tradition of the orations goes back to the days of the grammar school, and originally there were only Latin orations. The event was usually followed by an entertainment, held in a local public house or hotel, for which accounts survive for the 1813 and the 1814 events (see Chapter 9, reference 45). 1853 programme image © Highland Council Archives

Figure 9.4: Early class medals: (left) for the English class; (right) for the Latin class. The exact purpose and dates of presentation of these medals is not known. The smaller English medal, commemorating the accession of George IV is dated 1821, and is the same size as a modern penny piece; the other one is slightly larger.

Figure 9.6: Dr John Inglis Nicol, painted by Robert Innes of Edinburgh, and presented to Inverness Town Council in 1849. The portrait hangs in the main hall of Inverness Town House. Dr Nicol was born near Beauly in 1788, and his degree of M.D. was granted by the University of Tubingen in Germany. He practised medicine in Inverness from 1812, until his death from cholera in 1849. He served as Provost of Inverness from 1840 to 1843. © Am Baile/High Life Highland

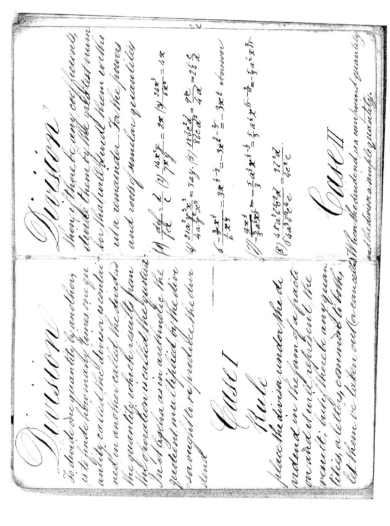

Figure 9.5: Sample page from George Macandrew's mathematical notebook from session 1835/36, as taught by Matthew Adam. Macandrew gained the Raigmore Silver Medal in 1837, although Adam felt that he should have got the Gold Medal, leading to a dispute. This was resolved in 1840, after which the gold and silver medals were awarded alternately for mathematics and classics.

The WRECK of the HINDOSTAN, EAST-INDIAMAN, on the WEDGE SAND, off MARGATE. Jan.11.1803.

shewing the Margate Boat saving part of the Crew.

Publish'd Jan.º 31.1803. by John

Fairburn. 116. Minories. London.

Figure 10.1 a-b: Two illustrations, from the collection of the National Maritime Museum, of the second *Hindostan*, Capt. Wm. Mackintosh's ship, but shortly after the time when he was its Captain. *Upper:* Nicholas Pocock's 'A Fleet of East Indiamen at sea' (1803), showing the *Hindostan* leading other East Indiamen. *Lower:* 'The Wreck of the *Hindostan* East Indiaman, on the Wedge Sand, off Margate, January 11 1803': a mounted aquatint print. © *National Maritime Museum, Greenwich, London*

EXCERPT FROM THE WILL

OF

CAPTAIN WILLIAM MACKINTOSH.

In the name of God, Amen.- I, WILLIAM MACKINTOSH, Commander of the Ship Hindostan, in the service of the East Indian Company, and now at sea, on her voyage to Bombay and China, declare this to be my Last Will and Testament,&c. It is my express Will that £5000 be vested in Trust with the Magistrates of Inverness for the time being, the interest of which sum is to be appropriated to the education of FIVE BOYS in succession, to be selected - first, from the descendants of the Family of Farr ; next, to those of Dalmigavie ; and thirdly, to those of the House of Kylachy, or their nearest relations, in the above order of consanguinity, but always of the name of Mackintosh ; **AND IT MAY BE HOPED THAT SOME OF THESE BOYS, IF THEY SUCCEED IN LIFE** (which this gives them a fair chance for), **WILL FOLLOW THE EXAMPLE, TO KEEP UP A RESPECTABLE THOUGH DECLINING CLAN.** It is to be remembered that they are to be educated at the Academy lately established in that town ; but if the Trustees think it advisable, on discovering marks of Genius, to send any of the boys to an University, they are not restricted from doing it. The said sum of Five Thousand Pounds, as soon as may be expedient, TO BE INVESTED IN LANDS in the County ; and

Perhaps it might not be improper to PASTE up the COPY of this BEQUEST in some part of the ACADEMY, which probably would stamp an impression, and stimulate to similar acts of liberality.

HUGH DOVE, Surgeon, }

C. S. DENNISON, Purser,} *Witnesses*　　　(SIGNED)　　**W. MACKINTOSH.**

Hindostan, at sea, the 5th of April, 1797.

N.B.- In the selection of the boys for education, my mother's family of Holm is to be preferred next to my father's, and, in succession, before that of Dalmigavie.

(Signed)　　**W. M.**

CODICIL II.

GOWER STREET, LONDON, June 10, 1800.

I leave her (Mrs Rae, sister of Sir George Dallas) the sum of £5000, that is to say, I leave the above £5000, in Trust, with the Magistrates of Inverness -- added to the £5000, in the first part of this Will, intended there for the education of certain boys -- the interest of which two sums, making, in all, £10,000, is to be regularly paid to her, during her natural life: and, after her decease, the sum is to be VESTED IN LANDS, for the education of boys, as above; but that my Will, with respect to the boys, may be put in immediate effect after my death, whatever sum of money may appear over and above the legacies in the instrument, which I expect will be considerable, I Will that the interest of such money shall be appropriated for the education of boys, during the life of Mrs Rae, and, after her death, this money, whatever it may be, to be then proportionally divided amongst my Brother and Sister's Children, or the survivors of them or their heirs; and the Ten Thousand Pounds, of which she is to enjoy the interest, to be then finally and forever SECURED IN LANDS, as soon as may be convenient, for the education of as many boys of the name of Mackintosh as it is adequate to - always observing that they are the descendants of the four families above - named, or their nearest kin.

(Signed)　　W. MACKINTOSH, S.S.

CODICIL IV.

MEMORANDUM.- I revoke the whole of that part of my Will relating to her (Mrs Rae); and hereby direct that the Ten Thousand Pounds, of which she was to enjoy the interest during her life, shall immediately after my decease be appropriated for the education of boys, as before described.

LONDON, 30th JUNE 1801.　　　　　(Signed)　　W. MACKINTOSH.

INVERNESS: *ORIGINALLY* PRINTED BY G. TAIT, ADVERTISER OFFICE

REPRODUCED BY J. STUART FINDLAY, 6M2
March 1992

Figure 10.2: The extract from Capt. Mackintosh's will which he ordered to be 'pasted up in the Academy' to encourage others to donate to the Academy. As the only known original print is damaged, with small sections missing, this version is a modern computer-generated print, produced at the time of the bicentenary of the Academy in 1992 by J. Stuart Findlay.

Figure 11.1: *Raigmore* steam engine, named after Mackintosh of Raigmore, an Academy Director. The drawing is from the school exercise book of Alexander Mackintosh of Farr. Although the book is dated 1852, the drawing cannot be earlier than late 1855, as the opening of the Inverness-Nairn Railway took place in November that year. Alexander died in 1853, so the artist must have been some other member of the family. The notebook is in the Highland Folk Museum Collection, Newtonmore. *Courtesy High Life Highland*

Figure 11.2: Peter Scott, classics master at the Royal Academy from 1824 until his retirement in 1862. He became Rector in 1853, and this photograph is the first known photograph of any Rector of the Academy. *Courtesy Highland Photographic Archive*

Figure 12.1: Bust of A. Penrose Hay, in the Town House, Inverness. Hay was Secretary and Treasurer of the Academy Directors from 1865 to 1887, when, with the change of management structure of the Academy, his son, Robert, took over as Clerk. © *Am Baile/High Life Highland*

302

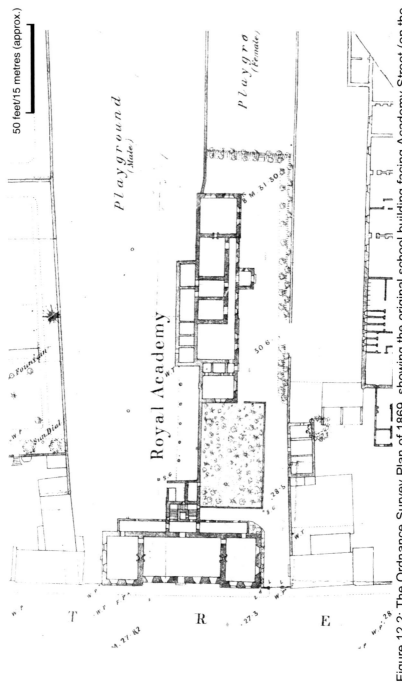

Figure 12.2: The Ordnance Survey Plan of 1869, showing the original school building facing Academy Street (on the left), with the Ladies' Institute to the rear, and at right angles. The building showing at the bottom of the map is the railway station. The top of the map is north-west.

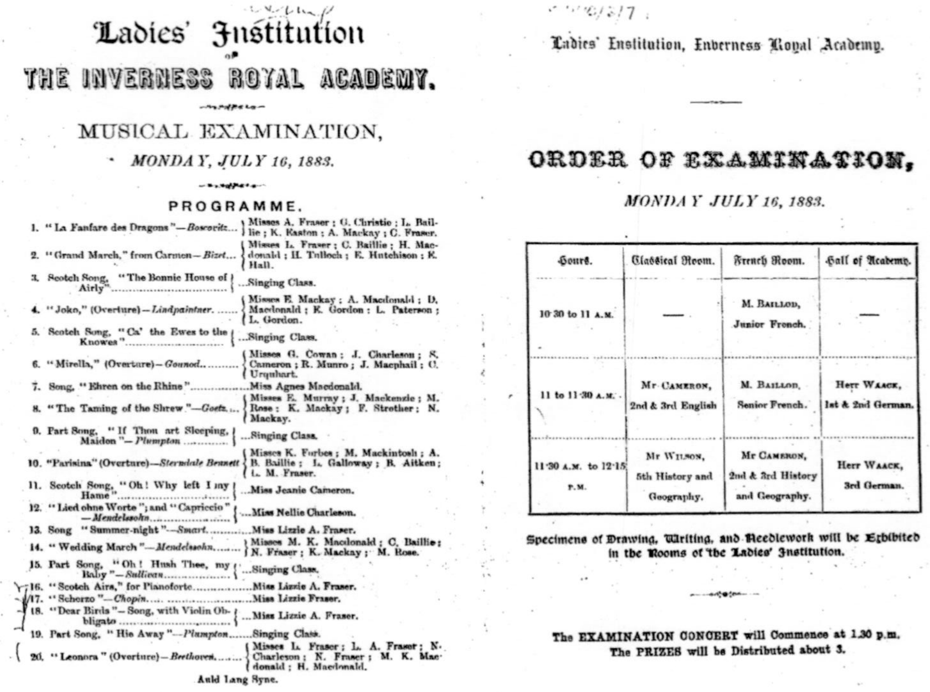

Ladies' Institution of THE INVERNESS ROYAL ACADEMY.

MUSICAL EXAMINATION,

MONDAY, JULY 16, 1883.

PROGRAMME.

1. "La Fanfare des Dragons"—*Boscovitz*... Misses A. Fraser; G. Christie; L. Baillie; K. Easton; A. Mackay; C. Fraser.
2. "Grand March," from Carmen—*Bizet*... Misses L. Fraser; C. Baillie; H. Macdonald; H. Tulloch; E. Hutchison; E. Hall.
3. Scotch Song, "The Bonnie House of Airly"... Singing Class.
4. "Joko," (Overture)—*Lindpaintner*. ...... Misses E. Mackay; A. Macdonald; D. Macdonald; E. Gordon; L. Paterson; L. Gordon.
5. Scotch Song, "Ca' the Ewes to the Knowes"... Singing Class.
6. "Mirella," (Overture)—*Gounod*.......... Misses G. Cowan; J. Charleson; S. Cameron; R. Munro; J. Macphail; C. Urquhart.
7. Song, "Ehren on the Rhine"...............Miss Agnes Macdonald.
8. "The Taming of the Shrew"—*Goetz*.... Misses E. Murray; J. Mackenzie; M. Rose; K. Mackay; F. Strother; N. Mackay.
9. Part Song, "If Thou art Sleeping, Maiden"—*Plumpton* ... Singing Class.
10. "Parisina" (Overture)—*Sterndale Bennett* Misses K. Forbes; M. Mackintosh; A. B. Baillie; L. Galloway; B. Aitken; L. M. Fraser.
11. Scotch Song, "Oh! Why left I my Hame"... Miss Jeanie Cameron.
12. "Lied ohne Worte"; and "Capriccio"—*Mendelssohn*... Miss Nellie Charleson.
13. Song "Summer-night"—*Smart*............Miss Lizzie A. Fraser.
14. "Wedding March"—*Mendelssohn*....... Misses M. K. Macdonald; C. Baillie; N. Fraser; K. Mackay; M. Rose.
15. Part Song, "Oh! Hush Thee, my Baby"—*Sullivan*... Singing Class.
16. "Scotch Airs," for Pianoforte...............Miss Lizzie A. Fraser.
17. "Scherzo"—*Chopin*.............................Miss Lizzie Fraser.
18. "Dear Birds"—Song, with Violin Obbligato ... Miss Lizzie A. Fraser.
19. Part Song, "Hie Away"—*Plumpton*.......Singing Class.
20. "Leonora" (Overture)—*Beethoven*........ Misses L. Fraser; L. A. Fraser; N. Charleson; N. Fraser; M. K. Macdonald; H. Macdonald.

Auld Lang Syne.

Ladies' Institution, Inverness Royal Academy.

ORDER OF EXAMINATION,

MONDAY JULY 16, 1883.

Hours.	Classical Room.	French Room.	Hall of Academy.
10·30 to 11 A.M.	—	M. Baillod, Junior French.	—
11 to 11·30 A.M.	Mr Cameron, 2nd & 3rd English	M. Baillod, Senior French.	Herr Waack, 1st & 2nd German.
11·30 A.M. to 12·15 P.M.	Mr Wilson, 5th History and Geography.	Mr Cameron, 2nd & 3rd History and Geography.	Herr Waack, 3rd German.

Specimens of Drawing, Writing, and Needlework will be Exhibited in the Rooms of the Ladies' Institution.

The EXAMINATION CONCERT will Commence at 1.30 p.m.
The PRIZES will be Distributed about 3.

Figure 13.1: The programmes for the Musical Examination and the General Examination by the local clergy and others for 1883. Parents and others interested would attend while the examination was in progress. An external examiner was first used in 1886, and it is very likely that the examination reports were rather uncritical up to that point, as discouraging remarks, or comments on poor performance, would tend to reduce the number of parents who would send their children to the Academy. Compare with Figure 9.3.

Figure 13.2: Senior English Class – Upper and Lower Divisions, session 1877/78. This is the first known photograph of a class group in the Royal Academy, and was presumably taken at the rear of the original building in Academy Street. The teacher in the centre is Mr Samuel Thomson, who taught at the Academy from August 1866 until summer 1883 when he was required to resign. The photograph was taken by D. Whyte of Church Street, who claimed on the photograph mount that he kept negatives for fifteen years, to allow duplicates to be ordered.

Figure 14.2: The first version of the school badge *(left)*, as prepared by Mr G. H. Gall, Architect; *(centre)* the version of the badge as used in the 1920's and 1930's, before matriculation with the Lord Lyon King of Arms; and *(right)* the official badge as matriculated in 1933.

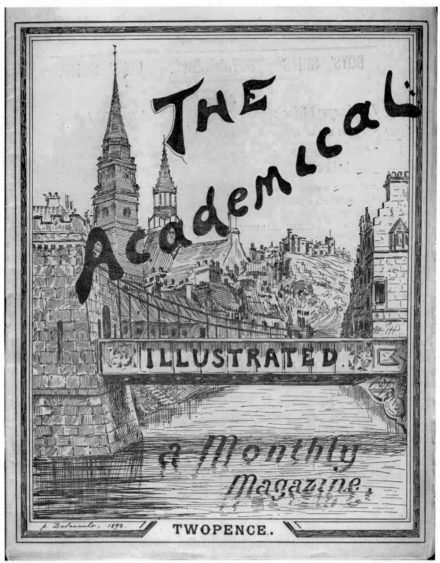

Figure 14.1: The cover of *The Academical*, the magazine first produced in February 1892, while George Bruce was Rector. The cover drawing is by Pierre Delavault, art master, whose signature can be seen in the bottom left-hand corner. The design is a montage of local landmarks of the time, and not an actual view of Inverness.

Figure 14.3: The staff of the Royal Academy probably in early 1894, shortly before George Bruce was dismissed as Rector. According to *Old Inverness in Pictures*, the names are:
Back row: Miss Mary C. Mackenzie (assistant, art), Mr William Gossip (junior English, geography, Latin), Miss Cosy Fraser (pianoforte), M. Pierre Delavault (art), Mr Charles Greaves (English and commercial subjects), Mr W. S. Roddie (singing), Mr Wallace (assistant elementary).
Front row: Miss Grace Middleton (sewing/needlework), M. Edouard Roubaut (modern languages), Miss Brown (Lady Superintendent, junior classes), Mr George Bruce (Rector, classics and English), Mr Thomas Cockburn (classics and English), Miss Annie Clegg (assistant elementary department), Mr J. Wilson Reid (mathematics).

INVERNESS NEW ACADEMY.

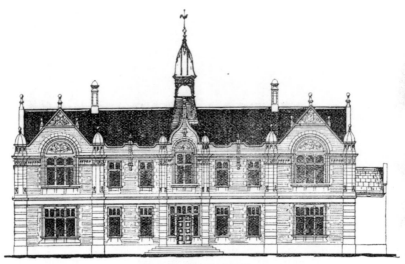

FRONT ELEVATION.

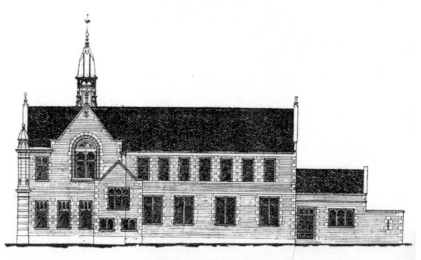

SIDE ELEVATION.

Figure 14.4 *(this page and opposite)*: The plans of the new building at Midmills, built between 1892 and 1895, as printed in *The Academical* at the start of 1892. The design was by Alexander Ross of the local firm of Ross and Macbeth. The structure is now a listed building, currently in use by Inverness College. The details of the captions are indistinct in the original.

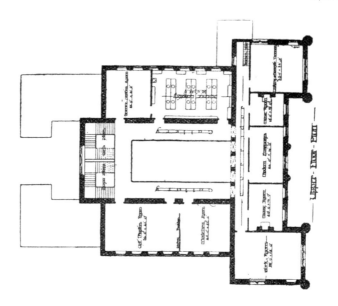

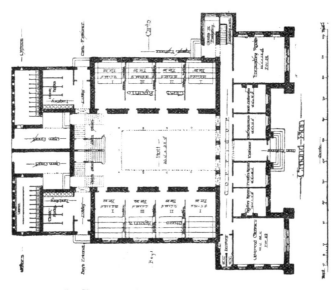

See Front and Side Elevation in last number.

Figure 14.5: The scene at the laying of the foundation stone of the new building at Midmills by the Grand Master Mason of Scotland, the Earl of Haddington, on 27th June 1893, in the presence of the Directors, the Town officials, members of the Burgh School Board, and a choir of pupils. It will be seen that, by this stage, sections of the walls were already several feet above the ground. The foundation stone apparently includes a copper plate (although more likely a box) containing recent newspapers, coins, a school prospectus, copies of *The Academical*, and the names of the Directors and officials.

Time Table of Upper School.

CLASS IV.—CLASSICAL.

	M.	T.	W.	Th.	F.	
9—9.45	English	English	English	English	English	1
9.45—10.30	Latin	Latin	Latin	Latin	Latin	2
10.35—11.20	Mathematics	Mathematics	Mathematics	Mathematics	Mathematics	3
11.20—12	Latin	Mathematics	Physics	Latin	Physics	4
1—1.45	Mathematics	Chemistry	Mathematics	Chemistry	Mathematics	5
1.45—2.30	Greek	Greek	Greek	Greek	Greek	6
2.35—3.20	Greek	Practical Physics	Drawing	Practical Chemistry	English	7
3.20—4	Drawing	Practical Physics	Drawing	Practical Chemistry	Drawing	8

CLASS IV.—MODERN AND SCIENCE.

	M.	T.	W.	Th.	F.	
9—9.45	English	English	English	English	English	1
9.45—10.30	German	German	German	German	German	2
10.35—11.20	Mathematics	Mathematics	Mathematics	Mathematics	Mathematics	3
11.20—12	Shorthand	Mathematics	Physics	Shorthand	Physics	4
1—1.45	Mathematics	Chemistry	Mathematics	Chemistry	Mathematics	5
1.45—2.30	French	French	French	French	French	6
2.35—3.20	English	Practical Physics	Drawing	Practical Chemistry	English	7
3.20—4	Drawing	Practical Physics	Drawing	Practical Chemistry	Drawing	8

CLASS IV.—GIRLS.

	M.	T.	W.	Th.	F.	
9—9.45	English	English	English	English	English	1
9.45—10.30	German	German	German	German	German	2
10.35—11.20	Mathematics	Mathematics	Mathematics	Mathematics	Mathematics	3
11.20—12	Drawing	Drawing	Drawing	Drawing	Drawing	4
1—1.45	Mathematics	Needlework	Mathematics	Needlework	Mathematics	5
1.45—2.30	French	French	French	French	French	6
2.35—3.20	Calisthenics	Needlework	Calisthenics	Needlework	English	7
3.20—4	Singing	Preparation	Singing	Preparation	Needlework	8

Inverness Royal Academy.

CLASS V.—CLASSICAL.

	M.	T.	W.	Th.	F.	
9—9.45	Mathematics	Mathematics	Mathematics	Mathematics	Mathematics	1
9.45—10.30	Greek	Greek	Greek	Greek	Greek	2
10.35—11.20	Latin	Latin	Latin	Latin	Latin	3
11.20—12	English	English	English	English	English	4
1—1.45	Mathematics	Mathematics	Mathematics	Mathematics	Mathematics	5
1.45—2.30	Chemistry	English	Latin	Chemistry	Latin	6
2.35—3.20	Greek	Drawing	Practical Chemistry	Greek	Greek	7
3.20—4	Latin	Drawing	Practical Chemistry	English	English	8

CLASS V.—MODERN AND SCIENCE.

	M.	T.	W.	Th.	F.	
9—9.45	Physics	Mathematics	Mathematics	Mathematics	Mathematics	1
9.45—10.30	French	French	French	French	French	2
10.35—11.20	Latin German Book-keeping	Latin German Book-keeping	Latin German Book-keeping	Latin Shorthand	Latin German Book-keeping	3
11.20—12	English	English	English	English	English	4
1—1.45	Mathematics	Mathematics	Mathematics	Mathematics	Mathematics	5
1.45—2.30	Chemistry	English	Chemistry	Drawing	Latin Arithmetic	6
2.35—3.20	Practical Physics	Drawing	Practical Chemistry	Drawing	Physics	7
3.20—4	Practical Physics	Drawing	Practical Chemistry	Drawing	English	8

CLASS V.—GIRLS.

	M.	T.	W.	Th.	F.	
9—9.45	Mathematics	Mathematics	Mathematics	Mathematics	Mathematics	1
9.45—10.30	French	French	French	French	French	2
10.35—11.20	German	German	German	German	German	3
11.20—12	English	English	English	English	English	4
1—1.45	Mathematics	Mathematics	Mathematics	Mathematics	Mathematics	5
1.45—2.30	Needlework	Drawing	Drawing	Needlework	Drawing	6
2.35—3.20	Calisthenics	Preparation	Needlework	Preparation	Mathematics	7
3.20—4	Singing	Needlework	Singing	Calisthenics	English	8

Figure 15.1: Part of the timetable for the Upper School from the Royal Academy Prospectus for 1899-1900.

Figure 15.2: School sports at the Northern Meeting Park, in either 1895 or 1896. This is the first known photograph of a school sporting event. The school sports were instituted by Wm. J. Watson, as he was a keen athlete himself. It is possible that the adult behind the athlete is Watson himself, as he had won a "Blue" at Oxford for the shot put. The bewhiskered adult right of centre has not been identified. *Courtesy Highland Photographic Archive*

Figure 16.1a: see opposite page.

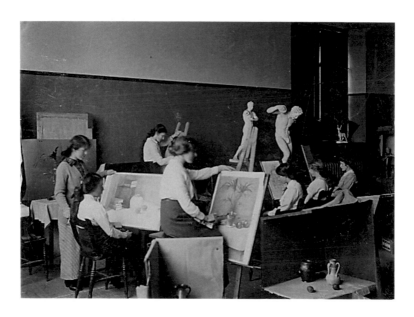

Figure 16.1 a-c: Three views of classrooms in the 1913 Science and Art School added to the Royal Academy: a *(opposite page lower):* a science laboratory; b *(above upper):* an art classroom; c *(above lower):* the gymnasium. Six interior shots by Paterson have survived, with the others showing another science laboratory, another art classroom and the upstairs corridor. All were taken in connection with the official opening.

Figure 17.1 a-b: Inverness Royal Academy War Memorial Hostel, opened 1922, with accommodation for about 60 girls. *Top:* hostel pupils and staff in 1924, with the matron, Miss Isabella Paterson, in the centre of the second row. *Bottom:* the senior girls' study in 1925. The girls' hostel was transferred to Hedgefield House in 1934, which was much more convenient for attending the Academy, then at Midmills.

Figure 17.2: The First World War Memorial Boards, now located in the Royal Academy building at Culduthel. These were paid for by subscriptions from members of the school's Old Boys' Club and other former pupils, and they were originally installed under the main window on the staircase at the east end of the original main hall at Midmills. The centre section records the names of 83 Old Boys and one member of staff who gave their lives in the war; the two side panels list the names of the 420 who served in one of the armed services. The boards were unveiled by Viscount Finlay, Lord Chancellor, on 10th October 1921. The War Memorial Hostel was also opened by Viscount Finlay later the same day [see Figure 17.1]. *Courtesy Am Baile/High Life Highland*

315

Figure 17.3: The sports pavilion at Millburn. In the 1930's the Royal Academy did not have sufficient space for sports at the Midmills site and additional land was fued at Millburn. To provide changing facilities, the pavilion was opened in 1938, mainly paid for from the school's endowments. This photograph dates from the time of the opening of the pavilion.

Figure 17.4: One of the Howden Medal Boards, now located at the Culduthel site. In 1913 Miss Elizabeth Ponton Howden had presented money to Inverness College to be used for medals for deserving pupils. As that school closed during the First World War, the Trust Fund and the medal were transferred to the Royal Academy, and are still awarded annually. Another display board records more recent recipients.

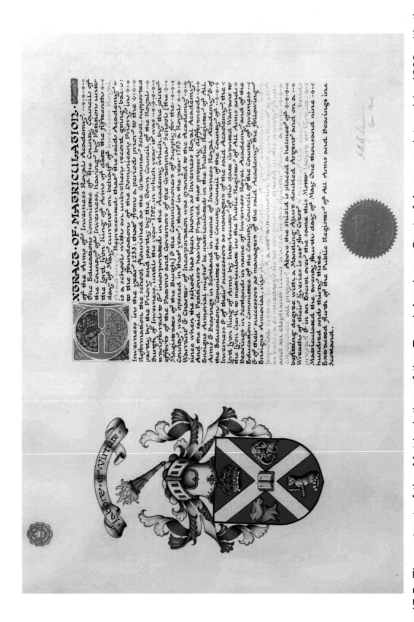

Figure 17.5: The extract of the Matriculation of the Royal Academy Coat of Arms, registered in 1933 with the Lord Lyon, King of Arms, at a cost of £17. This is the version of the badge and coat of arms still in use. See also Figure 14.2. *Courtesy Am Baile/High Life Highland*

317

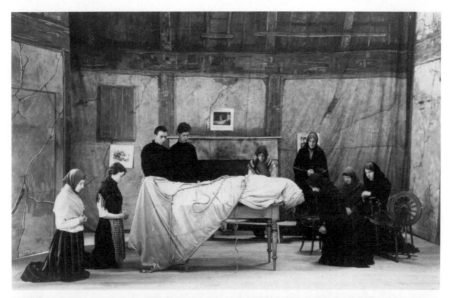

Figure 17.6 a-b: Two of the school drama productions during the 1930's. The upper picture is from a performance in June 1931 of *Riders to the Sea* (J. M. Synge). The lower picture shows the cast of a lower school (Primary School) production of one of three playlets which formed part of the same event.

Figure 17.7: Inverness Royal Academy Girl Guide Company was active from about 1923 until the early 1940's. This photograph shows the Guide Patrol Leaders in 1931, when Miss Mary Roy was Captain and Miss Jessie Horne was Lieutenant. This photograph appeared in the school magazine in June 1931. *Courtesy Highland Photographic Archive*

Figure 18.1: The War Memorial Gates at Midmills, soon after the time of their opening in November 1954. These central gates replaced the gates at the two front corners of the school which had been in use since the opening of the Midmills building in 1895. Pillars from the corner gates were reused. The cost was met from funds raised in an appeal by the Old Boys' Club. The identity of the man in the picture is not known. In addition to the gates, boards listing the names of those who died were erected in the central hall [see Figure 18.3].

Figure 18.2: The last Primary 7 class, photographed in the summer of 1961. Although the photograph was taken outside the front door of the Midmills Building, classes in the final two years of the phasing out of the Primary School were held in an annexe of the Crown School, across Midmills Road. The teacher on the right is Miss Kenetta Sinclair, who had been a member of the Academy staff since 1946. She moved to a post in the Crown School, next door to where she had been teaching.

Figure 18.3: The main hall of the Midmills Building in 1953, several years prior to the work to install a fireproof screen around the balcony and between the pillars. Once the new assembly hall was provided early in 1961, the central hall shown here was returned to use as the school library. The Rector, D. J. Macdonald, is at the podium. On either side of him can be seen the memorial boards recording the names of those killed in the Second World War. Seated at the side are members of staff. Above their heads are some of the school's Honour Boards. © *George Outram/The Herald and Evening Times*

Figure 18.4: A press photograph taken at the Christmas Dance in 1954. The location is probably in the gymnasium in the 1925 Primary School extension (later the girls' gymnasium), but it may have been taken in the gymnasium in the 1913 Art and Science extension (later the boys' gymnasium).

Figure 18.5: In the 1950's and early 1960's, summer term activities for senior pupils included the making of relief models of local landscapes. Second from the right is Mr James H. Johnstone, Principal Teacher of Geography, and also careers master. He later became Depute Rector. This photograph was taken in 1960, at the time of the opening of the new extension which included two classrooms specifically equipped for teaching geography. © *Highland News Group*

Figure 18.6: The Academy team from the 1962 radio series of 'Top of the Form'. This team only reached the second round of the contest. However in the televised show in 1970, the school team were runners-up and went on to win 'Transworld Top Team'. The members of the 1962 team shown are: Penelope Wilson (VI), Joan Ford (III), Fiona McWilliam (II) and Barbara Walker (II). © *Jimmy Thomson/Inverness Press Photos*

The Outdoor Centre

Figure 18.7: The old Primary School at Fort Augustus was taken over by the Academy as an outdoor centre in 1972. This view was drawn from Battery Rock which lies immediately behind the old school. For many years conversion work progressed to turn the building into basic accommodation for up to thirty-two pupils and four staff. Art, biology, geography and music groups used the centre, along with the Outdoor Club. However, an ageing staff and restrictions on outdoor activities eventually led to the school giving up the use of the centre in 2001.

Figure 19.1: The unveiling of the plaque on the original Academy building in Academy Street on 16th July 1992, to mark the school's bicentenary. *Left to right:* Provost William Fraser, Mrs Pat Hayden (Vice-President, Inverness Chamber of Commerce), Mr Eric Milne (President, Inverness Chamber of Commerce), Mr Ian Fraser (Rector). © *Aberdeen Journals, Ltd. (Press and Journal)*

Figure 19.2: The Earl of Inverness (Prince Andrew) unveils the commemorative plaque during his visit to the Royal Academy on 26th June 1992 to celebrate the school's bicentenary. On the left is Val MacIver, Chair of the Education Committee of Highland Regional Council, as it then was.

Figure A4.1: The contents of the grave in the 1975 archaeological discovery, after the cover slab had been removed. The find was made during site works for the new school building at Culduthel.

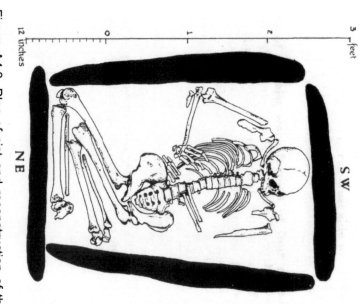

Figure A4.3: Plan of cist and reconstruction of the skeleton in the short cist discovered at Culduthel in 1928. From: *Proceedings of the Society of Antiquaries of Scotland, vol. LXIII (1928-29)*, p. 218.

Figure A4.2: The grave goods from the 1975 grave find at Culduthel: the beaker, the archer's wrist guard *(right)*, the arrowheads *(front)*, and the bone toggle or belt-ring *(centre)*, the flint implement and bead. See figure A4.1 for a view of the grave in which these items were found. © *National Museums Scotland*

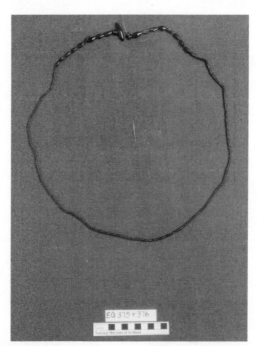

Figure A4.4: The beads and jet from the 1928 grave find, reconstructed as a belt, with the fragment of the bronze awl in the centre. The scale bar is in centimetres. See Figure A4.3 for a plan of the skeleton found in the grave. © *National Museums Scotland*

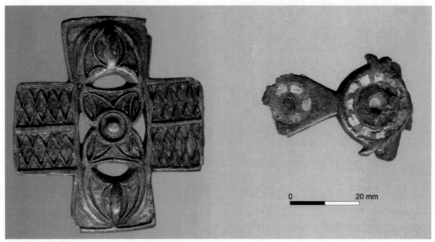

Figure A4.5: The cross, part of a horse-harness, and the brooch from the 2005 Culduthel dig. The scale bar is in centimetres. © *Headland Archaeology and Tulloch Homes, Ltd.*

References and notes

Chapter 1:

1: *Minutes of the Directors of Inverness Academy* (hereafter called *Directors' Minutes*), vol. 1, 16th July 1792, IRAA, A1

2: An extensive, but now rather dated, look at the Inverness's Church School appears in: Evan M. Barron: *Inverness Royal Academy: Some pages from a History of 650 years*, published in *The Inverness Academical, War Memorial Issue*, 1921 – the school magazine of the time; an identical article, apart from the introduction, appears in *The Transactions of the Inverness Scientific Society and Field Club*, vol. IX (1918-1925) with the title *An Old Inverness School*, which was Evan Barron's presidential address to the Society in November 1921.

3: Quoted by Barron, *op. cit.*, but source not stated.

4: D. E. R. Watt: *Education in the Highlands in the Middle Ages* in *The Middle Ages in the Highlands* (Inverness Field Club, 1981). Watt disagrees with Barron *(op. cit.)* as to what extent the school was open to laity.

5: Inverness Burgh Court Book, 19th July 1574, quoted on p. 239 of *Records of Inverness*, Publication of the New Spalding Club, Aberdeen, vol. 1, 1911; the original Burgh Court Books are in HCA, BI/1/1/1-3

6: I am very grateful to Dr Gordon J. Munro of the Royal Scottish Academy of Music and Drama in Glasgow for information about the early song school, taken from his University of Glasgow PhD Thesis: *Scottish Church Music and Musicians, 1500-1700* (1999), and also for commenting on this section of the text.

7: Quoted by John Durkan (p. 71) in *Education in the Century of the Reformation* in *Innes Review*, vol. 10, pt. 1, pp. 67-90 (1959), using a transcription in the Hutton Collection in National Library of Scotland, reference Adv. MS 29.4.2(xi), item 71, f. 103(r&v), with additional information from Dr Munro using a personal communication to him from Durkan; another 'obligation' for Auck(in)leck is in HCA, BI/1/19/3, with a date about one month earlier in which he is required to perform his duties as Parish Clerk, including keeping the song school, maintaining the clock and organ and taking part in services with the chaplains of the Parish Kirk; he is also to study music under Sir Walter Furthe or James Spens in Elgin until Beltane or until he is qualified; elsewhere in BI/1/19 are two 'obligations' for Sir John Waus in connection with his duties as a chaplain in the parish kirk in 1529 and 1544: all three are very difficult for the modern eye to read as they are in an early style of writing.

8: For a full discussion on the role of music in the 16th century church in Scotland see: Isobel Woods Preece: *Our awin Scottis use: Music in the Scottish Church up to 1603* (Universities of Glasgow and Aberdeen, 2000).

9: See: John Purser: *Scotland's Music* (Edinburgh: Mainstream/BBC Scotland, 1992) where the passage is translated from the original Latin.

10: NLS, MS Accession 11218, nos. 5 (the feudal law book – *Regiam Maiestatem*) and 6 (the music and the parts of the two Latin grammars): item 6 was conserved and reconstructed in 2000 with help from Dr Sally Mapstone of St Hilda's College, Oxford. She kindly gave me a copy of the lecture she gave in 2003 to the Edinburgh Bibliographical Society, and this material may form a forthcoming publication in the *Proceedings* of that Society. The comments on the law book and the Latin grammars are based on Dr Mapstone's work, which updates and amplifies aspects of Allenson's earlier paper (see note 11 below) which concentrates on the music. I am most grateful to her for her help with this material.

11: For a full account of the contents of the fragments and their musical and historical significance see: Stephen Allenson: *The Inverness Fragments: Music from a pre-*

Reformation Scottish Parish Church and School, in *Music and Letters*, vol. 70, no. 1, February 1989, pp. 1-45. James Ross has produced performance editions of part of the music, some of which has been publicly performed since 1991 by his music group, *Musick Fyne*, in Inverness and elsewhere.

12: Allenson, *op. cit.*

13: Now identified by Dr Mapstone as *In Primam Doctrinalis Alexandrini*, by John Vaux (one of Scotland's most distinguished early grammarians and humanists, and who lectured at Aberdeen University), published in Paris in 1522; a complete copy of this book exists in Aberdeen University Library, and is a commentary on a popular thirteenth-century Latin grammar. The unidentified grammar is entitled *Rudimentorum grammatices* and is probably from a slightly later date.

14: NLS, MS Accession 11218, no. 5 (see reference 10 above)

15: Quoted in Allenson, *op. cit.*: on folio 36 recto of the *Regiam Maiestatem* MS; the word 'boss' or 'bos' does not here mean 'the person in charge' or 'a pushy person', but is derived from a much older meaning of 'a leather bottle used as a drinking container', with an alternative meaning of 'empty' or 'hollow' and here figuratively means 'a empty worthless person'. I am grateful to Dr Mapstone for pointing this out.

16: Inverness Burgh Court Book, 3 February 1557, quoted in *Records of Inverness*, vol. 1, *op. cit.*, p. 5

17: Gordon J. Munro: The Scottish Reformation and its Consequences: chapter 12 of: Isobel Woods Preece, *op. cit.*, based on notes from Isobel Woods Preece

18: *Accounts of the Common Good*: Miscellany of the Maitland Club, ii: 50 (Edinburgh: Maitland Club, 1840)

19: Munro: *op. cit.*

20: Barron: *op. cit.*, p. 34

21: In the report of 9th June 1565: quoted in: *Records of Inverness,* vol. 1, *op. cit.*, p.125

22: Hew Scott (ed.): *Fasti Ecclesiæ Scoticanæ*, vol. 6 [of the 9 original vols.], pp. 454-455 (Edinburgh: Oliver & Boyd, 1926); see also: J. B. Craven: *History of the Episcopal Church in the Diocese of Moray* (London: Skeffington & Son, 1889), p. 231, for more information on Howieson.

23: *Records of Inverness*, vol. 1, p. xcix, *op. cit.*

24: 4th October 1564 and 13 January 1565: quoted in *Records of Inverness*, vol. 1, *op. cit.,* pp. 116 and 119

25: *ibid.*, p. 131

26: 17th February 1571: *ibid.*, p. 198

27: 29th January 1569: *ibid.*, p. 172

Chapter 2:

1: Inverness Burgh Court Records, as quoted on p. 117 of *Records of Inverness*, vol. 2, (Aberdeen: New Spalding Club, 1924)

2: *ibid.*, as quoted on p. 151

3: Taken from the Minutes of the Synod of Moray for 26th April and 3rd October 1636, in: Peter J. Anderson: *The Grammar School and Royal Academy of Inverness* (privately published in Inverness, 1907)

4: An unspecified manuscript source claimed by: John Soutar: *Memorabilia of Inverness* (reprinted from the *Inverness Courier*, 1822) (Inverness: Donald Macdonald, n.d.)

5: As quoted on p. 203 of *Records of Inverness*, vol. 2, *op. cit.*

6: *ibid.*, p. 20

7: Peter J. Anderson (ed.): *Officers and Graduates of University & King's College, Aberdeen, 1495-1860* (Aberdeen: New Spalding Club, 1893)

8: *Records of Inverness*, vol. 2., *op. cit.*, p. 204

9: 30th January and 12th February 1654, *ibid.*, p. 208

10: Rev. James Fraser: *Chronicles of the Frasers (The Wardlaw Manuscripts)* (Edinburgh: The Scottish History Society, vol. 47, 1905)

11: Norman Newton: *The Life and Times of Inverness* (Edinburgh: John Donald, 1996): quoted on p. 35 from *The Wardlaw Manuscripts*, p. 442

12: Anderson, 1907, *op. cit.*, section III; a copy of Fraser's Testament, dated 1730, is in HCA, L/M/1/5

13: As quoted on p. 205 of *Records of Inverness*, vol. 2, *op. cit.*

14: 3rd December 1663, 29th December 1663, 4th July 1664, as quoted on pp. 217-219 of *Records of Inverness,* vol. 2, *op. cit.*

15: 7th August 1665: *ibid.*, p. 222

16: Barron, *op. cit.*, p. 34

17: 3rd December 1663, as quoted on p. 217 of *Records of Inverness*, vol. 2, *op. cit.*

18: 20th September 1669, as quoted on p. 237, *ibid.*

19: 20th September 1669, as quoted on p. 236, *ibid.*

20: 20th September 1669, as quoted on p. 237, *ibid.*

21: *Presbytery of Inverness Records*, as transcribed on p. 24 of the *Publications of the Scottish History Society*, vol. 24 (1896)

22: 21st June 1671, as quoted on p. 248 of *Records of Inverness,* vol. 2, *op. cit.*

23: 6th October, 1673, as quoted on p. 256, *ibid.* [although the minutes of the Presbytery of Inverness (p. 42, *op. cit.*) claim he was "Alexander Ros of Earlesmill"]

24: 28th March 1682, as quoted on p. 303, *ibid.*

25: Bishop Falconar was one-time minister in Forres and then Bishop of Argyll, before coming back to Moray.

26: 16th February 1685, as quoted on p. 330 of *Records of Inverness,* vol. 2, *op. cit.*

27: 23rd March 1685, as quoted on p. 330, *ibid.*

28: 27th September 1686, as quoted on p. 346, *ibid.*

29: Anderson, 1907, *op. cit.*

30: ITCM, 20th June 1691 [From this point, quotations from the ITCM about the Grammar and other early schools are taken from Margaret MacDougall's typescript notes, prepared in 1955 for Evan Barron, but checked as far as possible from the original material]

31: Souter, *op. cit.*

32: Alexander Mitchell (ed.): *Inverness Kirk Session Records* (Inverness: Robt. Carruthers & Sons, 1902), p. 51

33: *Presbytery of Forres and Inverness*, 6th August 1707

34: *ibid.*, 5th May 1708

35: ITCM, 16th May 1709

36: Anderson, 1907, *op. cit.*

37: ITCM, 5th December 1709

38: ITCM, 9th January 1710

39: Barron, *op. cit.*, p. 43

40: HCA, CI/5/24/1/1 - 2

41: ITCM, 26th July 1710

42: ITCM, 18th August 1712 and HCA, CI/5/24/1/3

43: ITCM, 17th October 1712

44: *Presbytery of Inverness Records*, 5th February 1713, now housed in HCA

45: ITCM, 7th February 1717

46: *Inverness Kirk Session Records*, *op. cit.*, p.164

47: ITCM, 23rd February 1713

48: *Presbytery of Inverness Records,* 15th May 1718

49: *Inverness Kirk Session Records, op. cit.,* p.164
50: ITCM, 19th June 1723
51: ITCM, 6th November 1723
52: HCA, CI/5/24/2/3
53: HCA, CI/5/24/2/4
54: ITCM, 19th January and 22nd June 1730
55: ITCM, 8th August 1743
56: See HCA, CI/5/24/3 for a letter dated 14th April 1750 about Fergus(s)on's appointment to the Grammar School.
57: Inverness Burgh Treasurers' Accounts, HCA, BI/2/1/1
58: ITCM, 6th January 1755
59: NAS, GD23/4/175
60: ITCM, 27th February 1755
61: ITCM, 22nd September 1755
62: ITCM, 13th September 1756
63: ITCM, 13th April 1777
64: HCA, L/M/1/6b; the original will is item L/M/1/6a, and his wife's will is L/M/1/7
65: The inscription on the slab covering his grave is in Latin, and in translation reads:
Sacred to the memory of Hector Fraser, scholar of Classics and Mathematics, Rector of Inverness. With what conscientiousness, with what care, and with what success, he performed these duties for twenty-three years, the many young people who had imbibed his learning and teaching, and are now scattered throughout the various parts of the world, as well as those who have remained here at home, are witness. When will the town find his like again? He lived his life showing goodwill to all, pleasant to everybody, offensive to none. His death in his 74th year, A.D. 1786, was lamented by many good men, but by none more than the trustees of his will, who set up this gravestone, William INGLIS of Kingsmills, Simon FRASER of Faraline *[sic]* , Simon FRASER of Boblanie, and Alexander FRASER, minister of the Divine Word at Inverness. Here lies his wife Christian ROBERTSON.
66: *Edinburgh Evening Courant,* 1st September 1792
67: *Inverness Journal,* 11th September 1811
68: ITCM, 13th April 1777
69: ITCM, 20th December 1790
70: ITCM, 7th February 1791
71: Barron, *op. cit.,* p. 36
72: ITCM, 22nd October 1733
73: Inverness Burgh Accounts, 11th September 1738
74: ITCM, 28th January 1740
75: ITCM , 12th January 1747
76: HCA, CI/5/24/1/11
77: ITCM, 26th March 1744
78: HCA, CI/5/24/1/22 - 23
79: ITCM, 5th August 1754
80: Inverness Burgh Accounts, 1746-48: accounts were for two-year periods; ITCM on 1st October 1739 also records a payment of 40s [£2] to George Denoon who was going to Aberdeen College.
81: Inverness Burgh Accounts, 1746-1748
82: HCA, L/BI/BC/23/4, dated 11th April 1750
83: ITCM, 20th August 1792

Chapter 3:

1: ITCM, 14th May 1677, as quoted in *Records of Inverness,* vol. 2, *op. cit.,* p. 273
2: HCA, CI/5/24/1/5
3: HCA, CI/5/24/1/21
4: The material in the rest of this chapter is based in part on the unpublished essays [HCA, D390] produced in the 1950's by Margaret MacDougall, Inverness Burgh Librarian and Museum Curator. However she does not seem to have had access to all the documents now in the HCA, making use only of the ITCM.
5: HCA, CI/5/24/1/28
6: HCA, CI/5/24/1/19
7: HCA, L/BI/BC/6/6/1, 26th March 1773
8: ITCM, 13th April 1777
9: Inverness Burgh Accounts, 1779
10: ITCM, 14th July 1783 and 2nd August 1784
11: ITCM, 17th July 1721
12: ITCM, 22nd November 1725
13: See Donald J. Withrington: *Education and Society in the Eighteenth Century,* in *Scotland in the Age of Improvement: Essays in Scottish History in the Eighteenth Century* (Edinburgh: Edinburgh University Press, 1970), where he records a Robert Whytingdale as having taught navigation, book-keeping, arithmetic and writing in Glasgow from 1695 until at least 1704.
14: HCA, CI/5/24/1/12 - 13 and ITCM, 28th January 1740
15: HCA, CI/5/24/1/24, some time in early 1754
16: HCA, CI/5/24/1/16, dated about September 1743
17: Source not quoted by MacDougall.
18: HCA, CI/5/24/1/18, dated 23rd April 1853
19: ITCM, 4th January 1785
20: Accounts of the Common Good, *Miscellany of the Maitland Club,* ii, *op. cit.,* p. 50
21: ITCM, 20th September 1686, as quoted in *Records of Inverness,* vol. 2, *op. cit.,* p. 344
22: ITCM, 11th November 1687, as quoted in *Records of Inverness,* vol. 2, *op. cit.,* pp. 350-352
23: ITCM, 12th November 1687, as quoted in *Records of Inverness,* vol. 2, *op. cit.,* p. 352
24: Gordon Munro, *op. cit.,* 1999
25: John Hill Burton *et al.* (eds.): *The Register of the Privy Council of Scotland,* series 3, vol. 13, p. 217 (Edinburgh: HM General Register House, 1877-1898)
26: ITCM, 25th August 1699
27: MacDougall's notes on Robert Edwards are not fully correct as she does not seem to have realised that there were a father and son of the same name, a fact confirmed by a petition from the son preserved in HCA, CI/5/24/1/14.
28: HCA, CI/5/24/1/5
29: HCA, CI/5/24/2/5
30: HCA, CI/5/24/1/8 - 10
31: HCA, CI/5/24/1/14
32: ITCM, 1st October 1744
33: Inverness Burgh Accounts, 1744-46: payment listed amongst "Sallarys & Fees of Offices", alongside his salary for two years and the rent of the schoolroom for one and a half years, "he having had leave of absence for half a year"; there is mention in ITCM that the dancing master should also go to Edinburgh, but there is no corresponding payment for the dancing master, so he may not have gone.
34: In the middle to late eighteenth century, Edinburgh was by far the leading musical

centre in Scotland for both what might be called 'classical' and 'folk' music – there was a very active musical society: for an account of music in lowland Scotland at that time see: David Johnson: *Music and Society in Lowland Scotland in the Eighteenth Century* (2nd edition) (Edinburgh: Mercat Press, 2003).

35: HCA, CI/5/24/1/17

36: HCA, CI/5/24/1/25 - 26 (it is not clear if these represent two versions of the same document, or petitions presented at different times)

37: HCA, CI/5/24/1/29, dated 21st June 1756

38: Charles Fraser-Mackintosh, in *Letters of Two Centuries* (Inverness: A. & W. Mackenzie, 1890), pp. 331-332, states that the job was advertised in the *Caledonian Mercury* in January 1759, so the 1758 date may be incorrect.

39: NAS, GD128/37/16 – un-numbered in bundle (2 items); see also Fraser-Mackintosh, *op. cit.*

40: NAS, GD128/37/16, dated 9th February 1796 – un-numbered in bundle; see also Fraser-Mackintosh, *op. cit.*, where the letter is transcribed

41: HCA, CI/5/27/2; see also an article in *Inverness Courier* for 3rd May 1932 by 'W. S.' [William Simpson] which includes other details about Thomson

42: Isabel Anderson: *Inverness before Railways*, p. 59 (Inverness: A. & W. Mackenzie, 1885; reprinted: Inverness: Charles Leakey, 1984)

43: Quoted from MacDougall, *op. cit.*

44: HCA, CI/5/24/1/15

45: See note 33 above

46: Johnson, *op. cit.*

47: HCA, CI/5/27/3

48: NAS, CH1/2/53/20

49: *Inverness Kirk Session Records, op. cit.*, p.164-174

50: *The Compt Book of James Boynd, Chamberlain of the Bishopric of Orkney* (now in the Orkney Archives) has an entry for an Alexander Moncrief, "now schoolmaster at Inverness" who was due money for land in Stromness for the years 1727 to 1730; thanks to Christine Horne for bringing this reference to my attention.

51: HCA, CI/5/25 contains a variety of material relating to the school, its construction, and operation.

52: HCA, CI/5/25/1/5, dated 27th June 1757

53: For more information on the SSPCK schoolmasters, see A. S. Cowper (ed.): *SSPCK Schoolmasters 1709-1872* (Scottish Record Society, New Series 20, Edinburgh, 1997).

54: HCA, CI/5/24/1/33, dated 8th February 1783

55: NAS, GD248/369/7/23

56: HCA, CI/5/27/1

57: See, for instance, Donald [J.] Withrington: *Education in the 17th century Highlands* in *The Seventeenth Century in the Highlands* (Inverness Field Club, 1986) for references to schools in the country areas around Inverness.

58: For a general view of education in Scotland during the eighteenth century, see: Withrington, *op. cit.* (1970)

Chapter 4:

1: ITCM, 25th September 1786

2: *Minutes of the Commissioners of Supply for Inverness-shire*, 21st November 1786, HCA, CI/1/1/3a

3: *Directors' Minutes*, 29th January 1787: unfortunately the first eight-page section of this minutes book has been lost, but much, perhaps all, of the text is available in a transcript in IRAA, and this has been copied and was bound into the Minutes Book when it was rebound in 1996 [IRAA, A1 and A2].

4: A printed copy of the appeal for subscriptions is in NLS, J.133.c.1.11, and printed copies of the resolutions are in J.133.1.12 and 33

5: *Inverness Advertiser*, 13th August 1850, reproduces the text of his letter, but the original has not been traced

6: NAS, GD46/17/4 [Seaforth Papers], pp. 385-388: letter to Seaforth; a very similar letter to Mr Macleod is in *Directors' Minutes*; both are dated 13th March 1787

7: Withrington, *op. cit.*, 1970, discusses this influence throughout Scotland

8: Edward Smart: *History of Perth Academy* (Perth: Milne, Tannahill & Methven, 1932)

9: Aberdeen University MSS, 456, quoted in Withrington, *op. cit.*, 1970

10: Withrington, *op. cit.* (1970)

11: I am very grateful to Jim Brennan for information and rewrites of this section, based on his researches. These include sorting out the genealogy of the Cuthberts and all the other families to whom they were related by marriage; the history of Thomas Gilzean, and the financial links with the slave trade in Jamaica. Further research may affect some of the details of this work. See also note 19.

12: *Minutes of the Commissioners of Supply*, 30th April 1787, *op. cit.*

13: NAS, Seaforth Papers, GD46/17/4, pp. 385-388, dated 13th March 1787

14: *Directors' Minutes*, 1st May 1788

15: *Directors' Minutes*, 5th May 1788

16: NAS, GD128/34/1/17

17: NAS, GD128/37/16/a [also transcribed in: Fraser-Mackintosh: *op. cit.*] – MacPherson was appointed a member of the Supreme Council of Bengal in 1784 and created a baronet in 1786; he came back to Britain in 1787, not to return to India, and died in 1821; he was possibly a cousin of James "Ossian" Macpherson.

18: ITCM, 27th July 1789 and reply in NAS, GD128/34/1/16 (and also in *Directors' Minutes*)

19: Brennan (personal communications), using Gilzean's *Client Account Book* (see note 24 below), reckons that between 1786 and 1802 some 230 named individuals and two organisations subscribed to Academy funds: 61 had a West Indian connection, mainly Jamaica or Demerara; of the total of 230, 14 subscribed £100 or more (and these were often West Indian, including Lewis Cuthbert and the Wedderburn brothers) and 20 subscribed £50 or more – there may have been 20 to 30 others whose names were not recorded in the *Client Account Book*; little money came from Edinburgh or Glasgow; Douglas J. Hamilton: *Scotland, the Caribbean and the Atlantic World 1750-1820* (Manchester: Manchester University Press, 2005), chap. 8, sets these subscriptions in the context of Scottish activity in the West Indies at this time.

20: Smart, *op. cit.*

21: Brennan (see note 11)

22: *Directors' Minutes*, 1st May 1790

23: Derived from various entries in *Directors' Minutes* and Gilzean's *Client Account Book* (see note 24 below)

24: Thomas Gilzean: *Client Account Book 1782-1803*, pp. 255-256, HCA, D489: a vol. 2, covering Gilzean's transactions from 1803, cannot be traced, but most of the annual accounts survive in the *Directors' Minutes*.

25: *Directors' Minutes*, 21st April 1789

26: HCA, Cl/5/8/5/4, dated 4th May 1789, with associated letters in NAS, GD128/25/9/26 of 13th May 1789 and GD128/25/9/27 (draft, dated May, but no specific date)

27: *Directors' Minutes*, 15th March 1790 and 1st May 1790

28: *Directors' Minutes*, 20th October 1789

29: Brennan: in a letter to the *Inverness Courier*, 24th April 1998
30: Gilzean, *op. cit.*, p. 284 and *Directors' Minutes*, 22nd November 1790
31: Gilzean, *op. cit.,* p. 284
32: NAS, GD128/34/1/18
33: Gilzean, *op. cit.*, p. 284
34: Gilzean, *op. cit.*, p. 285
35: *Directors' Minutes*, copy letter of 10th December 1790 to Hugh Fraser in Jamaica, and minutes, 5th July 1791
36: *Directors' Minutes*, 5th October 1791
37: *Directors' Minutes*, 20th February 1793
38: Gilzean, *op. cit.*, various entries on pp. 284-286, 354-357, 392-395 and 426
39: (First) *Statistical Account of Scotland* (1793): Revs. Robert Rose, George Watson and Alexander Fraser: *Town and Parish of Inverness*, in: Sir John Sinclair (ed.):*The Statistical Account of Scotland 1791-1799,* vol. IX, pp. 603-635 (Edinburgh: William Creech, 1793); in the modern edition the relevant section is vol. XVII (Inverness-shire), pp. 98-99 (Wakefield: EP Publishing, 1981); a modern version is also available published by the Pentland Press (n.d.).
40: *Directors' Minutes*, 10th December 1792 and 14th January 1793

Chapter 5:

1: *Directors' Minutes*, 4th November 1791
2: *Directors' Minutes*, 1st February 1792
3: NAS, GD128/34/1/67, dated 17th May 1792
4: NAS, GD128/34/1/46 and 48
5: *Directors' Minutes*, 19th October 1792
6: *Minutes of the Commissioners of Supply*, 30th April 1792 and *Directors' Minutes,* 2nd May 1792
7: ITCM, 21st May 1792
8: NAS, GD128/34/1/67
9: NAS, GD128/34/1/63
10: *Directors' Minutes*, 10th January 1792
11: *Directors' Minutes*, 29th November 1792
12: *Directors' Minutes*, 29th June 1792
13: *Directors' Minutes*, 10th July 1792
14: *Directors' Minutes*, 16th July 1792
15: This statement is surprising as all other payments were by the session (a six-month period), and another hand has written in pencil in the Minutes Book, above the word 'year', the word 'session'.
16: *Directors' Minutes*, 28th January and 1st May 1789
17: *Directors' Minutes*, 1st May 1789
18: *Directors' Minutes*, 26th October 1791
19: *Directors' Minutes*, 6th October 1790
20: *Directors' Minutes*, 26th April 1793
21: *Directors' Minutes*, 26th April 1793
22: In the Royal Academy archive, in the Fraser-Mackintosh (book) Collection in Inverness Public Library, and in NAS, GD23/9/30; a manuscript version also exists in NAS, GD128/34/1, and a transcript appears in the Directors' Minutes Book.
23: *Directors' Minutes*, 29th June 1792
24: *Directors' Minutes*, 21st and 23rd July 1792
25: NAS, GD128/34/1/66
26: *Directors' Minutes,* 14th January 1793
27: *Directors' Minutes*, 15th March 1793

Chapter 6:

1: Gilzean: *op. cit.*, p. 356 and *Directors' Minutes*, 10th December 1792
2: A privately-published paper about Weir and his career was produced in 2002 by the current author, and is available on application to the Archivist at Inverness Royal Academy; a shorter version of the paper, *James Weir, Rector and Scientist*, was published in *University of Edinburgh Journal*, December 2002.
3: University of Edinburgh Matriculation Roll for Arts, Law and Divinity, 1775-1810
4: J. W. W. Stephenson: *Education in the Burgh of Dundee in the Eighteenth Century* (unpublished thesis, no date stated, courtesy Archive and Records Centre, Dundee)
5: Quoted in Stephenson, *op. cit.*
6: *Directors' Minutes*, 13th December 1791
7: Implied from NAS, GD128/34/1/48
8: NAS, GD128/34/1/46
9: *Directors' Minutes*, 14th January 1793
10: NAS, GD128/34/1/47
11: NAS, GD128/55/13/7, first item
12: *ibid.*, second item
13: NAS, GD128/34/1/62
14: NAS, GD128/34/1/64
15: *Directors' Minutes*, 15th March 1793
16: NAS, GD128/34/1/0
17: NAS, GD128/10 in five bundles
18: NAS, GD128/10/1/15: Rev. Harry Robertson was Minister of Kiltearn Parish from 1776 until his death in 1815; he married in 1772, and had ten children; Macgregor seems to have acted as a tutor to some of them, with whom he kept in correspondence until his death; for an outline of Harry Robertson's career, see *Fasti Ecclesiæ Scoticanæ*, vol. 7, p. 43.
19: NAS, GD128/34/1/80 and Inglis' reply in *Directors' Minutes* and GD128/34/1/81, dated July 1793
20: NAS, GD128/34/1/81
21: NAS, GD128/34/1/79, dated 13th November 1793, and rather inaccurate transcription in *Directors' Minutes*
22: *Directors' Minutes*, 14th December 1793, with the appeals in the minutes of 23rd December, and 21st January 1794; also letters in GD128/34/1/73, 77, 78 and 79
23: For more information on this work see the paper and article mentioned in note 2 above; a very brief account of Weir's work is also given in: E. G. R.Taylor: *The Mathematical Practitioners of Hanoverian England, 1714-1840* (Cambridge: University Press for the Institute of Navigation, 1966).
24: Dundee Town Council minutes for 1792, courtesy Archives and Records Centre, Dundee
25: NAS, GD128/10/1/7
26: NAS, GD128/34/1/72 and 75
27: NAS, GD128/34/1/76
28: NAS, GD128/34/1/74
29: NAS, GD128/10/1/25
30: The acceptance letter is NAS, GD128/34/1/37a
31: NAS, GD128/34/1/71 and *Directors' Minutes*, 28th March 1794
32: *Directors' Minutes*, 25th July 1794
33: *Inverness Kirk Session Records*, *op. cit.*, pp. 201 and 205
34: Implied from date of death of Thomas Macgregor given in Smart, *op. cit.*, and comment in NAS, GD128/34/1/70.
35: *Directors' Minutes*, 5th September and 20th December 1796

36: Copy letter in *Directors' Minutes*, 14th March 1798
37: NAS, GD128/34/1/56
38: *Directors' Minutes*, 15th June 1798
39: NAS, GD128/34/19
40: Old Parish Register – Inverness – Reel 45 OPR 98/6
41: *Inverness Courier*, 7th October 1819; an obituary also appears in *The Scots Magazine* for October 1819
42: *Directors' Minutes*, copy letters dated 6th and 15th April 1803
43: *Directors' Minutes*, 18th July 1803
44: *Directors' Minutes*, 16th January 1804
45: IRAA, B2; a manuscript version also survives as item B3, but seems to be of much later origin
46: IRAA, B1: this was ordered to be kept by decision of the Directors at their meeting on 27th February 1804; individual sheets for most of the classes in Autumn 1804 are also found in NAS, GD128/34/1/37 and 38; Hamilton *(op. cit.)* has studied the names and identified probable connections between some of the pupils, listed as coming from the Caribbean, and Inverness families such as the Inglis, Chisholm and Cuthbert families.
47: NAS, GD128/34/1/43
48: Tyro: from a Latin word meaning a beginner; the book is probably: *Tyro's Guide to Wisdom and Wealth, designed for the moral instruction of youth, with exercises in spelling ... to which are now subjoined the principles of English Grammar* by Alexander Barrie, *fl.* 1781-1810, teacher of English in Edinburgh: this book appeared in multiple editions around the start of the nineteenth century.
49: Flavius Eutropius (died *c.* AD 370) was the author of *Breviarum Rerum Romanorum ab urbe condita*; Cornelius Nepos was an author of historical works and a contemporary of Cicero, Atticus and Catullus.
50: *Voyage du jeune Anacharsis en Grèce* (1788): the best-known work by Jean Jacques Barthélemy (1716-1795)
51: See James Scotland: *History of Scottish Education*, vol. 1, for comments about the curriculum and books used in various other Scottish schools at different periods
52: NAS, GD128/10/4 and 5: about 14 items
53: NAS, GD128/10/3 (2 items) and 10/5 (1 item)
54: NAS, GD128/10/3/22 and 25
55: NAS, GD128/10/5/44
56: *Directors' Minutes*, 28th May 1793
57: HCA, CI/5/8/2/23, dated 23rd September 1793
58: NAS, GD248/686/1/4 [Seafield Papers]
59: *Minutes of the Commissioners of Supply,* 30th April 1794, *op. cit.*
60: *Directors' Minutes*, copy letter dated 21st October 1797
61: *Directors' Minutes*, 22nd November 1797: this was the school bursary instituted by Hector Fraser, not the bursary of similar name awarded for students at Aberdeen University instituted by Dr James Fraser, former pupil of the Grammar School.
62: IRAA, F3b
63: NAS, GD128/37/16: two unnumbered items; the bequest to the Town was for money for the deserving poor.
64: William Simpson: *Old Inverness Artists* in *Proceedings of the Inverness Scientific Society and Field Club*, vol. IX (1918-1925), pp. 31-49
65: *Directors' Minutes*, 10th September 1804
66: Fraser-Mackintosh: *op. cit.*, pp. 340-342
67: IRAA, F3b iii
68: *(First) Statistical Account of Scotland*, 1793: *op. cit.*

69: Thomas Garnet: *Observations on a Tour through the Highlands, etc. etc.*, vol. 2, pp. 2-5 (London: T. Cadell, Jnr. and W. Davies, 1800)
70: NAS, GD150/3420 [Earl of Morton Papers]

Chapter 7:

1: An early, but rather inaccurate, biography of Nimmo can be found in *A Biographical Dictionary of Eminent Scotsmen, volume V* (Blackie and Sons, 1856); a much more reliable one, but still with some minor errors, is by Ted Ruddock on pp. 483-489 of the *Biographical Dictionary of Civil Engineers in Great Britain and Ireland, volume 1: 1500-1830*, edited by the Institution of Civil Engineers (Thomas Telford, Ltd., 2002). The only full-length modern biography of Nimmo is: Noël P. Wilkins: *Alexander Nimmo, Master Engineer, 1783-1832* (Dublin: Irish Academic Press, 2009).
2: R. N. Smart: *Biographical Register of the University of St. Andrews, 1747-1897* (St. Andrews: St. Andrews University Library, 2004). Thanks to Noël Wilkins for tracing this information, and other information about Nimmo's early life and University career including reference 3 below.
3: Cupar [Fife] Town Council minutes, 2nd November 1796
4: Fortrose Academy was founded in 1791 but no detailed records, apart from the letter recorded in reference 5 below, survive from the first twenty or so years, so the date of Nimmo's appointment cannot be checked; however Wilkins (*op. cit.*) has identified from the Presbytery of Chanonry Session Minutes that Nimmo subscribed to the precepts of the Presbyterian Church in February 1802, a condition of taking up the job.
5: After a short gap, an Alexander Pollock almost certainly took Nimmo's place at Fortrose as second master in the autumn of 1805. In a letter from Pollock to a merchant in Glasgow, dated 10th September 1806, the new Rector is named as a Mr Todd. The letter says: "By a system of unparalleled rudeness, Mr Todd, our former Rector, had become obnoxious to the public feeling, as far as I can understand, he was a man conscientiously solicitous to push forward young people in the Dogmata of education; but his general treatment of students made him, as a teacher, contemptible in the eyes of the community." Todd resigned in December 1805 and Pollock was appointed in his place. Thanks to the Rector of Fortrose Academy for access to this document.
6: *Directors' Minutes*, 2nd April 1805
7: This Mr Pollock is almost certainly the Alexander Pollock of Glasgow who took Nimmo's place.
8: *Directors' Minutes*, 13th July 1805; the letter from the Edinburgh professors (quoted in the previous paragraph) follows the minute of the meeting.
9: ibid.
10: NAS, GD128/34/1/36
11: *Directors' Minutes*, 8th February 1810
12: HCA, CI/5/8/9/3/1/1: letter from Nimmo to the Directors, with inserted letter from Alexander Campbell, English Teacher, not dated – both letters are on the topic of schemes of work.
13: *Directors' Minutes*, 7th January 1811
14: *Directors' Minutes*, 20th May 1811
15: J. Playfair in the minutes of the Royal Society of Edinburgh (NLS, Acc. 10000/4), as quoted in Wilkins, *op. cit.*
16: Noted by Wilkins, *op. cit.*
17: Noted by Wilkins, *op. cit.*, from a paper in the *Transaction of the Royal Irish Academy*, vol. XIV (1825)
18: Highland Folk Museum collection, Newtonmore, catalogue no. X74; a note on a

separate sheet of paper reads: "Farr 23rd November 1864. The inclosed is a sketch of Fort George drawn by Mr. Nimmo Rector of the Inverness Academy in May 1864. Which I had with me in India it is worn out by having been carried many years in my pocket book. AM" – the date attributed to the drawing on this cover sheet is clearly wrong, as Nimmo died in 1832.

19: NLS, Adv MS 34.4.20: now published as part of: Noël P.Wilkins (ed.): *Alexander Nimmo's Inverness Survey and Journal, 1808* (Dublin: Royal Irish Academy, 2011), along with essays on the background to the survey and social conditions of the times.

20: *Third Report of Commissioners for Highland Roads and Bridges, 1807*, p. 57 – the Historical Statement forms Appendix U, from p. 75; Nimmo's fee is included in Appendix W on p. 97; a more detailed account of Nimmo's work appears in Arrowsmith's *Memoir relative to a Map of Scotland*, 1807 (published 1823), pp. 20-21.

21: See also: A. R. B. Haldane: *New Ways through the Glens* (Newton Abbot: David & Charles, 1962, with later reprints and new editions), p. 63

22: NLS, *ibid.*, ff. 51-54, inserted after Nimmo's *Journal*, and dated 12th October 1806; the letter goes on to say that he did not have enough time to sort out a dispute over the Caithness/Sutherland boundary at The Ord.

23: Ruddock, *op. cit.*

24: Joseph Mitchell: *Reminiscences of my Life in the Highlands*, vol. 1 (1883 and various modern editions)

25: *Rector's Report of the State of The Inverness Academy ... 30th April 1835*: IRAA, B2

26: Ruddock: *op. cit.*

27: A detailed study of his work in Ireland and elsewhere is found in: Wilkins: 2009 *op. cit.;* his work in the west of Ireland is also found in Kathleen Villiers-Tuthill: *Alexander Nimmo and the Western District* (Co. Galway: Connemara Girl Publications, 2006).

28: *The Times*, 26th January 1832

29: See *Treasures of the Royal Dublin Society*, compiled by James White and Kevin Bright (Dublin, 1998), item 270; the bust is 25 inches [about 62 cm] high, and was presented to the Society in 1846.

30: HCA, CI/5/8/9/3/1/5, dated 27th June 1811 – today, 2 George Street is on the edge of the old town of Glasgow, close to Glasgow Cathedral and the former buildings of the University, but no building is currently numbered '2' and it may have been either part of a tenement on the corner of the High Street, or on a now demolished site next to the tenement.

31: John Playfair: *Elements of Geometry: containing the first six books of Euclid, with a supplement on the quadrature of the circle and the geometry of solids; to which are added, elements of plane and spherical trigonometry* (Edinburgh: Bell & Bradfute, 2nd edition, 1804, or 3rd edition (enlarged), 1810): various copies and editions of this book are in the National Library of Scotland.

32: W. Innes Addison (compiler): *A Roll of the Graduates of the University of Glasgow* (Glasgow: James MacLehose & Sons, 1898), and the University records: thanks to Glasgow University's Archive and Business Records Centre for tracing this material.

33: *Directors' Minutes*, 29th July 1811

34: *Directors' Minutes*, 3rd September 1811

35: HCA, CI/5/8/9/3/1/25

36: *Directors' Minutes*, 3rd June 1812

37: *Directors' Minutes*, 5th September 1816

38: *Directors' Minutes*, 15th January 1812: consideration must have been given to purchasing these during Nimmo's time as Rector, as on the front of the letter from Nimmo to Rickman (folio 51, *op. cit.*, reference 19 above) the price of certain maps is given in another person's handwriting: "World on roller £1 16s; North America £1 10s;

illegible (probably Asia) £1 5s."

39: HCA, CI/5/8/9/3/2/19 and 20, dated 9th June 1812 and an unspecified Tuesday night, but clearly the same day or a day or two later.

40: IRAA, part of L3

41: HCA, CI/5/8/9/3/2/22

42: HCA, CI/5/8/9/3/3/1: this is a bundle of five letters, handed in for the meeting of 5th January 1813, covering various matters, not just the salary claim.

43: *Directors' Minutes*, 5th January 1813

44: HCA, CI/5/8/9/3/3/8 and 9

45: *Directors' Minutes*, 22nd June 1814; some of the details of the dispute have survived in the legal papers listed in reference 47 below.

46: *Directors' Minutes*, 4th October 1814

47: NAS, CS271/75293, covering the period December 1814 to July 1815; the Directors' submission to the Court of Session, prepared in February 1815, is a 78-page manuscript document; the final judgement is a 25-page printed document.

48: *Directors' Minutes*, 2nd May 1822, from Adam's statement about not being allowed to vote in the Glengarry affair (see Chapter 8)

49: *Directors' Minutes*, 5th September 1816

50: HCA, CI/5/8/9/3/3/13, dated 29th June 1819

51: *Directors' Minutes*, 1st May 1822

52: *Directors' Minutes*, 4th December 1827

53: *Directors' Minutes*, 24th December 1821

54: Adam's weather registers for 1821–1824 and his summary for 1825, prepared for the Royal Society of Edinburgh, survive in NLS, Acc. 10069/10.

55: *Directors' Minutes*, 1st May 1821

56: Adam's weather register for 1821, NLS, *op. cit.*

57: *Directors' Minutes*, 9th January 1824: copy of letter from Dr Brewster of the Royal Society of Edinburgh dated 29th December 1823

58: *Directors' Minutes*, accounts for 1827

59: (Sir) Thomas Dick Lauder: *Great Floods of 1829* (Edinburgh: Adam Black, 1830 [2nd edition]; modern reprint: Forres: Moray Books, 1998). The early editions list Adam's readings – in the 2nd edition these appear on p. 411. The readings were used by the present author to interpret the weather patterns that caused the Moray Floods in: *Historic Floods in the Scottish Highlands* in *Scottish Association of Geography Teachers' Journal*, no. 22, 1993.

60: NAS, GD128/19/7 [Raigmore papers] – 2 items in bundle

61: Board of Longitude Papers from the Royal Greenwich Observatory at Cambridge University Library [RGO] 14/30/349

62: RGO 14: specific references are given in other notes

63: *Inverness Courier*, 23rd January, 30th January, and 3rd April 1823

64: RGO 14/51/150-151

65: *Inverness Courier*, 3rd April 1823, and RGO 14/51/152

66: RGO, *op. cit.*, and RGO 14/51/154-155

67: For information on the voyage on *HMS Clio* see *Inverness Journal* of 10th October and 14th November 1823, and *Inverness Courier*, 6th November 1823.

68: RGO 14/30/356 mentions this report, but the report itself has not been traced.

69: RGO 14/3/107r, 14/4/173v-174r, and RGO 14/8 p. 14, are the rough minute, fair copy and confirmed minute respectively of this information.

70: RGO 14/30 p. 360

71: Adam published his report in the *Edinburgh Journal of Science*, vol. 4, no. vii (1825), pp. 95-99, with illustrations on plate I; David Brewster was editor of this Journal. There had also been brief mention of the work in vol. 1, no. ii (1824), p. 179.

The description of the instrument is repeated in Brewster's *Edinburgh Encyclopædia* (1830 edition), vol. 18, pp. 72-73 and with the illustrations as part of plate CCCCLXXXVII No. II, in an article on sextants. This article also includes Brewster's own suggestions on how Adam's development could be improved, material which had also appeared in the *Edinburgh Journal of Science* in vol. 6, no. xii (1827), pp. 250-251.

72: For further information on this work see a privately-published paper about Adam and his career, produced in 2003 by the current author, and available on application to the Archivist at Inverness Royal Academy; as with Weir a very brief account is also given in: E.G.R. Taylor: *The Mathematical Practitioners of Hanoverian England, 1714-1840* (Cambridge: University Press for the Institute of Navigation, 1966), but this account is inaccurate.

73: *Directors' Minutes*, 18th July 1822
74: *Directors' Minutes*, 24th December 1821
75: *Directors' Minutes*, 24th December 1821 and 3rd January 1822
76: *Directors' Minutes*, 18th July 1822
77: *Directors' Minutes*, 30th December 1823, and also NAS, GD128/34/1/25 - 26, 29 and 33
78: *Directors' Minutes*, 7th December 1824
79: *Inverness Journal*, 5th November 1824
80: I am grateful to Christine Horne for the information on Adam's marriage and about some of his children, identified from the Old Parish Register for Inverness (on microfilm); thanks also to the Highland Family History Society for assistance with locating his family grave in the Chapel Yard, Inverness; see also *Inverness Journal* for 14th July 1826 for the marriage announcement, which seems to give the wrong date of the marriage.
81: From personal communication from Jim Brennan, using information from University College, London.
82: Addison: *A Roll of the Graduates of the University of Glasgow, op. cit.*
83: *Rector's Report on the State of the Inverness Academy to the Annual Meeting of Directors, May 1835*: IRAA, B2
84: *Directors' Minutes*, 23rd February and 2nd March 1836
85: *Directors' Minutes*, 22nd March 1839
86: *Inverness Courier*, 8th May 1839
87: *A Roll of Graduates of the University of Glasgow, op. cit.*

Chapter 8:

1: *Directors' Minutes*, 12th November 1808
2: *Edinburgh Evening Courant*, 1st December 1808 (an original press cutting is in IRAA, F3c)
3: NAS, GD23/6/451/1 [Bught Papers], dated 1st February 1809; the donation however is not recorded in the *Directors' Minutes* until 8th February 1810.
4: *Directors' Minutes*, 7th January 1811
5: NAS, GD128/34/1/14 [Fraser-Mackintosh Papers]
6: *Directors' Minutes*, 16th February 1809; see also *Inverness Journal*, 12th August and 23rd December 1808
7: *Directors' Minutes*, 7th May 1810
8: *Directors' Minutes*, 29th July 1811
9: *Directors' Minutes*, 28th September 1811
10: *Directors' Minutes*, 12th February 1812
11: HCA, CI/5/8/9/3/3/2
12: *Directors' Minutes*, 15th December 1813

13: HCA, CI/5/8/9/3/3/5

14: "Invernessicus" [Lachlan Mackintosh of Raigmore]: *Observations of Objects interesting to the Highlands of Scotland* (Edinburgh: The Caledonian Press, 1814); at least three editions (probably more reprints than editions) of this book were produced – copies are in IRAA F4, Inverness Public Library Fraser-Mackintosh Collection (both a first and second edition copy), Dundee and St. Andrews University Libraries, and the National Library of Scotland.

15: HCA, CI/5/8/9/3/3/10

16: William Simpson: *Newspapers in Inverness in the 19th century* in *Proceedings of the Inverness Scientific Society and Field Club,* vol. IX (1918-1925), pp. 204-220

17: *Reply for the Rector and Teachers of the Inverness Academy to certain erroneous statements ... upon prizes bestowed by Teachers ...* (Inverness: no publisher stated, 1817) – the only known copy is in IRAA, G15

18: *Inverness Courier,* 2nd July 1818, where there is a moving, although brief, obituary, saying that former pupils would read the notice "with affectionate regret".

19: *Directors' Minutes,* 1st and 14th May 1817

20: *Inverness Journal,* 2nd August 1822 and subsequent editions

21: NAS, GD128/34/1/28

22: *Directors' Minutes,* 30th December 1823

23: Quoted by Barron, source not stated: see note 24 for reference

24: Evan Barron: *Ewen Maclachlan and Inverness Royal Academy* in *Proceedings of the Inverness Scientific Society and Field Club,* vol. VII (1906-1912), pp. 131-156

25: NAS, GD128/34/54, and copied into *Directors' Minutes* of 23rd February 1820

26: Barron, *op. cit.*

27: NAS, GD128/34/1/9 and copied into *Directors' Minutes* of 23rd February 1820

28: For an account of this matter, see: James Miller: *Inverness* (Edinburgh: Birlinn, 2004), chapter 11

29: *Directors' Minutes,* 23rd February 1820 and also result listed on NAS, GD128/34/1/12

30: *Inverness Courier,* 23rd March 1820 (quoted by Barron, *op. cit.*), and *Inverness Journal,* 24th March 1820

31: *Directors' Minutes,* 2nd May 1820, and quoted by Barron, *op. cit.*

32: Barron, *op. cit.*

33: NAS, GD44/43/354/9 [Gordon Castle Muniments]

34: *Inverness Courier,* 4th May 1820

35: *Directors' Minutes,* 3rd May 1820

36: Barron, *op. cit.*

37: For further information on Carmichael's career after leaving Inverness, see: Magnus Magnusson: *The Clacken and the Slate – the story of Edinburgh Academy* (London: Collins, 1974).

38: Mitchell, *op. cit.*

39: An obituary of Gilzean appeared in the *Inverness Courier* for 5th April 1843.

40: *Directors' Minutes,* 1st June 1833

41: *Inverness Journal* and *Inverness Courier* of various dates in the period July to September 1833

42: Inverness Royal Academy: *Report of a Committee appointed by the Directors to enquire into the State of the Institution* (Inverness: printed by R. Carruthers, 1834). Both a bound and an unbound copy survive in IRAA F5a; a copy also exists in the Fraser-Mackintosh book collection in Inverness Library.

43: *Directors' Minutes,* 1st May 1834

44: *Directors' Minutes,* 6th May 1835

45: The fourth Directors' Minutes Book finishes after the meeting of 9th July 1834, and the fifth book was missing from the Highland Council Archive when this was first catalogued by the first Inverness-shire County Council archivist – it was claimed to be in Inverness Town Library, but was located in early 2011 in Inverness Museum. However, a transcript of parts of the minutes, prepared by Evan Barron in the early twentieth century, is available in IRAA A2, and had originally been used in writing about the period from 1834 to 1847. By comparing the transcript with the actual minutes books it became clear that all the main events had been transcribed. The sixth minutes book does not start until 1847.

46: *Rectors' Report of the state of the Inverness Academy to the Annual Meeting of the Directors on 1st May, 1835*, IRAA, B2

47: *Code of Regulations for the Management of Inverness Academy, 2nd September 1835*, HCA, ED/IB/3/6; four copies are available: one appears to be a draft, two are handwritten copies, and one is a printed poster with manuscript amendments, indicative of further changes which were made to the regulations in 1836.

48: The text of the "Reasons for Protest" does not appear in the minutes book.

49: *Directors' Minutes*, 15th April 1836

50: *Directors' MInutes*, 2nd May 1836

51: IRAA, B4

Chapter 9:

1: *Directors' Minutes*, 2nd May 1807

2: *Directors' Minutes*, 31st December 1807

3: *Directors' Minutes*, 9th November 1811

4: NAS, GD128/34/1/36

5: NAS, GD128/34/1/55

6: IRAA, B1. According to the *Oxford Dictionary of National Biography*, vol. 39, pp. 639-640 (Oxford, 2004), where his name appears as 'Mudie', he went to Dundee High School about 1808 as drawing master, and then teacher of arithmetic and English composition, later becoming a newspaper editor and author, as well as a keen ornithologist, dying impoverished in 1842, aged 54 – however the information in this *Dictionary* concerning his time at the Royal Academy says he was the Gaelic master from 1802 (the post did become vacant then), and this information does not agree with what is found in the *Directors' Minutes,* where he is not considered for any appointment until 1804.

7: *Inverness Journal*, 9th June 1809

8: *Inverness Journal,* 22nd July 1809

9: HCA, CI/5/8/9/3/2/1, dated 2nd January 1812, and *Directors' Minutes*, 12th February 1812

10: *Directors' Minutes*, 8th May 1812

11: *Inverness Courier*, 8th July 1819

12: Isabel Anderson, *op. cit.*, pp. 50-51 of the modern reprint

13: *Inverness Courier*, 15th October 1912, in a letter from 'C.H.M.', following an article on the Clark family in the edition a week earlier

14: NAS, GD128/34/1/27 and *Directors' Minutes*, 2nd and 30th December 1823

15: James Kennedy, M.A.: an account of his early days written in 1886: although a photocopy of the relevant pages (pp. 72-81) of this book is in the Academy archive (IRAA, M9), it has not been possible to trace the proper title and details of the publication of this work.

16: *Directors' Meeting*, 7th January 1811. Some background on Villemer appears on a French-language internet forum board, *www.genealogie.com*, dated 2005, which says that he was probably born in Vire in Normandy between 1775 and 1780, and, following the French revolution, when he did not like the turn of events, he escaped to

England via Spain. He was married in London in May 1804 to a Mary Bore, and the daughter, Mary Magdaline, was born in November 1805, in London. However this site suggests that the Bishop of Béziers helped Villemer get the job in Inverness, whereas the school records suggest that it was the Bishop of Rodez, Seignelay Cuthbert, who recommended Villemer.

17: *Directors' Minutes*, 6th December 1825

18: *Directors' Minutes*, 15th July 1819

19: NAS, GD128/34/1/11, with an added date of either 1820 or 1829, but as Villemer died in 1825 the date should be 1820, and this is confirmed by the content of the letter.

20: Pierre Villemer (Maître de Langues à l'Académie Royale d'Inverness): *Astronomie: poëme*, seconde édition, élargie et revisée (Édinbourg *[sic]*: P. Villemer, 1824) – the only known original copies of this poem are in Inverness Public Library reserve stack, and in the National Library of Scotland: both are of the second edition; a photocopy of the second edition of the poem is also available in IRAA, L9.; copies of the first edition, *Poëme sur l'astronomie ...*, published in London in 1808, before Villemer came to Inverness, are in the National Library of Scotland and the British Library.

21: *Directors' Minutes*, 1st May 1827, and subsequent meetings; also relevant transcript excerpts in IRAA, A3c

22: *Directors' Minutes* and NAS, GD128/34/1/13; there was also a further appeal (NAS, GD128/34/1/53) on 5th June 1837.

23: *One Hundred Exercises to be translated into French for the use of the students of the Inverness Academy* (Inverness: printed by Robert Carruthers, 1838) – this booklet consists of fairly standard, graded, translation sentences, reflecting in terms of content the interests and attitudes of the time.

24: *Directors' Minutes*, 1st May 1833

25: Some of the documents are in Aberdeen University Library (Thomson 275/8), and NAS, GD16/46/81 [Papers of the Earls of Airlie]; the General Assembly hearing is reported in the *Inverness Journal* for 5th June 1818.

26: *Directors' Minutes*, 8th August 1833, and report in the *Inverness Courier* of 14th August 1833

27: Isabel Anderson, *op. cit.*, p. 54 of the modern reprint

28: HCA, CI/5/8/9/3/3/3, dated 4th May 1813

29: NAS, GD23/6/527/1 and 2 [Bught Papers], dated 4th October and 24th June 1813 respectively

30: *Directors' Minutes*, 15th June 1824

31: *Directors' Minutes*, 8th April and 1st May 1829

32: *Directors' Minutes*, 14th July 1829, and subsequent meetings

33: HCA, CI/5/8/2/23: the discharge is on the reverse of the original bond

34: *Directors' Minutes*, 7th June 1814, and subsequent meetings

35: *Inverness Journal*, 1st September 1815

36: *Directors' Minutes*, 24th December 1821

37: NAS, GD128/34/1/2

38: *Directors' Minutes*, 20th May 1811

39: *Directors' Minutes*, 3rd January 1822

40: *Directors' Minutes*, 2nd May 1831

41: *Directors' Minutes*, 29th July 1834

42: Extract © *Fraser of Reelig Papers*, NRAS 2696, reproduced with permission of the copyright holders. Terence was an early Latin comic dramatist; the Duke de Sully was a French statesman who was active around 1600.

43: Kennedy, *op. cit.*

44: NAS, GD128/28/34/1/35, with transcript in *Directors' Minutes* of 20th November 1821

45: HCA, CI/5/8/2/25/1 and 2

46: *Inverness Courier*, 24th May 1821

47: *Directors' Minutes*, 20th and 26th July 1838

48: IRAA, G1: this typescript list was probably prepared for P. J. Anderson towards the end of the nineteenth century, and covers the period from 1813 to 1861; the details must have been taken from the Directors' Minutes Books and the press advertisements following the examinations – a few names have pencil notes alongside giving details of subsequent success in public life; there are several typing errors.

49: A list of these is available in IRAA, G21

50: In correspondence with Andrew Macmillan of Edinburgh in 1993, Mr Macmillan indicated that he had come across other examples of the Latin medal from the Royal Academy, but could offer no views on the use or date of such a medal or token: the number 'XXXII' is unlikely to be the date (18)32; the George IV medal is one of a type in common use in the 1820's, and they were handed out so as to encourage learning, perhaps to pupils doing well in class, or undertaking tasks beyond the usual call of duty.

51: IRAA, D2 (1885/86 prospectus), L1a (P. J. Anderson's booklet: *The Grammar School and Royal Academy of Inverness, op. cit.)* and M5 (handwritten notebook) all contain lists of the early medal winners; Anderson's list also gives brief biographical notes on the recipients.

52: *Directors' Minutes*, 8th August 1836

53: Isabel Anderson, *op. cit.*, p. 81 of the modern reprint

54: D. Nairne: *Memorable Floods in the Highlands during the Nineteenth Century ...* (Inverness: Northern Counties Printing and Publishing Company, 1895), based on a report in the *Inverness Courier*.

55: IRAA, I2

56: IRAA, B4

57: *Directors' Meeting*, 8th December 1830

58: Kennedy, *op. cit.*

59: Letter from Dr. Bethune to an Academy Director (almost certainly Mackintosh of Raigmore) dated 15th November 1822, but printed in *Inverness Journal* on 23rd June 1826

60: *Rector's Report of the State of The Inverness Academy ... 30th April 1835*: IRAA, B2

61: *Inverness Journal*, 5th October 1832; thanks to Janet Guthrie for help with locating the references relating to cholera and its effect on the Academy.

62: *Inverness Courier*, 24th October 1832 and *Inverness Journal*, 2nd November 1832

63: For more information on the effects of cholera on Inverness, see Miller, *op. cit.*, chapter 12.

64: *Inverness Courier*, 28th March 1827

65: For more information on the effects of the Reform Bill in Inverness, see Miller, *op. cit.*, chapter 11.

Chapter 10:

1: Tom M. Devine: *Scotland's Empire, 1600-1815* (London: Allen Lane, 2003 [hardback]; London: Penguin Books, 2004 [paperback])

2: I am grateful to the staff of the National Maritime Museum, Greenwich, for supplying references on Capt. Mackintosh's biography and the details of the ships in which he sailed.

3: See: J. L. Cranmer-Byng (ed.): *An Embassy to China, being the Journal kept by Lord Macartney during his Embassy to Emperor Ch'ien-lung 1793-1794* (London: Longmans, 1962, reprinted by Folio Society, 2004), which makes several references to Capt. Mackintosh and the East Indiaman *Hindostan*.

4: The National Maritime Museum has originals of at least four items showing the first *Hindostan* and the replacement ship.

5: *Will of Captain William Mackintosh of the Hindostan East Indiaman ... (as printed by order of Captain Mackintosh's Trustees in 1844)* (Inverness: Mackintosh & Co., 1850), in IRAA, E2d – the book also transcribes many of the later court decisions up to 1842; a manuscript copy of the Will survives in the *Mackintosh Farr Fund Record Book, vol. 1: 1797-1820* in HCA, CI/5/9/1.

6: National Maritime Museum, PU6362

7: NAS, GD128/34/1/20 [Fraser-Mackintosh Papers]

8: HCA, CI/5/9/22

9: NAS, GD23/6/649 [Bught Papers]

10: *Directors' Minutes*, 8th August 1836

11: *Directors' Minutes*, 20th October 1843

12: Most Mackintosh Farr Fund material is found in HCA, CI/5/9; CI/5/9/1 - 7, and covers the administration of the Fund up to the change in management of educational endowments in 1887. This includes vols. 3 and 4 of the minutes books (vols. 1 and 2 are missing), record books (vols. 1 (1797-1820), 2 (1820-1825) and 4 (1862-1883), but 3 (presumably 1825-1862) is missing), a letters book from 1876 until 1885, and a list of bursars from 1843 until 1856. CI/5/9/8 - 13 contain ledgers from 1887 until 1935; CI/5/9/31 - 36 contain rental registers for land and housing from 1925 until 1976; correspondence about the misappropriation of funds by the clerk and factor in the 1880's is in CI/5/9/37 - 41; other material is located in CI/3/38/2/22 - 24; CI/5/1/5/4/41 - 43, CI/5/19/4/4 and D1152/1.

13: The section on Bell and the Bell's Institution is based on: Andrew Grant: *An Inverness School: Ninety-six years of Fruitful Work in Farraline Park Institution* (Inverness: Highland News, 1937).

14: *Directors' Minutes*, 6th April 1835

15: Joseph Mitchell: *A Letter to the Directors of the Royal Academy and Town Council of Inverness ...*, 22nd April 1835: no copy has been traced, but the letter was summarised in the *Inverness Courier* on the same day, with support for his proposals from the Editor.

16: *Inverness Courier*, 30th October 1839

17: Copy in *Directors' Minutes*, 21st March 1848

18: HCA, CI/5/11/6 contains a leaflet and memoranda 3 and 4; memoranda 1, 2 and 5 have not been traced; a copy of the leaflet without any of the memoranda is also to be found in the Fraser-Mackintosh book collection in Inverness Public Library Reference Room.

19: HCA, CI/5/9/28 - 30 includes material on this scheme.

20: See the reports of the meeting in *Inverness Advertiser* of 29th January 1850 and *Inverness Courier* of 31st January 1850

21: Both the terms of the protest and the *Answer for the Town Council* appear in the *Inverness Advertiser* for 22nd January 1850; the *Answer for the Town Council*, written by William Simpson, Bailie W. Dallas and G. Anderson, is also available in HCA, CI/5/9/29

22: *Inverness Courier*, 14th February 1850, and an offprint or reprint in NAS, GD176/1908

23: See note 5 above: based on the evidence given to the House of Lords committee, this version of the booklet was probably produced by Dr Welsh Forbes, a well-known local doctor, Town Council member and philanthropist.

24: A petition exists as HCA, CI/5/9/30, and it seems likely that, although undated, this is the petition as presented to the Town Council.

25: *Inverness Advertiser*, 23rd and 30th July and *Inverness Courier*, 1st August 1850 (no copy of the *Courier* for 25th July, which presumably carried the first report, is available in Inverness for reference)

26: *Inverness Advertiser*, 3rd September, and *Inverness Courier*, 5th September 1850

27: *Inverness Advertiser* and *Inverness Courier*, various editions from late December 1850 until August 1853

28: *Inverness Courier*, 24th March 1853

29: 25 & 26 Vict c.2: The Mackintosh Farr Fund Act 1862 (granted Royal Assent, 29th July 1862)

30: NAS, CS275/5/5/39 of 18th July 1843, and the financial accounts of the action in CS275/6/231

31: *Inverness Journal*, 26th April 1844

32: *Directors' Minutes*, 17th January 1845

33: *Inverness Courier*, 17th January 1845

34: *Inverness Courier*, 2nd and 23rd August 1849

Chapter 11:

1: *Directors' Minutes*, 1st May 1839

2: *Directors' Minutes*, 19th September 1839

3: (Lord) Henry Cockburn: *Circuit Journeys* (various editions, including a modern facsimile reprint): the relevant quotation is in the account of the Northern Circuit journey of spring 1845.

4: *Directors' Minutes*, 24th July and *Inverness Courier*, 29th July 1840

5: *Inverness Courier*, 14th July and 3rd November 1841

6: *Directors' Minutes*, 17th January 1845

7: *Inverness Journal*, 16th May 1845

8: *Inverness Courier*, 24th January 1845

9: Perth and Kinross Archives B59/24/6/71: testimonials for Peter Scott

10: *The Scotsman*, 30th August 1843

11: *Directors' Minutes*, 7th July 1843

12: Isabel Anderson: *op. cit.,* p. 55 of the modern reprint

13: *Inverness Courier*, 9th October, and *Inverness Journal*, 11th October 1844

14: *Inverness Journal*, 23rd September 1842

15: *Directors' Minutes*, 2nd May 1853

16: *Directors' Minutes*, 24th July 1846 onwards

17: John Fraser: *Reminiscences of Inverness* (Inverness: published by the author, 1905; with modern reprint: Inverness: Charles Leakey, 1983); the incident is also reported in the *Inverness Courier*, 26th February 1840

18: *Directors' Minutes*, 7th July 1848

19: *Directors' Minutes*, 22nd March 1849

20: *Inverness Courier*, 28th December 1842

21: Highland Folk Museum collection, Newtonmore, catalogue no. CC17; images of some pages are available on-line as part of the Highland Council's *Am Baile* project.

22: *Directors' Minutes*, 30th January 1850

23: Isabel Anderson, *op. cit.,* p. 52 of the modern reprint

24: *Directors' Minutes*, 21st July, and *Inverness Courier*, 24th July 1851

25: *Directors' Minutes*, 29th August 1851

26: Background information on Jastrzebski has been supplied by David Henry of the

Pinkfoot Press in Angus.

27: Isabel Anderson: *op. cit.*, p. 56 of the modern reprint
28: *Directors' Minutes*, 9th May 1853
29: *Inverness Courier*, 24th February 1853
30: *Inverness Courier*, 21st February 1856
31: *Inverness Courier*, 19th May 1853
32: *Inverness Courier*, 29th December 1853
33: *Inverness Courier*, 25th May 1854
34: *Inverness Courier*, 24th May 1855
35: *Inverness Courier*, 31st January 1856
36: *Directors' Minutes*, 1st May 1855
37: *Directors' Minutes*, 1st May 1857
38: *Directors' Minutes*, 3rd and 10th January 1846, and various other meetings thereafter
39: *Directors' Minutes*, 14th December 1853
40: HCA, CI/5/8/5/5 - 7, with maps from 1855 and 1858
41: Various accounts of the construction of railways in Inverness are available, one of the most recent being: Keith Fenwick: *The Inverness and Nairn Railway* (Cookham: Highland Railway Society, 2005).
42: *Directors' Minutes*, 2nd August 1858
43: *Directors' Minutes*, 1st February 1861, and HCA, CI/5/8/5/7
44: *Directors' Minutes*, 1st February 1861
45: *Directors' Minutes*, 16th November 1861

Chapter 12:
1: *Inverness Courier*, 6th February 1862
2: *Directors' Minutes*, 13th February 1862 and subsequent committee meetings on 17th and 20th February
3: *Directors' Minutes*, 1st May 1862
4: *Directors' Minutes*, 8th May 1862 – report of committee meeting
5: James Kennedy: *op. cit.* (see chapter 9, note 15)
6: Isabel Anderson: *op. cit.*, pp. 48-49 of the modern reprint
7: *Inverness Courier*, 24th December 1863
8: *Directors' Minutes*, 7th November 1862
9: Robertson's works prior to arriving in Inverness were: a translation into English of part of Theodor Mommsen's *Römisch Geschichte (Roman History)* [in NLS and British Library], and *A Compendium of Latin Syntax* (1861) [in British Library].
10: *Directors' Minutes*, 10th January 1863 – report of committee meeting
11: *Directors' Minutes*, 16th April 1863 – report of Special General Meeting
12: *Inverness Courier*, 2nd July 1863
13: Source of the statistics: 1863 and 1864 figures from Rector's reports in *Directors' Minutes*; 1868 figures from *Report of Burgh Schools* (see note 33 below), as the 1868 figures were left out of the Directors' Minutes Book.
14: IRAA, B5 onwards
15: *Directors' Minutes*, 20th December 1864
16: *Directors' Minutes*, 3rd February 1864
17: *Inverness Courier*, 5th March 1863
18: *Inverness Courier*, 25th February, 3rd, 17th and 24th March 1864
19: See: W[illiam] J. ('Bobo') Mackay, J.P.: *The Freemen of Inverness* (Inverness: The Highland Herald, 1975)
20: *Inverness Courier*, 24th August 1865
21: *Directors' Minutes*, 11th March and 20th April 1865

22: *Directors' Minutes*, 29th and 30th August 1865: due to severe water damage to the edges of the pages of this minutes book, some of the values are unreadable.
23: *Inverness Courier*, 31st August 1871
24: From this date, the number of staff appointed to the school, in both the Academy and the Ladies' Institution, is too numerous for all to be mentioned specifically, and names will only be given where there is reason to do so.
25: *Directors' Minutes*, 29th November 1865
26: *Directors' Minutes*, 20th January 1866
27: *Directors' Minutes*, 2nd August 1866
28: *Scotsman*, 18th August and *Inverness Courier*, 24th August 1871
29: *Directors' Minutes*, 13th and 24th February 1869
30: *Second Report of the Royal Commissioners appointed to inquire into the Endowed Schools and Hospitals* (Colebrooke report), 1874: although not published until 1874, the report names Miss Haswell as the Lady Superintendent, but, as she resigned in 1871, this information must date from that year or perhaps late 1870.
31: "Recollections of the Old Academy, 1869-1873" in *Inverness Academical*, Christmas 1911, pp. 20-23, reprinted from *Inverness Courier*, 5th March 1895, by a 'well-known member of the Scottish legal profession'
32: For detailed studies on nineteenth century education including the 1872 Education Act see standard histories of Scottish education such as: James Scotland: *The History of Scottish Education, vols. 1 and 2* (University of London Press, 1969); for more critical studies see: Robert D. Anderson: *Education and Opportunity in Victorian Scotland* and *Education and the Scottish People* (Oxford: Clarendon Press, 1983 and 1995).
33: *Third Report of Her Majesty's Commissioners appointed to inquire into the Schools of Scotland – Burgh and Middle-Class Schools [Volume 1]*, and *Volume II: Special Reports*, Education Commission (Scotland) [Argyll Commission], 1868: Parliamentary Papers 1867/8, xxix – this report was written by Thomas Harvey (who was later to become Rector of Edinburgh Academy) and Alexander Craig Sellar (an advocate, later to be a Liberal M.P. active in educational matters).
34: *Inverness Courier*, 11th January 1866
35: *Schools Inquiry Commission*, 1868 [Taunton Commission]: vol. VI, p. 154 (the full report is on pp. 144-156)
36: Taunton Commission: *op. cit.*, vol. VI, p. 151 (IRA) and p. 206 (Inverness High School); also quoted in R. D. Anderson: *Education and Opportunity, op. cit.*, pp. 138-139, as part of a table covering eight Scottish schools.
37: Argyll Commission: *op. cit.*, vol. 2, p. 86
38: See R. D. Anderson's *Education and Opportunity, op. cit.*, p. 135, for a review of this attitude across Scotland in the 1860's and 1870's.
39: Argyll Commission: *op. cit.*, pp. 291-299
40: Argyll Commission: *op. cit.*, p. 299
41: *Inverness Courier*, 8th April 1869
42: *Directors' Minutes*, 21st February 1871
43: 35 & 36 Vict c. 62: Education (Scotland) Act, 1872: An Act to amend and extend the provisions of the law of Scotland on the subject of education (granted Royal Assent, 6th August 1872)

Chapter 13:
1: Copies of the statement are in IRAA, F7a and NAS, GD176/2382/2
2: *Second Report of the Royal Commissioners appointed to enquire into the Endowed Schools and Hospitals* (Colebrooke Report), 1874: the school submission, in response to a questionnaire sent out by the Commission, appears on pp. 495-502.

3: James Grant: *History of the Burgh Schools of Scotland, volume 1* (London: Collins, 1876) – volume 2 was never published; figures for the number of pupils in the most advanced classes of the Academy appear on p. 442, and these are: classics, 20; mathematics, 20; modern languages, 14; statistics for 1874 about the various burgh schools throughout Scotland are provided on pp. 443 and 508-510.

4: *Directors' Minutes*, 11th May 1875

5: *Inverness Courier*, 20th May 1875

6: NAS, GD176/2382/1 [Mackintosh papers], dated 30th July 1875

7: IRAA, F10a/1: the opinion of Counsel was not recorded in the Minutes Books, but is found in the *Inverness Courier* of 13th January 1876.

8: *Inverness Courier*, 3rd April 1879

9: *Inverness Courier*, 29th May 1879, with comment on how the editor thought the Act should operate.

10: NAS, ED13/392: *Endowed Institutions (Scotland), Inverness Academy, County of Inverness*, Abstract, vol. 12, p. 209

11: *Inverness Courier*, 12th February 1880

12: *Directors' Minutes*, 19th February 1880

13: *Memorial for an opinion of Counsel on the interpretation of the Academy Charter as affecting the Rights of the Board of Directors, and the Opinion of Counsel*, dated April 1881 [IRAA, F10a/2]

14: *Directors' Minutes*, 10th May 1881, and also IRAA, F10b/1

15: *Directors' Minutes*, 6th May 1882, and a letter from Charles Innes to John Mackintosh of Union Street in IRAA, E10b/2

16: *Inverness Courier*, 9th November 1882

17: *Directors' Minutes*, 12th and 19th December 1882

18: *Directors' Minutes*, 23rd January 1883

19: HCA, CI/5/9/1: Mackintosh Farr Fund Minutes Book, vol. 3, 1861-1883, meetings dated 16th, 19th and 28th February 1883

20: *Directors' Minutes*, 12th March 1883

21: Mackintosh Farr Minutes Book, *op. cit.*: meeting of 9th April 1883

22: (September) 1884: *Memorandum by the School Board of the Royal Burgh of Inverness for the Information of the Commission including Draft Scheme for the Establishment, Regulation and Government of the Royal Academy of Inverness, with two schedules* [IRAA, E6b]; *Submission by the Trustees of the Mackintosh Farr Fund to the Commissioners, and Abstract of Accounts from 1862 to 1884, with notes on the use of Fund* [E6c]; *Statement submitted to the Commissioners by the Directors appointed to represent the Directors and Managers of the Royal Academy, Inverness* [E6d] – a transcript of the evidence appears in the *Report of the Educational Endowments (Scotland) Commission*, Second Report (1885), pp. 532-575.

23: *Statement by the Directors in Reference to the ... Scheme ... now lying on the table of the House of Commons, and to the motion to be submitted by C. Fraser-Mackintosh, Esq., M.P. to the House on Monday, February 28th, ... praying Her Majesty to withhold consent from the said Scheme, in so far as concerns the Mackintosh Farr Fund, 1886* [IRAA, E6f i)] and *Memorandum by the School Board of the Burgh of Inverness, in reference to the ... Scheme ... now lying on the table of the House of Commons, and to the motion to be submitted by C. Fraser-Mackintosh, Esq., M.P., to the House on Monday, February 28th, ... praying Her Majesty to withhold consent from the said Scheme, in so far as concerns the Mackintosh Farr Fund, 1886* [E6f ii)].

24: *Educational Endowments (Scotland) Act, 1882: Copy of Scheme for the Management of the Endowments in the Burgh and County of Inverness ... , 1887* [IRAA, E6g]

25: A transcript of the full document is available in IRAA, E5, and *Directors' Minutes* records the significant details around October 1872.

26: *Directors' Minutes*, 6th May 1882 and *Inverness Courier*, 11th May 1882

27: ITCM, 4th May 1886

28: NAS, GD176/2809/21, 23 and 24 contain an invitation letter, the programme of the musical examinations and the order of examination and programme of orations for June 1880; HCA, CI/5/8/9/6 has a ticket of admission for the 1881 event, and the Order of the Subject Examination and Musical Examination Programme for 1883.

29: IRAA, O3b

30: *Directors' Minutes*, 23rd July 1879

31: *Inverness Courier*, 7th June 1940, p. 8

32: Letter from Thomas Cockburn to a former pupil, dated 1st October 1933, now in the possession of Inverness Royal Academy; see also *The Academical*, vol. 1, no. 1, February 1892: T.C. [Thomas Cockburn]: *A Reminiscence of Robert Louis Stevenson*.

33: Cockburn's obituary by Baillie appears in *The Scotsman*, 21st October 1947, and was followed by at least four letters to the editor from other people adding their own tributes; the memorial library to Cockburn, paid for by money donated by former pupils, was opened in the Academy in November 1956, being handed over by Evan Barron, of the *Inverness Courier*, representing the subscribers.

34: NAS, GD176/2820/27, dated 19th March 1881

35: *Directors' Minutes*, 7th July 1882

36: *The Inverness Academical*, February 1913: "Memories 1888-1895" by an 'Old Boy'

Chapter 14:

1: *[Tentative] Regulations and Standing Orders by the Directors of the Royal Academy and Governors of the Inverness Educational Trust ...* – this document is undated but clearly belongs to this date [IRAA, E6g ii]

2: *Inverness Courier*, 3rd January 1888, and, on 6th January, a letter of support from P. J. Anderson, who was to become librarian at King's College, Aberdeen, and one of the school's most famous former pupils.

3: *Inverness Courier*, 31st December 1889

4: *Directors' Minutes*, 13th December 1887

5: *Inverness Courier*, 1st May 1888

6: A profile of Delavault appears in *The Academical*, vol.1, no. 5 (June 1892) (see note 10 below)

7: *Inverness Courier*, 21st June 1889

8: *Directors' Minutes*, 19th July and 5th September 1888

9: *The Scotsman*, 18th May 1889

10: IRAA, K1 contains copies (some as photocopies) of all issues of *The Academical*; the only known complete set, but without the covers with Delavault's artwork, is a bound volume in HCA, D311/3/4

11: *Directors' Minutes*, 6th April 1892, and *Inverness Courier*, 8th April 1892

12: *Inverness Courier*, 12th April 1892

13: *Directors' Minutes*, 1st June 1892

14: *Inverness Courier*, 23rd December 1892

15: *Directors' Minutes*, 16th January 1893

16: *Directors' Minutes*, 14th March 1893

17: *Directors' Minutes*, 5th July 1893

18: Some material relating to this conference is in IRAA, F11.

19: *Directors' Minutes*, 8th May 1894 and subsequent meetings

20: *Inverness Courier*, 3rd August 1894

21: *Directors' Minutes*, 14th August 1894
22: *Directors' Minutes*, 6th June, 29th June and 4th July 1888
23: *Directors' Minutes*, 7th November 1888
24: *Directors' Minutes*, September 1891, and also IRAA, F13; an estimate for the work is in HCA CI/5/17/8.
25: *Inverness Courier*, 26th February 1892
26: *Directors' Minutes*, special committee meeting of 12th May, and special general meeting of 17th May 1892
27: Letter to the Directors from Ross and Macbeth dated 31st May 1892, as a printed copy in *Directors' Minutes*, and as part of IRAA, F13
28: *Inverness Courier*, 10th June 1892
29: *The Academical*, January and March 1893 in IRAA, K1; the drawings were reprinted in the June 1893 issue.
30: Both photographs have been traced in the National Archive at Kew, where they were registered for copyright, at: Copyright Office: Entry Forms, etc. COPY 1/413/34
31: *Directors' Minutes*, Special General Meeting of 13th November 1893
32: *Inverness Courier*, 26th February 1895
33: *Highland News*, 7th January 1971
34: *Inverness Courier*, 8th March 1895

Chapter 15:
1: *Directors' Minutes*, 1st February and 1st March 1899
2: *Inverness Courier*, 3rd June 1898
3: *Directors' Minutes* (inserted amongst minutes for 1896), and advertisements in *Inverness Courier*, 4th and 7th August 1896
4: School Log Book, IRAA, C1
5: School prospecti, IRAA, D10 and subsequent items, and staff lists, IRAA, L4
6: Tabulated lists of staff in IRAA, L4
7: *Inverness Courier*, 8th September 1903
8: School Log Books, IRAA, C1 - 6
9: *Directors' Minutes*, 27th July 1896
10: *Directors' Minutes*, 7th September 1897
11: *Inverness Courier*, 9th March 1897
12: *Inverness Courier*, 18th May 1897
13: *Inverness Courier*, 16th July 1897
14: *Inverness Courier*, 6th January 1905
15: *Inverness Courier*, 28th December 1906 and 18th January 1907; lists of headmasters and Fraser Bursars were also published, all of which were later gathered together into P.J. Anderson's pamphlet *The Grammar School and Royal Academy of Inverness*, IRAA, L1, and Inverness Library reference room.
16: *Inverness Courier*, 21st December 1906 and 20th December 1907
17: *Inverness Courier*, 8th May 1903 (in the absence of the Directors' Minute Book covering the period)
18: *Inverness Courier*, 11th December 1903 (in the absence of the Directors' Minute Book covering the period)
19: *Directors' Minutes*, 10th September 1906 and *Inverness Courier*, 11th September 1906
20: *The History of the Inverness Royal Academy*, IRAA, F14 – this pamphlet is not a history of the Academy but an account of the Burgh School Board meeting of 15th November 1906 with a full account of Kenneth Macdonald's statement using the history of the Academy to try to establish it was wrong to transfer the Academy to the control of the Burgh School Board; see also *Inverness Courier*, 16th November 1906.

21: *Directors' Minutes*, 7th December 1906
22: *Inverness Courier*, 14th December 1906
23: *Directors' Minutes*, 9th January 1907
24: The various stages of the legal process are in NAS, HH33/209 and HH80/193; the Order is also in IRAA, F14, the *Directors' Minutes*, and the Burgh School Board's minutes book.
25: *Directors' Minutes*, 6th November 1907
26: For a full understanding of the educational debate that was taking place at this time see: Anderson: *Education and Opportunity in Victorian Scotland*, chap. 6, and Anderson: *Education and the Scottish People*, chap. 10.
27: For an account of the development of the Leaving Certificate in its early years, see for example: Scotland: *The History of Scottish Education*, vol. 2, chap. 5

Chapter 16:
1: *Burgh School Board Minutes*, 13th May 1910 *et seq.*
2: *Inverness Courier*, 14th January 1913, and *Inverness Academical*, vol. 2, no. 1, February 1913
3: *Burgh School Board Minutes*, 9th June 1909
4: W. J. Watson: *The Place Names of Ross and Cromarty* (Inverness: Northern Counties Printing and Publishing Co. Ltd., 1904)
5: W. J. Watson: *The History of the Celtic Place Names of Scotland* (original edition 1926; reprinted: Edinburgh: Birlinn, 1993)
6: See, for example, *The Scotsman*, 10th March 1948 and *Inverness Courier*, 12th March 1948
7: Reminiscences by Archie Dobbie, in *Historical Folio*, Document 21, issued by Inverness Royal Academy at the time of the Bicentenary, 1992
8: *Inverness Courier*, 7th January, 10th January, 17th January and 11th April 1913; *The Scotsman*, 8th and 9th January 1913
9: *Inverness Courier*, 14th June 1912
10: *Inverness Courier*, 30th June 1908
11: His Majesty's Inspector of Schools: reports on Inverness Royal Academy, September 1909, September 1910 and September 1911
12: Some of Barron's material has been used in the preparation of Chapters 1 to 3 of this book.
13: Reports appear, for example, in *The Scotsman*, 1st August 1912 and the *Inverness Courier*, 6th August 1912, with a photograph of the team in the *People's Journal (Northern Edition)*, 3rd August 1912; similar reports appear in 1913.
14: *Burgh School Board Minutes*, 11th June 1913
15: Edinburgh University Library, Baillie Project – the Baillie brothers were both theologians, and the collection also contains some school essays by John Baillie.
16: *Burgh School Board, Finance Committee*, 19th April 1915
17: *Inverness Courier*, 9th and 13th June 1916
18: *Inverness Academical*, vol. 2, no. 2, June 1916 – War Services Number
19: For an account of the war service of some former pupils, see: Bannerman: *Further Up Stephen's Brae*.
20: *Burgh School Board Meetings*, 21st December 1914 to 6th January 1915
21: *Burgh School Board, Finance Committee*, 8th February 1915
22: *Burgh School Board Minutes*, 23rd June 1915

Chapter 17:
1: For more extended comment on life in the school hostel, see: Bannerman: *Further Up Stephen's Brae*.

2: *Inverness-shire County Education Committee minutes*, 29th July 1919; CI/5/19/2/3/1 includes most of the surviving references and letters relating to the establishment and running of the Girl's Hostel in the early years.

3: *Inverness Courier*, 22nd October 1920

4: *Historical Folio*, Document 17, issued by Inverness Royal Academy at the time of the Bicentenary, 1992

5: *County Education Committee minutes*, 11th January 1939

6: An appreciation of Hugh Robson's career up to his retiral as a teacher in early 1934 is to be found in *Inverness Royal Academy Magazine*, March 1934

7: *Inverness Burgh Schools Management Committee meeting*, 1st October 1920

8: See *Inverness Courier*, 4th December 1925, and *Inverness Citizen*, 3rd December 1925, for reports of the opening ceremony.

9: School Log Book, 17th September 1938

10: *Inverness Courier*, 6th November 1923; *Inverness Citizen*, 8th November 1923

11: *County Education Committee minutes*, November 1923 and January 1924

12: *Inverness Royal Academy Magazine*, June 1931

13: An appreciation of Andrew Harrow Watson appears in *Inverness Royal Academy Magazine*, June 1935.

14: *People's Journal*, 9th July 1938

15: For comments and anecdotes on many of these staff, see Bannerman: *Further Up Stephen's Brae.*

16: *County Education Committee minutes*, February/March 1938

17: NAS, ED23/231, ED23/371, ED23/606 and ED23/2253/3 cover the various stages in the preparation of the revised scheme.

18: *Inverness Courier*, 2nd and 6th October 1931

19: *Inverness County Council Education Committee minutes*, 3rd and 4th May 1932, and *Inverness Courier*, 13th May 1932

20: Papers on the history and activities of the Howden Trust can be found in IRAA, E9 and E10; HCA, CI/3/38/2/10, CI/5/8/3/1 and CI/5/19/2/3/4, and in NAS, ED23/1028 and ED23/1029.

21: *Inverness Courier*, 6th January 1931

22: HCA, CI/5/19/2/3/9 contains some of the correspondence on the process of matriculation of the Coat of Arms.

23: References not specifically noted in this and later sections are gleaned from issues of the School Log Books and the *Inverness Royal Academy Magazine*, with some from relevant issues of the *Inverness Courier*. See also, for more extended comment on school life in the 1920's and 1930's: Bannerman: *Further Up Stephen's Brae*

24: Ross, Father Anthony: *The Root of the Matter* (Edinburgh: Mainstream, 1989)

25: Located in 2008 at: igcdads memoirs.blogspot.com; part 1, chap. 9, covers his time at the Academy

26: See: Lt. Col. Stewart Roddie: *Peace Patrol* (London: Christophers, 1932)

27: *Inverness Courier*, 19th December 1930

28: Reports of the visit are printed in *Inverness Royal Academy Magazine*, June 1931.

29: A report of the 1934 camp is printed in *Inverness Royal Academy Magazine*, December 1934.

30: *Inverness Royal Academy Magazine*, December 1933 and December 1934, contain reports of the voyages.

31: *Inverness Courier*, 23rd December 1924

32: *Glasgow Herald*, 19th May 1938

33: *Inverness Royal Academy School Magazine*, July 1929

34: Lists of evacuees admitted to the Academy are to be found in IRAA, B22 and B23.

35: School Log Book, 11th October 1941
36: Some information on this is available in IRAA, F19b.
37: *Inverness Royal Academy Memorial Magazine*, 1947

Chapter 18:

References not specifically identified are mainly taken from the relevant volume of the School Log Book and from editions of the school magazine, starting with the Memorial Magazine in the summer of 1947.

1: *Inverness Courier*, 20th September 1957 and *Highland News*, 21st September 1957
2: For a more light-hearted look at some other aspects of life in the Academy at this period, see: Bannerman: *Further Up Stephen's Brae.*
3: *Inverness Courier*, 26th November 1954, and the 1954 edition of the school magazine
4: Inverness County Council Education Committee, minutes of 7th to 9th June 1955, and *Inverness Courier*, 10th June 1955
5: Inverness County Council Education Committee, minutes of 3rd to 5th May 1948, and *Inverness Courier*, 7th May 1948
6: Inverness County Council Education Committee, minutes of 11th to 13th May 1952 *et seq.*
7: *Inverness Courier*, 23rd September 1955
8: Inverness County Council Education Committee, minutes of 13th to 15th May 1957
9: Education (Scotland) Acts, 1939 to 1956: County of Inverness: Inverness Royal Academy Trust Scheme, 1960
10: For some of the sports highlights, see Bannerman: *op. cit.*
11: HCA D144/1
12: Inverness County Council Education Committee, minutes of 4th to 7th July and 5th to 8th December 1966
13: *Inverness Courier*, 26th January 1971 et seq., and *Highland News*, 28th January 1971
14: Highland Regional Council Education Committee, minutes of 8th December 1976
15: Inverness County Council Education Committee, minutes of 8th to 11th October 1973

Chapter 19:

1: *Highland News*, 24th March 1977
2: HCA, CI/3/38/1/24: Proposed new Secondary School at Culduthel
3: Full details of the construction are to be found in *Building*, 23rd June 1978, and in an offprint from that source in the school archive.
4: *Inverness Courier*, 21st April 1978, and other newspapers
5: HRC Education Committee meeting, 22nd July 1981, the full Highland Regional Council meeting, 10th September 1981, and subsequent meetings
6: HRC Education Committee meeting, 20th September 1978
7: *Highland News,* 15th and 22nd December 1977 and *Inverness Courier*, 23rd December 1977 and 3rd February 1978
8: HRC Education Committee meeting, 8th February 1978, and *Inverness Courier*, 10th February 1978
9: HRC Education Committee meeting, 1st November 1978
10: Material related to the bicentenary is to be found in IRAA M18 and elsewhere.
11: *Inverness Courier*, 25th June 1993

Appendices

Appendix 1: Masters and Doctors of the Grammar School
(from after the Reformation)

The list of masters is based on the original list in P. J. Anderson: *The Grammar School and Royal Academy of Inverness* (1907), updated and corrected with material located up to December 2010. In P. J. Anderson's own copy of the booklet in Aberdeen University Library there are various amendments and some correspondence, which leave some unresolved questions especially about John Cuthbert, Alexander Ros(e) and George Dunbar.

The list of doctors or ushers is based on an anonymous typewritten list in the Inverness Royal Academy archive, again updated with material located up to December 2010.

In both lists there are various gaps, and some of the material is doubtful. All references to King's College and Marischal College are to the ones in Aberdeen. References quoted do not necessarily provide all the stated information. For the definition of certain words, e.g. dispute, stallanger, see the text in chapters 1 and 2.

MASTERS OR RECTORS:

c. **1562**   Master Thomas Heweson/Howieson: appointed a Burgh clerk, 25th June 1561; still in overall control of the school in 1570 *[Records of Inverness, vol. 1, p. 92]*

c. **1564/65**   Master Martyne Logie: admitted stallanger, 4th October 1564; may only have been doctor, although record says master *[Records of Inverness, vol. 1, p. 116]*

c. **1617**   William Ross *[Records of Inverness, vol. 1, p. 151]*

c. **1636**   John Duff: M.A., King's College, 1624; Master of Elgin Grammar School, 1629-1633 *[Minutes of Synod of Moray, 26th April and 3rd October, 1636]*

1649   Robert Forbes: possibly M.A., King's College, 1649; appointed after trial; resigns 1650 *[Records of Inverness, vol. 2, pp. 201 and 203]*

1650   Alexander Dunbar: possibly M.A., King's College, 1649 or 1650 (two people of the same name appear); appointed as he was found to be qualified; resigns probably late 1653; possibly then minister of Inveraven (Speyside) and then Delting (Shetland) (if M.A., 1649), or alternatively minister of Kinloss (if M.A., 1650) *[Records of Inverness, vol. 2, pp. 204 and 208, and Fasti Ecclesiæ Scoticanæ, vol. 6, p. 344]*

1654   Alexander Fraser: son of Alexander Fraser, litster *[dyer]*: to take over until a more qualified person is available; by 1660 confirmed in post; M.A., Marischal College, 1657 (a class-fellow of Gilbert Burnet, Bishop of Salisbury, and Professor James Gregory, the astronomer); drowned Inverness harbour,

August 1661 *[Records of Inverness, vol. 2, p. 208* and *Wardlaw Manuscripts, p. 442]*

c. 1662/63 William Cumming: possibly from Morayshire and M.A., King's College, 1661; resigns Martinmas 1663; may have become minister at Dores and then Halkirk (Caithness) *[Records of Inverness, vol. 2, pp. 214 and 216, and Fasti Ecclesiæ Scoticanæ, vol. 6, p. 451]*

1663 James Stewart/Stuart: native of Strathdon; M.A., King's College, 1663; won the dispute to be appointed; resigned autumn 1669; ordained minister of Inveraven (Speyside), 1669, moving to Fordyce (Banff) by 1681 *[Records of Inverness, vol. 2, pp. 217 and 237, and Fasti Ecclesiæ Scoticanæ, vol. 6, p. 344]*

1669 John Cuthbert: native of Inverness; M.A., King's College, 1669; chosen from three candidates; resigned or forced to resign following preaching without authority at Daviot (Strathnairn) *c.* August 1673 *[Records of Inverness, vol. 2, pp. 237 and 256, and Minutes of the Presbytery of Elgin, 19th February 1673]*

1673 Alexander Rose/Ros: son of David Rose/Ros of Earlsmill/Earlfinlay, Morayshire; M.A., King's College, 1667 or 1673; presumably resigned 1680, and then ordained minister of Botarie (Strathbogie*) [Fasti Ecclesiæ Scoticanæ, vol. 6, p. 303]*

1680 George Dunbar: native of Ross-shire; M.A., King's College, 1671 or 1673; signs Test Act in 1681; resigned early 1682 *[Records of Inverness, vol. 2, p. 303, and Inverness and Dingwall Presbytery Records, p. 332]*

1682 John Munro: native of Inverness-shire; M.A., Marischal College, 1672; previously schoolmaster at Kiltarlity; resigned May 1685 *[Records of Inverness, vol. 2, pp. 303, 320 and 325]*

1685 Alexander Sutherland: native of Inverness-shire; M.A., King's College, 1681; replaced John Munro, and appointed with approval of Bishop of Moray; resigned 1690 *[Records of Inverness, vol. 2, pp. 330 and 216]*

1690 Thomas Jaffrey: native of Aberdeenshire; M.A., King's College, 1679; previously Master of Elgin Grammar School; from March 1691 assisted minister notwithstanding a previous act against schoolmasters preaching; died in late 1706/early 1707

1707 Robert Thomson: synod bursar 1705-1709; temporary until dispute in 1708; resigned 1709 to continue his studies; ordained minister of Clyne (Sutherland), 1713, and of Kirkhill, 1716 *[Fasti Ecclesiæ Scoticanæ, vol. 7, p. 80]*

1709 Alexander Matthew: replaced Robert Thomson; resigned after poor report

1709 John Laing: replaced Alexander Matthew; possibly M.A., King's College, 1693; previously doctor of the Grammar School of the Canongate (Edinburgh); resigned on health and cost of living grounds 1712; contributor to Monteith's *Theater of Mortality*, 1713 edition, p. 202

1712 Alexander McKenzie: possible temporary appointment for three months

1712 James Mackenzie: previously schoolmaster at Ferintosh (Ross-shire); may never have signed Confession of Faith; resigned Whitsun 1718

1718 George Steele: M.A., Marischal College, 1715; Chaplain to the Laird of Lethen; resigned 1723 so that he could travel abroad for his further instruction

1723 David Fraser: native of Inverness; first bursar at King's College, 1718; M.A., 1722; previously doctor in the school; seems to have resigned 1727

1727 Thomas Macpherson: native of Inverness; first bursar at King's College, 1721; M.A., 1725; previously doctor in the school; died probably early 1750

1750 Alexander Ferguson: native of Insch; M.A., King's College, 1738; previously schoolmaster at Prestonpans; imprisoned 1755 for defamatory remarks and immorality; dismissed

1755 Hector Fraser: son of Alexander Fraser, Inverness; Fraser Arts bursar  at Marischal College, 1728; M.A., 1732; Fraser Divinity bursar and librarian at King's College, 1740; left for London and became master of an academy at Bethnal Green (now in east end of London); first Inverness Grammar School master to be styled 'Rector'; retires on a pension of £20 stg., April 1777; died 1786; grave in Chapel Yard, Inverness; founded a bursary in Inverness Grammar School for sons of burgesses of the name of Fraser; donated school bell; bust sculpted by Richard Westmacott is still in the school

1777 Alexander Simpson: native of Aberdeen; M.A., King's College, 1771; previously usher in school; resigned 1790; died in London, 16th July 1814

1791 Ebenezer Young: previously Rector of the Grammar School, Queensferry; in 1792 became classics master in the Royal Academy until his death in 1808; grave in Chapel Yard in Inverness

DOCTORS OR USHERS:
1566 Sir Patre [Patrick] Anderson: previously chaplain of St Michael's Chapel in the Parish Church, Inverness; resigned perhaps in 1570 *[Records of Inverness, vol. 1, pp. 131-132]*

1571 Andrew/Andro McPhail: minister (Barron suggests he was not accepted by the Town Council, but this may be a misreading of the original text) *[Records of Inverness, vol. 1, p. 198]*

1671 John Munro: may only have been in post for a year; may be same person as the schoolmaster from 1682

1713 Kenneth Tuath: resigned 1715; left Inverness in about June 1715

1715 Alexander McPhail: son of Alexander McPhail; M.A., Marischal College, 1714; resigns 1717

1718 William MacKay: but resigns later that year, and may have gone to Lothian, as Inverness Synod recommend a William McKay to Lothian Synod in 1719; possibly a Gaelic speaker

1719 William Porteous: resigns in the same year

1721 ..... Maclean resigns

1721 David Fraser: native of Inverness; first bursar at King's College, 1718; M.A., 1722; becomes master 1723

1723 Alexander McBean: son of Gilles McBean, glover and burgess, and later Deacon Convenor; resigns 1725

1725 Thomas MacPherson: native of Inverness; first bursar at King's College, 1721; M.A., 1725; becomes master 1727

1728 ..... Paterson

1729 Robert Niddrie/Neddry (sub-doctor): from Elgin; M.A., King's College, 1720; schoolmaster at Alves 1719-1720; Presbytery of Elgin seek to appoint him 1728; resigns 1736

1736 Hector McPhail: native of Inverness; first bursar, King's College, 1733; M.A., 1737; "student of philosophy"; resigns 1748; minister of Resolis, 1748-1774

1748 David Denoon: native of Inverness; Town bursar in 1746; M.A., King's College, 1748; resigned 1752; minister Killearnan, 1758-1792; bequeathed £100 for maintenance of a bursar at Inverness Academy

1752 George Watson: free scholar 1744; probably second doctor at this point; son of James Watson, tailor; resigned 1753 to continue his studies *[see 1754]*

1752 John Boyd: first usher, but salaried from 1753 only (but backdated); resigned without notice, probably 1754

1754 George Watson: reappointed; M.A., Marischal College, 1755; resigns 1756; minister Kiltearn, 1770-1775, Inverness (third charge), 1775-1778, Inverness (second charge) 1778-1798

[no information on Hector Fraser's ushers until 1777]

before 1777 Alexander Simpson; becomes Rector 1777

[it seems likely that there was no usher/doctor for the remaining period of the Grammar School, but rather separate teachers of the different schools, loosely linked together]

Appendix 2: Rectors of Inverness Royal Academy

The early part of this material is based on information in part 1 of *The Grammar School and Royal Academy of Inverness*, by P. J. Anderson, published in 1907, but these entries have been extended and corrected where other information has come to light. Entries for Rectors in post since 1906 have been compiled from many sources, including copies of the school magazine, press cuttings and references from published books (many of which are indicated in the text below). The Royal Academy archive maintains files on each of the Rectors, with material such as press cuttings, photocopies of key documents, and photographs (where available).

This list was first published by the school as a pamphlet in 1994, with a revised reprint in 1999. This appendix incorporates many amendments and additions to the 1999 edition. Further information and corrections are always welcome.

1. 1792 - 1793 James Weir

From Craignethan, near Lanark. Student at Edinburgh University, 1780-1783. Rector, Dundee Academy (1786-1792). Appointed April 1792, to allow for preparations for opening; and much of his first session (till Christmas 1792) was spent purchasing apparatus in London and elsewhere. Employed to teach natural and civil History, Natural Philosophy, Chemistry, Astronomy. Had severe epilepsy in summer 1793: advised in July 1793 to take voyage from Leith to London and then London to Inverness. However he only went to Edinburgh from where he went to Lanarkshire. Dismissed December 1793 (ill health), as he had not attended since July and Directors thought it unlikely he would be fit to return. Later in London in conjunction with the Board of Longitude he conducted experiments on artificial horizons to assist in determining longitude at sea. Died 1797.

2. 1794 - 1803 Dr John McOmie

Also spellings of McOmie or M'Comie. Born in Perth. Previously assistant Rector, Perth Academy. Took up appointment July 1794. Taught Geography and Drawing, also Natural Philosophy and Chemistry. LL.D., Marischal College, 1795. Censured for his conduct, and then devoted more time to his work. Resigned through ill health, 1803, and returned to Perth. Became Secretary, Literary and Antiquarian Society of Perth, and gave private instruction in Drawing and Geography. Died in October 1819, aged 63. Obituaries in *Inverness Courier*, 7 October 1819 and *Scots Magazine*, October 1819.

3. 1803 - 1805 Alexander MacGregor

From Perth. Appears to have married and had child in Renfrewshire around 1789. Taught at Grammar School in Alness prior to 1792. Applied for job at Dundee Academy but turned it down, 1792. Appointed Mathematics master of Inverness Royal Academy 1793, becoming Rector ten years later. Estranged from his wife by 1801 when settlement agreed. Died at Inverness, 24 March 1805, aged 35, and apparently in debt. Appreciation in *Scots Magazine*, April 1805.

4. 1805 - 1811 Alexander Nimmo

Born probably in Cupar, Fife, in 1783 but moved to Kirkcaldy where his father became a shopkeeper. Gained bursary to St Andrew's University in 1796, attending for two years, followed by two years at Edinburgh University. A tutor in Edinburgh, then taught at Fortrose Academy (Mathematics) from early 1802. Appointed to Academy in

autumn 1805 by the Professors of Latin, Logic, Natural Philosophy and Chemistry at Edinburgh University. Taught Mathematics, Geography and Natural Philosophy. During summer of 1806 he surveyed the Highland county boundaries, and was paid £150 by the Government; boundaries used in Aaron Arrowsmith's map of Scotland (published 1807); his diary kept during his surveying was published by the Royal Irish Academy (2011). In 1808 or 1809 he surveyed the route for a road from Kylerhea to Killin in Perthshire, although the road was never built. Resigned 1811 after his appointment as assistant engineer to Telford, and then worked in Ireland as a surveyor and engineer. Died in Dublin in 1832. See *Memoir* by Arrowsmith in *Reports of the Commissioners for making Roads and building Bridges in the Highlands of Scotland* (1809). Biography: Wilkins, Noël P.: *Alexander Nimmo, Master Engineer 1783-1832* (2009). See also *New Ways through the Glens* (Haldane), p. 63, and *Reminiscences of my Life in the Highlands, vol. 1* (Mitchell), p. 44 – but wrong reason is given for resigning as Rector. Some early biographies are misleading or wrong.

5. 1811 - 1839 Matthew Adam
Born in Dailly, Ayrshire, 20th February 1780. M.A. Glasgow 1808. Taught in school of his own in Glasgow, 1808-1811. Appointed from August 1811. In dispute with Directors in 1812 concerning the emoluments due to his situation, his possible dismissal and compensation for loss of situation: Court of Session decided in favour of life tenure in 1815 (see *Inverness Journal*, 14 July 1815). Taught mathematics and geography: see class registers in IRAA. In 1823 spent three periods at sea making experiments on board *HMS Cherokee*, on the frigate *Seringapatam* and the sloop of war *Clio*, by directions of the Admiralty, perhaps with permission of the Chairman of the Directors (see *Inverness Courier*): hence he did not conduct his Geography class in the autumn that year. Took weather readings, and some of his figures were used by Lauder (1830) in the book *Great Floods of 1829*. Pensioned on £60 per annum in 1839, following alleged misconduct; taught in Glasgow 1840-1850; died at Ayr, 10 December 1853. For comments see *Inverness before Railways* (I. Anderson), p. 52, and *My Early Days* (Kennedy), p. 75.

6. 1839 - 1845 David Gray
Native of Kirkcaldy. M.A., Edinburgh, 1829; Dollar Academy (Mathematics), 1833; Professor of Mathematics, University of New Brunswick, 1837. Selected by Lords Cockburn and Moncreiff. Taught Mathematics and Geography. Appointed Professor of Natural Philosophy, Marischal College, Aberdeen, 1845; married 5th January 1842, and had at least one child; died 10 February 1856, aged 45 (see *Inverness Courier*, 14 February 1856).

7. 1845 - 1847 Peter Wilson
Probably from Roxburghshire; studied at St Andrew's College and Glagow. Previously Professor of Natural Philosophy at Andersonian University, Glasgow (now University of Strathclyde). Also selected by Lords Cockburn and Moncrieff. Appointed Rector in April 1845. Taught Mathematics and Geography. Resigned 1847 on taking up appointment in Glasgow, then became Rector of Tain Academy. Died August 1854, aged 48 (see *Inverness Courier*, 17 August 1854).

8. 1847 - 1851 James Steele
L.R.C.S.Ed., 1839. From Bell's Institution, Inverness. Appointed in summer 1847 by Directors as he was known to them. Afterwards practised medicine in Wishaw. See comments in *Inverness before Railways* (I. Anderson), pp. 52-54.

9. 1851 - 1853 Robert Harper
From Yorkshire. B.A.(Cantab.), 1850: 15th Wrangler (= 1st class Mathematics).
Appointed August 1851. Became Second Master, Dudley Grammar School, 1853;
Headmaster, Dudley Grammar School, 1854-1878; retired on pension of £90, Feb
1878. Took with him to Dudley his colleague John Scott Hoppert, Second Master at
Dudley, 1854-1895. Was later Rev. Robert Harper, and became Rector of Great
Tubney, Berkshire. Died 1898, aged 74. See *Dudley Herald*, 28 September 1878.

10. 1853 - 1862 Peter Scott

Classics Master at Inverness Royal Academy since 1824. Acted as
MC of the Academy Ball over many years. Suggested as Rector in
1851 but not appointed then. Appointed January 1853; resigned 1862
on a pension, through poor health. Died 31 December 1863, but
pension paid until May 1864; buried in Greyfriars Cemetery, Inverness.
Regarded as a very good teacher. For other comments see *My Early
Days* (Kennedy), pp. 75-77, notes by Joseph Cook and a feature in
Inverness Courier "Old Inverness" series, 10 December 1991.

11. 1863 - 1866 George Robertson
From Grange House School, Edinburgh. Appointed from April 1863. Became
Headmaster, Edgbaston Proprietary School, Birmingham, and Warrender Park
School, Edinburgh. LL.D., Glasgow,1874. Translated part of Theodor Mommsen's
Römische Geschichte (London, 1858), under the title *The Earliest Inhabitants of
Italy*; wrote *Compendium of Latin Syntax*, (Edinburgh, 1861). See *Inverness Courier*,
4 March 1910 for a letter from P. J. Anderson looking for his photograph.

12. 1866 - 1888 William Eadie
M.A. Edinburgh, 1861. Mathematics Master at Inverness Royal Academy from 1861;
appointed Rector August 1866; retired 1888. See *Academical,* Christmas 1911, p. 21,
for comments. Photograph mentioned in letter of 1932 cannot now be traced.

13. 1888 - 1894 George Taylor Bruce

Born 1857 in Aberdeen; educated at New and Old Grammar Schools;
M.A. Aberdeen, April 1880. Taught Classics in Enfield; English at
Crieff Academy; then Classics and senior English at Robert Gordon's
College, Aberdeen. Chosen from nearly 100 candidates; started
February 1888. At time of Academy centenary proposed introduction
of school badge. Resigned 1894, after disagreement with Directors.
Then for 10 years Principal, New Glenmoriston College (Inverness).
Later farmed in Canada. Died 1947. See *Academical* for March 1892
and School Report for 1893/94 in *Academical*, June 1894.

14. 1894 - 1909 William John Watson

Born Kindace, Easter Ross, 1865. Native Gaelic speaker. Educated
at local school and Grammar School of Old Aberdeen; scholarship to
King's College, Aberdeen; M.A. 1st class Hons. Classics (Aberdeen)
and Gold Medal for best Latin scholar of the session, 1886;
Exhibitioner, Merton College, Oxford; B.A.(Oxon.) Litterae
Humaniores (1st class Honours), 1893; with "blue" for shot put.
Previously taught at Kelvinside Academy, Glasgow, 1891-1894.
Appointed August 1894. Sought to introduce Gaelic as an
examinable subject in the Leaving Certificate. Introduced annual
sports day in 1895. Rector, Royal High School, Edinburgh, 1910-

1914. Became leading scholar on Celtic Studies, and Professor of Celtic, Edinburgh University, 1914-1938. LL.D. (Aberdeen), 1910. His major work was *The History of the Celtic Place-Names of Scotland* (1926), but also edited anthologies of prose (*Rosg Gàidhlig*, 1915) and verse (*Bàrdachd Ghàidhlig*, 1918) and was general editor for the series *Leabhraichean Sgoile Gàidhlig* (c. 1920-1923). Founded the Scottish Gaelic Texts Society. Honorary Secretary of the Gaelic Society of Inverness for 44 years; at various times Secretary and President of Inverness Field Club. Died 9 March 1948; buried Tomnahurich Cemetery, Inverness, as he regarded Inverness as his "spiritual home".

15. 1909 - 1910 Gilbert Watson

Born November(?) 1882, attended Royal High School (Edinburgh); M.A. (Edinburgh); from 1904 at Lincoln College, Oxford, becoming Senior Scholar; B.A. (Oxon.). In 1908 became assistant in Humanities Department of Edinburgh University. Appointed from 31 August 1909; resigned as of 2 December 1910. Junior Inspector of Schools, 1910-1919; H.M. Inspector of Schools, 1919-1942; Chief Inspector of Schools (Southern Division), 1942-1945; then Senior Chief Inspector of Schools, 1945-1948. Retired 1948, when he wrote extensively. Spent his final years in Edinburgh; acknowledgement of 100th birthday greetings is in Royal Academy archive; died 5 October 1987 shortly before his 105th birthday. See Lincoln College Record (1985(?)) and *School Inspection in Scotland, 1840-1966* (T. Bone).

16. 1910 - 1920 George A. Morrison

M.A. 1st class Hons, Classics; Simpson and Liddel Prizeman; LL.D.., F.E.I.S. Was Senior Classics Master, Robert Gordon's College, Aberdeen. Appointed as from 12 December 1910. Photograph as insert to *Academical*, Autumn 1911. Shown in undated Staff photo in 1910's. Resigned as of 30 June 1920. Became Headmaster, Robert Gordon's College, Aberdeen. Was a President of the Educational Institute of Scotland. Accomplished musician, giving lecture-recitals to Debating Society during First World War – either pianist or violinist or both (Schubert & Purcell). Retired 1934; was M.P. for Scottish Universities, 1934-1945 died Lossiemouth, September 1956, aged 86; obituary in school magazine, 1957.

17. 1920 - 1944 Wm. Crampton Smith

Born Sunderland 1879; B.Sc. Durham, winning Charles Mather Scholarship in Mathematics; distinction in Mathematics and Physics (London). First post in Peterhead; then Principal Teacher of Mathematics and Science, Keith Grammar School, soon becoming second master; came to Inverness Royal Academy in 1915 as Second Master and Principal Teacher of Mathematics; also for some time head of Science Department. Appointed Rector from 1 September 1920; retired on 28 January 1944. Awarded O.B.E. in 1938. President of Educational Institute of Scotland, 1939 and 1940; became F.E.I.S. Member of Secretary of State's Advisory Council on Education from 1943 to 1946. Founding Scoutmaster of 3rd Inverness (Crown) Boy Scout Troop from 1916-1919. See *Memorial Magazine* 1947 (with photograph). Died 1 December 1949, aged 70.

18. 1944 - 1962 Donald John Macdonald

Born 9 June 1900. From Lochcarron (Ross-shire). Native Gaelic speaker. Educated

Lochcarron School (to 1915), Dingwall Academy (1915-1918); attached to a junior Battalion, Gordon Highlanders, 1918; M.A.(Hons) (Aberdeen), English Language and Literature, 1923; outstanding student at Training College, winning MacGregor Prize for teaching, 1924. President, Aberdeen University Celtic Society, 1923-1924. Assistant teacher of English from 2 September 1924, becoming head of department, 25 April 1929; became Second Master, 25 August 1942; then Rector from 31 January 1944. Introduced prefects to School. Retired on 12 January 1962. J.P.; Honorary LL.D., 1957; F.E.I.S., 1960. Member of the Rotary Club of Inverness; member of Culloden Battlefield Committee of the National Trust for Scotland; member and Chairman of Inverness Hospitals (later Northern Hospital) Board of Management, 1943-1971. Elder of West Church of Scotland, Inverness, from 1946. Chief of the Gaelic Society of Inverness, 1964. President of Inverness Battalion of the Boys' Brigade for two years. Died 14 June 1993. See *Magazine* 1947 for photo (as younger man) and *Magazine* 1958 and 1962 for later photograph and more details.

19. 1962 - 1971 William S. Macdonald

Born in Caithness, but soon his family moved to the South of Scotland. M.A. (1st class Honours) French and German, Edinburgh; B.A. (1st class Honours) History, London; B.Ed. Played football for Queen's Park; captain, Scottish Amateur International Team, 1939. During Second World War became Commander of an antisubmarine corvette; senior interpreter of U-boat survivors; mentioned in despatches and decorated M.B.E., D.S.C. Started teaching at Govan High School before Second World War. After War became Principal Teacher of Modern Languages, Mortlach Secondary School, Dufftown. Then to Coatbridge until 1952. Rector of Campbeltown Grammar School, 1952-1961. Appointed from 15 January 1962; retired 27 August 1971 to Caithness. Was an elder of the Crown Church, Inverness, and for some years President of Inverness Battalion of the Boys' Brigade. After retiral trained for Ministry at Trinity College, Glasgow. Became Regional Councillor for John O' Groats ward, 1974; was Vice-Chairman of Highand Regional Council Education Committee; visited Brussels on European Economic Community business. See *Magazine* 1971 for photographs and more details. Died 21 January 1978 in Caithness, aged 66. Obituary in *Inverness Courier*, 24 January 1978.

20. 1971 - 1993 Ian R. Fraser

Born Carmyle, near Glasgow. Educated Aberdeen Grammar School; M.A. (Hons.) Geography, Aberdeen University, 1953; M.Ed. (1955); prizewinner in Geography, Education and Psychology; winner of MacGregor Prize for Teaching at Aberdeen Training College. Taught at Stirling High School; Head of Geography, Elgin Academy (1960-1966); Rector, Waid Academy, Anstruther, 1966-1971; appointed Rector 6 September 1971. President, Headteachers' Association of Scotland, 1977-1978; Vice-Chairman, Scottish Consultative Council on the Curriculum, 1987-1991; O.B.E. for services to Education, 1989. Retired 15 August 1993.

21. 1993 - 2010 John Considine
Took up appointment on 16 August 1993.

22. 2010 -   Alastair McKinlay

Royal Warrant
for a
Charter
incorporating
The Directors of the Academy of Inverness

George R.

Our Sovereign Lord considering, That an humble petition has been presented to his Majesty by and on behalf of William Mackintosh Esq; Provost of the burgh of Inverness, John Mackintosh Esq; William Inglis Esq; Alexander Mackintosh Esq; and James Clark Esq; Bailies, and James Shaw Esq; Dean of Guild of the said burgh of Inverness; of Simon Fraser of Farraline Esq; his Majesty's Sheriff-depute of the county of Inverness; and of Lachlan Macgillivray Esq; William Mackintosh Esq; Thomas Fraser Esq; Alexander Fraser Esq; and Angus Mackintosh Esq; being a committee chosen by the Commissioners of Supply of the county of Inverness for superintending the management and direction of the affairs of the Academy therein after mentioned; and also of John Baillie of Dunean Esq; Alexander Baillie of Dochfour Esq; James Smith Baillie younger of Dochfour Esq; James Baillie of Bedford Square in the county of Middlesex Esq; Evan Baillie of the city of Bristol Esq; Alexander Chisholm of Chisholm Esq; the Right Reverend Seignelly Cuthbert, late Bishop of Rhodez in the Kingdom of France, Lewis Cuthbert of Castlehill Esq; Duncan Davidson of Tulloch Esq; Arthur Forbes of Culloden Esq; the Honourable Archibald Fraser of Lovat, Simon Fraser of Nesscastle Esq; James Fraser of Culduthel Esq; Hugh Fraser of the island of Jamaica Esq; the Right Honourable Lord William Gordon, James Grant of Redcastle Esq; Charles Grant, late of Bengal Esq; Colin Macdonald of Boisdale Esq; John Lachlan Macgillivray of Dumnaglass Esq; Æneas Mackintosh of Mackintosh Esq; Phineas Mackintosh of Drummond Esq; Francis Humberstone Mackenzie of Seaforth Esq; Colonel Norman Macleod of Macleod, Sir John Macpherson Baronet, Sir Hector Munro of Novar, Knight of the most Honourable order of the Bath, John Ogilvie of Argyle Street in the county of Middlesex Esq; John Wedderburn of Leadenhall Street, London Esq; James Wedderburn of the island of Jamaica Esq; and of the Reverend the Moderator and Ministers of the Presbytery of Inverness, being subscribers of fifty pounds and upwards towards defraying the expence of erecting, building and endowing the said Academy; SETTING FORTH, That the petitioners, and sundry other persons did, in the year One thousand seven hundred and eighty-eight, form themselves into a Society for the purpose of founding and endowing an Academy for the instruction of youth within his Majesty's royal burgh of Inverness: That they had raised considerable sums of money by voluntary subscription, and had already in part applied these sums agreeable to the plan of their institution, particularly in purchasing a convenient area within the said burgh of Inverness, and in erecting buildings thereon for the accommodation of the different classes proposed to be taught at the Academy, the property of which area and buildings stands now vested in the Magistrates and Town-council of Inverness, as trustees for the petitioners and other members of the society: That the petitioners had proposed certain regulations set forth in the petition for the better conducting the Academy: That they humbly conceived the institution would be highly beneficial, not only to the Highlands and Islands of Scotland, but to the nation at large: And that they were advised, that if they and their successors were formed and erected into a body corporate, so as to be enabled to hold property, and to manage the funds of the Academy in a regular manner, their exertions would be rendered still more extensive and beneficial to the public: AND THEREFORE PRAYING, That his Majesty would be graciously pleased to grant his Royal charter or letters-patent, under the Seal appointed by the treaty of Union to be kept and used in Scotland, in place of the Great Seal formerly used there, NOMINATING, CONSTITUTING, and APPOINTING, the Provost, four Bailies, and Dean of Guild, of the burgh of Inverness for the time being, the Moderator of the Presbytery of Inverness for the time being, and five other persons, to be from time to time annually elected by the Commissioners of Supply of the county of Inverness, in manner after mentioned, together with such other person or persons as already have, or who hereafter shall or may subscribe and pay to the extent of fifty pounds of lawful money of Great Britain, for the purposes of the said institution, and the heirs-male of lawful age, of such person or persons as shall subscribe and pay to the extent of one hundred pounds of like lawful money, or upwards, agreeable to the rules of the Society, INTO ONE BODY POLITIC AND CORPORATE, by the name and title of THE MANAGERS AND DIRECTORS OF THE ACADEMY OF INVERNESS, and under the regulations set forth in the said petition: AND HIS MAJESTY being satisfied, that the design of the petitioners, and of the other persons associated with them, is laudable, and deserves encouragement, DOES THEREFORE ORDAIN a charter or letters-patent to be passed and expede under the Seal appointed by the treaty of Union to be kept and used in Scotland in place of the Great Seal formerly used there, CONSTITUTING, ERECTING and INCORPORATING, as HIS MAJESTY, by his Royal prerogative, and of his special grace, does hereby, for himself and his Royal successors, CONSTITUTE, ERECT and INCORPORATE the Provost, four Bailies and Dean of Guild of the burgh of Inverness for the time being, the Sheriff-depute of the county of Inverness for the time being, the Moderator of the Presbytery of Inverness for the time being, and five other persons to be from time to time annually elected by the Commissioners of Supply of the County of Inverness, in manner after mentioned, together with such other person or persons as already have, or who hereafter shall or may subscribe and pay to the extent of fifty pounds of lawful money of Great Britain for the purpose of the said institution, and the heirs-male of lawful age of such other person or persons as shall subscribe and pay to the extent of one hundred pounds of like lawful money, or upwards, agreeable to the rules of the Society, INTO ONE BODY POLITIC AND CORPORATE, or legal incorporation, by the name and title of THE MANAGERS AND DIRECTORS OF THE ACADEMY OF INVERNESS; and as such, and by such name, to have perpetual endurance and succession, and to be able and capable in law to purchase, take, hold and enjoy lands, tenements and hereditaments, not exceeding one thousand pounds of lawful money of yearly rent, and also to take, hold and enjoy goods, chattles, and other personal property, and to receive donations and legacies for the uses and purposes of the Academy, and to lend out and employ the money so acquired or to be acquired and received: And by the name and title aforesaid, to sue, plead, defend and answer, and to be sued, impleaded, defended and answered, in all or any of his Majesty's courts of judicature: And to appoint treasurers, cashiers, factors, stewards, and other necessary officers, to act for them: And to have and use a common seal, and the same to change from time to time as to the said Incorporation shall seem expedient: And otherwise, and in all other things, to act and do, and proceed in such manner as the law permits, and is usual in the case of persons incorporated, and with all the privileges incident to such Incorporations: AND FURTHER APPROVING, as his Majesty hereby APPROVES, of the following REGULATIONS made by the said Society; THAT IS TO SAY, *First,* That the directors of the Academy shall consist of the Provost, the four Bailies and Dean of

Guild of the burgh of Inverness for the time being, the Sheriff-depute of the County of Inverness for the time being, the Moderator of the Presbytery of Inverness for the time being, together with five persons, to be annually chosen by the Commissioners of Supply of the county of Inverness, at their general annual meeting on the thirtieth day of April, or such other day as they shall by law be appointed to meet for the purpose of assessing and levying the land-tax; *2dly,* That each person who already has, or hereafter should or may subscribe and pay to the extent of fifty pounds of lawful money of Great Britain for the purposes of the institution, shall be a director during his natural life, and that each and every person or persons who shall or may subscribe and pay to the extent of one hundred pounds of like lawful money, or upwards, and their heirs-male of lawful age, shall be perpetual directors; *3dly,* That the functions of the directors shall be to elect proper teachers for the different branches of education proposed to be taught at the Academy, to appoint salaries to these masters out of the funds of the Academy, to dismiss any of them upon proper grounds, and elect others in their places, to form regulations for both masters and students, and in general to regulate and govern the Academy in every respect; *4thly,* That seven directors shall make a quorum, and all questions shall be determined by ballot; *5thly,* That there shall be a rector and four other masters in the Academy, and the directors shall have it in their power to appoint from time to time such additional masters as the funds of the Academy shall permit, and the number of students attending it may require, and to allot to the rector and other masters such departments as their particular qualifications may, in the opinion of the directors, render expedient; *6thly,* That the directors shall meet annually on the first lawful day of May in each year, in order to examine the accounts of the treasurer or cashier, and other officers to be appointed by them, and to receive from the rector reports of the state of the Academy; and the directors, or a quorum of them, shall also meet on such other day or days, and at such other time or times, as to them shall seem expedient for the purpose of examining the different schools, and regulating the other business of the Academy; AND HIS MAJESTY APPOINTS the said regulations to be duly observed; GIVING and GRANTING nevertheless, as his Majesty hereby GIVES and GRANTS to the members of the said Incorporation and their successors, at their general meetings, from time to time to be assembled annually on the said first lawful day of the month of May, full power to make such other and so many bye-laws, constitutions, orders and ordinances, as they, or the majority of them present at such meetings, shall judge proper and think necessary for the better government and direction of the Academy; and the said regulations, herein above recited, as well as the bye-laws, constitutions, orders and ordinances, to be made in the future, or any of them, to alter or annul, as the members of the said Incorporation so assembled, or the major part of them present shall deem proper and requisite: AND HIS MAJESTY WILLS AND DIRECTS, That all the bye-laws, constitutions and ordinances, made as aforesaid, shall, until altered, be duly observed and kept, provided that the same are noways contrary to the laws of the realm, and the general purport and meaning of his Majesty's said charter and letters-patent: AND HIS MAJESTY, for himself and his Royal successors, DECLARES, That the said charter or letters-patent shall be valid and effectual in law, according to the true intent and meaning thereof, and shall be taken, construed and adjudged, in the manner most favourable and beneficial for the said Incorporation, notwithstanding any misrecital, defect or imperfection in the same: AND HIS MAJESTY WILLS AND COMMANDS, That the said charter or letters-patent shall pass the Seal appointed by the treaty of Union to be kept and used in Scotland, in place of the Great Seal formerly used there, without passing any other Seal; for doing whereof, these presents shall be to the director of his Majesty's Chancery in Scotland, and to the keeper of the said Seal and their deputies, a sufficient warrant. Given at his

Majesty's Court at St James, the 6th day of March 1793, in the thirty-third year of his Majesty's reign.

By his MAJESTY'S Command,

HENRY DUNDAS.

The actual Charter (CHARTA Academiæ de Inverness) is in Latin – the basic text is the same as that of the warrant, except for an introduction declaring:

George, by the grace of God, King of Great Britain, France and Ireland, Defender of the Faith, To all honest men, both clergy and lay, of all his kingdoms, Greetings: Considering that an humble petition...

There are also adjustments in the tense of some of the verbs, the use of the Royal 'We' in place of 'His Majesty', and in the final few words. It concludes:

Per Signaturam S. D. N. Regis supra script.

Written to the Seal, and registered the 9th day of April

THOMAS MILLER, *Sub.*

Sealed at Edinburgh, the ninth day of April,
One thousand seven hundred and ninety-three years.
GEO. CUMIN, Subt. L.80 Scots

Henry Dundas, born 1742, was a powerful politician in Scotland for thirty years or so around 1800, holding most legal offices. He was Member of Parliament for Midlothian, and then Edinburgh, until elevated to the peerage in 1802, to become 1st Viscount Melville. He was Lord Advocate from 1775 to 1783, and also at times Keeper of the Signet and of the Privy Seal. He basically managed the political patronage of the nation. Opposed to reform, he was the product of a corrupt system, but was impeached in 1805 and acquitted for the irregularities of a subordinate. He is sometimes called 'The Uncrowned King of Scotland' or 'Henry the Ninth'. He died in 1811. The King of the time was George III.

Appendix 4: The Archæological Finds at Culduthel

In the twentieth century there were three finds of cists [pronounced 'kists'] on or near the current site of Inverness Royal Academy at Culduthel. These can be dated to the Bronze Age, roughly between 2400 and 1750 B.C. In addition there are various other sites of archæological interest in the locality. These sites are only about a kilometre from the original site of the well-known sculptured Boar Stone in Essich Road (now on display in the foyer of the Highland Council Chamber in Glenurquhart Road, Inverness).

The 1975 find

The most recent short cist find, made during excavations for the building of the new school at Culduthel in 1975, is a very important example of this type of feature. The site lies on slightly higher land south of the former loch whose name is recalled in the local place-name of Lochardil. The precise location of the cist was on the site of the present-day main car park at the north-east corner of the school site. The site was discovered when a contractor's vehicle broke through the cover slab to reveal the skeleton [Figure A4.1]. The initial excavation was carried out by Laurance Wedderburn, at that time Assistant Curator at Inverness Museum, assisted by Dorothy Grime, a local amateur archæologist.

During the Early Bronze Age, from about 2500 to 2000 BC, the usual form of burial in Scotland was an individual, finely-made stone cist, unlike the small barrow cemeteries found further south in the British Isles. The majority of the cist graves and single burials have no grave goods whatsoever, but some contain fine pottery beakers, often associated with archery equipment. In Scotland nearly all of those with beakers (there are nearly four hundred of them) have been found on the eastern coast or in the Western Isles. These are some of the more fertile regions of the country. Only half a dozen include metal objects, and there are also only a few more with items such as wristguards or barbed or tanged arrowheads.

In the cist found in 1975 were both a skeleton and various important grave goods. The skeleton was not properly studied until 1988, when it was taken to the Department of Anatomy at Aberdeen University. Examination showed it to be that of an adult male, probably aged between 35 and 40, of average height (approximately 5 foot 7 inches or 1.71 metres) and build. Dating of the skeleton by C_{14} analysis has now been carried out, confirming the period of his life and burial.

He still had all his teeth in good condition, and he was obviously a well-nourished individual. Recent strontium and oxygen isotope analysis of his molar tooth enamel has shown that he was not local, but instead came from Ulster. One interesting feature was that, at the back of the left knee joint and tibia (calf bone), there had been an injury which affected the lower leg from the knee to the Achilles tendon in the heel. The cause of death is not known.

The grave goods include [Figure A4.2]:
- a beaker of the typical northern style
- a flint implement, perhaps a strike-a-light
- eight barbed and tanged flint arrowheads
- an archer's wristguard decorated with gold-covered bronze rivets
- an amber bead with hourglass perforation set to one edge
- a bone toggle or belt-ring

The beaker was unfortunately broken by the contractors' vehicle before it was realised that this was an archæological site, but it has now been entirely reconstructed. The beaker is a typical example of a northern British beaker decorated in two major sections: from the rim to the neck, and in a lower section from the shoulder towards the base. The ornament consists of bands of horizontally comb-stamped lines alternating with vertical or oblique stamps applied with a stouter comb. On the base is the impression of a grain of barley.

The flint implement is made from a thick flake of mottled grey cherry flint, which is iron-stained from contact with gravel in the grave. It is roughly chipped along the edges and the broader end, and worn thin at the thinner end.

The arrowheads are mainly of browny flint. The flakes are of very high quality, carefully thinned. The colour of the flint is the result of changes whilst the materials have been buried.

The wristguard of mottled green and grey stone is highly polished with a convex upper and concave lower surface. It has four copper or bronze rivets, each with a solid conical head capped with sheet gold. The stone has recently been been sourced. The wristguard was used in archery, and was attached to a leather wristband. It is possible that it was made and worn for display or burial only, replacing an everyday leather one which has not survived.

The toggle or belt-ring is 'napkin-ring' shaped and originally had flanges at each end, and a pair of central ribs spanned by two or more loops of which only one survives intact. Around the outside of the surviving flange, and in the concave zones between the ribs, are rows of decorative dots about 5 mm apart.

This concentration of grave goods implies that this was a male of high status amongst his community. The items are now on display in National Museums Scotland in Edinburgh, in the 'Death' section, so as, to quote Dr Alison Sheridan, 'to illustrate the point that funerary practices could emphasise various aspects of the deceased's identity' [personal communication, 1999]. The skeleton is now housed in Inverness Museum.

Main references:

D. V. Clarke, T. G. Cowie and A. Poxon: *Symbols of Power at the Time of Stonehenge* (Edinburgh: National Museum of Antiquities of Scotland, 1985)

Richard J. Harrison: *The Beaker Folk: Copper Age Archæology in Western Europe* (London: Thames and Hudson, 1980)

Alison Sheridan: personal communications, 1992, 1999 and 2011, held in the school archive

The 1928 find

This find is also of great importance, as it contained unique grave goods. In August 1928 workmen were digging a sand pit at the rear of Culduthel Farm, only metres from the present school fence and to the west-south-west. They found a large stone slab covering a short cist containing a skeleton with some grave goods. The discovery was examined by Prof. Alex. Low, M.A., M.D., F.S.A.Scot., and he gave a report on it to the meeting of the Society of Antiquarians of Scotland in February 1929.

The site of the cist was in a pebbly gravel knoll, about 0.5 metre below the ground surface, in a field which had been under cultivation for many years. The cover slab was about 1.1 metres long, 1 metre at its broadest and about 0.1 metre thick, with its long axis running roughly south west to north east, similar to the 1970 find (see below). The skeleton lay on its back in the contracted position, with the skull at the south west [Figure A4.3], the opposite way round from the 1970 find. The legs were greatly bent with the knees to the individual's right, with the hands lying over the lower abdomen. The skeleton was fairly complete, but with some decay. It was of a young woman of about 5 foot 1 inch or 1.55 metres in height. She was in her early twenties, a view based on information from her skull and from her limbs.

Also found in the grave were:
- a large number of beads
- a fastener made of jet
- a small fragment of a bronze awl
- a small flake of obsidian
- several small pieces of charcoal

A total of 538 beads were found, with fragments of others, around the waist region of the woman. Most of the beads are in the form of small, perforated, circular discs, on average 4 mm in diameter and 2 mm in thickness, and are made of an unusual lignitic material, perhaps of local origin from the Jurassic rocks of the Black Isle. Six of the beads are large, and eighteen are long fusiform (barrel-shaped) ones, all made of cannel coal. The awl may have been used for the working of items such as the beads.

There is also a large V-perforated boat-shaped piece of jet about 30 mm in length and 11 mm in breadth, which comes from a deposit of jet found at Whitby in north-east England. The flat under-surface is pierced on either side of the centre with two holes running obliquely into each other, forming the V-shaped passage. This is probably a type of toggle that could be passed through a loop.

In total the beads and the piece of jet probably formed a belt [Figure A4.4], although when first assembled in the 1930's they were turned into a necklace. It is possible that the original owner changed the larger beads from a necklace into a belt, by adding the smaller beads. It would have been the property of an high status woman.

The belt is currently on display in National Museums Scotland around a figure sculpted by Eduardo Paolozzi. The skeleton and another four beads are in the Marischal Museum of the University of Aberdeen, reference ABDUA:14221.

Main references:

Alex. Low: *A Short Cist at Culduthel, Inverness*, in *Proceedings of the Society of Antiquaries of Scotland*, vol. LXIII (1929), pp. 217-224

Alison Sheridan: personal communications, 1992 and 1999, held in the school archive

The 1970 find
Just under 1 kilometre west-south-west of the school, another cist was found in July 1970 by Richard Milne, then Curator of Inverness Museum, on the edge of a gravel pit. It was about half a metre below the ground surface and consisted of four side slabs and a covering slab, measuring 1.1 metres long by 0.8 metre wide by 0.6 metre deep. It contained a crouched burial, with the skeleton laid on the left side. However, unlike the two other local cist finds, there were no other objects in the grave. Mr Milne took photographs, and the grave is still in place.

The 2005 discovery of the site of an iron-smelting community
In the first decade of the 21st century major house building has taken place on the slope on the south side of the Southern Distributor Road which now runs immediately to the south of the school. In 2005, during preparatory siteworks, one of the most significant Scottish archæological finds for many years was made when the remains of an iron-smelting community were located. Seventeen round houses were discovered on a terrace commanding clear views across the valley at the northern end of the Great Glen. Underneath the iron-age finds were some cists, probably dating back to the Bronze Age.

Of great significance was the discovery that some of the buildings had had industrial use. One was identified as a grain mill, but five were identified as smithies. Specially-designed hearths, with large edge-set stones forming a box, designed to collect the slag and iron bloom, were excavated. A significant amount of slag was found in surroundings deposits, as well as some copper slag.

The settlement was clearly one of high status. Some Roman coins were found, as well as some weapons. Particularly significant were some copper-alloy objects, including a Romano-British bow and fantail brooch, an intricately decorated cross (part of a horse harness) [Figure A4.5] and a decorated sword-hilt guard.

At the time of preparing this summary, the final report of the excavation had not been published, and this summary is based on a short article by Ross Murray of Headland Archaeology in *History Scotland*, September-October 2006.

The other archæological finds in the locality
During preparatory work in 2001 for the construction of the Southern Distributor Road which now runs immediately to the south of the school, excavations revealed about 90 fire-pit sites. The pits were either circular/sub-circular or egg-shaped, and the largest of them measured roughly two metres by one metre. However these pits did not produce any particularly important finds, and it proved difficult to date the fire-pits with any precision. Also found was about 12 metres of a palisade trench probably from the Iron Age, designed to contain an upright closely-spaced wooden fence. Most of the finds were on the level terrace area at about 50m above sea level, on the better-drained land. On the poorer-drained land around 40m above sea level there was little archæological evidence. Excavations were carried out by Ian Suddaby of CFA Archæology Ltd. For more information see: *Archæological Watching Brief Data Structure Report no. 650*, published by CFA Archæology Ltd.

About half a kilometre north east of the school site, on the land below Lower Slackbuie farm buildings, aerial photography has revealed what may be an unenclosed settlement, comprising a pit-circle 7 metres in diameter and a ring-ditch 13 metres in diameter. The north-east arc of the ring-ditch has been destroyed by road construction.

Roughly halfway between the 1928 and 1970 finds are the remains of a Neolithic cairn of the Clava type. It lies at the edge of a patch of woodland, but it has been so completely robbed that only a few stones of the stone circle remain in their original location, and a few more lie where they have fallen outwards in their original positions. They are most likely the southern arc of a cairn kerb, although they are not in a true circle. The 1871 Ordnance Survey map of the area showed the circle as being much more complete. For more information see: Audrey S. Henshall: *Chambered Tombs of Scotland* (Edinburgh: University Press, 1963 and 1972). This cairn is listed as site 22 on pp. 372-373 of the 1963 edition of the book.

Two other sites near to the school have produced small finds. In the field immediately to the south of the main building, now crossed by the Southern Distributor Road, a riveted piece of bronze and several flints were found in 1985. Two retouched pieces of flint and a blue glass bead were found in the field close to the remains of the chambered cairn. All of these items are now in the collection in Inverness Museum.

Thanks are due to the following for help in preparing this summary:
Dr. Alison Sheridan, Head of Early Prehistory, National Museums Scotland
Catharine Niven, formerly Curator, Inverness Museum and Art Gallery
Dr. Robin Hanley, formerly Assistant Curator (Archæology), Inverness Museum and Art Gallery
Ian Suddaby, CFA Archæology Ltd., Musselburgh
Ross Murray, Headland Archaeology, Edinburgh
Neil Curtis, Marischal Museum, University of Aberdeen
Janet Waller, formerly Librarian, Inverness Royal Academy
Carol Taylor, formerly Librarian, Inverness Royal Academy

As research continues, further information is likely to become available. With the building work in connection with future housing developments, there may also be further archæological discoveries in the area around the school. It is hoped to update this summary on the Royal Academy website from time to time.

Bibliography

1. Primary sources:
a) Manuscript:
Inverness Royal Academy Archive:
> A1: Directors' Minute Book, 1787-1798
>
> Other documents in the Royal Academy archive, as noted in the chapter references

Highland Council Archive: the main references are:
> CI/5/4/1: Inverness School Board minutes, 1907-1918
>
> CI/5/8: Inverness Royal Academy, 1789-1907, including:
> > CI/5/8/1: Directors' Minutes' Books, 1798-1907 (excluding 1834-1847 which is in Inverness Museum, and 1901-1904 which is missing)
> >
> > CI/5/8/2: accounts ledgers and fee books
>
> CI/5/9: includes material on the Mackintosh Farr Fund
>
> CI/5/11: proposed amalgamation of Dr Bell's Institution with Royal Academy, 1848-1849
>
> CI/5/24: Inverness Grammar School and other early schools, 1710-1852
>
> CI/5/24: Trust funds and bursaries, 1788-1862
>
> CI/5/19 and CI/3/38 include material from Inverness County Council files relating to the Academy

National Archives of Scotland: the main references are:
> GD128/10/1 - 5: Alex. Macgregor's private correspondence, 1789-1805
>
> GD128/34/1: items relating to the Academy, 1789-1827
>
> GD128/37/16: 7 items, 1789-1801, in a bundle of assorted material
>
> GD128/55/13/7: 2 items, 1793

b) Transcriptions of, and compilations from, early Documents:
Anderson, Peter J. (ed.): *Officers and Graduates of University & King's College, Aberdeen, MVD-MDCCCLX* (Aberdeen: New Spalding Club, 1893)

Anderson, Peter J. (vol. 2) and Johnstone, James F. K. (vol. 3) (eds.): *Fasti Academiae Mariscallanae Aberdonensis* (Selections from the Records of the Marischal College and University) *MDXCIII-MDCCCLX*, vols. 2 and 3: Officers, Graduates and Alumni (Aberdeen: New Spalding Club, 1898)

Fraser, James: *Chronicles of the Frasers* [commonly known as *The Wardlaw Manuscripts*] (Edinburgh: Publications of the Scottish History Society, vol. 47, 1905)

Mackay, William (ed.): *Records of the Presbyteries of Inverness and Dingwall 1643-1688* (Edinburgh: Publications of the Scottish History Society, vol. 24, 1896)

Mackay, William and Boyd, Herbert Cameron (ed.): *Records of Inverness,* 2 volumes: *Volume 1 – Burgh Court Books, 1556-86; Volume 2 – Burgh Court Books, 1602-37, and Minutes of Town Council, 1637-88* (Aberdeen: New Spalding Club, 1911 and 1924)

c) Government Reports and Enquiries:
Educational Endowments (Scotland) Commission (Balfour Commission), Second Report, 1885, pp. 532-575

Endowed Schools and Hospitals (Scotland) Commission, Second Report (Colebrooke Commission), 1874, pp. 495-502 (report on the Royal Academy)

Report on the State of Education in the Burgh and Middle-Class Schools in Scotland

(Argyll Commission), *volume 2 – Special Reports, 1868* (written by Thomas Harvey and Alexander Sellar), pp. 291-299 (report on the Royal Academy)

Schools Inquiry Commission Report (Taunton Commission), *volume 6, part 5* (written by Daniel R. Fearon), 1868, pp. 144-156 (Royal Academy) and pp. 205-208 (Inverness High School)

2. Secondary Material on Inverness:

Anderson, Isabel Harriet: *Inverness before Railways* (Inverness: A. & W. Mackenzie, 1885; modern reprint by Charles Leakey, Inverness, 1984)

Barron, James: *The Northern Highlands in the Nineteenth Century* in 3 volumes (Inverness: Robt. Carruthers & Sons, 1903, 1907, 1913) [Essentially a selective index to the *Inverness Journal* and the *Inverness Courier* from 1800 to 1841]

Fraser, John: *Reminiscences of Inverness, its People and Places* (Inverness: published by the author, 1905; facsimile reprint: Inverness: Charles Leakey, 1983)

Hamilton, Douglas J.: *Scotland, the Caribbean and the Atlantic World* (Manchester: Manchester University Press, 2005)

Lawson, Alan B.: *Church and School in the Century after Culloden,* in *Loch Ness and Thereabouts* (Inverness: Inverness Field Club, 1991)

Lawson, Alan B.: *Comments on the Minutes of the Presbytery of Inverness, 1745-1748, Presidential Address,* in *An Inverness Miscellany* [volume 1] (Inverness: Inverness Field Club, 1984)

Miller, James: *Inverness* (Edinburgh: Birlinn, 2004)

Mitchell, Joseph: *Reminiscences of my Life in the Highlands, vol. 1* (1883) (modern reprint available: Newton Abbot: David and Charles Reprints, 1971) [but contains incorrect information about Nimmo's reason for resignation as Rector]

Newton, Norman S.: *Inverness – Highland Town to Millennium City* (Derby: Breedon Books Publishing Company, 2003)

Newton, Norman S.: *The Life and Times of Inverness* (Edinburgh: John Donald, 1996)

Suter, James: *Memorabilia of Inverness* (Inverness: Donald Macdonald, n.d., but based on material first published in the Inverness Courier in 1822)

Wilkins, Noël P. (ed.): *Alexander Nimmo's Inverness Survey and Journal, 1806* (Dublin: Royal Irish Academy, 2011)

3. Secondary material on Schools and Education:
a) Specifically on Inverness Royal Academy:

Anderson, Peter J.: *The Grammar School and Royal Academy of Inverness: Headmasters, 1636-1906; Gold Medallists, 1811-1906; Fraser Bursars, 1725-1906* (Inverness: privately published, 1907) [a fourth section: *Raigmore Silver Medallists 1810-1888*, was published as a pamphlet a short while later, of which the only known original copies are in Inverness Public Library and Aberdeen University Library]

Bannerman, Charles: *Up Stephen's Brae – Midmills Days at Inverness Royal Academy* (Inverness: Inverness Royal Academy, 1995)

Bannerman, Charles: *Further Up Stephen's Brae – The Midmills Era at Inverness Royal Academy, 1895-1979* (Inverness: St Michael's Publishing on behalf of

Inverness Royal Academy, 1999)

Barron, Evan M.: *Inverness Royal Academy – Some Pages from a History of 650 Years* (published as part of *The Inverness Academical* [the Magazine of Inverness Royal Academy] in 1921, and in an almost identical version under the title *An Old Inverness School* in vol. 9, 1918-1925, of *The Transactions of Inverness Scientific Society and Field Club*, 1927)

See also the many illustrations with captions, relating to Inverness Royal Academy, which appear on the *Am Baile* website: http://www.ambaile.org.uk/en/index.jsp. Some of these appear as illustrations in this book.

b) Scottish and Highland Education in general:

Allenson, Stephen: *The Inverness Fragments: Music from a pre-Reformation Scottish Parish Church and School*, in *Music and Letters*, vol. 70, issue 1 (February 1989), pp. 1-45

Anderson, R. D.: *Education and the Scottish People, 1750-1918* (Oxford: Clarendon Press, 1995)

Anderson, R. D.: *Education and Opportunity in Victorian Scotland – Schools and Universities* (Oxford: Clarendon Press, 1983)

Cockburn, Lord Henry: *Circuit Journeys* (first published1888; facsimile reprint: Edinburgh: Mercat Press, 1975)

Craigie, James: *A Bibliography of Scottish Education in 2 volumes: before 1872* (Edinburgh: Scottish Council for Research in Education, 1970) and *1872-1972* (Edinburgh: Scottish Council for Research in Education, 1974)

Grant, James: *History of the Burgh and Parish Schools of Scotland, volume 1: Burgh Schools*, (London, Glasgow: Collins: 1876) (vol. 2 was never published)

Humes, Walter M., and Paterson, Hamish M. (eds.): *Scottish Culture and Scottish Education, 1800-1980* (Edinburgh: John Donald, 1983)

Knox, H. M.: *Two Hundred and Fifty Years of Scottish Education* (Edinburgh: Oliver and Boyd, 1953)

Lawson, Alan B.: *Education*, in *The Hub of the Highlands* (Inverness: Inverness Field Club, 1975) [a brief survey concentrating on developments in and around Inverness from the 1872 Education Act to the date of publication]

Preece, Isobel Woods: *Our awin Scottis use – Music in the Scottish Church up to 1603* (Glasgow: Universities of Glasgow and Aberdeen, 2000)

Scotland, James: *The History of Scottish Education*, in 2 volumes (London: University of London Press, 1969)

Watt, D. E. R.: *Education in the Highlands in the Middle Ages in The Middle Ages in the Highlands* (Inverness: Inverness Field Club, 1981)

Withrington, Donald [J.]: *Education in the 17th Century Highlands*, in *The Seventeenth Century in the Highlands* (Inverness: Inverness Field Club, 1986)

Index

Certain topics, e.g. the Academy Directors as a group, occur so frequently through the text that they have been omitted from the index. The spelling of people's names did not become standardised until the end of the 18th century, so some entries have two or more spellings for a person's name. Academy staff, and those from the earlier schools, are listed by surname with their subject specialisation(s) in brackets. Not all staff of the former Inverness Grammar School are given in this index: see Appendix 1 for a full chronological list of these staff; the biographies of Rectors are also not fully indexed here: see Appendix 2. Page numbers in **bold** refer to illustrations/photographs, with text or caption.

383

School hostels 239, 241-242, 243-246, 249, 254, 257-258, 263-264, 265-266, 271, 281, **314** (*see also* Drummond Park *and* Hedgefield House)
School leaving age 242, 250, 276
School Vennel (Inverness): *see* Bank Lane
Schoolmaster's salary (early) 17-19, 21, 25-30, 32, 35-40, 42-47
Schoolmasters (early): method of appointment 22, 24, 25, 26
Schools (early):
  Adventure School 36
  Dame School 36
  Dancing School 35, 43, 44-45, 65
  Free Church Institution 46, 193, 202
  Girls' Boarding School 46-48, 89
  Latin School 13, 16
  Mathematics School 29, 30, 32, 36, 37-38
  Music School 17, 29, 35, 38-44, 59
  Reading School 13, 16, 17, 35
  Song School/Sang Schuile 14-16, 17, 38, 282
  Writing School 13, 30-31, 33, 35, 36-37, 39, 53, 63
Scotsman, The 208, 263
Scott, Peter (classics, Rector) 103, 130-132, 136, 138, 139, 142, 143, 161-163, 165, 168-169, 170-173, 174, 179-180, **296**, **302**, **361**
Scott, Roderick (clerk) 200
Scottish Association of Young Farmers' Clubs 264
Scottish Education Board (Edinburgh) 195
Scottish/Scotch Education Department (SED) 198, 204, 210, 213, 220, 223, 226, 230-233, 236, 240, 242, 244, 247, 263, 267, 272, 276
Scottish Episcopal Church 171, 178
Scottish Society for the Propagation of Christian Knowledge (SSPCK) 45, 46, 48, 190-191
Seafield Estate (Inverness) 32, 147, 224, 251
Secondary education 192, 194-196, 201-205, 211, 215-217, 232, 250, 270, 281-282
Secretary of State for Scotland 259, 270
Sellar, Provost Alan 278
Sellar, Alexander (Government Commissioner) 194-196
Session clerk: *see* Precentor/session clerk
Schaefer, Heinrich (French/German) 169, 170
Shaw, John (father of pupil) 34
Shaw, Maxwell (music) 42
Shaw, Mr .... (Dean of Guild, Director, trustee) 151-152
Shiels, Maxwell (wife of Alex. Macgregor) 82
Shier, Mr .... (lecturer) 143
Shipland Estate (Inverness) 40, 57
Sibbald, William (superintendent of works) 60-61

Simpson, Alex. (usher/doctor, later schoolmaster) 32, 357, 358
Simpson, Alexander (Factor to Mackintosh Farr Fund) 213
Simpson, James (writing/arithmetic/book-keeping) 137
Simpson, John (Dean of Guild) 115-116
Simpson, William (Inverness Scientific Society) 84
Slavery 56-57, 104, 282
Smith, James (minister at Avoch) 53
Smith, Janet (servant to Alexander Macgregor) 81
Smith, John (son of merchant) 108
Smith, Mackintosh (pupil) 224
Smith, Robert (Academy Secretary) 105, 137, 175-176, 183
Smith, W. Crampton (mathematics, Rector) 241, 243, 247, 248, 250, 252, 258-259, 264, 362, **362**
Smith, Provost William 205, 278
Society in Scotland for Propagating Christian Knowledge: *see* Scottish Society for the Propagation of Christian Knowledge (SSPCK)
South Kessock Farm (Inverness) 251
Southern Distributor Road (Inverness) 274, 371-372
Spalding Club, Aberdeen 154
SS Neuralia 254
SS Uganda 269
Statistical Account of Scotland, First 61, 85
Steele, George (schoolmaster) 28, 357
Steele, James (Bell's School/Academy Rector) 150, 157, 161, 165, 167-168, 360
Stevenson, Robert Louis (author) 207, 213
Steward, Robert (Highland Council archivist) 282
Stewart, Charles (Brin, Director) 188
Stewart/Stuart, James (schoolmaster) 24, 356
Stuart, Ellis (French) 249, 272
Sundial on old Burgh bridge 37
Suter, Isabella (pupil) 140
Suter, James (wine merchant, Director) 150-151
Suter, John (junior classics) 184
Sutherland, Alexander (schoolmaster) 25, 356
Sutter, Hugh (mason) 60-61
Synod of Moray 132, 355

Tain Academy 161, 168, Table 4.1 (53)
Taunton Commission: *see* Royal Commissions
Telford, Thomas (engineer) 91, 92
Textbooks (outwith Royal Academy) 15-16, 35, 46
Tey, Josephine: *see* Mackintosh, Elizabeth
Theft: *see* Vandalism
Thomson, J. E. ('Jess') (former pupil, classics) 272
Thomson, Keith (music) 42-43

389